The Craft
of a
Chinese Commentator

SUNY series in
Chinese Philosophy and Culture

David L. Hall and Roger T. Ames, editors

The Craft
of a
Chinese Commentator

Wang Bi
on the
Laozi

Rudolf G. Wagner

STATE UNIVERSITY OF NEW YORK PRESS

Published by
State University of New York Press, Albany

© 2000 State University of New York
All rights reserved

Printed in the United States of America

For information, address the State University of New York Press, State
University Plaza, Albany, NY 12246

Production by Ruth Fisher
Marketing by Nancy Farrell

Library of Congress Cataloging-in-Publication Data

Wagner, Rudolf G.
    The craft of a Chinese commentator: Wang Bi on the Laozi/Rudolf
G. Wagner.
        p.   cm.—(SUNY series in Chinese philosophy and culture)
    Includes bibliographical references and index.
    ISBN 0-7914-4395-7 (alk. paper).—ISBN 0-7914-4396-5 (pbk.:
alk. paper)
    1. Lao-tzu. Tao te ching. 2. Wang, Pi, 226–249. Lao-tzu tao te
ching chu. I. Title. II. Title: Wang Bi on the Laozi.
III. Series.
BL1900.L35W29   2000
299'.51482—dc21   99-40511
                                                               CIP

10 9 8 7 6 5 4 3 2 1

Contents

Preface

It has taken many years, and several other books, to finish this study of which the present book is the first of three volumes. In fact, the writing of this study took as many years as Wang Bi, its subject, lived, namely twenty-three. Debts of gratitude for spiritual and material support and critical discussion have accumulated. The core ideas were developed in Berkeley in 1971 where I spent a wonderful year as a Harkness Fellow. The first of many drafts of an extrapolative translation of the *Laozi* through the Wang Bi *Commentary* was begun then, and continued in the following year in Berlin with a habilitation grant from the German Research Association (DFG). A position as assistant professor at the Free University of Berlin began a long detour. My education had been exclusively in the field of classical Chinese studies; the focus of the Berlin Institute was modern China. While gaining some expertise in this new field, work on Wang Bi remained active, but on the back burner. After the job in Berlin had run its course in 1977, I worked part-time as a science journalist and consultant on Chinese agriculture, and finished the first full draft of this study. In 1980 I submitted it (in German) as a habilitation thesis, and it was passed in 1981 with my late teacher Prof. Wolfgang Bauer (Munich) and Prof. E. Zürcher (Leiden) as external referees. Cornell University was generous enough to invite me as a fellow into its Society for the Humanities in the same year, which resulted in a book on Taiping religion. In the subsequent years I was a Research Fellow at Harvard University and a Research Linguist at UC Berkeley, working on two books on the politics of modern Chinese fiction. Only small segments of my Wang Bi study were published in English during these years. In 1987 I began to teach at the University of Heidelberg in Germany at an institute in urgent need of a major development effort. A stipend from the Stiftung Volkswagenwerk made possible another year at Harvard working now at the English version of this study. In the meantime, scholarship had revived in mainland China, and a sizable amount of new work had come out. I was relieved that my core arguments seemed solid enough to survive, and developed new sections, such as the analysis of Wang Bi's commentarial strategies contained in this volume, the critical edition of the texts, and the chapter on textual transmission, while reworking all the rest. In short bursts of feverish work between long stretches of other equally feverish work that study finally was completed.

It will appear in three separate volumes of which the present volume is the first. They are:

1. *The Craft of a Chinese Commentator: Wang Bi on the Laozi;*

2. *Wang Bi's Commentary on the Laozi. Critical text, Extrapolative translation, Philological Commentary;*

3. *Language, Ontology, and Political Philosophy: Wang Bi's Scholarly Exploration of the Dark (Xuanxue).*

Much of the emotional cost of such a study is not borne by the author but by those on whom this kind of work imposes painful deprivations. My older daughter Martha was born in 1971. When I eventually told her the manuscript was now finished, she seemed unbelieving. Since the day she was born, this manuscript had hung over her head with the eternal and never fulfilled promise that, after one last effort, it would be finished. I wish to thank her, her sister Tina, and their mother for their many years of bearing the burden of this work with me, and I wish to apologize for the deprivations and disruptions of their lives coming with it.

Catherine Vance Yeh with her unflinching optimism and support is thanked not only for the study's eventual completion but she managed that this protracted, tumultuous, and often very frustrating work lost its grim colors, and ended up in enriching our lives.

My thanks to the foundations and universities that have generously supported this work at various stages such as the German

Research Association (DFG), the Stiftung Volkswagenwerk, and the Universities of Cornell, Harvard, and UC Berkeley who offered me research opportunities; to the members of the research group "Text and Commentary" in the Institute of Chinese Studies in Heidelberg who gave much needed spiritual support and critical advice, and to Dr. Johannes Kurz and Holger Kühnle who during the last stages helped as research assistants to finish the manuscript and the bibliography. Florence Trefethen eventually applied her firm and gentle pen in an effort to make my English more understandable and economical. Finally, the readers have been exceedingly helpful with their comments, pointing out weaknesses in argument and prompting me to rethink some important premises. Two of them were kind enough to go through the manuscript in painstaking detail and as they gave permission that I could know their names, I can express my sincere gratitude for this labor of scholarly collegiality and friendship to Robert Henricks and Robin Yates.

The book is dedicated with gratitude to my mother, Renate v. Weyrauch. Her firm and unconditional belief in the right of her children to develop their own potential and interests has enabled me to enter Chinese studies, a field in which I have never for a minute been bored.

Introduction

During my dissertation work on early Chinese Buddhist thinkers, especially Shi Daoan 釋道安 (312–385) and Shi Huiyuan 釋慧遠 (334–416), I found Buddhist arguments were often understood and expressed in a language originating in third century Xuanxue 玄學, the "scholarly investigation of that which is dark," to use a cumbersome translation.[1] Though the importance of Xuanxue in Chinese philosophy, including Chinese Buddhist philosophy and even Song-dynasty Neo-Confucianism, was acknowledged, and though its general outlines were mapped and arguments about its presumable sociopolitical orgins and purposes were available, there were no detailed critical studies of particular texts and issues. It seemed natural to take up the study of Wang Bi, unquestionably the most sophisticated and influential Xuanxue thinker.

There is a dearth of critical editions of Chinese texts and of detailed studies of individual philosophical works. In studies of the Western classics, there has been a division of labor between scholars collating, editing, commenting, and perhaps translating texts, and scholars mostly bent on analyzing the works thus made available. There were some scholars, however, such as Rudolf Bultman in the study of the Christian Testament who had managed to span the entire breadth of the enterprise, from painstaking philological research through broad analyses of religious, social, and political currents, to hermeneutical explorations of the internal logic of philosophical texts and religious beliefs. This model I set out to emulate, assisted by some years of studying hermeneutics with Hans-Georg Gadamer at the University of Heidelberg.

The resulting work includes:

— A volume with critical textual editions of Wang Bi's *Laozi* text, Wang Bi's *Commentary to the Laozi*, and his *Structure of the Laozi's Pointers, Laozi weizhi lueli*; translations of all three texts, and studies on the textual transmission and philology of these works. These will form a volume separate from the present book, but this volume will contain the editions on which the textual analyses presented here are based;

— The present volume, which is dealing with the art and technique of Wang Bi, the commentator of the *Laozi*, and the intellectual currents from and against which his approach developed;

— A study of his philosophy of language that is underlying his treatment of the classical texts, of his ontology that marked a watershed in the history of Chinese philosophy, and of his political philosophy for which his ontology provided the model and logic.

It is quite a modest enterprise, the many pages notwithstanding. The length only reflects a certain backwardness of Chinese studies in terms of securing their philological fundaments. My study does not even include the entirety of Wang Bi's oeuvre, leaving out as it does most of his work on the *Zhouyi*.

The study of Chinese philosophical commentaries has suffered much from the European disdain of the Reformation and Renaissance period for the dark ages of "scholasticism," which has been regarded as second-hand thought. The Urtext, the original meaning, and the author's original intention have since been extolled as the only proper focus of scholarly research, while the "prescientific" commentators and exegetes have been summarily denounced as subjectivist and unscholarly, bent on making their own points instead of explaining what was "really" meant by the text. This trend has directed large and often brilliant energies into consolidating this "scientific" approach. The weakness of the uncritical transfer of these Renaissance prejudices to China (and their acceptance by much of the Chinese scholarly community) lies in having created large desert areas summarily denounced as second-hand thought not worthy of the best scholarly energies.

We do know that, at least since the second century CE, classical texts were generally read in China through commentaries. We do know that a very large segment of the best Chinese minds since pre-Qin times have focused on the interpretation of the classical texts as the only available heirloom of the Sages of antiquity. And we do know that to check the meaning of a fifth- or tenth-century reference to the *Spring and Autumn Annals* or the *Laozi*, it obviously makes little sense to go back to a reading presumably focusing on the Urtext and the original intention; the person quoting the passage as well as his readers will have read it through a particular commentary or commentaries which probably situated it within a completely different context than what might be construed as the "original meaning."

Sadly, to this date, not even have a sketch of the early history of the Chinese commentary is available, although it most certainly is the genre that most Chinese thinkers and philosophers used to exercise their talents. Already by the time of Confucius the understandability of certain oral or written statements from earlier times had become a problem that was being discussed. The utterances and gestures of Confucius seemed to his disciples to both contain and hide their deep meaning and the *Lunyu* records how they asked him, or each other, about it. The *Laozi* purports in many passages to present explanations to what was meant by words and actions of the "Sage" or "those of olden times," and goes so far as to occasionally insert commentaries on his own statements, starting with the phrase "what is meant by . . . 何謂?" The "four chapters" of the *Guanzi* develop this structure further by containing an extensive "internal commentary."[2] These internal commentaries are not just restatements of the original phrase in other words. They use a different argumentative register, and the two interact to create a structure of meaning that is both more complex and more stable.

With some texts gaining the status of writings of a higher order directly associated with the Sages of old who are credited with measuring up to Heaven in their understanding of the mysteries of the world, the interpretation of their coded messages became the privileged access to truth. Mengzi already structures his own arguments by having them result in a quotation from the *Book of Odes, Shijing*. In this manner they become—even if they do not have the form of a commentary—exegeses explaining and unfolding what was understood as being compressed and encoded in the poetry of this text. The *Shi* had already achieved the status of being the subject-matter of exegesis at the time of Confucius, but the exegetical leeway was not restricted by either context or historical meaning. Eventually it was the story of the last of the Sages, Confucius' himself, selecting and editing the *Shi* that made it into a canon of Sagely wisdom at least for the evolving "Confucian" or *Ru* tradition. As other texts and groups of texts were inserted into the same canonical register they also became the object of exegesis. This exegesis might take on the form of a commentary directly attached to the text itself that was eventually seen as an integral part of it as was the case with the "wings" of the *Zhouyi*; or it took on the new form of direct and separate commentaries as was the case with the *Gongyang zhuan* and the *Guliang zhuan*, the first surviving separate commentarial works, both of which comment on the *Chunqiu*; or it might take on the form of a collection of anecdotes or arguments indirectly illustrating the meaning. Nor was this development during the fourth and third century BCE restricted to what the Han court later made into the classical Ru or "Confucian" canon. All surviving texts share a wide array of common themes, approaches, and practices and it makes little sense to retroactively impose "school" divisions on them. The *Laozi*, *Guanzi*, or the recently discovered *Wuxing* 五行[3] were discussed and submitted to exegesis; the statements of Laozi, for example, being discussed in many pre-Qin texts such as the *Zhuangzi*, and the text *Laozi* being quoted, interpreted, and commented upon in works such as the *Wenzi* 文子[4] and the *Hanfeizi*.

The reading of these authoritative texts became a part of school instruction since the time of Confucius, and their exegesis part of a learned and often very politically charged debate. In this manner reading and understanding became a public act, and had to prove plausibility toward a community of other exegetes of the same canon. The shared assumption that these texts were authoritative but compressed and coded statements by the Sages that no effort could ever completely translate into the fixed terms of regular mortals created a triple bind: authoritative statements had to be derived from a reading of these authoritative texts of old; the reading had to be plausible and convincing to other readers who might want to derive other conclusions from these canonical texts; and any reading was open to challenge due to the inexhaustibility *in princi-*

ple of these texts. The consequence was the development of a set of highly sophisticated and publicly defensible strategies of reading and decoding these texts.

The *Gongyang zhuan* and the *Guliang zhuan* both retain traces in their didactic questions and answers of actually having originated in exegetical teaching about the *Chunqiu*. For the benefit of the students they make the rules for their exegesis explicit. They assume the *Chunqiu* to consist of entries of events of importance to the court in Lu. For each type of entry there is assumed to be a standard formula prescribing its form and content. The matrix formed by these formulas is not a really existing handbook but a set of practices inferred from the totality of entries as well as some other ritual sources as they survive in the *Zhouli*, *Liji*, and *Yili*.[5] The specific entries are held against this matrix, and any deviation requires an explanation. The deviation is marked by these two commentaries with standard phrases such as "why does [the *Chunqiu*] write [XX instead of the YY to be expected here] 何以書" or "why does [the *Chunqiu*] not write [the ZZ to expected here] 何以不書." The very first *Chunqiu* entry only marks the date of a new reign in Lu beginning, but does not record an event. The *Gongyang* starts out by establishing an exegetical rule "if there is no event, there will be no entry 無事不書." The question then is "why does [the *Chunqiu*] make an entry 何以書 [of the date only]?" A comparison with the first entry for many of the other dukes of Lu shows that they contain "an event," namely the information "he ascended the throne 即位." As only events are recorded, the non-accession is the event recorded here. The absence of information in a formula where a particular kind of information is to be expected gives the clue to the encoded information, namely that Duke Yin did not formally accede to the throne but took on a caretaker role for his brother who was higher in the line of succession but too young to accede himself. This then reflects on Duke Yin's impeccable character and foreshadows the evil character of his younger brother who had him killed because he was afraid Duke Yin was himself vying for the throne.

In their effort to prove a consistent and plausible exegetical strategy for the entire *Chunqiu*, not just a random phrase, the *Gongyang* and *Guliang* commentaries signal the stress coming from the existence of a exegetical community vying for control over the reading of the canonical texts. The high analytical quality and scholarly achievement of these commentaries signals the level of this stress. The commentator could not claim the privilege of a teacher handing the truth to his students, nor of a school insisting on its idiosyncratic reading. By congealing into the written medium, the commentary became a public exegetical event, and had to survive potentially hostile challenges. We see similar efforts at scholarly systematization in the *Zhouyi* "wings," and eventually in the prefaces and commentaries attached to the *Shangshu* and the *Shi*. Under the assumption that the encoded meaning in the canonical texts had to do with a social practice of the emperor or his officials, and was, by implication, providing general rules through indirect praise or criticism, the decoding consisted mostly in extracting these judgments and in formulating general rules of acceptable behavior. While the *Laozi* also attracted much comment and explanation, the reading of this text or this body of texts in pre-Han and Han times neither seemed to call for similar efforts at finding a unified, verifiable, plausible, and in this sense scholarly strategy of "decoding," nor for the extraction of moral guidelines.

These efforts at preserving and actualizing some understanding of the bequests of the Sages' coded insights inserted themselves into a story of growing desperation that spread during the former Han. It seemed to many that the time of the Sages was gone forever, and that a nearly natural decay would result in the later born ending up in complete incomprehension of their bequest. Already the students of Confucius, wrote Ban Gu, failed to understand the Master, and after their death even the broad outlines of his teaching were being forgotten. For him, the physical demise of the book manuscripts with their destruction under the Qin, and the rotting of the recovered manuscripts under the Former Han was just the material manifestation of this decay; and its intellectual manifestation was the simultaneous presence of many different currents of exegesis of the classics, all state efforts at creating a unified reading through the institution of official doctors of the classics notwithstanding.[6] The "subtle words" left behind by the Sages were "subtle" because the truth was hidden in them. This also meant that a plain reading of the surface text would not yield this truth. The surface text was but an unreliable if unavoidable medium of communication. The unreliability of the surface text called forth scholarly and intercommunicable ways of extracting the subtle truths, but also made these extractions open to challenge at any moment.

Two sets of commentarial devices were developed during the latter part of the Western Han to cut down on this unreliability, and seal the truth. The first was the decoding key made up of two factors merged into one structure, the Yin-Yang system and the Five Elements. It was imputed that this structure reflected that of the universe, and therefore was the natural key used by the Sages to code their bequests. A conscious application of the linkages between different realms provided by this structure would allow the rational extraction of meaning from seemingly trivial canonical texts. The second was the full lexical explanation of the surface language of the texts, especially the elements referring to institutions, ritual, and material culture. In a pragmatic sense, this latter type of commenting could be justified by the time-lag between the canonical texts and the readers, and the ensuing changes in grammar, terminology, and social reality that needed bridging.

The efforts of the court and the doctors of the classics notwithstanding, this attempt at fixing both the texts classified as canonical, and the strategies for their decoding never was unchallenged. Other texts such as the *Laozi* and the *Chuci* pushed their way into the generally accepted core canon, and other commentarial strategies evolved. During the Eastern Han the two sets of commentarial devices mentioned above seem to have been congealed into the genre of the *zhangju* 章句 commentary. As will be detailed in chapter 2, a rapidly growing number of men of letters expressed their frustration with what they saw as the excessive attachment of the *zhangju* commentaries to the surface text, and their concomitant disregard for the ultimate "meaning," *yi* 義, of the Sages' bequests.

The collapse of the Han eliminated state patronage for these *zhangju* commentaries, and created a few years and decades of an interstice during which the search for the philosophical rather than the moral bequests of the Sages, for the subtle meaning rather than the vocabulary of the surface text, could be pursued by irreverent young men from the best families in an environment of open and relatively friendly competition. These young men were no paragons of modesty; they were brilliant, and they knew it. They felt they were up to the task of coming up with "subtle words" of their own and as a group might match the depth and historical importance of Confucius and his students. The few decades of their blossoming with the *zhengshi* era (240–249) at their heart were the golden age of a new type of "meaning" oriented commentary, and Wang Bi certainly was its most admired and emulated practitioner. A biographical sketch of this young genius will be given in chapter 1. His type of commentary was rigidly philosophical in its questions; it rejected the doxographic traditions that set the various "schools" apart in favor of a pursuit of a truth beyond the schools and the texts they had appropriated for themselves; including into the core canon of philosophically relevant texts above all the *Zhouyi*, the *Laozi*, and the *Lunyu* (only later to be joined by the *Zhuangzi*), and by dismissing the Yin-Yang /Five Elements decoding as speculative constructs not supported by the material itself, it set for itself the highest possible standards of scholarly exegesis. Chapters 3 and 4 will analyze the craft of this exegesis that has in many respects remained unsurpassed in the sheer intellectual quality of its textual analysis to this very day. With this focus on the scholarly craft of exegesis and its rules, the main part of this book aims to become part of a history of the process of textual and cultural understanding in China that remains to be written. The results of the exegesis both in terms of textual decoding and philosophical analysis will be reserved for the two other volumes of this project where the translation of the *Laozi* as extrapolated from Wang Bi's commentary will be presented together with this commentary, and where the development of Wang Bi's philosophy out of an analysis of the *Laozi* will be outlined.

Wang Bi's work shows the extraordinary analytical sophistication and philosophical depth of the best of the Chinese commentators. It is a worthy object of study, and the precision of his exegesis certainly thwarts the presumptions of many a modern reader who attributes the fogginess of his own translations to his Chinese author's thinking rather than to his own hermeneutic skills.

As a picture for the cover I have chosen Liang Kai's 梁楷 (first-half-thirteenth cent.) painting of the Sixth Patriarch shredding the sûtras.[7] Hui Neng's act is depicted as the epitome of a process of reading the sûtras, learning them by heart, reciting them, having them explained by a teacher and commentators, having poured over them oneself, and having in turn become a teacher. Hui Neng's act undoes what his students might attach themselves to as the holy writ, and in the act signals that only by forgetting and literally destroying the poor medium that is their language can their intended meaning be reached. By acting in public, he gives a shocking and supreme commentary performance to all in his (and the painting's) presence. While Wang Bi is a stranger to Hui Neng's concept of enlightenment, the two men share an understanding of their purpose.

Chapter One

Wang Bi

A Biographical Sketch

Wang Bi's Life

Martin Heidegger is said to have reacted to a request by students to provide some introduction to Aristotle's life by starting his next lecture with the words: "Aristotle was born, worked, and died." He then continued to hold forth on the philosopher's philosophy.

Heidegger's attitude talks back to a fashion of reducing intellectual to social history and philosophical pursuits to high-register articulations of particular economic, political, or personal interests. This fashion corresponds to some commonly held assumptions about the nature of man, but it still has to prove the particular ways in which social interests might translate into particular philosophical or religious constructs; and it also has to account for the fact that often these constructs survive the demise of the social group whose interests they once seemed to advocate, and exert a profound influence on later generations with a completely different "social interest" and agenda. In some of my previously published studies on Wang Bi I was less disturbed by such reductionism. But in the end the link could neither be verified nor falsified, while the fact remained that Wang Bi remained a valid intellectual force for many centuries to come, and this under substantially changed circumstances. Heidegger's implied argument that in a philosopher only his philosophy counts has a point. It counters an old and widespread tendency to evade the challenge of a philosopher's thought by reducing it to "school" tenets, political affiliation, or legitimation of the socioeconomic interests of the class or segment to which he is thought to belong.

On the other hand it is commonplace that many Chinese philosophers—and not only they—have been involved with their thought in political and factional debate in their time. Still, the survival and fame of their work in later times can hardly be attributed to their political stance in this or that battle, and the question remains what their philosophical contribution might have been that makes it worthwhile for a modern reader to study their works.

Wang Bi 王弼 (226–249), then, was born, worked, and died very young.[1] At the time of his death he had barely reached the age of twenty-three, and had written *Commentary to the Laozi, Commentary to the Zhouyi,* two tracts analyzing the structure of these two works, a critical supplement to the *Collected Commentaries on the Lunyu* edited by He Yan 何晏 (?–249), and a number of other philosophical tracts. The commentaries and the structural analyses have survived the fierce battles for textual patronage to this day, and are unanimously described as being a watershed in the history of Chinese philosophy. His *Commentary to the Zhouyi* became the standard commentary in Kong Yingda's edition of the *Correct Meaning of the Five Classics,* and his *Commentary to the Laozi* dominated the scene with an interruption during the Tang dynasty.

The historical and social environment in which Wang Bi lived certainly facilitated the development of his philosophy. Born just after the collapse of the Han dynasty and at the beginning of an extended period of "disunion," he grew up in a postwar world with states that were only gradually trying to establish new institutions and orthodoxies, and where both thought and social forces were much in flux. It was a world suddenly without stern and authoritative teachers since the system of state and private academies so prominent in the second century, with official "doctors of the classics" and private teachers such as Ma Rong or Zheng Xuan, had collapsed. While some now complained that education was at its worst, it certainly was a moment when individual talent supported by a good environment had a rare chance to flourish, and the number of young geniuses in Wang Bi's generation became the envy of centuries to come. They would come out with lasting works at an age when their forebears would have barely had the time to memorize the first commentary to one of the classics. It was a time when original and even outrageous thought, speech, and behavior brought notoriety and fame, a time when young scholars such as Wang Bi not only produced brilliant contributions to Chinese philosophy, but also self-confidently thought they were doing so, and behaved with appropriate pomp. The members of Wang Bi's generation were not ill at ease with their originality, but cherished, fostered, and stylized it.

Wang Bi certainly had both the talent and the environment. Although born in the Capital Luoyang, he hailed from the Wang clan in Gaoping 高平 in the Shanyang District of today's Shandong.[2] The clan belonged to the magnate families of the Later Han who were to form the core of the "aristocracy" dominating much of the upper echelons of the succeeding centuries.[3] Fan Ye calls the Gaoping Wangs "magnates," *haozu* 豪族.[4] The clan rose to fame with Wang Gong 王龔 (d. 140) who became one of the three highest officials, *sangong* 三公, and established the affiliation with the "Pure Ones," *qing* 清, who were united in their battle against the eunuchs' influence at court. His son, Wang Chang 暢 (d. 169) was in turn promoted by protégés of his father, and continued the latter's affiliations. He was a member of the "Eight Geniuses" 八俊, a group that was in close connection with similar groups such as the Three Gentleman 三君 and the Eight Perspicacious Ones 八顧, which included Guo Tai 郭泰 (128–169), the man renowned to be the founder of *qingtan*, "pure talk," a type of highly allusive and elliptical characterization of a man's character and quality through which the members of these groups were portraying each other, or, in the opinions of some contemporaries, flattering each other.[5] While five of the eight members of Wang Chang's group were killed during the purges against the "Pure Ones" in 169, he was not touched, perhaps protected by the status of his family.

It was Wang Chang who established the intellectual renown of the clan. His most prominent student was Liu Biao 劉表 (d. 208), also from Gaoping, a member of the imperial clan who later became governor of Jingzhou. During the collapse of the Han dynasty, Liu Biao attracted many of the leading lights to Jingzhou and set up an academy there. The political clout and intellectual renown of the

Wang clan was by now so well established that Wang Chang's son Qian 謙 refused to marry the daughter of his superior He Qin, the commander-in-chief of the army and brother of the empress dowager. He Qin owed his rise to his sister, a concubine of the emperor who had borne him a son; but originally the family had been butchers. A Wang from Gaoping would not go for such a *mesalliance*. Qian's son Can 粲 (177–217) could bank on this ancestry. When in 190 Dong Zhuo transferred the capital to Chang'an, Wang Can, still a small boy, followed the train. Before he was fifteen, he had a memorable and fateful meeting with the famous poet Cai Rong 蔡邕 (132–192) who was so excited to meet a scion of the Gaoping Wangs that in his rush to greet the young visitor he put his shoes on the wrong way.

> When [Emperor] Xiandi was abducted westward, [Wang] Can followed [the Court] to Chang'an. The Leader of Court Gentlemen on the Left Cai Rong met and admired him. At the time the talent and scholarship of [Cai] Rong were famous, he was held in high esteem by the Court, and the street [in front of his] house was constantly clogged by carriages [of visitors] and guests filled the seats [in his house]. When he heard that Wang Can was at the door, he rushed towards him with his sandals on the wrong feet. When Can came in, still young and weak, small and frail of stature, the guests were all quite stunned [by the flattering reception he had been given]. [Cai] Rong said: "This is Mr. Wang [Chang's] grandson, his talents are exceptional, and mine are no match to his. The books and documents, letters and essays [held by] my family shall be eventually [after my death] given to him."[6]

This library must have contained a very broad spectrum of Han classical learning, and must have reflected the interest of one of Cai's forebears, Cai Xun 蔡勳 (fl. during the first decades CE) in "Huang-Lao" thought as well as the musical and poetic interests of Cai Rong himself.[7] When Cai was eventually killed as an accomplice of Dong Zhuo in 192, this priceless collection in about 10,000 scrolls was carried off in "several carriageloads" to Jingzhou by young Wang Can. It is the only library that we positively know survived unscathed the burning of Luoyang in 190 and the civil war marking the end of the Han. It must have been an important asset for Liu

Biao's Jingzhou Academy in Xiangyang. When Wang Can arrived, his family stature nearly resulted in him being chosen as Liu Biao's son-in-law, but in view of his unattractive physique and lax behavior, his cousin Wang Kai was honored in this way. When Cao Cao's military superiority became evident, Wang Can advised Liu Biao to capitulate. In return Cao Cao gave him an honorary title. He became a court poet, and a friend of Cao Cao's son Cao Pi. The very personal relationship prevailing among members of the new Wei court established in 220 is highlighted by a fine anecdote:

> Wang Zhongxuan [= Can] loved the braying of donkeys. When he was buried, Emperor Wen [= Cao Pi] went to the tomb and said to his entourage: "Wang Can loved the braying of donkeys. Each of us should bray once as a farewell for him." Thereupon each one of the guests brayed once like a donkey.[8]

During his stay in Jingzhou, Wang Can seems to have married. Two of his sons, the inheritors of the library, were involved in an early rebellion against Cao Cao led by a certain Wei Feng, and were executed in 219.[9] Cao Cao refrained, however, from annihilating the entire clan, and installed Wang Kai's son as the heir of this prominent family that Miyazaki classified as belonging to the second highest rank among the aristocracy.[10] Not much is to be said of the heir to the library, Wang Ye 業, apart from a modest career, a friendship with Pei Hui 裴徽 (fl. 230–249), scion of another important *haozu* clan that, like the Gaoping Wangs, became a founding family of the Jin dynasty in 265, and his fathering two sons, Wang Hong and Wang Bi.

Wang Bi's education probably followed that of the offspring of similar families such as the Zhongs 鐘 or the Xuns 荀 from Yingzhou who claimed to be descendants of Xunzi; it has been movingly described by Zhong Hui in the biography he wrote of his mother.[11] By the time Wang Bi came of age, the approach and style for the intellectuals of Wei had been set by Xiahou Xuan 夏侯玄 (209–249), He Yan 何晏 (ca. 190–249), and others. Little of the writing of these latter two thinkers survives but it is enough to understand that they set the new canon for their and the following generations that combined the *Laozi*, *Zhouyi*, and *Lunyu*, and in this very selection rejected the rigid school affiliations that had prevailed during much of the Han dynasty. So they would study these works guided by their mothers, a firm belief in their own genius, and the privilege of youth to be recklessly brilliant, unburdened by too much knowledge. Wang Bi began to make his mark as a sophisticated interpreter of the new canon when he was barely ten years old. He did not have to be a loner, there were other youngsters in families of similar status with similar interests, but more importantly there were many from the first postwar generation who enjoyed talking to him. He was received by his father's colleague Pei Hui, and discussed philosophy with him;[12] had big debates with Xun Rong 荀融;[13] and had contact with Wang Chen 王沉;[14] and talks with Fu Jia 傅嘏 (205–255?), another scion of an old family that was eventually to side with the Jin.[15]

The Cao court had become increasingly wary of the growing economic and cultural powers of the scions of these *haozu* clans. Following the economic recovery after the civil war, these clans had begun to regroup during the 230s; their young men had again formed loose associations under names that sported their claim to genius, sometimes including upstarts such as He Yan, who had grown up in Cao Cao's household but whose great-grandfather had been a butcher and whose family rose to prominence through the fact that the butcher's daughter became an imperial favourite concubine and that his son, He Qin, became minister of defense as a consequence. These young men were clamoring for a role in government. Emperor Mingdi (r. 227–239) saw them as enough of a threat to commission a special examination code to make sure that people with this intellectual orientation would not pass. A coup by his secretaries at the time of his death installed a child on the throne and made an associate of these groupings and uncle of the emperor, Cao Shuang, the regent together with General Sima Yi, whose son would found the Jin dynasty. With this change and the beginning of the Zhengshi era 正始 (240–249) the members of these former groupings were recruited en masse into the government with He Yan himself as *libu shangshu* in charge of civil personnel.[16] He Yan tried to forge a coalition between the *haozu* clans and upstart families from the environment of the Cao court such as his own by appointing prominent members of the *haozu* clans such as Wang Bi to the *shangshu* under his direct tutelage. The *Shishuo xinyu* preserves the story of the first encounter between He Yan and Wang Bi:

When He Yan was heading the *shangshu* [after 240], he had status and renown, and the debaters 談客 of the time filled his seats. [Commentary: The *Wenzhang xulu* says: [He] Yan was skilled in "pure talk," and at this time his power extended over the entire empire. The debaters all adored him.] Wang Bi had not yet been capped [to become an adult], but he went to pay [He Yan] a visit. He Yan had heard about Wang Bi's fame. Accordingly he laid down a series of arguments which he had hitherto considered unassailable, and said to Wang Bi: "These arguments I consider the ultimate. Are you capable of refuting them?" Whereupon [Wang] Bi refuted him, and all guests were of the opinion that He Yan had suffered defeat. Thereupon Wang Bi himself assumed the roles of both master and guest [that is, he himself both proposed arguments, and refuted them], and that for several rounds; not one of the guests was capable of matching him.[17]

He Yan was Wang Bi's elder by some decades and the most influential government official at the time. Worshiping brilliant youths such as Wang Bi was a new feature of the time, and He Yan would immortalize himself not so much through his own work but through his willingness to cede the first place to the genius of youth. Another anecdote shows He Yan going as far as visiting Wang Bi to test the commentary of the *Laozi* he was about to finish.

When He Yan had not yet finished his commentary of the *Laozi* he visited Wang Bi. [During the visit, Wang] himself explained the purport of the *Laozi*. He Yan's interpretation still had so many deficiencies that he did not even dare to make his own [opinion] heard, but only repeated "Yes! Yes!" As a consequence, he did not continue with his commentary but made the *Essays on Tao and De* 道德論 out of it.[18]

He Shao 何劭 tells us in his biography of Wang Bi:

Already as a child [Wang Bi] was sharp witted and intelligent; barely beyond his tenth year he loved Mr. Lao [Laozi]; he was proficient in argumentation, and was a skilled speaker. . . . At the time He Yan was *libu shangshu* [minister in charge of government affairs and personnel] and truly found [Wang] Bi extraordinary. He sighed in admiration about him: "Confucius [already] said that 'young people should be treated with respect [because they might end up very learned].'[19] But with this fellow [Wang Bi] it is possible to talk [already now when he still is so very young] about [problems as deep as] the connections between [the order of] Heaven and [that of] men."[20]

In this cult of youthful genius that suddenly replaced the previous respect for the old scholar who had spent most of his life memorizing the classics before starting to venture opinions of his own, He Yan was more than a man of fashion. With his social prestige as someone who had grown up in Cao Cao's household, and had stunned his foster father with his precocious intelligence; with his powerful position in the office controlling all civil appointments in the center; with his fame as one of the leading lights of the Scholarly Exploration of the Dark, Xuanxue, that became the dominant trend with this generation; with his stylized elegance and otherwordly paleness; with his use of the mind-expanding drug *hanshi san* 寒石散, and finally with these highly publicized gestures of bowing to the superior intelligence and originality of the youthful genius, He Yan was the man to set this fashion for the Zhengshi era rather than being a mere follower.[21] The constant borrowings from statements referring to Confucius and his students signal not only the historical envy with which the Xuanxue intellectuals saw this group, but also the attempts to claim for themselves a status akin to Confucius or his preferred students, especially Yan Hui, who was the most brilliant and died so young.

At the same time, the Zhengshi era marks an era of fundamental reforms in government philosophy and practice. Very little material survives that lets us understand these changes, but it seems that when the Sima took effective control through a *coup d'état* in 249, they killed most of the prominent leaders, above all He Yan himself, but by and large continued their policies.[22]

While philosophers such as He Yan, Xiahou Xuan, and young Wang Bi were engaged in crafting a new lifestyle for aristocratic youth that was to be followed and emulated for centuries, they at the same time brought their political philosophy to bear on political problems of the day. He Yan, apart from being the editor of the new *Lunyu* commentary for the *zhengshi* era, would write poems to criticize the extravagance of the court under the child-ruler;[23] and

Wang Bi would go "several times" to Cao Shuang himself to "talk about the Dao," in other words, to give advice on matters of principle in government (to the utter consternation and hilarity of Cao Shuang).[24] He Yan saw a triumvirate supervising the new politics. A third-century source reports about his assessing some of the most prominent figures of his time in the manner much practised by *qingtan* amateurs:

> In his youth when Xiahou Xuan, He Yan, and the like were the most famous in their time, Sima Jingwang [= Sima Shi] was also on the rise. [He] Yan once said: "[What the *Xici* refers to as] '[reaching] deep he is able to penetrate the [hidden] impulses of the world'—this is true for Xiahou Taichu [= Xiahou Xuan]. [What the *Xici* refers to as] '[getting to the] subtle [convergences of developments], [he] is able to manage all the affairs of the world'—this is true for Sima Ziyuan [Sima Shi 司馬師]. [What the *Xici* refers to as] 'being spirit, [he] is able to be fast without hurrying, to arrive without going'—I know this phrase, but I have not met such a person."[25]

He Yan modeled himself with the last phrase on a statement by Confucius in the *Lunyu*. There was much speculation among Confucius' entourage as to whether Confucius was a Sage. In an indirect reaction to these discussions, Confucius answered that one might meet a *junzi*, but that he never managed to meet a person qualifying as a Sage.[26] This has been read by commentators as a modest admission/denial that he himself might be one of the rare beings qualifying for a Sage. He Yan put himself into the same speaker's position as Confucius himself, and by repeating the last phrase at a time where there was universal consensus that Confucius indeed was the last of the Sages, the claim by Sima Guang (1019–1086) that He Yan wanted to indicate that this highest role of the "spirit" was indeed his, He Yan's, does not seem entirely unfounded.[27] The *Xici* passage referred to here outlines how the *Zhouyi* enables the Sage to penetrate the mysteries of the world. The *Xici* quotes the "Master," who is read as being Confucius himself, as saying that the three qualities named here—reaching deep, getting to the subtle, and being like a spirit—are the "Way of the Sage." In this triumvirate, Sima Shi is to run the world, Xiahou Xuan is to understand the hidden mechanisms of the world, and He Yan might

have flattered himself to match the role of the supreme spirit of the
new politics. Thus it seems that He Yan rather than appropriating
the role of the new Sage for himself, assumed that neither of the
three men alone qualified, but the three together might. Sima Shi
for one certainly proved He Yan to be correct in his assessment of
him. Prodded by his father, Sima Shi secretly amassed troops for the
coup in 249 during which He Yan in all his "spirituality" was executed and which set the stage for the coming of the Jin dynasty
under the Sima family.

It was a part of this great store being set on youth, originality,
style, and brilliance that relations between the individuals involved
took a new turn. In this heated intellectual and political climate, the
traditional expectations of deference to a sponsor, respect for status
and age, and other forms of self-control were not part of the interior
decoration of the leading spirits of the Zhengshi era. This was true
intellectually as well as politically. Wang Bi was appointed by He
Yan to an official position, but had no qualms about coming out with
his own corrections to He Yan's *Lunyu* commentary, and to give it
the rather brazen title *Lunyu shiyi* 論語釋疑, *Explaining the Doubtful Points in the Lunyu.* Contemporary sources are full of reports of
philosophical disagreements and polemics, a sign of a relatively
untrammeled freedom of expression during these few years from
240 to 249. Wang Bi had been promoted by He Yan, but when he
died in Luoyang in the same year in which He Yan was executed by
the Sima, none other than Sima Shi wept for him, donning on the
occasion the big coat of Confucius and making Wang Bi into his
gifted youthful disciple who died so early.

> When Wang Bi died the [later] Emperor Jing of the Jin [that is,
> Sima Shi] sighed for days on end, and said [as Confucius had
> said when his most gifted student Yan Hui died, *Lunyu* 11.9]
> "Heaven destroys me!"[28]

One might expect that with this environment, Wang Bi would
have opted for a literary form of expressing himself that would
reflect the new leeway given to youth and genius. Instead, he chose
the form of philosophical reflection imposing the most stringent
constraints on the author, the commentary, and the analytical essay
outlining the literary and argumentative structure of the two main
texts he dealt with, the *Laozi* and the *Zhouyi.* The use of these forms

forces the author to spend most of his mental energies in under-standing another text and making a unified sense out of it instead of allowing him to explore his own ideas. At the same time, a success-ful bid for interpretive control over a text such as the *Zhouyi* or the *Laozi* would bring a status similar to the first commentator and editor of the classics, Confucius himself, and the authority coming with a successful unified explanation of those texts that were unani-mously regarded at the time as the philosophical foundation pieces, quite apart from the renown of having succeeded to find satisfying and convincing explanations where all others had failed. On this count, Wang Bi was conservative and followed Han traditions. He was a brilliant debater, but he stuck with the conservative form of the written word and the conservative genre of the commentary, while many of his peers gained their fame as profound philosophers through short oral interjections and epigrammatic remarks that, with all the liveliness of orality and sense of situation, truly imitated Confucius' form of communicating "subtle words"; the brightest indi-cator of the Master's deep understanding of the weaknesses of the written word being his ostentatious non-writing of a book.

Still, by challenging tradition on the very ground where it had established its stronghold, the commentary to the classics, Wang Bi lived up to the iconoclasm to be expected from a man like him at that historical moment. His commentaries were a most devastating cri-tique of the Han tradition, and he attacked Zheng Xuan, whose commentaries had reigned supreme during the last decades of the Eastern Han, in a thinly veiled passage of his *Zhuoyi lüeli*.[29] A fine anecdote about the ultimate encounter with the ghost of Zheng Xuan that has escaped the attention of the many scholars who have tried to write a biography of this young man, highlights this chal-lenge. It also shows the dangers coming with writing commentaries that challenge the spiritual authorities that be. It is contained in the *Youming lu* 幽明錄, a compilation by Liu Yiqing (403–444), the same author to whom we owe the *Shishuo xinyu*.

> When Wang Bi wrote his *Commentary on the Zhouyi* he made fun without qualms of [a scholar as important as] Zheng Xuan because of his Ru-theories, saying: "This old fuddyduddy is completely without brains." Thereupon he heard, in the middle of the night, suddenly steps outside the door, and a moment later something stepped forth and introduced itself: Zheng

Xuan. [The ghost of Zheng] accused him: "You are so young how dare you poke holes into my writings and pick at my phrases, going so far as make fun of this old man [me, ironically Zheng Xuan calls himself *laozi* 老子]?" He looked very angry and left straight away. Fear and worry rose in Wang Bi's heart. After a short while he fell sick and died.[30]

Zheng Xuan's ghost was to hound him to his death.

The excerpt from a "Biography of Wang Bi" by He Shao quoted in the Commentary to the *Sanguo zhi* drily remarks that because of the political events surrounding the regent Cao Shuang and He Yan in 249, Wang Bi withdrew from office. In the fall of this year, he died from an epidemic. He "had no son." His tomb outside of Luoyang was a haunted spot for centuries to come.[31]

Wang Bi's Afterlife

The above short sketch of a biography of a philosopher who died very young suggests some conditions that may have had their impact on Wang Bi's thinking. His family background put him into a group of wealthy and very exclusive elite clans with a long tradition of intellectual and literary pursuits, close connections with each other and the highest political echelons, and opposition to an overly invasive central government, a feature that might have had an impact on his political theory.[32] While this family background opened for him the doors to the most fashionable philosophical salons at the time, his library allowed him uniquely easy access to a very broad spectrum of philosophical texts, among them a rarity at the time, a *Zhuangzi*, and the manuscript on which some decades later Zhang Zhan based his famous *Liezi* edition.[33] The collapse of the Han had done away with the institutional structures that had kept the old learning in place, his link with Jingzhou put him into contact with the early challenges to Han orthodoxy, and the infatuation of his time with the brilliance of a youth unpolluted by stuffy rote-learning created a preciously short historical moment that allowed him a very early exploration of his analytical skills in an extremely open and competitive environment. Together with other Xuanxue philosophers, he engaged in an envious replay of the situation of the Sage Confucius and his followers as revealed in the *Lunyu*'s emphasis on oral and situational communication of "subtle words," *weiyan* 微言. The different roles in the model set-up of Confucius and his disciples were much contested, especially that of Yan Hui, but some, such as He Yan in the quotation given above, would even stake a claim at matching Confucius himself. While Wang Bi gained much of his fame in oral philosophy, he continued to use the complex communication structure of a written text with a written commentary as a flawed but unavoidable tool of philosophy. His strong emphasis on philosophy of language signals the stress coming from critics who argued that language was intrinsically unable to handle the problem of the Dao, and therefore treated the classics as mere "debris" and useless fallout from the wisdom of the sages of old.[34]

Wang Bi's life might have been short, his afterlife was not. Although he was not executed together with He Yan but died while withdrawing from the political turmoil of 249, the two together came to symbolize the Xuanxue philosophy of the *zhengshi* era. The leading intellectuals of the Jin emulated their philosophy and style, and tried to live up to the high standards of this era in the same manner as He Yan and his friends tried to live up to the circle of Confucius and his disciples.[35] Wang Bi's philosophical tenets were much discussed with some such as Zhong Hui 鐘會 (225–264) siding with him, and others such as Xun Rong 荀融 attacking his *Zhouyi* reading, or Ji Zhan 紀瞻 holding forth on his philosophical system.[36] In the battle for the interpretive control of the *Zhouyi*, Wang Bi won out against Zheng Xuan's commentary with which it had been taught side-by-side during the Southern dynasties.[37] In the four academic subjects newly established in Song in 439 and again during the Jianyuan era (479–483) in Qi, namely Xuanxue, Ru, Literature, and Histories, Wang Bi's *Commentary to the Laozi* must have belonged to the official core curriculum of the first discipline, Xuanxue, as Wang Baoxuan has convincingly argued.[38] Eventually, Kong Yingda 孔穎達 (574–648) chose Wang Bi's *Commentary to the Zhouyi* for his edition of the *Wujing zhengyi*. In his introduction, he bluntly stated that Wang Bi's commentary "alone stood out among [all available commentaries] of former and recent times" 獨冠古今.[39] In view of these merits, Empress Wu Zetian 武則天 in the last full year of her rule in 704 enshrined Wang Bi among the worthies whose name tablets were hung up in the Confucius temple; there he would join Zuo Qiuming, Mengzi, and his old adversary Zheng Xuan.[40] While his *Laozi* commentary was eclipsed by the Tang emphasis on the Heshang Gong and eventually Emperor Ming's own commentary, he continued to dominate the *Zhouyi* reading, and it was through his eyes that the Neo-Confucian scholars of the Song dynasty had first read this foundational text of their own endeavor.

It will be noticed that Wang Bi became enshrined, after some controversy, in the Confucian tradition for his *Zhouyi* commentary. As the persona of this text, he would be part of the Confucian canon, and make it into the Confucius temple as a worthy, *xian* 賢; it helped that he had regarded Confucius as being superior to Laozi even if his reasons would hardly have pleased Confucian scholars. The person to be enshrined here was emulated for the overpowering analytical quality of his commentaries, which set the new standard for a "commentary of meaning" as opposed to a learned commentary supplementing a text with data about such things as terms and implements mentioned in the text. Although most of the early praise for Wang Bi's commenting was bestowed on his *Zhouyi* commentary, this had much to to with the prominent role of the *Zhouyi* in Confucian education. We are justified to argue that the praise was bestowed on Wang as a commentator, and held true as well for his *Commentary on the Laozi* as well as his *Solving Doubtful Points in the Lunyu*.

All his youth notwithstanding, Wang Bi still was given a second afterlife and persona, and this one mostly connected with the politics of the Zhengshi era. In this second afterlife, Wang Bi joins He Yan to form a villain called He Wang 何王. There is a certain division of labor among the two. He Yan is here said to have used his powerful political position to push through the great reform project of the Zhengshi era of which, apart from a few shallow polemics, the Jin historians seem to have obliterated nearly every trace that would allow us to understand its particulars; He Yan furthermore gave the model for a style of living reputedly characterized by effete decadence, drug-taking, and boastful emptiness. Wang Bi for his part is said to have managed through his commentaries to spread the concepts of Negativity 無 and the Dark 玄 as the only relevant topics of philosophic discourse, and thus to have turned away the minds of the country's elite from the pragmatic problems of keeping the country together and the people in order. This image began to emerge very early.

A few decades after the North had been lost to various non-Chinese-speaking groups and confederations and a part of the Chinese elite had fled south, Fan Ning 范甯 (339–401), an otherwise marginal Confucian devotee from a Buddhist family whose tireless efforts to restore the old rituals made him such a nuisance that he was eventually forced to withdraw from office, made his claim for immortality through a treatise in which he argued that the spiritual causes of China's recent demise were to be found in He Yan and Wang Bi. The treatise was written in the then popular form of a dialogue; the glorification of He Yan and Wang Bi by Fan's dialogue partner reflects to what degree Fan Ning's opinion was marginal at the time. His biography claims: "Because at the time the frivolous 浮 and empty 虛 were heaping praise on each other, the Confucians and the learned 儒雅 were daily more superseded. [Fan] Ning was of the opinion that this all had begun with Wang Bi and He Yan, the crimes of whom were greater than even those of Jie and Zhou [the notoriously vicious last emperors of the Xia and Shang dynasties]. As a consequence, he published a treatise." Given the importance of this little treatise in later times, it is appropriate to translate in full what survives of it.

> Someone said: Once the Yellow Emperor and Emperor Yao receded into the distance, and the highest Way fell into decay; once [Zhuangzi and his friends at the two rivers] Hao and Pu stopped singing, and style had no prop to support it anymore, contention for mastery manifested itself with regard to "humaneness" and "righteousness," and what was right and wrong was fixed between the Confucians and the Mohists. [Compared to these latter] [He] Pingshu's [= Yan's] spiritual grasp was beyond comparison, [Wang] Fusi's [= Bi's] sophisticated thinking penetrated the most subtle [words] [with the effect that] they resucitated the decayed structures [of Zhuangzi] from a thousand years ago and set into place the structures from the Duke of Zhou and Confucius that had crumbled. They are thus the highest achievers among court officials [by restoring the traditions of the Duke of Zhou and Confucius], the master craftsmen of the bridge over the Hao River [where Zhuangzi and his friends conversed]. I have heard, however, that you argue that [their] crimes are worse that those of Jie and Zhou. How [can] that be?
>
> Answer: Do you believe indeed, sir, that [theirs] are words of Sages? Generally speaking it is true that the Sages' capacity

德 matches that of Yin and Yang, and that they are on top of the Three Powers [of Heaven, Earth, and Man] in their Way 道; even though the [Sage] emperors of old have different appellations, and even though their inner character and outer form had different organization, in [their] unified control over the world and the completion of governmental duties they kept to the same orientation for endless generations.

Wang [Bi] and He [Yan] [on the other hand], discarding the classical texts and without respect for the system of ritual, strung words together playfully and argued frivolously, and threw the later born into confusion; they embellished and adorned [their] words so as to obscure reality, and recklessly dressed up [their] writings so as to bewitch their contemporaries. [As a consequence] people in official positions were swept off their feet and changed course, and the intellectual style of [Confucius' tradition who was teaching in Shandong near] the Shu and Xiu rivers has long since fallen into oblivion. As a consequence they brought about that humaneness and righteousness went into decline, Confucian learning sank into dust, ritual collapsed, and [court] music went under. [In short, it is due to them] that the Central Plain [= China] was overturned [= conquered]. These [two] are the kind of fellows people of antiquity referred to when they spoke of those whose words are false but sophisticated, and whose deeds are vicious, but pursued with obstinacy!

When in former times the Master [Confucius] had Shaozheng [Mao] beheaded in Lu and Taigong had Huashi executed in Qi, was this not a punishment for the same crime in distant times? The brutal repression by Jie and Zhou was truly sufficient to bring disaster upon [their] persons and topple [their] dynasty; it was a warning example for later generations and certainly could not avoid being perceived by the Hundred Families [the people]! Wang [Bi] and He [Yan] enjoyed the frivolous acclaim from all in the empire; they banked on the loud boastings from the wealthy; painting man-eating hobgoblins they considered smart, and getting agitated about reckless behaviour they considered vulgar. Truly, [theirs] is a case of the tunes of Zheng bringing chaos to [correct] music, of sharp-witted tongues toppling a state! I am most decidedly of the opinion that it is a lighter offense to bring misfortune to a

single generation [as Jie and Zhou had done], and a heavier
offense to commit crimes against an entire series of generations [such as He Yan and Wang Bi had done]; that the griev-
ance of bringing about one's own demise is small while the
transgression of leading the multitude into error is great.[41]

Fan Ning's own admissions about the overpowering intellectual
quality of the writings of these two thinkers highlight the helpless-
ness of his criticism, a quandary shared by other Jin writers such as
Sun Sheng 孫盛 (302–373).[42] Fan Ning's outcry against the wealthy
and powerful elite of his time could not be more desperate and
passionate. He Yan's and Wang Bi's frivolous and cliquish lifestyle,
their disregard for the transmission of reading the classics handed
down among the Ru, the Confucians, and their development of
sophisticated and alluring readings had besotted this elite, had led
to a dissolution of social standards, the disempowerment of the
natural leaders of the state, the Confucians, and eventually brought
about the national disaster of the occupation of the Central Plain by
northern nomadic warriors since 316. While Jie and Zhou might
have lost their lives and dynasties, He Yan and Wang Bi had lost
China proper altogether for generations to come. Thus their crime
was worse than that of these two vicious last emperors. In this way,
Wang Bi and He Yan became guilty for bringing about the perceived
tragedy of the "period of disunity," and Fan Ning's statement became a stock-in-trade in later Confucian polemics against people
from other currents of thought trying to assume responsibility for
the preservation of the state and the maintenance and transmission
of orthodoxy.

It took many generations until scholars would venture a bolder
view that tried to do justice to the intellectual and scholarly achievements of Wang Bi, and to merge his two personae back into one. Gu
Yanwu 顧炎武 (1613–82) might have had the situation of his own
lifetime, which saw the demise of the Ming, in mind when he stuck
to the old view, and roundly blamed the scholars of the Zhengshi era
for "the demise of the state, the downfall of [proper] teaching, and
the occupation of China by barbarians"; they had not only caused
the demise of the dynasty but that of the empire.[43] Zhu Yizun 朱彝尊
(1629–1709) a few years later already was bold enough to challenge
such views and their implied assumption that any slackening of
Confucian control over state ideology meant national disaster. In his

"On Wang Bi" he asserted "criticism and praise are the common [prerogative] of everybody," and should not be decided by the partial view of a single person. Fan Ning's claim was "exaggerated," but "scholars had put too much faith in it." Song scholars of highest renown such as the Cheng brothers, Cheng Hao (1032–85) and Cheng Yi (1033–1107) had admitted their indebtedness to Wang Bi, and no one could deny his intellectual contribution. While Han-dynasty Confucian commentators of the *Zhouyi* "had by and large been lost in speculations about Yin and Yang, natural disasters and odd appearances, [Wang] Bi was the first to highlight its [the *Zhouyi*'s] meaning" 始暢其義理.[44] Qian Daxin 錢大昕 (1727–1804) followed in Zhu's tracks and bluntly disclaimed the traditional charge that He Yan and Wang Bi had put Confucianism down and elevated Laozi and Zhuangzi.[45] These scholars explicitly rejected Fan Ning's facile link between Xuanxue and national disaster, and restored Wang Bi as the major philosophical and commentarial event following the end of the Han dynasty. The remaining chapters of this book will focus on this Wang Bi, Wang Bi the commentator.

Chapter Two

The System of the Classics

W
ang Bi's biographers, as well as his opponents, have described him as a philosopher bent on establishing a coherent and systematic argument through his commentaries and treatises. In his "Biography of Wang Bi," He Shao writes: "Wang Bi wrote a commentary to the *Laozi* and made a Zhilüe 指略 of it which works out that [the *Laozi*] has order and system" 致有理統.[1]

Sun Sheng 孫盛 (299–369), a critic of Wang Bi's and author of several historical works such as the *Jin yang qiu* 晉陽秋,[2] writes in his treatise entitled "The *Xiang* 象 in the [*Zhou*]*yi* are More Subtle than Visible Forms" 易象妙於見形論:

As the [*Zhou*]*yi* as a book "penetrates the spirit and knows about the changes" [an ability defined in the *Xici* 下3 as "the epitome of capacity" 德之盛], who but the most sublime [person] in All Under Heaven could be a match to it? Sadly enough, the commentaries and elucidations [on the *Zhouyi* circulating] today are altogether useless. How true is this even for [Wang] Bi who aspired to an all-encompassing systematization of the purport of the Dark by means of [his] argumentative devices of fitting and combining [arguments and terms in different places

of the text] 世之注解殆皆妄也　況弼以附會之辨　而慾籠統玄旨者乎!³
Thus, when he is lining up esoteric meanings [of the hexa-
grams], the brilliantly wrought phrases dazzle the eye, and
when he is holding forth on Yin and Yang one subtle and fine
point follows another; but as to the transformations of the six
lines, the premonitions contained in the *xiang* 象, the periods
of the day and the months of the year as well as the sequence
of the 5 ethers [associated with the five elements], *wuqi* 五氣,
[Wang] Bi completely leaves them out, and does not concern
himself with most of them. Although there are indeed passages
deserving attention [in Wang Bi's *Commentary to the Zhouyi*],
I am afraid he [basically] obscures the Great Way.⁴

The core problem in this passage lies with the Chinese term
fuhui. It often comes with negative connotations in the sense that
this technique imposes an extraneous system and structure on
texts. Sun argues that Wang Bi indeed does impose such a structure
and thereby neglects and discards the traditional and established
interpretation of the late Han, which seems to him to be the natural
way of reading this text. Basically, however, the term denotes an
interpretive technique elucidating the very structural core of a text.
In this sense it is used by Liu Xie 劉協 (465–522), who devotes a
chapter of his *The Literary Mind and the Carving of Dragons*,
Wenxin diaolong 文心雕龍 to this concept. There, he writes:

What is the meaning of *fuhui* 附會? It denotes the systematization of the literary and the argumentative [elements] 總文理 [of
a text], the integration of [its] beginning and end 統首尾, the
fixing of what is to be added and at is to be taken away, the
harmonization of the [text's] boundaries [so that] a single "encompassing" piece of work [comes about, which is, according to
Xici 上3, encompassing as the *Zhouyi* is able to "encompass the
ways of Heaven and Earth,"], which, "while [its words are]
diverse, will not [have them] encroach on each other" [in the
same way in which this is solved with the words of the *Zhouyi*
according to *Xici* 下5]. It is as in the building of a house where
a basic plan is needed and as in the tailoring of a dress where
a pattern is required. It is a fact that, when a gifted child
studies the art of writing, he should get the structure 體製
straight; for this he should take the feelings and intentions as

the spiritual core, events and meanings as the bone and the marrow, phrases and words as the musculature and the integuments, and the *gong* and *shang* [notes] as the sound and breath; he will then give proper value to the yellow and the dark [the color pattern] and apportion metal and jade [the sound pattern], offer what is appropriate, and replace what is not, and thus achieve [that it corresponds to] the Mean—this is the lasting art of connecting thoughts. It is generally true that a large-scale literary text has manifold branches and currents; he who regulates the currents, takes his orientation from the source, and he who orders the branches goes by the trunk. Therefore, in putting together phrases, *fuci* 附辭, and combining concepts, *huiyi* 會義 one (has to) go by the general guiding principle, force the ten thousand "paths" to "the same goal," and guide "the hundred thoughts" to "the same purport," [which, according to *Xici* 下 3, is how the *Zhouyi* is organized] so that, the variety of the many arguments notwithstanding, they will not have the awkwardness of getting into each other's way, and, the great quantity of the many words notwithstanding, there will not be the chaos of their all getting mixed up. Whether elements go by the Yang and stand out, or whether they follow the Yin and hide their tracks, when beginning and end are closely connected, and the manifest as well as the hidden are one unified whole, then this is the art of *fuhui*.[5]

In Liu Xie, *fuhui* refers to the establishment of homogeneity in the organization of a text in the process of its being written. In this sense it is also used by He Shao for Wang Bi's own writings:

[Wang Bi] had a nature [that accorded] with the principle of harmony 性和理,[6] he enjoyed entertainments and festivities, he had much understanding of musical pitches, and excelled in [the drinking game] of pitching arrows into a pot. In discoursing about the Way, he was no match for He Yan as far as putting together and combining literary patterns and expressions 附會文辭 is concerned, but in his natural endowment 自然 he had something clearly superior to He Yan.[7]

In Sun Sheng's statement, *fuhui* is a term for an interpretive device through which the commentator extracts a structural and systematically coherent core from a text, and elucidates it through his commentary. Sun implies that Wang Bi constructs his own meaning, disregarding the indications of the text itself, so that he is in fact superimposing a rigid structure over the text by means of *fuhui* as though he was writing the text himself. Reading the same statement without sharing Sun's polemical edge, Sun Sheng confirms what other authors of the period have also stated, that Wang Bi attempted a systematic literary as well as argumentative interpretation of the various parts of the *Zhouyi* in his efforts to arrive at a unified meaning. Sun Sheng mentions the core and trunk around which Wang's argument is constructed, namely the "purport of the Dark" 玄旨. With this reference to a core notion from the *Laozi*, he indicates his opinion that Wang Bi's philosophic project focused on certain key philosophic issues through the perusal of a variety of texts such as the *Laozi*, the *Zhouyi* and the *Lunyu*, with the implied assumption that they all deal with the same problem so that the way to a systematic elucidation of this concept is to comment on all of these texts.

The very structure of the texts with which Wang Bi is dealing seems to belie that systematic purpose. The *Laozi* is made up of some eighty short sections, *zhang* 章. Each chapter is independent of the next, and, while one might discern a common philosophic concern in many of them, the presentation is anything but systematic. The *Lunyu* consists of twenty chapters referred to as scrolls or chapters, *juan* 卷, each consisting of a fair number of mostly disconnected short passages each containing an anecdote about or a statement by Confucius or some of his disciples. The *Zhouyi* consists of sixty-four hexagrams with no apparent sequence or direct connection among them,[8] to which a great mass of interpretive material has gradually been added. The last such addition was indeed by Wang Bi himself, whose *Zhouyi lüeli* 周易略例 had, by the Tang dynasty, become the tenth chapter of the *Zhouyi*.[9]

If the structure of the individual texts seems to resist any effort at philosophic systematization, the "canonical" texts as a group are so disconnected in their topics of presentation, time of origin, and philosophic background as to make any effort at a systematic interpretation seemingly hopeless. Nonetheless, since the early Han, many of the best minds have attempted to tackle the problem of the system of the classics, and, while Wang Bi might be considered a class apart in terms of philosophical and philological sophistication, he certainly did not invent the idea that there existed a "system" in the classics. This idea had become all too well established during the Former Han. There, it might be seen as mirroring in the spiritual realm of the unity and intellectual homogeneity that this dynasty aimed to establish throughout the realm. Wang Bi's contribution was to put this common assumption of a "system of the classics" on a philosophic footing. His attempt is to be read against the established notions that he challenged. Only by reading his positive statements and commentaries as implicit discussions on or polemical rejections of other, usually not mentioned, assumptions will we be able to reconstruct the environment within which his own text operates.

Tang Yongtong's study about Wang Bi's relationship with the Jingzhou Academy established by Liu Biao at the end of the Eastern Han stressed the radical break of the scholars in the Jingzhou Academy—and of Wang Bi—with many Eastern Han interpretations of the classics, in particular those by Zheng Xuan 鄭玄 (127 CE–200 CE).[10] Yu Yingshi, on the other hand, has amassed evidence to show that a rebellion against the state-sponsored interpretation of the classics had been underway throughout the Eastern Han with Zheng Xuan one of the main protagonists.[11] This would put the scholars in the Jingzhou Academy into the tradition of Zheng Xuan. We shall shortly review the evidence.

A Sketch of Commentary Strategies during the Han Dynasty

The efforts at establishing the Five Classics as the ideological foundation of the state under Han Wudi since 136 BCE were based on the widely shared assumption that these texts were in some ways coherent. This thought was expressed through a variety of etymological and historical narratives.

The term *jing* 經 for "classics," already widely used for certain types of texts during the pre-Qin period, was defined in Han etymological explanations as being the thread going through the holes pierced on both ends of the bamboo strips that were used for writing, and holding them together.[12] In this way the generic category under which these texts were subsumed symbolically implied that the different elements that might seem to be as disconnected as separate bamboo strips are linked by a common meaning. The *Shiming*

釋名 dictionary of the Eastern Han explains *jing* 經 "classics," as *jing* 徑, "throughfare, an continuously [valid] text, [that is,] a throughfare that leads you everywhere and that can be used continuously."[13] With these two definitions three elements are described: first, the coherence of the classics; second, the universal applicability of the classics; and third, their continuous applicability. The state institution of the "Professors for the Five Classics," *wujing boshi* 五經博士, each of whom would be in charge of the interpretation of one of these classics, put the five texts into a common institutional framework, and it became a habit to speak of the "Five Classics."

In terms of content, the homogeneity of the classics was expressed through the story that Confucius himself had edited them. A story furthermore found wide acceptance according to which the main philosophic treatise in this body, the *Xici* appended to the *Zhouyi*, had been written by Confucius himself, as had the *wenyan* 文言 commentary to the first two hexagrams.[14]

The main problem, however, still remained to be solved. The accessible textual surface of the classics failed to provide either theoretical or practical guidelines for running the empire. Already the first generation of Confucius' students had wondered whether the Master revealed to them all his insights; they had gone so far as to ask his son about the father's private teachings.[15] They assumed there was some secret teaching that remained unarticulated because language could not handle such arcane matter. Confucius himself had exclaimed that he "would rather be without words,"[16] pointing to Heaven's regulation of the seasons, which resulted in perfect order without a single word uttered. The Master's refusal to commit himself to words, and his refusal to write a book of his own proved that he was aware of the limitations of language. The texts edited by him had existed previously as some kind of raw material. Through his editing, he had coded them with symbolic freight, and it was the duty of the later-born to decode the secret text and keep the insights encoded there accessible. Various schools and texts in fact claimed to possess and know the "secret" teachings of the Master. They passed them on as "traditions," *zhuan* 傳, and, since the end of the Former Han, an entire body of texts arose that even claimed to be and to divulge this secret transmission of the Master's teachings, the *chan wei* 讖緯 texts.

The form of communication chosen by Confucius is the very form through which the dead ancestors, Heaven, and the Lord on High communicated with the living, namely the dark symbolic language of the dream, portents such as the eclipse of the sun, or the crack in the tortoise shell, and similar forms of nonexplicit communication. These "texts" have to be deciphered and decoded, translated and interpreted, and retain an irritating challenge because they can never be entirely reduced to their open form. Confucius' use of this method of communication proved him to be that superior being and regulator of the world that is the "Sage," *shengren* 聖人, and it put the interpretation of the classics into the same category as the reading of the expressions of Heaven's will through auguries, oracles, and signs.

Various techniques for the interpretation of different "classical" texts had been developed already prior to the establishment of the Han dynasty, not all of them in the relatively late form of the commentary. The early *Chunqiu* commentaries such as the *Gongyang zhuan* for example extracted from the entries of these *Spring and Autumn Annals* of the court of Lu, Confucius' home state, a routine for making such entries, something like a virtual handbook for the scribes; they held the actual entries against these standard entries and if there was deviation they explained it as fraught with specific meaning that required commentary and interpretation, often accompanied by the insertion of additional historical information that could shed light on the implied meaning. This particular highly rational system of interpretation that could be negotiated in intersubjective communication, was not applicable to other texts such as the *Shi* 詩 or the *Zhouyi*. For these text, however, other exegetical strategies were developed that also proceeded on a basis of rational intersubjective communication. For the *Shi* one of the key strategies used by the *Chunqiu* commentaries, namely to reset the item in question into a historical context for purposes of textual enrichment and specification, was widely used, for example in the interpretations of the *Shi* by Mengzi and later in the prefaces to the Mao edition of this text. The keys to the *Zhouyi* provided by the different "wings" established the status of the text as a product of the Sages of old, and then proceeded to show the unified dynamics underlying the hexagrams.

These readings of the different classics rested on the assumption that the surface text in and of itself might seem trivial. Only the imputed author- or editorship by the Sages guaranteed that it did contain the truth, but it did not and could not show it.

From the surviving sources, it appears that the standard official interpretive strategy to decode the classics, as much as heavenly portents during the Later Han period, was based on the system of Yin and Yang and the Five Elements, *yinyang wuxing*, a theoretical construct that developed centuries after the material going into the classics themselves had been written and edited. With its elaborate structure of correspondences between the most varied realms such as colors, materials, heavenly bodies, and dates, it allowed for the creation of a rationally controlled, and in this sense "scientific" and communicable metatext. Applied to the *Spring and Autumn Annals*, *Chunqiu*, the lead classic of the Han since Dong Zhongshu's intervention with Han Wudi,[17] it allowed for the development of moral standards for political action that could be applied in court discussion and law cases.[18] Eventually, from the end of the Former Han, the *yinyang wuxing* theory even turned from a device to decipher texts into a device to code them. The prognostication texts, *chan wei* 讖緯, operated on the basis of this theory. It was even claimed that they represented the secretly transmitted teaching of Confucius.[19] Generally speaking, this school of interpreting the unified "system of the classics" held sway until the end of the Later Han.[20] Philologically, the system had to live with increasingly irritating anomalies. Ever more elaborate constructs were necessary to submit the entire corpus to this unified interpretive system. Once an agreement had been reached on the underlying mechanics of the coding of the classics, innovation could only be found in ever more detailed and erudite notes on the terminology used in the classics, especially with regard to such matters as ritual objects, old institutions, or rare plants and beasts. In the process, the ultimate "meaning" of the classics was taken for granted, and got lost. At least this is what the critics claimed as little of these *zhangju* 章句 commentaries survives.[21]

Opposition against this prescribed orgy of unity, homogeneity, orthodoxy, and learned loquaciousness came in various forms. The discovery of manuscripts of the texts written in "old writing" with their textual differences from the manuscripts in the "new script" gave rise to philological inquiry and undermined the validity of the current texts although the importance of these divisions has been greatly exaggerated by much modern scholarship unde the impact of the late Qing controversy.[22] The interpretive artistry of the ever-longer "phrase by phrase" commentaries, *zhangju*, was subjected to ridicule.[23] The term *zhangju* used for this style of commentary took on a meaning indicating that these lacked any consistent meaning whatever, and were just dissipating themselves in ever more elaborate interpretations of single phrases without any connecting thought.[24]

Critics who reviled these *zhangju* commentaries would break with their paradigm here or there, but in most cases, as in Zheng Xuan's, would continue to follow the basic interpretation strategy of the *yinyang wuxing* scheme. In order to thwart the intrusion of such new interpretive matter as the *chan wei* texts into the body of the bona fide classics, some scholars from the latter part of the Former Han attempted to read the classics through the much earlier *zhuan*, which in fact already had been done with the *Chunqiu* for which the *Gongyang zhuan* had provided the main reading strategy during the Former Han. The monopoly of the *Gongyang* had been broken since Liu Xin 劉歆 (first century BCE) began to read the *Zuozhuan* as something like a commentary to the *Chunqiu*, a process eventually concluded by Wang Bi's contemporary Du Yu 杜預.[25] Bi Zhi 費直 (first century BCE) read the "wings" of the *Zhouyi* as commentaries to the main body of the text, a tradition eventually followed and systematized by Wang Bi. Eventually, the relative weight of the different classics was challenged, and, during the Later Han, the *Zhouyi* with its much more philosophical bent gradually replaced the *Chunqiu* as the lead classic.[26]

An alternative to this return to the older exegetical material was the development of exegetical methods not based on the *yinyang wuxing* scheme to reach a unified understanding of the classical lore; an early example by the circle around Liu An, the Prince of Huainan, is recorded in the *Huainanzi*.

Finally, many Later Han scholars began to openly reject the *zhangju* commentaries and proceeded to find the ultimate "meaning," *yi* 義, of the classics beyond the learned casuistry and political pragmatism of current interpretations. The *yinyang wuxing* scheme had originally been intended to give just such a unified meaning to a wide body of communication be it in the form of natural event or text that derived its authority from its heavenly or sagely origin, but this original impetus was lost on the later critics, who only saw the scholastic focus on the particular.

The proponents of this commentary of meaning constructed their own pedigree. Liu Biao's Jingzhou Academy never claimed for itself the honor of having begun the search for the ultimate "meaning" of the classics, or to have rearranged the canon's priorities and contents. Many of its scholars focused their work on Yang Xiong 揚雄 (53 BCE–18 CE) and wrote commentaries (now lost) on his works, in particular the *Classic of the Great Dark, Taixuan jing* 太玄經.[27] Their own endeavor, they implied, began with this philosopher, or rather his teacher Zhuang (Yan) Zun 莊 (嚴) 遵 (59 BCE–24 BCE), whose original family name, Zhuang, was tabooed so that he became known later as Yan Zun.[28] Yang Xiong, the *Han shu* writes, studied "when he was young with Yan Zun and in this way became famous in the capital; officials at the court would often praise him as a 'man with the capacity, *de* 德, of a [Yan] Junping [= Yan Zun]'."[29]

Zhuang Zun was a specialist on the *Zhouyi* and earned his livelihood in Sichuan Province as a teacher and by fortune-telling on the basis of this book. He wrote a *Commentary to the Laozi, Laozi zhu* 老子注, of which fragments survive.[30] He furthermore wrote a treatise *The Purport of the Laozi, Laozi zhigui* 老子指歸, of which a large fragment survives in the Taoist canon.[31]

Zhuang Zun is the first known philosopher to combine an interest in the *Laozi* and in the *Zhouyi*, although the two strands seem to have been connected much earlier, as can be seen from the fact that, in the Mawangdui tombs, both texts or parts of them were found.[32] The reference to the *Zhuangzi* in the doxographic statements about Zhuang Zun might not carry much weight, and the term Lao Zhuang used here by Ban Gu refers to a school denomination rather than to the writings of the two philosophers.[33]

As seen from the comment on Yang Xiong quoted above, Zhuang Zun achieved considerable fame. In his home province, later generations would bring sacrifices to his grave and would go so far as to compare his contribution in the *zhigui* with that made by Confucius through his editing the *Spring and Autumn Annals*.[34] His intellectual stature among the contemporaries of Wang Bi can be gauged from a statement by Zhao Kongyao 趙孔曜, who described the achievements of another famous scholar from the Zhengshi 正始 period (240–249 CE), Pei Hui 裴徽, in the following terms:

His talent and his gift for systematization are pure and bright, and he is capable of explaining the Dark and the Empty. When he holds forth on the way of the [Zhou]yi, Lao[zi] and Zhuang[zi], he is in every instance more refined than people like Yan [Zun] and Qu 瞿 [?].[35]

Even two centuries after his death and during a period that regarded itself as the very peak of philosophic insight, Zhuang Zun was still so well known that he provided a standard against which to measure the intellectual acumen of scholars dealing with the *Laozi* and the *Zhouyi*. In the quotation, it is assumed that Zhuang Zun, too, dealt with the "Dark" and the "Empty," these terms obviously denoting the ultimate meaning of the *Laozi* and the *Zhouyi*.

Chao Yuezhi 晁説之 (1059–1129) writes in his *Fuzhi ji* 鹿畤記 that Wang Bi himself "followed the tradition of Yan Zun" in his own *Commentary to the Laozi*.[36] This assessment is borne out by the comparison between Zhuang Zun's commentaries and those of Wang Bi in another section of this study.[37] On the other hand, Zhuang Zun's *Laozi* interpretation made some use of the *yinyang wuxing* system, which also led him to another line of division between the two chapters. In this respect, Wang Bi did not follow his precedent.

By writing both a *Commentary* and his *Purport*, Zhuang Zun found a way out of the conflict between the phrase-by-phrase commentary with its danger of getting lost in the particular, and the grand perspective of the general essay, with its danger of losing contact with the text. Wang Bi himself appreciated this solution by following its pattern in his work on both the *Laozi* and the *Zhouyi* with his *Laozi weizhi lüeli* 老子微旨略例 and his *Zhouyi lüeli* 周易略例.

Zhuang Zun's disciple Yang Xiong followed his teacher in combining an interest in both the *Laozi* and the *Zhouyi*, to which he added a third text, the *Lunyu*, which he emulated with his *Fayan, Model Sayings*.[38] No explicit statements survive that would make clear why this third text was added. We can only surmise the assumption that Confucius was somehow at the center of all three texts. Yang Xiong did not follow his teacher in the form of his philosophizing. Instead of writing commentaries and essays about the three texts, he wrote new versions of all three that imitated their structure and in this conscious imitation allowed for an understanding of his own way of reading the original versions.

Yang Xiong's imitation of the *Zhouyi*, the *Taixuan jing*, the *Classic about the Great Dark*,[39] operates on the assumption transmitted in the *Rites of Zhou, Zhouli*, that there had been two earlier forms of this oracle handbook used in the dynasties preceding the Zhou, called Lianshan 連山 and Guizang 歸藏 respectively.[40] The *Zhouyi* itself as the *Book of Changes of the Zhou Dynasty* was thus adjusted to that dynasty as the earlier versions had met the needs of earlier dynasties. With the advent of the Han dynasty, or, as may be suggested, with the coming of Wang Mang's Xin [New] dynasty marking the end of the Former Han in 9 CE, a new *Book of Changes* was needed. In fact, Wang Mang made use of the work for divination.[41] At the core of this new book was the notion of the *taixuan*, 太玄, of the Great Dark. This notion also dominates Yang Xiong's replica of the "five-thousand-character text" as the *Laozi* was commonly referred to, in his *Taixuan fu*, 太玄賦, *Fu [prose poem] about the Great Dark*.[42]

The three texts show links beyond their emphasis on the Dark. The number of tetragrams in the *Classic of the Great Dark* is 81, which is the number of *zhang* 章 into which the *Laozi* had been divided (although Zhuang Zun proposed only seventy-two chapters with forty in the first and thirty-two in the second book), a number often seen as based on numbers speculation within the *yinyang wuxing* system.

With the concept of the Dark, *xuan* 玄, Yang Xiong established the key concept for the philosophers of the generations following the end of the Later Han. In his own work, however, this notion had not matured into a full philosophic term. For Yang Xiong and his commentators, the Dark was defined as Heaven, as it originally referred to the dark color of Heaven.[43] As Heaven was the regulating principle of nature and society, the definition of this body as being "dark" held the potential of a philosophic term and a political theory dealing with the relationship of a ruling center and the diverse social forces; this potential, however, was only touched upon in Yang Xiong's own work.

With the demise of Wang Mang's reforms and the reestablishment in a much altered form of Han rule in 25 CE, the political and philosophic conditions for the further exploration of the Dark as the possible nucleus of the "meaning" of the classics were now given. It seems that the *yinyang wuxing* system was now increasingly seen as an official doctrine associated with the *zhangju* commentaries. Their constructions of discrete meanings for different passages increasingly ran counter to the search for a unified meaning of the classics compatible with a new pair of criteria—economy and rationality—for the credibility of a textual analysis. In times of often harsh suppression of political criticism from scholarly circles, the rejection of the *zhangju*-type commentary became a marker for the mutual recognition of people or even social forces sharing a similar scholarly, philosophical, and political agenda. We will now try to define these forces.

Already in Yang Xiong's biography we find the opposition between *zhangju* and "penetrating the meaning," *tong* 通. "Since his early youth Yang [Xiong] loved to study [the classics], but he did not go in for *zhangju* [style commentaries]. In his interpretations he attempted nothing but to penetrate [to the meaning]" 雄少而好學不為章句訓詁通而已. Yan Shigu 顏師古 (579–645) explains the term *gu* 詁 as *zhiyi* 指義, "to point at the meaning," a reading that is justified in view of the surviving work of Yang Xiong.[44]

In a statement linking all the markers of intellectual independence and broad-minded critical spirit, Ban Gu is said by Fan Ye to have had "a thorough grasp of the Nine Currents and the Hundred Schools. In his studies he had no permanent teacher and did not go in for the *zhangju* 不為章句 but went after nothing but the overall meaning" 舉大義而已.[45]

Wang Chong 王充 (27 CE–100 CE) linked up with this tradition by supporting the Old Text school; philosophically he questioned the notion that Heaven was directing society through omens and other portents and developed a concept of a self-regulatory nature without strong intervention by some central activist body, a concept he explicitly linked with Huang/Lao thought.[46]

Huan Tan 桓譚 (43 BCE–28 CE), a contemporary of Yang Xiong's and, like him, sometimes associated with the so-called Old Text school, had actually been in Wang Mang's service as had Yang Xiong. According to his biography, he was "widely read, and had deep insights in many areas; he was learned in the Five Classics [as opposed to the state-appointed scholars of the classics who specialized in only one], but in all [Five Classics] he only interpreted the grand meaning, *dayi* 大義 and did not think much of the *zhangju*."[47] He seems to be one of the first scholars to formulate the thought that the Five Classics, all their differences notwithstanding, in fact had only one common "grand meaning." His *Xin lun* 新論, perhaps better translated as *Treatises on the New* than *New Treatise*, opened another avenue of implied criticism.[48] In his political theory he stressed a modern, applicable government doctrine as much as did Yang Xiong and Wang Chong; in his opposition to a bureaucratized central power he also included elements of Huang/Lao thought in his political theory.[49]

The *yinyang wuxing* system had by now turned from an instrument for interpreting the classics into an instrument for writing new classics, the *chan wei*, many of which assumed the proud title of *jing* 經. The political character of this system had become more evident as the Later Han relied to a great extent on the concepts of this system to establish its own credibility. The new Emperor Guangwu had just established this reliance when Huan Tan's *Treatises on the New* began to circulate. The emperor ordered Huan Tan's immediate execution because his teachings "were in conflict with [those of] the Sage [Confucius]."[50] Although Huan Tan was eventually banished instead, the reaction shows to what degree philosophic dissidence could be seen as a threat to the legitimacy of the government and its policies.

The *Zhouyi* specialist Bi Zhi 費直 (first century BCE) treated the *Zhouyi* as a self-explanatory text by pioneering the reading of the "wings" as commentaries to the main body of the *Zhouyi*. Wang Bi inherited this tradition and established the modern text by actually inserting the "wings" into the main body. Bi Zhi also "rejected the *zhangju* [commentaries]."[51]

Bi Zhi's contemporary Gao Xiang 高相, another specialist of the *Zhouyi* "also rejected the *zhangju* in his studies."[52]

Xun Shu 荀淑 (83–149 CE), said to be a descendant of Xunzi in the eleventh generation, "had an elevated demeanor since his youth, was widely read, but did not appreciate the *zhangju*. Therefore he was often attacked by the Ru, while he was appreciated in his home area as a brilliant man."[53] The context signals that these Ru were scholars at the court upholding the exegetic mode of the *zhangju*. Wang Bi's great-grandfather Wang Chang 王暢 had studied with Xun Shu, whose sons and grandsons continued his tradition, especially Xun Shuang 荀爽. With the Xuns we have for the first time members of one of the great magnate clans of the Later Han entering the fray. The Xuns were referred to as *xihao* 西豪, the Western Magnates,[54] and Ch'en Ch'i-yun has even suggested the possibility of a strongly political reading of Xun Shuang's *Commentary to the Zhouyi,* although his textual evidence seems to support this claim only in part. According to Ch'en's reading, Xun Shuang used his commentary to evoke the threat of rebellion should the center continue to be run by weak emperors controlled by eunuchs.[55] With Xun Shuang, a further element is added; he belonged to the "Pure Ones"

清, like Wang Bi's ancestors. With this term a growing number of officials and scholars tried to define themselves in opposition to the eunuch-dominated center.

Han Shao 韓韶 (first century CE) also was one of the "Pure Ones," from the same circles and the same place as Xun Shuang. His son Han Rong 韓融 "was already in his youth capable of systematic interpretation and did not engage in *zhangju*" 少能辯理而不為章句.[56]

By the second century CE, the intellectual and political current mapped out here achieved hegemony, the persecutions of the 160s and 170s notwithstanding; the most famous scholars of the period were part of it. Ma Rong 馬融 (79 CE–166 CE), "scion of a magnate family related to the empress,"[57] followed in the tradition of combining the various classical traditions by writing commentaries to some of the classics as well as to the *Laozi, Huainanzi,* and the *Lisao*.[58] We have no explicit statement about his attitude toward the *zhangju* and the question of the common "grand meaning" of the classics, but, from statements about and by his disciples Lu Zhi 盧植 (?–192 CE) and the famous Zheng Xuan, we can surmise their teacher's attitude.

Lu Zhi "studied in his youth together with Zheng Xuan under Ma Rong. He was familiar with both the New and the Old Text Schools, but he preferred to look for the essence [of the classics] and did not go by the *zhangju*" 好研精而不守章句.[59]

Zheng Xuan stayed closer to the traditional techniques of interpretation than his teacher. He did not comment on the *Laozi* and stayed close to the official canon, which by this time included *chan wei* texts.[60] Fan Ye, author of the *Hou Han shu*, however, writes in an analytical statement, *lun* 論, at the end of his biography about Zheng Xuan's intentions:

As to the [interpretation of] the classics, there are many schools, and each one of them gives numerous [different] interpretations; in the worst case a *zhangju* [commentary] might have more than a million words. The students labor, but the results are scanty, and so the later-born harbor doubts and have no firm guidelines. Zheng Xuan has condensed the whole, has gathered up [the best from] the different schools, has torn out the weeds, and filled in the gaps. Since [he completed this labor], the students understand by and large what the classics amount to 略知所歸.[61]

Fan Ye imputed to Zheng Xuan the desire to establish a complete system of "what the classics amount to" by homogenizing and integrating earlier efforts. This attempt presupposes a common endeavor of the various schools justified by the unified sense and meaning of the classics which they tried to decipher and spell out. The "meaning of the classics" would be found not by rejecting the readings of the different schools but by taking their best and leaving out the dregs, an interpretive principle underlying He Yan's *Lunyu jijie* 論語集解, *Assorted Commentaries to the Lunyu*,[62] a few decades later. He Yan here picked for each phrase from the available commentaries the one that seemed best suited, assuming that all previous commentators were after the same truth and in perfect disregard for their possible "school" affiliations. Fan Ye's assumption is confirmed by Zheng Xuan's letter to his son. There he writes that he "intended only to transmit what the earlier sages originally had in mind, and thought [only of] rectifying the disunity among the Hundred Schools" 但念述先聖之元義思整百家之不齊.[63] This emphasis on the "original intent" of the former sages [or the long-gone Sage Confucius] presupposes such a unified intent. In his philologic work he "gave preference to the [reading in either the Old Text School or the New Text School text] that was superior in terms of meaning" 取其義長者, writes Fan Ye.[64] In terms of philosophic economy, Zheng Xuan argued in his *Preface to the Shipu* 詩譜序 in a passage elaborating on Confucius' statement about the *Book of Songs* in *Lunyu* 2.2 that, by grasping this ultimate meaning, all other things would fall into place:

In pulling the one line [of the fishing net], all meshes will open. Little force is needed [for pulling the line].

In understanding one chapter, many scrolls will become clear.

Few thoughts are needed [to understand one single chapter]. What could be more enjoyable for the scholar?[65]

Cai Rong 蔡邕 (132 CE–192 CE), the most prestigious poet of his generation, linked to these scholars by many political, intellectual, and personal bonds, provides the direct link to Wang Bi's family. In Cai Rong's family there was a tradition of admiring and perhaps worshiping Huang/Lao,[66] and Cai Rong might have been the calligrapher writing the *Laozi ming* 老子銘, the Laozi tablet inscribed on

orders of the emperor in 165 CE.[67] At the same time, he was a scholar
of the classics and wrote the text for the New Text edition of this set
engraved in Luoyang between 175 CE and 183 CE.[68] It seems that he,
much like Zheng Xuan, tried to get beyond the factional trivia of the
Old and New Text schools.

His biography stresses that he was one of the "Pure Ones." The
politician presiding over the demise of the Later Han, Dong Zhuo
董卓, pressed Cai Rong into his service. As we have seen, Cai, in the
turmoil of imperial collapse in the capital, gave his entire library of
ten cartloads to Wang Bi's uncle Wang Can 王粲 (177–217 CE), whom
he had met when the latter was still a young man.[69] Cai's own
reading of the classics may be inferred from a letter of recommendation he wrote for a certain Bian Rang 邊讓 to He Yan's 何晏 grandfather, He Jin 何進, then the Minister of the Army:

> Already upon his first reading of the classics, he perceived
> their root and understood their meaning 見本知義, his mentors
> proved unable to answer his questions, and the *zhangju* held
> no interest for his mind. 章句不能逮其意.[70]

It had now become so common to disdain the *zhangju* that this
disdain would be mentioned by way of recommendation in certain
high circles.

Xu Gan 徐幹 (171–218), who later joined the intellectual circle
around Cao Pi and Cao Zhi to which Wang Can also belonged, and
who had close relations with the Wang Clan throughout,[71] summed
up these efforts to get at the ultimate meaning of the classics in his
Essay on the Mean, Zhong lun 中論:

> Generally, [true] scholars will make the grand idea [of a classic
> or of the classics] the primary concern [of their comments] and
> put [the explanations] of the names of things [as they occur in
> the classics and on which the *zhangju* commentaries focused]
> in second place. Once the grand idea has been brought out, the
> [explanation of the] names of things [may] follow. The poly-
> maths of vulgar Ruism, however, busy themselves with the
> names of things and give detailed explanations of vessels and
> instruments [appearing in the original text]. They brag about
> their detailed explanations and make extracts from their
> *zhangju* [commentaries], but they are unable to systematically

sum up what their [the classics'] grand meaning amounts to and thus to grasp what was at the heart of hearts of the former [Sage] kings.[72]

It appears from the material quoted above that the circles attempting to unearth the ultimate meaning of the classics were interlocked with other circles with seemingly quite unrelated concerns. Unlocked, these circles would seem to be the following:

- People persecuted in the Danggu persecutions of the "Pure Ones" since 160 CE.

- Scholars critical of the *zhangju* line of interpretation and concerned with the "ultimate" and unified meaning of the classics.

- Scholars attempting to deal with the new problems of Han China through the medium of new writing, be it in imitation of classical texts (Yang Xiong), in the new form of the essay, *lun* 論, or in the critical examination of the classical heritage (Wang Chong).

- Scholars shifting the focus of attention from the official lead classic, the *Chunqiu*, to the *Zhouyi*, which they read in the context of the *Laozi*, a group to which the *Lunyu* was eventually joined. Influence from "Huang/Lao" thinking was said to be prevalent among them.

- Highly educated members of the newly emerging magnate clans, who would recognize each other socially through intermarriage and other connections, morally by conferring the title of "pure" on each other, and politically by their common opposition to the personal exertion of power by the emperor through eunuchs and the families of empresses who were not part of the bureaucratic and social elite. These links would be above all between clans and only then between individuals. Holding and developing their social, political, and economic standing over many generations, these clans would build up intellectual family traditions and attract scholars as their guests.

- Scholars maintaining that the texts in the "old script" were the genuine text as opposed to the texts in "new script."

From the records quoted above, it is clear that each person belonged to at least two circles, and often to more. That these circles interlocked to form a fairly closed ring can be inferred: first, from their shared opposition to some of the many manifestations of the authority of the center; second, from the fact that, during the many persecutions of the Later Han, the center saw these circles as linked and persecuted them; and third, from the fact that these various and fairly distinct circles eventually, by the fourth or fifth decade of the third century, had coagulated into a rather homogeneous social stratum with a definable self-consciousness, social status, and ideology.

For the philosophic development of the search for the "meaning" of the classics, the Jingzhou Academy was of pivotal importance. Liu Biao 劉表, a member of the imperial Liu clan, was governor in Jingzhou 荊州 (comprising parts of Hunan, Hubei, Sichuan, Guizhou, Guangxi, and Guangdong) when the empire fell apart amidst warfare and unending destruction. His province was spared the ravages of war, and his academy offered shelter to scholars and their libraries. His own motive in this generous policy was probably to build up a claim to the throne as a man who knew how to honour worthies. Liu Biao himself came from the same Gaoping as the Wang clan, he had been the most famous student of Wang Chang 王暢, Wang Bi's great-grandfather,[73] and true to this intellectual schooling and background, he mostly attracted to Jingzhou Old Text School scholars with some family or political link to the big magnate families.

It is indicative of the strength of this current of thought and the social forces behind it that Liu Biao was willing to bank on them instead of inviting the official doctors of the Five Classics and their disciples. The Academy is said to have attracted over three hundred intellectuals of renown. Their responsibility was clearly to lay the intellectual foundations for the future empire after the imminent demise of the Eastern Han had become evident.

Not much of the original writing of this Jingzhou Academy survives, and we have to piece the record together from bibliographical entries and short fragments of doxographic material. From these materials, the following points emerge:

- The original impetus of Yang Xiong was rediscovered in Jingzhou. The most important scholars of the Jingzhou

Academy, such as Song Zhong 宋衷 (second–third century CE) wrote commentaries and guides to the *Taixuan jing*.[74] Wang Su 王肅 (?–256 CE) studied this text with Song Zhong;[75] Li Xuan 李譔, another student of Song's "wrote a *Purport of the Taixuan [jing], Taixuan zhigui* 太玄指歸. In all his works he based himself on Jia 賈 [Kui 逵] (30–101) and Ma 馬 [Rong 融] (79–166) and differed from Zheng Xuan."[76] The impact of this revival of *Taixuan* studies was not lost on the next generation. Yu Fan 虞翻 (164–233), whose fame as a *Zhouyi* connoisseur had national dimensions at the time and who again combined an interest in the *Zhouyi*, *Lunyu*, and *Laozi*, took exception not only to Zheng Xuan's reading, but also to the reading of Ma Rong and Song Zhong. Against the latter's "mistakes in explaining the [*Tai*]*xuan* and in order to establish [his] method he published an *Elucidation of Yang [Xiong]* 明揚 and an *Explanation [of the mistakes] of Song [Zhong]* 釋宋〔衷〕 in order to set those passages right where he [Song] had stalled."[77] The assembled scholars wrote a new standard commentary to the classics. At the same time, they worked on the *Laozi*.[78] In this manner they continued and merged the two techniques for exploring new philosophic questions, namely the commentary concerned with the grand meaning, and the "modern" *lun* 論, "essay."

- It was now generally accepted that the body of material containing elements of the unified truth definitely included matters outside the classics. Li Xuan "learned [in Jingzhou] under Yin [Mo, who had studied with Li Xuan's father under Song Zhong,] to debate about the meaning [of the classics and philosophers] and [its] systematic [exposition], and they went through the entire body of material from the classics to the different philosophers."[79]

- The technique of interpreting the classics not from the perspective of extraneous material, like the *yinyang wuxing* system, but from the more sober and rational *zhuan* [traditions] became prevalent. For the *Zhouyi*, the ten "wings" were used; for the *Shu jing (Book of Documents)*, the dictionary *Erya* was used; and for the *Chunqiu*, the *Zuo zhuan* was used.[80] Bi Zhi's exegesis of the *Zhouyi* was continued here;

Du Yu 杜預 (222–84), to whom we owe the interweaving of the *Chunqiu* and the *Zuo zhuan*, continued the Jingzhou tradition.

- The core group of lead texts was now, in the revived succession of Yang Xiong, composed of the *Zhouyi*, the *Laozi*, and the *Lunyu*.

- The key terms for commentaries were "meaning" and "system." This did not imply that all the various materials would merely be elucidations of one single theme, but rather that the different classics dealt with different aspects within a common and systematic framework, a reading going back to the *Lunyu*.[81] This reading of the classics has left its traces even in the writings of Wang Bi.

- There were important differences of opinion with the scholar who had dominated this avenue of interpretation a generation before, Zheng Xuan. However, Yu Yingshi has convincingly challenged Tang Yongtong's view that the break was complete.[82] The phrase from Li Xuan's biography quoted by Tang Yongtong, that his work on the classics "had altogether followed Jia Kui and Ma [Rong] and had deviated from Zheng Xuan,"[83] has to be reread. Zheng Xuan had studied with Ma Rong and followed his line of interpretation. In the points where student and teacher differed, Li Xuan would side with Ma Rong. This, however, meant that, in general, he would still be in the same general track as Zheng Xuan, whose commentaries had authoritative weight in Old Text–school circles. The criticisms stated by Wang Su in his *Sheng zheng lun* 聖證論 (*Vindication of the Sage*) seem also to have been directed against a blind acceptance of all that Zheng Xuan had written, because again Wang Su deals not with the model of interpretation but with individual passages.[84]

In support of his own argument that the continuity with Zheng Xuan prevailed in Jingzhou, Yu Yingshi quotes the comment of Yu Fan, according to whom "[Song] Zhong's and Zheng [Xuan's commentaries to the *Zhouyi*] differ a bit." Again, however, the context has to be respected. Yu Fan in fact praises the *Zhouyi Commentary* by Xun Shuang 荀爽 (128–190) (= Xun Xu 荀諝). After having said that Ma Rong, "who is known as a genius," still was no match for Xun Shuang "in explaining," he says: "As to Zheng Xuan from Beihai and Song Zhong from Nanyang, both of them have written a commentary [to the *Zhouyi*]; that by [Song] Zhong differs a bit from that by Zheng [Xuan], but still neither of them is a match [for Xun Shuang] and has hardly anything to show for himself [compared to him]."[85] The passage again supports the theory that, by and large, Zheng Xuan's commentary was a part of the mainstream standard before bold new readings made themselves heard.

Zheng Xuan was seen and continued to be seen as a pioneer of the "meaning-oriented" commentary. He continued to have many adherents during the following decades and centuries who would defend his heritage.[86] He Yan, editor of the *Lunyu jizhu* 論語集注 (*Assorted Commentaries to the Lunyu*) around 242 CE, showed the continuity of the new brand of meaning-oriented commentary, *yishuo* 義説, with the efforts of Han scholars like Zheng Xuan by including many of their commentaries in his selection of the best explanations. In his preface, however, he reserved the title of *yishuo* for Chen Qun 陳群 (d. 236), Wang Su 王肅, and Zhousheng Lie 周生烈, all his contemporaries,[87] thus indicating a qualitative change. His *Assorted Commentaries to the Lunyu*, in fact, marks both the indebtedness of the meaning-oriented commentary to the Later Han tradition and the break with this tradition. The result could not have been more different from the Han commentators, quite apart from the fact that He Yan and his co-editors claimed in their preface the freedom to "change a little" the wording of the commentaries they quoted if they were "not satisfied" with even the best available explanation, a claim substantiated by a comparison of the Tang MS of Zheng Xuan's with passages from this commentary quoted in the *Assorted Commentaries to the Lunyu*.[88]

The story quoted elsewhere that Wang Bi died after the ghost of Zheng Xuan had bitterly complained about his disrespectful treatment at the hands of the arrogant youngster shows that the battle with the *zhangju* commentaries was over for Wang Bi, and the father to kill was now Zheng Xuan. In the process, however, Wang Bi remained much indebted to Zheng Xuan.[89]

The differences between the various interpretations were far from being merely scholarly. Various groups claimed the authority of the classics for their own policies. In hindsight, from a perspective of a Ruism greatly deflated after the end of the Later Han, Zheng Xuan represented the Ruist reform, and reestablishing him in a position of authority meant strengthening the claim of the Ru for government offices. Thus, what originally were different and competing attempts to get at the deepest layers of the classics and the philosophers became precursors of factional fightings as we know from some later records. In this form, the conflict has become a standard trope in the polemics against the scholars from the Zhengshi era, in particular He Yan and Wang Bi, down to the *Siku quanshu congmu* editors late in the eighteeenth century who claimed that the theories of Wang Bi had been "attacking the Ru of the Han and touting themselves as Modern Studies" 新學. The editors thereby reduced a pivotal hour in the history of Chinese philosophy to the trivia of infighting between various factions of aspirants for government office.[90]

The *History of the Southern Qi, Nan Qi shu*, quotes Lu Cheng's 陸澄 (425–94) letter to Wang Jian 王儉, which reports on the efforts to establish a chair for the *Zhouyi* interpretation according to Zheng Xuan:

> In the fourth year of the era *Taixing* [321 CE], the *taichang* Xun Song 荀崧 asked for the establishment of a chair for the *Zhouyi* commentary of Zheng Xuan, which [as he said] had been widely read in earlier times. At the time, however, power was in the hands of the Wangs 王 and Yus 庾, altogether mighty spirits with refined knowledge, who were capable of discoursing about the Dark and the Recondite, and thus [the attempt] to have [Wang] Fusi['s] [= Bi's *Zhouyi Commentary*] rejected and [Zheng] Kangcheng[s] [= Xuan's] used, was a hopeless undertaking. Subsequently, during the Taiyuan era [376–397 CE] [a chair teaching the *Zhouyi* according to] Wang Su's *Yi* [*Commentary*] was established because [Wang Su] was about halfway between [Zheng] Xuan and [Wang] Bi. When, during the era Yuanjia [424–54 CE] the university was being established [under the Liu Song dynasty in the South], [chairs for teaching the *Zhouyi* according to] [Zheng] Xuan and [Wang] Bi coexisted side by side. When Yan Yanzhi 顏延之 was Director of the Imperial Banqueting Court [in 454], he abolished [the chair for] Zheng [Xuan] and established [a chair] for Wang [Bi],

because [Yan Yanzhi's] interest was only to stress the Dark, and he did all he could to damage the Ru. If today the approach of the Ru is not strongly propagated, it is not worthwhile to establish a university. All the classics are in the hands of the Ru; only the *Zhouyi* is [interpreted] with regard to the Dark. But the technique [of interpreting the *Zhouyi*] with regard to the Dark cannot be wiped out, and [on the other hand] we cannot leave the Ru with an incomplete [classical canon in their hands]—and this means one has to let [the two forms of exegesis of the *Zhouyi*] exist side by side.[91]

Control over the *Zhouyi* was never regained by the Ru for the next millennium. Wang Bi's *Commentary to the Zhouyi* became the official text during the Tang, and his explanation of the structure of this book, the *Zhouyi lüeli*, became the ninth chapter of the *Zhouyi* itself.

History seems to have conspired to put Wang Bi in about every possible advantageous position to live out his genius in the short twenty-three years of his life. Being an offspring of a famous magnate family, the Wangs from Gaoping, made him by birth a member of the most elite intellectual and social circles of his time. His family tradition linked him to the Old Text school, the Pure Ones, and the Jingzhou Academy. His education focused on the new "canonical core," the *Zhouyi*, the *Laozi,* and the *Lunyu* at a very early age. The Ru doctrine had not only lost its prestige, but with the demise of the Han, also its power. While general education seems to have been severely hurt, the magnate families had taken care to give their offspring the best they could offer so that an entire generation of irreverent young intellectuals with a common philosophic and social background competed in Wei for the laurel of the sharpest mind, which produced a challenging intellectual environment.

As the territory ruled by the Han split into three separate states, Wei, Shu, and Wu, with no new unified central government taking over with a need and capacity to give expression to its power by unifying the intellectual sphere, there was a breathing space for a young and appropriately arrogant philosopher to instigate a qualitative change in the history of Chinese philosophy and bring to maturity the diffuse and wavering attempts of the preceding generations. And, finally, history threw into the lap of the young man Cai Rong's library, the only collection known to have survived the conflagration of the Later Han, a disastrous burning of the capital and its collections. Cai Rong's collection must have included Han scholarship, materials from the Huang/Lao tradition, and poetry, and it must have been supplemented by Wang Can in Jingzhou with the new studies written there.

Chapter Three

Technique and the Philosophy of Structure

Interlocking Parallel Style in *Laozi* and Wang Bi

Wang Bi's 王弼 (226–49) commentary to the *Laozi* is not the first of its kind. By his time, the market was flooded with other commentaries, and Wang Bi's readers were most likely to have first read the *Laozi* through one or the other of these earlier commentaries. Whatever survives of these earlier commentaries does show a strong emphasis on understanding the purport and meaning of the *Laozi* but little emphasis on the language of the text as well as its statements on language.[1]

In this respect, Wang Bi fundamentally differs from the earlier commentators. He pays very close attention to the formal and structural devices used by the *Laozi*, and even more to the *Laozi*'s pronouncements on language and its limited capacities in dealing with the Dao. His analysis of the language and statement structures of the *Zhouyi* 周易 and the *Lunyu* 論語 shows the same focus. All three texts suggest through their often highly elaborate formal structure and their use of paraverbal means of articulation—which is especially marked in the *Zhouyi* hexagrams—a high consciousness of the limited uses of plain language in discussing the mysteries of the Dao, the universe, and the Sage. Their use of nonverbal means of expression such as formal stylistic patterns, hexagrams, or self-contradictory language can thus be read as a conscious effort to expand the means of articulation beyond words, and their explicit statements about language suggest that this is a conscious strategy.

In his diatribes against other commentators of the *Laozi* from different schools, Wang Bi claims that they do not understand the *Laozi*'s use of language, and that they disregard not only the actual features of the *Laozi*'s language, but also the explicit statements of the text on language. Instead, he claims, "according to what their eyes happen to perceive, they assign a name [of a school to which the *Laozi* purportedly belongs]; depending on what they like, they cling to that meaning."[2]

Against this attachment to the verbal surface of the text, Wang Bi quotes the *Laozi*'s explicit warnings against such a procedure. His criticism of the "school" reading of the *Laozi* implies a program of his own: Wang Bi will extract his own strategy of reading the *Laozi* from the implicit and explicit parameters provided by the text itself. The *Laozi* itself has to provide the key to its proper reading, and Wang Bi will articulate and make explicit the features of this key. While Wang Bi presents his own hermeneutic procedure in stark contrast to that of all others, Han-dynasty commentators of other texts such as the *Mengzi* and the *Chuci* have started to move into this direction. This is especially true for Zhao Qi 趙岐 (?–201) who reads *Mengzi*'s strategy of reading the *Shijing* as an advice to the reader about how to read the *Mengzi* itself, an advice that, sure enough, had not been heeded by previous readers of the *Mengzi*.[3] Again these previous readers stuck to the surface text with the result of missing the intended meaning of the *Mengzi*. The hermeneutic procedure of extracting the strategy for reading a text from the indicators given in the text itself will claim the authority of an authentic reading, and will from this position reject other readings as being wantonly imposed. At the same time, it subjects itself to a rigid set of rules and procedures that dramatically reduce the interpretive leeway of the commentator by making his readings falsifiable on the basis of its own standards. While this more scholarly approach might on occasion seem to signal a reduction in the vitality of appropriating a text to contemporary needs, it certainly makes it more compatible with modern hermeneutic approaches, and inserts these commentaries as serious participants into a modern scholarly discussion about the reading of classical Chinese texts. In other words, Wang Bi's handling of the *Laozi* transcends in terms of method the historical limits of his own time, and his discoveries concerning the coding features of the *Laozi* or the *Zhouyi* have the potential of being tested and verified/falsified by modern scholarly methods of textual research.

This chapter will begin at the margins of Wang Bi's analysis of the *Laozi*, namely with his analysis of an important stylistic feature of the *Laozi* that I will call interlocking parallel style. Given the high status of the *Laozi* among Xuanxue scholars, this feature eventually became the basic stylistic mode of discourse on the Dark, *xuan* 玄, and the Dao. The start at the margin rather than at the center has the advantage of being more economical in highlighting some core elements of Wang Bi's handling of the text; the focus on the formal elements of the style of the *Laozi* and of Wang Bi himself has the advantage of precluding the danger of a unified deformation that is always present with the core content of a text as influential and much commented-upon as the *Laozi*.

We thus begin the analysis of Wang Bi's commentarial interpretation of the *Laozi* with a study of the features of interlocking parallel style that he extracts from the *Laozi* text, and reproduces in his own writings.

The Discovery of Parallel Style in Western Scholarship

In 1892, the eminent Dutch Sinologist Gustave Schlegel gave a first description in a Western language of the rules governing Chinese parallel prose, followed in 1896 by his critical retranslation of Zhang Yue's 張説 (667–730) preface to Xuanzang's travel account.[4] He focused on the rigid numerical and grammatical parallelisms dominating much of elevated and profound prose for texts such as prefaces. The understanding of this parallelism would help in unraveling difficult textual passages by relying on a parallel phrase for elucidations of grammar and for educated guesses about textual corruptions and emendations. His rule was:

> In two parallel or juxtaposed phrases the laws of Chinese style demand that all parts of the statement correspond to each other: subject to subject, verb to verb, noun to noun, adjective to adjective, adverb to adverb, place name to place name, genitive sign to genitive sign, object to object, etc., etc.[5]

The parallel phrases in his sample are simple pairs whose core elements would normally be antithetical and complementary.

The little volume was well received by scholars such as Erwin von Zach and J. Legge, and his discovery has long since become part of a classical sinologist's education. Schlegel's description of this rhetorical device, however, useful as it is, can be viewed as only a beginning of the study of the forms, history, intellectual origins, and function of parallel style in Chinese. As Schlegel's line of inquiry has not been continued, however, his description of a rather mechanical and crude parallelism has resulted in the complacent view that his rule is all there is to parallel prose. Schlegel seems to have been unaware of the relevant Chinese scholarship and reading practice. By now, many Chinese books have been written on Chinese "parallel prose," *pianwen* 駢文, its features and history, and collections of works in this style have been put together.[6] They have accumulated much evidence on the pervasive use of parallelisms in both poetry and prose before the Qin, have pointed out the lift in status given to this pattern through its use for the majestic tone of imperial edicts, *zhizhao* 制詔 since the Early Han,[7] have shown that its use became more widespread during the Later Han to peak in Cai Rong 蔡邕 and have not failed to notice the presence of the pattern in the *Laozi*, in He Yan and Wang Bi.[8] Their focus has been on the aesthetics of the pattern; their analysis of the core structural features of the pattern, however, has not gone beyond the rule set up by Schlegel; and there is no analysis of the much more intricate pattern of interlocking parallel style and its philosophical implications.

While it would be rather unusual to find a qualified sinologist nowadays mistranslating a phrase because a parallelism has been overlooked, I contend that the lack of understanding, among sinologists, of the more sophisticated forms of parallel style has resulted in misreadings of many texts and, worse, in a social practice of attributing the seeming lack of coherence in Chinese philosophical arguments to inconsistent thinking by the Chinese authors. For reading third-century Xuanxue 玄學 texts, Schlegel's rule is clearly insufficient. It covers only the variant with the poorest endowment, the blank parallel pair; the authors studied here, however, used a rich variety of stylistic devices rooted in parallel style and linked to the philosophical problematic of overcoming the limits of definitory language in handling core philosophical categories.

This chapter will argue that very many of the *zhang* (chapte_ _,
paragraphs) of the *Laozi* are entirely or in part written in interlocking parallel style (IPS); that Wang Bi made a conscious and sophisticated use of his understanding of this pattern in his commentary
to the *Laozi*; that his own writing mostly uses this pattern and
contributed greatly to make it into the standard literary form of
philosophical Xuanxue writing; and that the application of the
rules of this pattern, which I shall try to extract from the *Laozi* and
Wang Bi's writings, will solve a number of riddles both texts
have offered translators and scholars, and will open another—
structural and nonverbal—dimension of these texts' philosophical
argumentation.

As will be seen from the outset, this chapter takes seriously
Wang Bi's hermeneutical claim of a reading based on verifiable and
falsifiable features and indicators of the *Laozi* itself, and accepts his
reading of interlocking parallel style as a legitimate hypothesis to be
subjected to regular procedures of falsification. Or, to put it negatively, it does not from the outset reduce Wang Bi's reading to being
a historical event of at best marginal interest to a modern scholar
interested not in Xuanxue but in *Laozi*.

The Problem: Molecular Coherence

There has been consensus that what is seen as the overall philosophical consistency of the basic tenets of the *Laozi* to be found in a
number of overarching and general statements is not matched by
argumentative and rhetorical coherence within the individual sections. Among the hypotheses offered to account for this riddle were:
the text might be badly transmitted, the bamboo strips on which it
was written having fallen apart and been reassembled in the wrong
order (Yan Lingfeng); there has been a misunderstanding of the
textual structure, which is looser, more like a series of largely
disconnected proverbs (D. C. Lau, Kimura Eiichi); or, the text's
profundity eludes common understanding altogether.

While the last hypothesis is a matter of belief only, the first has
been disproved, and the second badly shaken by the three *Laozi*
segments recently found in the Chu tomb at Guodian 郭店, a tomb
perhaps closed as early as 310–300 BCE,[9] and the two nearly complete *Laozi* manuscripts found in the Mawangdui 馬王堆 tomb near

Changsha, both dating from the first decades of the second century BCE. The Guodian *Laozi* segments show a sequence of the sections, *zhang* 章, of the *Laozi* that has hardly more than an accidental connection to the sequence preserved in all variations of the received text and already largely prefigured in both Mawangdui *Laozi*.[10] This might indicate that the familiar sequence has become fixed after 300 BCE—if the Guodian *Laozi* do not present one or several separate lineages, which is quite possible. The texts preserved in both finds, however, have in the main confirmed an amazingly high level of stability of the transmitted *Laozi*, and thus have done nothing to solve the problems of connections between individual phrases within a given *zhang* of this text, and certainly have not provided us with a loose pile of proverbial utterances that were later linked into what is known as the *Laozi*.[11] Most important, the stability of the *zhang* of the *Laozi* has been confirmed by interpunctuations especially in the Guodian texts and by the very fact that the *zhang* are in different sequences. The Guodian texts themselves already present two different sequences, both altogether unconnected to the received text. Guodian *Laozi* A and C overlap in reproducing the same segment from *Laozi* 64 in the received text. In A, this segment is in the sequence 46, 30, 64, 37, 63; in C it is in the sequence 35, 31, 64, and this is the end of what survives from this segment. In other words, even the *Laozi* texts found in the Guodian tomb have different sequences of the *zhang*, but the segment of *zhang* 64 given there clearly has the same structure with minor variants. The Mawangdui texts also have in many places a sequence of the *zhang* that differs from the received text, quite apart from an inverted sequence of the two chapters, *pian* 篇. The *zhang*, however, reappear by and large intact in their new places which confirms their stability as independent textual units.[12] The transfer of entire *zhang* to new locations proves that, at this early date, the stability of these *zhang* as textual units was high even where no formal markers such as dots separated them in manuscripts. This leaves us with the problems of understanding the rhetoric of their internal structure.

The hypotheses quoted are, in my opinion, the product of uncertainty expressed by many scholars about the specific connection linking individual phrases within a given *zhang* of the *Laozi*. The problem is thus one of molecular coherence within a body of philosophical thought otherwise seen as being quite consistent. This uncertainty has led to translation strategies that assume that the

Laozi consists of proverbs and similar popular sayings glued together by a more or less incidental *hence* and *therefore* or an occasional conclusion.[13] The recent retranslations, often based on the Mawangdui manuscripts and including one by D. C. Lau, have not readdressed this problem.[14]

Attempts to proceed with the proverb theory and eliminate the problems of cohesiveness within the *zhang* have not proven very successful; both Kimura Eiichi and D. C. Lau are forced, for reasons of rhyme, to leave passages together even where their translation cannot provide much meaning. D. C. Lau does not seem to stand too firmly by his own analysis. After saying "individual chapters are usually made up of shorter passages whose connection with one another is at best tenuous,"[15] he suggests "if the reader can see the connection between parts that I have separated, he can simply ignore my section markings."[16]

Beyond the analytical problems of the proverb theory looms the questionable relevance of this solution for understanding the *Laozi* as a Chinese text handed down, read, and reread over more than two thousand years in various strands of Chinese tradition. If we assume that the *Laozi* "originally" was an anthology of loosely connected proverbs to which a helpful editor added more connecting *"thus*'s" and *"therefore*'s," *gu* 故 and *shiyi* 是以, than the text could support, we would still be faced with the fact that not a single historical reader read the text in this manner. For the understanding of this *Laozi* as part of Chinese traditions the proverb argument would be of little help; we would still be forced to reconstruct the *Laozi* as it was read by different commentators, traditions, and groups at different times. Such reconstruction would have to be based on a shared perception that the text was coherent both in terms of its overall argument and the detailed connections within a *zhang*. This chapter will argue that Wang Bi read the *Laozi* as a text largely written in a firm pattern—interlocking parallel style—the knowledge of which allows for understanding the argumentative connections within the *zhang*, and that he and other eager students of the *Laozi* copied this style in their own writings.

It will not be disputed that the reconstruction of a historical reading of a text is a valid hermeneutical endeavor. The modern scholar, however, has given the historical reader, and especially his own predecessor, the commentator, short shrift insofar as understanding the "original meaning" of the text is concerned. With characteristic bluntness, Arthur Waley has summed up this view in the comments to his *Laozi* translation: "All the commentaries, from Wang Pi's onwards down to the 18th century, are 'scriptural'; that is to say that each commentator reinterprets the text according to his own particular tenets without any intention or desire to discover what it meant originally. From my point of view, they are therefore useless."[17] Waley expresses a view widely shared to this day and responsible for the sorry state of research in one of the most sophisticated and philosophically rewarding sources of Chinese intellectual history, the commentaries. Historical Chinese commentaries are used by modern (including modern Chinese and Japanese) scholars at best as quarries from which to pluck an occasional note about a tricky passage. If their own theories are presented as they are in studies on Xuanxue, their statements are mostly quoted as stand-alone phrases torn from their original commentarial context and purpose.

This attitude does not seem to result from a long history of scholarly research on these commentaries; little such research is in evidence. Its roots, therefore, must be sought in European intellectual history. One marker of the Reformation and Renaissance was to reject the commentarial authority of the Church, and to establish the *Urtext* as the only valid point of reference. This European prejudice against commentaries as second-hand scholastic thinking without basis in the text, which was the result of European theological polemics, eventually came to dominate scholarship worldwide. It was this prejudice that has earned for Chinese commentarial literature the harsh words of Arthur Waley, and the general scholarly disregard.

The implied fundamental difference between modern scholarship and premodern commentaries is decidedly too flattering for the former. Elsewhere I try to make the point that Wang Bi and other commentators did interpret the *Laozi* in the context of their own philosophical, political, and ideological concerns and struggles, but, with the authority of schools or religious communities at a low ebb after the end of the Han, a high degree of scholarly and rational treatment of the text was essential to enhance their own positions as compatible with the "ancients." If these commentaries had been just random notes jotted down here and there, they would have ended up in oblivion—and would have had no effect.[18] At the time of Wang Bi, there was an intense struggle between various political trends as to who could justly inherit the authority imparted by this text; the commentaries were therefore closely scrutinized and criticized. That Wang Bi's commentary remained influential through the ages is not owing to the political position he represented, but to the fact that he presented it as a close interpretation of the *Laozi*, which, in its sheer analytic quality, earned him respect, even from his opponents.

The language of the following analysis will leave it open whether we are describing an important rhetorical feature in the *Laozi* as imagined by Wang Bi (which still would make it important for the understanding of Wang Bi's own thinking), or one that can actually be found in the text and thus marks a verifiable scholarly discovery on Wang Bi's part. Only in the end will I try to come to a conclusion about Wang Bi's hypothesis. The reader is thus asked to reserve his or her judgment and to first evaluate the evidence provided.

My overall project is mainly concerned with the political philosophy of Wang Bi. One of the first obstacles here is the structure of his own writing and argument; the second, that of the text(s) he was commenting upon. In the presentation of the argument I shall start with the model of Wang Bi's own style, namely the *Laozi*.

There are several levels of coherence in a text, depending on the questions it is exposed to. It may be coherent within the framework of the political and ideological discussion of a given time, coherent with other works by the same author; coherent in presenting a comprehensible and more or less consistent ensemble. Finally there is the question of the word-for-word, sentence-for-sentence coherence within a given segment of a text; it is in this field of molecular coherence here that most problems with the *Laozi* arise. Wang Bi dealt with the overall consistency of the *Laozi*'s philosophy in the *Laozi weizhi lüeli* 老子微指略例, translated and analysed elsewhere. I will focus here only on the problems of molecular coherence.

All current editions divide the *Laozi* text into *zhang*. While the old manuscripts such as the Guodian and Mawangdui MSS sometimes use spacing or dots as visible limits between the *zhang*,[19] their length, as we have seen, is largely determined by content and elements such as initial and final particles. The *zhang*, accordingly, present relatively stable textual units that have remained largely unchanged since the first available manuscripts early in the third century BCE. Their rhetorical structure is the issue here.

Open Interlocking Parallel Style in the Laozi

A number of passages in the *Laozi* are written in "open interlocking parallel style." The *Laozi* text used here is my reconstruction of the *Laozi* as used by Wang Bi. This will be published in a separate volume. As far as relevant for the argument, I will refer to other, earlier, *Laozi* texts. *Laozi* 64.5–6 says:[20]

```
1  為者敗之
2  執者失之
3  是以聖人
4  無為故無敗
5  無執故無失
```

A minimalist translation that leaves aside the problem of the points of reference for the different *zhi* 之 may run:

    1 He who interferes, destroys them;
    2 He who holds fast, loses them.
  3 That is why the Sage
      4 does not interfere and thus does not destroy
      5 does not hold fast and thus does not lose.

It should be noted that I deal here with structure, not with the particulars of translation. Even if someone should prefer a different choice of translation terms, the argument would stand so long as the structural analysis was not falsified.

Phrases 1 and 2 are rigidly parallel according to Schlegel's rule, as are phrases 4 and 5. This formal parallelism linking the pairs 1/2 and 4/5 is crossed by a linkage of content: The words *wei* 為 and *bai* 敗 from phrase 1 are taken up in phrase 4; the words *zhi* 執 and *shi* 失 from phrase 2 in phrase 5. Parallelisms with this explicit linkage are the rule in open IPS. We thus have two pairs 1/4 and 2/5 openly linked by common language and content, yet not parallel with each other. Phrases 1–5 therefore consist of two pairs of phrases linked by parallelism, 1/2 and 4/5, and two pairs of phrases linked by content, 1/4 and 2/5. The divide between the two parallel pairs is formed by "that is why the Sage." This element does not link the immediately preceeding and the immediately succeeding phrase, which would give an absurd sequence "He who holds fast, loses them. That is why the Sage does not interfere and thus does not destroy," a sequence absurd because it connects the disconnected phrases 2 and 4 instead of the pairs 1/4 and 2/5. Phrase 3 accordingly links the two pairs, and must in fact be read as two identical phrases "that is why the Sage" compressed into one, and linking phrase 1 with phrase 4 as well as phrase 2 with phrase 5. Phrase 3 thus establishes the connection between the pairs of phrases linked by content. Trivial as this might sound, it establishes a vital reading strategy for a proper handling of IPS, namely spatial instead of linear reading.

While in terms of form, the text might be described as two sets of parallel pairs, I and II, linked by a nonparallel phrase, in content the text consists of two interlocked strains, *a* and *b*, with a nexus formed by a third element. Focusing on content alone as visible in the words, one might unlock the text into two long parallel statements:

a He who interferes, destroys them. That is why the Sage does not interfere and thus does not destroy.
b He who holds fast, loses them. That is why the Sage does not hold fast and thus does not lose.

The formal parallelism and the compression of the two uses for "that is why the Sage" into one are not just elegant and economical ways of expressing a thought. They express, through silent and structural means, a second layer of thought. This can be verbalized. The two strains *a* and *b* are not merely juxtaposed. In subject matter they are complementary opposites which together form the entirety of a realm of entities. Strain *a* with interference 為 and destruction 敗 is mainly related to a ruler's power of social action; the *b* strain is mainly related to his wealth. These two are the mainstay of his position. The same antonymic pair appears in formulas containing the notions of "fame" and "wealth" abounding in other sections of the *Laozi*. This is not too evident in the present case, but will become clearer further along. Here we shall establish a hypothesis that, as a rule, a relationship of complementary opposition prevails between the core notions of parallel pairs like the *a* and *b* here. Together these form a whole in the manner of Heaven and Earth or Yin and Yang.

The parallelism indicates formally and nonverbally a similar, even identical, structure of two opposite realms. He who "acts on it" would normally have some achievement in the end, but he "destroys"; he who retains would normally have much in his possession, but he "loses." The two opposite realms share the same structure, and this is expressed in the form of parallelism.

The separation of the two pairs by the "that is why the Sage" signals a different status for these pairs. The first represents a set of universal rules as might be operative for Heaven and Earth, or the Dao. The second marks the conscious application ("that is why . . .") of this universal rule in the Sage's action and gives its results. There is thus reason to give separate numbers to these pairs. Section I (phrases 1 and 2) of the quoted passage gives the general rule, section II (phrases 3 and 4), its application by the Sage.

This short piece deals with three issues. First, the consequences of "interfering" and "holding onto." Second, the parallelism prevailing between the dynamics of the power of "interfering" and the wealth that is being "held onto." Third, the basis of the Sage's behavior in universal rules. Only one of these three is verbalized. The other two are expressed formally through structural arrangements such as parallelisms and pair groupings.

A linear reading would typically follow the tunnel prescribed by the sequence of the characters along the lines of the text to get at the meaning. A variety of devices are often used to overcome the limits this linearity imposes on a thought that as a rule is full of complex three-dimensional correlations among its constituent parts. In classical Chinese texts these devices might include section markers or final particles to define the borders of one argument or thought; terms such as 夫 in the beginning of a phrase to mark a statement of a general validity as opposed to a statement functional only in a particular context; explicit references to earlier or later statements within the same text to bolster an argument while avoiding reduplication; implicit quotations from authoritative texts to prove consistency of the argument with tenets of the classics, and so on. Outside and beyond these devices, statements have been developed that are silently encoded in the structure. The most evident form of a spatial text is the *Zhouyi*, but IPS opens the way for spatially organized statements that add to the linear surface text a new organization and a rich new layer of implicit argumentative matter. In the process of the cultural transfer any modern reading of the *Laozi* and of Wang Bi's *Commentary* entails, this silent structure and argument has to be made explicit because its decipherment is not anymore part of the modern reading routine. In the example given above the same phrase "he who interferes destroys them" appears simultaneously in three different contexts without moving an inch from its position in the linear sequence of characters: it is grammatically and thus structurally parallel to the phrase "he who holds fast, loses them," it is the first half of a statement the second half of which ("does not interfere and thus does not destroy") comes only three phrases further down, and it is part of a segment I describing a universal dialectics as opposed to its application by the Sage in segment II. None of these three texts are verbalized, but the three are in fact more important ingredients of the statement than the words themselves.

This passage from *Laozi* 64 has been selected for detailed presentation because some key factors of interlocking parallel style are distinctly visible here. The passage consists of two interlocked complete utterances, a (1/4) and b (2/5); their subjects are opposites and together form a whole. This is the vertical structure of the text. Its horizontal structure is marked by two sets of parallels, 1/2 versus 4/5, pointing to the identical structure of the opposite phenomena dealt with in a and b. The passage is written in "open" interlocking parallel style in that there is an explicit verbalized link between the constituent elements of the two strains, in this case through the vocabulary *wei* 為 *bai* 敗 in a, and *zhi* 執 *shi* 失 in b.

After this pedantic analysis, I shall go one step further and propose to make the silent structure as explicit as nonverbally possible through a form of structural writing:

I 1a He who interferes destroys   2b He who holds fast loses
       them;   them.
                    3c That is why the Sage
II 4a does not interfere and   5b does not hold fast, and
       thus does not destroy.   thus does not lose

or

I 1a   2b
       3c
II 4a   5b

In this structural writing, horizontal correspondence indicates parallelism, vertical correspondence indicates the strain to which a phrase belongs. That phrases such as 3c here that are written in the middle indicates that the phrase refers equally to both strains and must be treated as two identical phrases compressed into one. Arabic numerals such as 1, 2, 3 indicate the sequence of phrases in the Chinese text; roman numerals such as I, II, III, mark blocks of phrases sharing the same argumentative status. In the present case, "that is why the Sage" not only links the first pair of parallels with the second, but also serves as the marker for the status difference in content between blocks I and II. Since, in the great majority of cases, there are two strains and there are general statements pertaining to both, I have formalized the names of the strains into *a* and *b*, and refer to the statements pertaining to both as *c*.

Wherever applicable, the full translation of Wang Bi's *Laozi*, his *Laozi Commentary*, and his "The Structure of the *Laozi*'s Subtle Pointers" will be written in this form in the volume containing the translations of Wang Bi's work on the *Laozi*. Read as it appears in the linearity of the text, the sequence of the passage will be 1a, 2b, 3c, 4a, 5b. Read in terms of parallelisms, the reading would be 1a/2b as one pair, 3c as a nonparallel piece referring to both strains, and 4a/5b as the second pair. Read in terms of content, the unlocked strains would require a reading 1a/3c/4a and 2b/3c/5a, 3c appearing twice. Read in terms of the macrostructure of the argument, section I would mark the general statement, section II its application.

The analysis of this short piece shows that the Schlegel rule is far from sufficient for understanding the intricacies of parallel style. It refers only to pairs of phrases, while, in the present case, we have a much more complex structure, interlocking phrases that require a very particular reading strategy. The conventional unilinear reading of phrase after phrase must be abandoned in favor of a spatial reading aimed at mentally constructing the complex macro- and microstructures of the statement; only the understanding of this structure will enable the reader to grasp the meaning of the statement. This integrated use of verbal and structural devices of communication, of articulate and silent text, is highly economical. Its most elaborate form is found in the *Zhouyi* 周易, where the structural devices are actually made visible in the form of hexagrams and thus cannot be overlooked, unlike the form used in the *Laozi* (and many Xuanxue writers). The innocent example with its open interlocking parallel style given here can hardly be said to present grand challenges to understanding. This will change once we move toward closed IPS.

The following section from *Laozi* 27.6 in open IPS presents a more developed *c*-section. More important, it will show how the position of identical referential terms such as 其 within the IPS structure might change their point of reference and thus force radically different translations for identical terms. Again the reader is asked to disregard the translation, the identification of the subject, and other matter within the brackets. They are based on Wang Bi's readings. At this point, however, we are interested only in the structure of the *Laozi* statement, not in different commentators. The numbers indicate the sequence of the textual elements and phrases:

1 故
2 善人不善人之師
3 不善人善人之資
4 不貴其師
5 不愛其資
6 雖智大迷

A first translation may run according to Wang Bi's commentary:

1 That is why [the Sage]
2 [makes] the good ones into the teachers of the not good ones, and
3 [makes] the not good ones into the material of the good ones, [but the Sage]
4 does neither honor their [the not good ones'] teachers
5 nor does he love their [the good ones'] material.
6 Even having knowledge, it would be a great error [to do this, that is, honor and love them respectively].

The text presents two pairs of parallels, namely 2/3 and 4/5. With phrase 4 taking up the key term *shih* 師 from phrase 2, and phrase 5 taking up the key term zi 資 from phrase 3, we have two openly interlocked texts, a (2/4) and b (3/5). This modest observation has serious consequences: The same term qi 其 in the parallel phrases 4 and 5 each time refers to something different, the 其, "their," in phrase 4 refers to "the not good ones" 不善人 of phrase 2, and the 其, "their," in phrase 5 to the "good ones" 善人 of phrase 3. The rendering given above is based on Wang Bi's commentary. Other Chinese commentators construct this passage differently, but they all must read the same qi 其 in two parallel phrases as referring to two different things.

The text contains several c elements, namely 1 and 6. The 故 stands alone, and links not just phrase 2 but the pair 2/3 with the preceding text. Phrase 6 again is without a parallel and again refers to both strains a and b. We see that, as a rule, elements in texts written in IPS that are lacking a parallel can easily be identified as c elements and thus read in the appropriate way as referring to/summing up/drawing conclusions from both strains of IPS. Phrases of the c type are often, especially at the end of a sequence, not simply compressions (such as the 故 in this example) but have the function of expressing an overall conclusion concerning both strains. Such a conclusion is rhetorically possible and argumentatively prepared for by the identical structure of the two strains as expressed in their rigid parallelism, a structure that signals that an identical process is at work about which overarching statements are possible.

In the Wang Bi reading on which my translation is based, the Sage is retained as the subject for phrases 4 and 5, which means that another c element "but he [the Sage]" has to be inserted between the two pairs.

Using the structural writing proposed above, the passage reads:

1c That is why [the Sage]

2a [makes] the good ones into the teachers of the not good ones,   and

3b [makes] the not good ones into the material of the good ones,

[but he]

4a does neither honor their [the not good ones'] teachers   nor

5b does he love their [the good ones'] material.

6c Even having knowledge, it would be a great error [to do this].

or:

```
     1c
2a        3b
     [ ]
4a        5b
     6c
```

The importance of this rhetorical structure and its ensuing structural reading strategies will become clearer from the next example, from *Laozi* 70, which presents a *pars pro toto* construction and a first introduction to closed IPS. Closed IPS means that there are no explicit references to link the phrases belonging to the same strain.

    Laozi 70.1–70.3:

1 吾言
2 甚易知
3 甚易行
4 而人
5 莫之能知
6 莫之能行
7 言有宗
8 事有主
9 夫唯無知是以不我知

It is immediately evident that the piece contains three parallel Schlegel pairs, 2/3, 5/6, and 7/8. It is also evident that the piece contains two strains. Phrase 5 takes up the 知 from phrase 2, and phrase 6 takes up the 行 from phrase 3. While we thus have a segment of open IPS with the strains 2/5 and 3/6, it is unclear whether and how the next pair, 7/8, might fit into these strains, since there is no open and explicit term from the two established strains that is being taken up. The passage also contains 3 phrases without parallel, namely, 1, 4, and 9.

    A first translation may read:

1 My words
2 are very easy to understand [and]
3 are very easy to put into practice,

4 but of the others
5 no one is able to understand [and]
6 no one is able to put into practice.
7 [My] words have the principle.
8 [My] activities have the ruler.
9 It is [hence] a fact that only those without any
   understanding will therefore not understand me.

At first glance, this might look like a rhetorical mess. The "words" 言 in phrase 1 are in a stand-alone phrase, but reappear in phrase 7, which is a paired phrase having the counterpart of "activities" 事. Similarly, the notion of "understanding" 知 appears in a paired phrase 5 as the counterpart of "put into practice" 行 in phrase 6, but is taken up in phrase 9, a stand-alone phrase. Finally, after having only heard about the "words" in phrases 1–6, we suddenly find them paired with "activities" 事, not mentioned hitherto.

From the three examples given hitherto there can be no doubt that the *Laozi* contains passages written in IPS. From the elements of open IPS (2/3 and 5/6) in the present example, it is also evident that this passage at least contains IPS elements. The conflict remains, however, between the structural status of phrases 1 and 9, which marks them as *c* phrases referring to both strains, and the fact that their core terms, 言 and 知 respectively, appear as being part only of one of the two strains in phrase 7 and 5 respectively. The tight symmetrical structure of the entire statement makes it improbable that it should be matched by a loose arrangement of the actual argumentative structure. I therefore propose to turn the argument around and, instead of extrapolating the rules of IPS from these examples, proceed now to apply them.

First, then, the linkage of the 7/8 pair with the two existing strains. The core terms in phrases 7 and 8 are "words" 言 and "activities" 事. The interlocking sequence may be a regular *ab ab ab*, but as we shall see further down inversions such as *ab ba ab* might also occur. Testing the regular sequence, we would get a strain *a* linking "understanding" 知 in phrase 2 with inability to understand them 莫之能知 in phrase 5 and the "words" of phrase 7 as the object to be understood or not to be understood. Similarly, we would get a strain *b* linking the "putting into practice" 行 of phrase

3 and the inability to put into practice 莫之能行 from phrase 6 with the "activities 事" of phrase 8. The linguistic association of "activities," *shi* 事, and "putting into practice," *xing* 行, is as common in Chinese as that between "words" 言 and their being "understood," *zhi* 知. Thus we have a first case of closed IPS: in the third pair we do not have terms quoted explicitly to establish the links between elements of the same strain, but key terms culturally and rhetorically associated with the key terms of the existing strains. The linkage of the third pair with the strains established by the first two, a linkage the rules of IPS prompted us to discover, is satisfying both structurally and culturally. The text has two strains, 2/5/7 and 3/6/8.

Since phrase 4 as a marker of transition between two segments does not present a problem, there remain the stand-alone phrases 1 and 9. Phrase 9 is the easier to solve. Its status in IPS signals that it should be a *c* phrase. It comes at the end of two strains interlocked in three pairs, and dominated by "understand/word" and "put into practice/activity" respectively. IPS structure requires that the *c* phrases refer to both strains. We have to assume that the term "understand" 知 in phrase 9 is a short form, a *pars pro toto* construction, for the key terms "understand" 知 and "put into practice" 行 of the two strains. This type of construction might be used for lack of a term of a higher order that would encompass both 知 and 行, and so as to avoid cumbersome repetition. It is a frequent device in IPS. A modern translator will have to supplement the economized parts in brackets to prevent the reader from interpolating his own cultural prejudices.

Once it is established that the *pars pro toto* construction is a standard option for *c* phrases in IPS, the solution for phrase 1 is easy. Its core term, "words," 言, is made rather explicit as being another *pars pro toto* construction by the pair 7/8, where "words," 言 and "activities," 事 are juxtaposed. "Words" in phrase 1 is a *pars pro toto* construction for "words and activities," and the immediately succeeding phrases refer with "understand" to the "words" and with "putting into practice" to the unspoken, structurally supplemented "activities," which again a translator again will have to put into brackets. The two *pars pro toto* constructions in this piece both select key terms from the "*a*" strain, thus reducing structural confusion about this device.

The segment reads in structural writing:

    1c My
  words   [and   my activities]
2a are very easy to understand
         and   3b very easy to put into
                              practice.
    4c But [still, even these easy words and activities]
      of the others
5a no one is able to understand 6b no one is able to put into
  and   practice.
7a [My] words have the principle. 8b [My] activities have the
                              ruler.
    9c It is [hence] a fact that only those without any
      understanding will therefore not
      understand me   [and ditto for practice].

To indicate the *pars pro toto* character of "words" in phrase 1 and "understand" in phrase 9, I have indicated to which side they belonged and have supplemented the remaining part.
Fully formalized, the statement has the structure:

    1c
  a [b]
2a   3b
    4c
5a   6b
7a   8b
    9c
  a [b]

IPS is not a crude and mechanical stylistic form but encompasses a fair variety of rhetorical devices. As I shall document, both closed IPS and *pars pro toto* constructions are common in IPS, providing statements well wrought both structurally and argumentatively, and fitting well into pre-Qin conventions of philosophical rhetoric.

We now move to the analysis of entire *zhang*, beginning with *Laozi* 26, which operates with a *pars pro toto* construction, and introduces a rarer variant of IPS, a pair that does not follow Schlegel's rule.

1 重為輕根
2 靜為躁君
3 是以君子
4 終日行不離輜重
5 雖有榮觀宴處超然
6 如之何萬乘之主而以身輕於天下
7 輕則失本
8 躁則失君

A translation may run:

1 The heavy is the basis of the light.
2 The calm is the lord of the impetuous.
3 That is why the gentleman
4 does not leave the heavy carts [of the army where the weapons and provisions are carried even if] the march continues through the whole day,
5 remains calm and aloof even when there are [enemy] camps with watch towers [where he marches with his army].
6 What will happen if someone [is] lord over ten thousand war chariots but is with his own person light toward All Under Heaven?
7 Being light [toward it], he will lose the basis.
8 Being impetuous [toward it], he will lose his princely [position].

In this *zhang*, we have two fully parallel pairs, 1/2 and 7/8, both operating with the same core vocabulary, 輕 and 躁. This suggests open IPS with two strains, 1/7 and 2/8. While phrases 3 and 6 are clearly stand-alone elements, phrases 4 and 5 present more difficulties. Technically they are not parallel in Schlegel's sense. However, they are a pair in a text partly structured in open IPS, and their core terms have close links with those of the two strains. Phrase 4 explicitly takes up the term "heavy" 重 from the 1/7 strain, the "calm and aloof" 宴處超然 in phrase 5 might be seen as echoing the notion of "calm" 靜 in the 2/8 strain. Phrases 4 and 5 have a loose parallelism in terms of their numbers and general form. The odd end is the character 雖 in phrase 5. In fact, something like it has to be supplemented in the beginning of phrase 4. Things would be simpler if 雖 would actually appear at the end of phrase 3, referring to both phrases 4 and 5. I have seen no textual evidence for this reading in any edition or manuscript. Still, both statements begin with a segment in 3 characters (終日行／有榮觀) and end with a segment in 4 (不離輜重／宴處超然). Both mark a contrast between their first and second sections. They are close enough in vocabulary and content to merit their integration into the grid with phrase 4 joining the 1/7 strain, *a*, to form a strain 1/4/7, and phrase 5 the 2/8 strain, *b*, to form a 2/5/8 strain. A survey of some translations of the *Laozi* indicates that translators like Waley, Duyvendak, Lau, Kimura Eiichi, and Debon have assumed phrase 5 to refer to phrase 2 (and, of course, phrase 4 to phrase 1).

Phrase 3 does not present problems. It separates the universal rule spelled out in the first pair from its application by the gentleman (who here has the same status of showing the model of philosophically correct behavior as the Sage), and thus marks the status difference between the two segments. Phrase 6 is more complicated. With *qing* 輕 it seems to link up with the 1/4/7 strain. The immediately succeeding pair, however, which argumentatively spells out the consequences of the general statement in phrase 6 returns to the original grid with both *qing* 輕 and *zao* 躁. This pair obviously treats the statement concerning 輕 in phrase 6 as a condensed form of two analogous phrases about 輕 and 躁, that is, as a *pars pro toto* construction. Again, the proper reading strategy for phrase 6 hinges on a correct understanding of the status of this phrase within the structure of IPS. Only in this manner will the statement be understood as being two statements compressed into one, with a second about the ruler's being "agitated" about his empire hidden within the readable statement about his being "light" toward his empire. By introducing a new subject, the "lord over ten thousand war chariots," and inserting him into the argumentative grid with pair 7/8, phrase 6 marks the beginning of a third segment of this text, characterized as the deficient mode of the ruler who has it wrong.

In structural writing the *zhang* reads:

I   1a The heavy is the basis   2b the calm is the lord of the
       of the light   excited.
II   3c That is why the gentleman
       4a does not leave the heavy   5b remains calm and aloof even

carts [of the army where the weapons and provisions are carried even if] the march continues through the whole day,	when there are enemy] camps with watch towers [where he marches with his army].

III   6c What will happen if someone [is]
             lord over ten thousand war chariots
             but is with his own person
     light   [and   impetuous]
             towards All Under Heaven?

7a Being light [toward it],   8b Being impetuous [toward it],
   he will lose the basis!   he will lose his princely
                [position]!

While IPS is a highly structured and formalized way of philo-sophical writing, it allows for structures, as in the pair 4/5, which follow IPS rules only in a broad sense.

A frequent variant within IPS, the change of the sequence *a b a b* into one such as *a b b a* does not present problems in open IPS. Sometimes it does so in the closed form because the linkages be-tween elements of the same strain are not immediately evident to a modern scholar coming from a different cultural background. In manuscripts such as the Mawangdui MSS, in quotations from the *Laozi* in various early sources, and in texts printed over different commentaries such as those by Wang Bi or Heshang gong, the sequence of the phrases within a parallel pair is often inverted.[21] This might indicate that, for the copyist, the essential thing was the parallelism of the pair, not the sequence of the two phrases. From the available record, *a b b a* sequences are frequent, but in the *Laozi* do not occur in open IPS. One example, however, the beginning of *Laozi* 73, is open enough in terms of content to serve as an example.

The text:

1 勇於敢則殺
2 勇於不敢則活
3 此兩者
4 或利
5 或害

A translation:

1 If someone is courageous in daring [to do], he will be killed.
2 If someone is courageous in not daring [to do], he will live.
3 Of these two [kinds of courage]
4 one is beneficial
5 one is harmful.

The piece consists of two pairs 1/2 and 4/5 linked by a c element in phrase 3. There are no open links between the two pairs, but the text in phrase 3 explicitly links the first two with the last two phrases, and phrases 4 and 5 itemize their affiliation through 或／或. Culturally it is clear that "living" referred to in phrase 2 would be considered the point of reference of the "beneficial" 利 in phrase 4, and being "killed" in phrase 1 would be the point of reference for the "harm" 害 mentioned in phrase 5. This gives us a sequence ab c ba for this little segment, in structural writing:

1a If someone is courageous in daring [to
    do], he will be killed.   2b If someone is courageous in
                              not daring [to do], he will live.
          3c Of these two [kinds of courage]
              4b one is beneficial,
5a one is harmful.

The inverted sequence is graphically indicated by the 4b being on a higher level than 5a, like this

1a   2b
  3c
     4b
5a

I think the sequence *a b b a*, which appears in the next *zhang* to be analyzed, must be counted among the regular features of IPS.

Closed Interlocking Parallel Style in the Laozi

I believe I can prove through my translation that a solid part of the *Laozi* is written in interlocking parallel style. Many of the *zhang*, however, do not show the open form of this style, which prevails in the passages analyzed hitherto; these have not led to much disagreement among sinologists. The more complicated analysis of the closed form should be based on the knowledge of the rules of this style as extracted from the examples written in open IPS. In discussing some recent translations I shall try to analyze some *zhang* of the *Laozi* with the instrument developed above.

Zhang 68 of the *Laozi* runs:

1 古之
2 善為士者不武
3 善戰者不怒
4 善勝敵者不與
5 善用人者為之下
6 是謂不爭之德
7 是謂用人之力
8 是謂配天　古之極也

Laozi 68 seems to consist of four more or less parallel phrases, 2–5, after an initial 古之, followed by another set of three more or less parallel phrases, 6–8. It is not immediately clear how the first four phrases are related—some military orientation notwithstanding—and it is not clear what the formula *shiwei* 是謂 in its triple repetition might refer to. The general thought of *Laozi* 68 might be that the best military strategy consists in doing exactly the opposite of what common understanding would expect of a military man. Before starting my own analysis, I shall try to see how far readers get without a clear notion of IPS. D. C. Lau translates:

166　One who excels as a warrior does not appear formidable;
　　　One who excels in fighting is never roused in anger;
　　　One who excels in defeating his enemy does not join issue;
　　　One who excels in employing others humbles himself
　　　　before them.
166a This is known as the virtue of non-contention;
　　　This is known as making use of the efforts of others;
　　　This is known as matching the sublimity of Heaven.[22]

D. C. Lau proceeds from the assumption that the *Laozi* is composed of proverbs; he dismantles the *zhang* and numbers the text in a sequence of what he considers independent proverbial statements. In this view, *Laozi* 68 consists of two such statements, rather closely related so that they do not receive successive numbers 166 and 167,

but are treated as close relatives, 166 and 166a. Punctuation provides some information about the translator's interpretation of the
structure.[23] His first four phrases are separated by semicolons, and
end with a full stop. This indicates that the four form a single
statement, each of the four elements repeating the same thought in
a different fashion, and the translation stressing their similarity in
content. His last three phrases in 166a again are separated by
semicolons and form another unit, this time of three similar statements. Again the reading and translating strategy stresses their
similarities, not their differences in structure and content. A full
stop separates 166 and 166a; they seem to have only a casual
relationship. Since no other indication is given, the threefold "this is
known as" must each time refer to the same thought or argument.
Having translated 166 as multiple expressions of the same thought,
the 是謂 in 166a are made to refer to this collective entity created by
the translation. The translator has been successful in illustrating
his point—that the text consists of disconnected elements held together by some general common framework of meaning. His translation shows a loose sequence of disconnected phrases, put together
into batches with parallel structures, and with references pointing
into some void.

In 1934, long before Lau's widely distributed translation, Arthur
Waley had translated:

> The best charioteers do not rush ahead;
> The best fighters do not make display of wrath.
> The greatest conqueror wins without joining the issue;
> The best user of men acts as though he were their inferior.
> This is called the power that comes of not contending,
> is called the capacity to use men,
> the secret of being mated to Heaven, to what was of old.[24]

The punctuation again gives important clues to the structure as
seen by this translator. Waley separates his first and second statement by a semicolon, and does the same for the third and fourth. We
thus get two parallel pairs, and he marks their border by a full stop.
The second set is seen as a single clause. The triple repetition of *shi
wei* 是謂 is read as a rhetorical device for emphasis, the point of
reference for *shi* 是 remains open. Although Waley sees that, in the

Laozi, statements might come in pairs rather than foursomes, he does not establish any link between the two pairs and, like Lau, translates them in a way that brings out their general similarity. This does not seem satisfactory.

Leon Hurvitz has rendered the translation of Kimura Eiichi into English:

> [There is an ancient proverb which says] "He who plays the part of a warrior [truly] well is not brave; he who fights [truly] well does not get angry; he who defeats a rival realm [that is, a country evenly matched with his own] truly well does not rely on the help of an associated realm [that is, an allied country]; he who employs others [truly] well [humbles himself and] occupies a position inferior to them." This is called "The virtue of non-contention" [or] it is called "using the strength of others" [or] it is called "matching heaven," and it is the ultimate of the way of antiquity.[25]

The text reprinted in Kimura Eiichi's original study as well as the translation give only formal markers between units in the form of inverted commas, but they do not differentiate between the semicolon and the full stop. Still, Kimura Eiichi encloses his first four phrases in quotation marks as being what he sees as the "ancient proverb" and thus marks them as a single statement in four parallel parts. This view impels him into a translation strategy that emphasizes the similarity among these four elements. The next three statements, exclusive of 古之極也 at the end, he defines through his inserted "or" (*mata*) quite explicitly as three attempts at defining the general essence of what has been said in the "ancient proverb." The last element, 古之極也, he sees as a statement by the presumable author or editor who, having used three phrases already in circulation, now adds his own assessment.

This analysis of translations could easily be continued to those most recently published. Even the translators of the Mawangdui texts have not been able to get out of the inherited assumptions about the looseness of the *Laozi*, and thus have not contributed much toward an understanding of the rhetorics of this text. I shall start with the last three phrases. Formally phrases 6 and 7 are structured in the same way, but phrase 8 is not. Kimura Eiichi has noted this, but his solution, to cut off the end, 古之極也, leaves us with 是謂配天, which also is not parallel to phrases 6 and 7:

6 是謂不爭之德
7 是謂用人之力
8 是謂配天　古之極也

Given the binary genetic code of IPS, the integration of phrase 8, which is nonparallel and would be the third in the set, is highly unlikely. The formal accoutrements of *Laozi* 68 with its parallel pairs make it likely that the text is written in IPS with phrase 8 structurally a *c* phrase referring to two previously established strains. Do these strains exist?

The text contains some elements of open IPS that can help in establishing the links. *Yong ren* 用人 in phrase 7 用人之力 takes up the same expression in phrase 5 善用人者. *Bu zheng zhi de* 不爭之德 in phrase 6, the "capacity not to fight," takes up, though with a different term, what phrase 4 says with 善勝敵者不與, "he who is good at overcoming enemies does not engage with them." Accordingly, we have a solid link to establish two strains, 4/6 and 5/7, and a probable *c* phrase in 8. As things stand now, we are in fact forced to insert the remaining pair, phrases 2 and 3, into this grid. The officer in phrase 2 is the only candidate who can be said to be "employing" or "using" other people to do the fighting, and he does it best by not strutting about in a martial manner but by humbling himself before them. This gives us a strain, *a*, consisting of phrases 2/5/7. Luckily, he who according to phrase 3 manages to be "good at war" because he "does not get angry" (善戰者不怒) is an excellent candidate for the second strain which deals not with the art of making use of others in the military but with the art of overcoming the enemy. This gives us a second strain, *b*, consisting of phrases 3/4/6.

The first *c* element, 古之, evidently refers to the subsequent pair 2/3. The last *c* element sums up what has been said previously about the two strains. We have already had a case where the point of reference of an identical *qi* 其 in two parallel phrases changed according to the structural position of the phrase. The same is true here with *shi* 是 in the last three phrases. Far from having a common but unnamed point of reference in the vague general meaning of the first set of phrases, each of the three *shi wei* 是謂 gets its specific point of reference from its structural position. *Shi wei* 是謂 in phrase 6, 是謂不爭之德, refers to the art of the subject of strain *b*, the person good at war and at overcoming enemies; 是謂 in phrase 7 是謂用人之力 refers to the officer in strain *a* who is good at employing others by not lording it over them in a martial manner, but by humbling himself. And the third *shi wei* 是謂 in phrase 8, 是謂配天　古之極也, structurally cannot but refer to the two previous strains and mean "these two." In the light of the rules of IPS, *Laozi* 68 is tightly structured, highly coherent, and economically argued, a reading well in tune with the rigors of its parallelisms. The *zhang* has an inverted sequence in the middle, *c a b b a b a c*. The impact of the structural understanding on eliminating fogginess and ambivalence in the translation will be stronger here than in the chapters discussed earlier.

A structured translation would run:

1c Those of old
2a who were good at being
officers were not martial.   3b who were good at fighting did
not get angry.

[This is so because]   4b he who is good at overcoming
enemies, does not engage.

5a he who is good at using
others lowers
himself under them.   6b This [not engaging in fighting]
is called the capacity
of not fighting.

7a That [lowering oneself
as an officer under one's
men] is called making
use of the strength of
others.

8c These [two abilities] are called matching Heaven.
[They are] the ultimate [achievement] of antiquity.

or:

1c
2a   3b
          4b
5a   6b
7a
          8c

Quite apart from clarifying the points of reference for the three 是謂, the integration of the parallel pairs into the binary grid of IPS prompts a different translation strategy. It does not emphasize the similarity with the parallel phrase, but the content link to the other members of the same strain, hence their difference. The fact is that, as a rule, the two strains are designed as complementary opposites, in the present case dealing with one's men, and dealing with the enemy. The strategic orientation for a reader and translator is to bring out the opposition between the two strains, not the similarity within the parallel pairs.

The influence of understanding structure on understanding content and the consequent translation can be still more clearly shown in an analysis of *Laozi* 44:

1　名與身孰親
2　身與貨孰多
3　得與亡孰病
4　是故
5　甚愛必大費
6　多藏必厚亡
7　知足不辱
8　知止不殆
9　可以長久

At first sight, it is clear that *Laozi* 44 contains two pairs of parallel phrases, 5/6 and 7/8. It begins with a set of three phrases that have structurally much in common, such as 與 and 孰 in the similar positions. We shall again proceed via earlier translations. Waley translates this *zhang*:

Fame or one's own self, which matters to one most?
One's own self or things bought, which should count most?
In the getting or the losing, which is worse?
Hence he who grudges most pays dearest in the end;
He who has hoarded most will suffer the heaviest loss.
Be content with what you have and are and no one can
　　despoil you;
Who stops in time, nothing can harm.
He is forever safe and secure.[26]

Waley is the only translator I have seen who has spotted the structural difference between the first pair and phrase 3. The nouns 名／身 and 身／貨 in the first pair have no counterpart in the at best nominalized verbs 得／亡 in phrase 3.[27] There is a probability that the two verbs 得 and 亡 in phrase 3 refer to the "getting" 得 of "fame" 名 and "riches" 貨 and the "losing" 亡 of one's "own person" 身 in phrases 1 and 2. This is what Waley, in my view correctly, suggests; it would make phrase 3 a *c* phrase referring to the preceding two strains.

From this first segment of three phrases on, the text seems to fall apart in this translation. After having posed three questions, Waley's text proceeds with a logically quite nonsensical "hence."[28] The two phrases on "grudging" and "hoarding" both seem to refer to material goods. They do appear in phrase 2 as 貨 but, according to this reading, the rest of the *zhang* never again talks about the issue of line 1, fame 名. Waley's next pair does not improve the situation. "Be content with what you have" would seem at best to refer again to the goods, but with regard to what he "who stops in time" will stop remains unclear. Waley essentially went by the commonly held notion that parallel style means saying the same thing twice, and by the accepted dictionary meanings of the terms; since *ai* 愛 in line 5 also means "to save" or to be "parsimonious" and *cang* 藏 in line 6 means "to hoard," he has every reason to assume that both must have to do with the issue of material goods and wealth. In this manner, we end up with a sad *zhang* that announces itself through the parallelisms as a highly crafted and structured affair, but drops half its issues by the wayside in a space of 9 short phrases with thirty-nine characters altogether.

If the piece is written in IPS, the structural information about the status of each line and its relationship with the others, not just the dictionary meaning, must play a vital role in determining the meaning and point of reference of the core terms. We have experience with such matters everyday in speaking. We use nondescript words like *thing* and leave it to the contextual understanding to identify its particular meaning at the moment. And we often intend the particular meaning of a term not as its dictionary definition but as the possible meaning it can have in a particular context. Once it is understood that a piece is written in IPS, such contextual structural information becomes a relevant and essential part in establishing the meaning of the terms.

Laozi 44 has all the markers of IPS with parallel pairs and nonparallel elements. If it is written in IPS, it would be the closed form, since no explicit cross-references link the strains.

First, we shall deal with the oddity of "therefore" or "hence" 是故 after three questions. An analysis of the *Laozi*'s use of *shu* 孰, the interrogative term in all three questions here, shows that it is used only in rhetorical questions where the answer is supposed to be perfectly obvious.[29] The "hence" or "therefore" makes sense after the answer implied in the rhetorical question is clear.

Second, "therefore" implies that a direct connection should exist between what came before and what comes after it. This connection between the first three phrases of the *zhang* and the rest after "therefore" is not visible in any of the translations I have consulted. Fan Yingyuan 范應元, a compiler of "old manuscripts" of the *Laozi* from the second half of the thirteenth century and perhaps the last to base his reading of the *Laozi* on a positive understanding of IPS, inferred from the structural position of 愛 that it must not mean "grudging" or "parsimonious" with regard to money and goods, but must refer to the "name/fame" 名 of the first line. He wrote:

甚愛名者則必大費精神
多藏貨者則必重失身命

Someone truly obsessed with fame will by necessity suffer
   great loss in his spiritual energy.
Someone grandly hoarding goods will by necessity suffer
   heavy losses in terms of his life.[30]

Fan Yingyuan explicitly defines the "name/fame" as the point of reference for 愛 in line 4, and the "goods" as the point of reference for 藏 in line 6. There is hardly any trouble with associating the "hoarding" with the "goods," because the term 藏 could, by any stretch of its meaning, hardly be associated with "name/fame." By default *ai* 愛 seems predestined to refer to "name/fame" in the sense of "being besotted with." Fan Yingyuan bases his suggestion on a familiarity with the regular textual environment of *ai* 愛 because the combination *aiming* 愛名, "being besotted with fame," in fact occurs in texts such as the *Zhanguo ce* 戰國策, the *Hanshi waizhuan* 韓詩外傳, or the *Sanguo zhi* 三國志.[31]

In this manner, we have two strains 1/5 and 2/6 with a *c* element in phrase 3. The problem of the correct linkage with the existing strains appears again in phrases 7 and 8, rendered by all consulted translations according to the idea mentioned already—namely that parallelism basically means that the same thing is said twice with different words. Waley's translation of the two lines refers only to riches, although some of the terminology used in these phrases occurs elsewhere in the *Laozi*, which might give some hint. *Laozi* 33.3 also uses the expression 知足 in the formula *zhi zu zhe fu ye* 知足者富也, "He who knows how to have enough will be wealthy." This shows that the *zhi zu* 知足 is associated in the *Laozi* with riches, so that it is plausible that phrase 7 should be linked in an inverted sequence to the strain 2/6 with "goods" 貨 as its key word. The 知止 from phrase 8 occurs in *Laozi* 32.3, 始制有名　名亦既有　夫亦將知止　知止所以不殆. Extrapolating from Wang Bi's commentary, this would translate as: "With the beginning of [social] regulation [I, the Sage, will] have names. Once the names are there, [I, the Sage,] set out to have an understanding about [how to] put a stop [to the ensuing developments]. [Only] having an understanding about [how to] put a stop [to them] is what gets [me] out of danger."

It is not relevant whether this translation or another is followed, because the point is very simple: 知止 has as implied object the term *ming* 名 in this passage, and this is all we need. It allows us with some confidence to link phrase 8 with the strain 1/5 around the core notion of *ming* 名. Phrase 9 stands alone and evidently is a *c* phrase. However, the paired terms 長久 in this phrase probably again take up the two strains, 長 being used here in the sense of "to excel" and referring to the strain associated with 名, and 久 in the sense of "lasting long," linking up with the argument concerning 貨. Our reading for phrases 7 and 8 is graciously supported by Fan Yingyuan who, in the commentary already quoted, explicitly links 知足 and 知止 to the very strains suggested above.

The segments of the text are easily delineated. The general principles are stated in the form of rhetorical questions in the first pair and summarized in phrase 3. This is followed by segment II with phrases 5 and 6, which show the consequences of ignoring the insight contained in the rhetorical questions of segment I. This second segment is followed by segment III which deals with the proper application of the insight following from the initial pair. In structured writing the *zhang* could be translated as follows if Wang Bi's commentary were to be followed:

I 1a When fame is joined to the
body, which [of the two] does
[in fact] become dearer?!
[Fame, of course.]   2b When the person is joined by
                                 goods, which [of the two] is [in
                                 fact] increased?! [The goods, of
                                 course].

    3c If [in this manner] getting [more fame and
        goods] and losing [on the side of one's person]
        come together, who is it [after all] that causes
        the affliction [done to one's person?!
        The others in their envy, of course].

II   4c That is why
5a too much craving [for fame]
    inevitably leads   6b too much hoarding [of goods]
    to great expenditure;   inevitably leads to ample loss.
III   [Consequently, it is he]

                                 7b who knows how to be satisfied
                                     [with what goods he has] will
                                     have no loss!

8a who knows how to halt
    [the craving for ever greater
    fame] will be without danger!
        9c [In this way] it is possible to
            excel   and   last long.

Laozi 44 has a sequence with an inversion, the sequence being
a b c c a b b a c. In formalized writing, it has the structure

    I 1a   2b
          3c
    II   4c
       5a   6b
    III   7b
       8a 9c

The pair defining the two strains, *ming* 名 and *huo* 貨, represents
the two big classes of entities in pre-Buddhist Chinese philosophy,
事 and 物. By and large, they provide the basic grid for the binary
strains in IPS.[32] An analysis of *Laozi* 7 will help to fortify these
arguments. In the Wang Bi recension of the *Laozi*, it runs:

1　天長
2　地久
3　天地所以能長且久者以其不自生故能長生
4　是以聖人
5　後其身而身先
6　外其身而身存
7　不以其無私邪故能成其私

The text has two clearly visible pairs 1/2 and 5/6. There are no explicit references linking the phrases. If it is written in IPS, suggested by the parallel pairs and the inserted c phrases, it is closed IPS. It is clearly divided into two segments, the first three phrases establishing a cosmic principle, the second segment beginning with phrase 4 showing its application by the Sage.

Kimura Eiichi's translation is rendered by Hurvitz as follows:

"Heaven and Earth never perish." The reason that heaven and earth are able to be eternal is that [they are unselfish and mindless, and that] they make no attempt to prosper by their own devices: therefore they live forever. Thus the sage [in obedience to this universal truth] "[places others first and] himself last, but [as a result he automatically] finds himself in the fore. [He attempts to save others while] ignoring himself, but [as a result he automatically] remains in existence." Is [this] not because the sage "has no personal desire"? For this very reason [the result, contrary to all expectation,] is that he is "able to satisfy his personal desires fully."[33]

The translations presented by D. C. Lau, Duyvendak, Waley, and others are similar. It remains unclear why 長 and 久 are repeated if they mean the same thing or how the Sage of the second part imitates Heaven and Earth with his actions; in these translations Heaven and Earth only provide a model for his "remaining in existence" but none for his "finding himself in the fore." *Shi yi* 是以 would seem to promise that both statements concerning the Sage that follow would be based on the principles stated in the beginning of this *zhang*. According to this and other translations, the *Laozi* 7 seems helter-skelter; a phrase is written but not taken up, another is taken up twice—and this notwithstanding a seemingly rigorous formal structure warning the reader that the writing was conscious and planned.

From the general rules of interlocking style it has to be hypoth-
esized, in view of the parallel pairs and nonparallel segments, that
Laozi 7 is written in interlocking parallel style. There is not a single
example of simply reduplicating parallel style in the *Laozi*.

Given the general stylistic model of IPS, we have to translate
the two phrases of the first pair with a view to their difference, not
their similarity. The text prompts us to do this by insisting on twice
repeating 長 and 久, which the translators merge into a single
word. The point of orientation in establishing the difference between
phrase 1 and 2 is the second pair, namely, 5 and 6, supposedly the
applications of phrases 1 and 2. There, the core terms are *xian* 先
and *cun* 存. The semantic leeway we have with *jiu* 久 beyond "long
endurance" is very small, and it only fits *cun* 存 in phrase 6. In
"disregarding his own person" 外其身 the Sage would thus imitate
the Earth. This gives us a strain 2/6 with allusion to this strain in
phrase 3.

By default, the Sage must imitate Heaven in "putting his own
person into the background" and thus managing to be in the fore.
This links 先 and 長. Heaven, said to 長, however, is the model for
the emperor and the Sage in that it is high above all entities. The
example shows that in determining the meaning of a term in the
Laozi it it not enough to look at its intrinsic range of meanings; its
position and linkages in the structured set-up of IPS has to be taken
into account as an important, and occasionally determining feature.
From the connection with *xian* 先, "coming to the fore," it becomes
clear that 長 must mean here something like "being on top of" or "to
excel," quite apart from its being the opposite of *duan* 短 in the
sense of "being excellent at . . ." as opposed to "being bad at . . .". This
formulates a second strain, namely 1/5, also with elements in phrase
3, and a sequence *a b c a b c*. A problem remains with line 3. All
received *Laozi* text over the Wang Bi commentary as well as both
Mawangdui MSS and Fu Yi's" Old Manuscript" write *changsheng*
長生, "live long," instead of the *chang jiu* 長久 that one might expect
here. Shima Kuniō has suggested an emendation to 長久. Given the
consistency of the tradition, I believe changsheng has to be kept and
to be read as a *pars pro toto* construction for the pair "persisting
long" and "excelling."

The basic dividing line separating the strains is again the
complementary opposite of wealth and social status similar to that
dominating *Laozi* 44, just analyzed. The argument in both chapters
is similar. If greed and interest in material goods and social status

are openly displayed, there will be animosity from others; they will attack the person openly displaying his fame and wealth, which may considerably shorten his life and endanger his status; a correct application of the universal laws will secure life and status. This is handled in phrases 3 (for Heaven and Earth) and 7 (for the Sage).

The *zhang* presents a well-structured, completely understandable argument, presented with the dialectical turn against common-sense understanding characteristic of the *Laozi*.

I 1a Heaven excels.   2b Earth persists.
      3c That by which
    Heaven   and   Earth
         are able to
   excel   and   persist
      is that they do not live for their own interests.
      That [indeed] is the reason why they are able to
            persist long
   [and excel].
II   4c This [pattern of Heaven and Earth] is the
      reason why the Sage [as is well known]
5a puts his own person in the
  background and [manages in
  this way] that his own person
  comes to be to the fore.   6b disregards his own person and
                manages in this way] that his
                own person will last.
      7c Indeed, is it not because of his being without
         private interests that he is able to accomplish
         his private interests?
Or:

I 1a   2b
    3c
II   4c
  5a   6b
    7c

A last example illustrates the use of the standard forms of IPS in the *Laozi*. Notwithstanding the rigors of its formal organization, it has left translators and readers baffled. It is one of the few examples where Wang Bi helps out by explicitly establishing the proper links. *Zhang* 9 of the *Laozi* runs in my reconstruction of Wang Bi's text:

1　持而盈之不若其已
2　揣而鋭之不可長保
3　金玉滿室莫之能守
4　富貴而驕自遺其咎
5　功遂身退天之道

There are two parallel pairs, 1/2 and 3/4, with one *c* element in phrase 5. There are no open links between the lines, and the blunt metaphorical statements do not facilitate the search for links. A first translation extrapolated from Wang Bi might run:

1 In maintaining [it] and then even adding to it one is not as well off as if one [had] nothing.
2 By polishing [it] and then grinding it, one will be unable to protect [oneself] for long.
3 No one who fills [his] palace with gold and jades will be able to preserve them.
4 Someone who is wealthy and honored but arrogant brings calamity upon himself.
5 To withdraw with one's person once the task is completed—that is the Way of Heaven!

Again the translations consulted present a confused picture. Waley separates clause 1 and 2 by a semicolon, but 3 and 4 by a period, thus indicating a different relationship between these pairs. D. C. Lau ends clauses 1 and 2 with a semicolon, thus indicating that the first three clauses belong together; he ends 3 and 4 with a period each. Chan does not see any relationship among the clauses and separates them all by periods, as though they were a series. None of the translations I have seen establishes a structure for the first four clauses beyond a simple series.

While open links do not exist in the text, there is no dearth of connections via related terms and contents. *Man* 滿, "be full," in phrase 3 evokes *ying* 盈, "to overflow," in phrase 1 which is the term the Guodian A and MWD A MSS use here. The content of phrase 2— to pass over a knife with the finger and furthermore sharpen the knife—is taken up in phrase 4 about someone who is not only rich and famed but arrogant to boot. Wang Bi uses a simple and very effective technique of explicitly establishing the links and help the reader out of the conundrum: His comment to phrase 3, "one is not as well off as if one [had] nothing 不若其已," is taken verbatim from phrase 1, and his comment to phrase 4, "he will be unable to protect [himself] for long 不可長保," is taken verbatim from phrase 2 *Laozi* 9 thus consists of two strains, 1/3 and 2/4, held together by a *c* element, phrase 5. A translation in structural writing, the inserts derived from the structural analysis, could look like this:

1a In maintaining [one's capacity] and then even adding to it one is not as well off as if one [had] nothing.

2b By polishing [a sword] and then grinding it, one will be unable to protect [oneself] for long.

[Accordingly,]
3a no one who fills [his already sumptuous] palace with gold and jades will be able to preserve [these riches].

4b someone who is [already] wealthy and honored but [in addition turns] arrogant brings calamity upon himself.

5c To withdraw with one's person once the task is completed—that is the Way of Heaven!

Again, a conscious application of the rules of IPS—and Wang Bi's help—changed a seemingly unstructured jumble of disconnected clauses into a tightly coherent text.

One further important and elegant variant of IPS in the *Laozi* still has to be introduced, the binary series. Diagrammatically, such a series would look like this:

1a
2b
3c
4d
5e

6a
 7b
  8c
   9d
    10e

.

Instead of pairs of parallel phrases linked to other pairs of parallel phrases, here we have two series of parallel phrases (1/2/3/ 4/5/6 . . . and 6/7/8/9/10 . . .), the corresponding members in each series linked to each other 1a to 6a, 2b to 7b, 3c to 8c, and so on. As usual, the two series would be held together by a stand-alone element, which in this case will be called X.

One of the most intriguing *zhang* of the *Laozi*, *Laozi* 22, is structured according to this pattern, a discovery that seems to have been made by Wang Bi, who also uses this variant in his own writing.[34]

The text of *Laozi* 22 runs:

1 曲則全
2 枉則正
3 窪則盈
4 敝則新
5 少則得
6 多則惑
7 是以聖人抱一為天下式
8 不自見故明
9 不自是故彰
10 不自伐故有功
11 不自矜故長
12 夫唯不爭故天下莫能與之爭
13 古之所謂曲則全者豈虛言哉誠全而歸之

The text shows a series of four parallel phrases 8–11. It begins with a series of six parallel phrases; the first four are not visibly anti-thetical to each other, but the last two are. Phrases 5 and 6 are different in character from the rest and may be part of an analytical summing up of the first four. We thus have two sets of four parallel phrases each in this *zhang*, 1–4 and 8–11. There is no explicit linkage between the two sets, but we are forced to look for one through the "this is why . . ." 是以 in phrase 7.

Two hypotheses seem possible. The two blocks of four parallels each consist of two pairs of parallel phrases. However, their terminology and content seem so disconnected that it would be hard to establish clear criteria for two strains of connected interlocked phrases. Wang Bi here suggests a brilliant variant. His commentary to phrases 1–4 consists verbatim of the *Laozi* text of phrases 8 through 11. In this manner he establishes the basis for a reading strategy that pulls the linked phrases toward each other. This very plausible suggestion results in a dramatic reduction in fuzziness, and brings out a clear structure of this argument, taking full care of the promise of coherence made in "that is why" 是以 in phrase 7, which also indicates the status difference between the two halves— the universal truths in the beginning, and the Sage's application after "that is why." The following translation is again based on the extrapolation from the Wang Bi commentary. The decisive connection between the two sets of four, however, is independent of the specifics of Wang's commentary.

A translation extrapolated from Wang Bi may run as follows. The phrase numbers, especially for the X-phrases, have been rearranged to match the argument above:

1a Hiding results in completeness.
  2b Bending results in correctness.
    3c Being a pothole results in getting full.
      4d Being worn out results in getting new [things].
        5X [In short,]
          reduction results in attaining,
          increase results in delusion.
          This [last general principle] is why
          the Sage holds on to the One, and makes
          the empire [take it as] a model.
6a [The Sage follows the first maxim, that is why] he does not show himself, and therefore [his] enlightenment [becomes complete].
  7b [The Sage follows the second maxim, that is why] he is not self-righteous, and therefore [his being right] shines forth.
    8c [The Sage follows the third maxim, that is why] he does not brag, and therefore he has [his] achievements [uncontestedly].
      9d [The Sage follows the fourth maxim, that is why] he does not praise himself, and therefore [his capacity] grows.

> 10X [In short,] only because he does not struggle no one in All Under Heaven is able to struggle with him. How could it be empty chatter, that which the people of old called "hiding results in completeness" [and so forth]? To him who is in truth complete, [All Under Heaven] will render itself.

Or:

1a
  2b
    3c
      4d
        5X
6a
  7b
    8c
      9d
        10X

Phrase 10 obviously stands without parallel and is of the c type; the reference to phrase 1 in phrase 10 ("hiding results in completeness") is a *pars pro toto* construction; phrase 1 is made to represent the entire set of 1–4.

The reasons for this coordination presented by Wang Bi are still not entirely convincing to me. Yet a translation turning this obviously structured text into an accumulation of witticisms does not bring us anywhere. Wang Bi's attempt starts from the basically sound assumption that between the two sets of four parallel phrases, 1–4 and 8–11, there must be a correlation, because the latter are said to follow from the former. One must start from this structural insight in making a translation. At the same time, this text shows clearly that knowledge of interlocking parallel style does not immediately lead to an understanding of a text's structure. The concrete analysis of each passage is still necessary, especially in closed IPS passages. However, the instruments of analysis become more specific and permit the falsification of certain reading strategies.

To recapitulate, parts of the *Laozi* are written in interlocking parallel style, in open and closed form, and contain a regular variant that inverts the sequence (abba instead of abab). Stand-alone phrases often use material from one of the two strains in *pars pro toto* constructions. Frequently rhymes are used as an additional method to stress parallelism.[35] Binary strains are based, as a rule, on complementary opposites. In this manner the style is predestined for arguments dealing with analogous structures of different fundamental realms of entity, and with principles underlying those analogous strains. IPS is, therefore not merely a formal device but is linked to certain philosophic concepts and pursuits to be dealt with in my study on Wang Bi's philosophy.[36] The knowledge of the rules of IPS helps to articulate the silent text encoded into the structure of these *zhang* with two important consequences. First, an understanding of IPS prompts reading with a focus on opposition and complementarity instead of commonality between parallels, and on links with other elements of the same strain. Second, the positive definition of the unnamed points of reference of key words in both parallel pairs and stand-alone phrases becomes important in the process of defining the meaning of these points.

It is my understanding that about half—39 out of 81 *zhang*—of the *Laozi* are wholly or partially written in interlocking parallel style: 1, 2, 3, 5(?), 7, 9, 10, 13, 19, 22, 23, 25, 26, 27, 29, 33, 38, 39, 41, 44, 47, 49, 50, 51, 53, 56, 57, 61, 62, 63, 64, 65, 67, 68, 70, 73, 76, 77, 80. There are a few *zhang* containing an *abc* hierarchy of phrases but no interlocking structures such as *Laozi* 75 and 81. Documentation will be found in the translation, also to be published separately. There might be other *zhang* where IPS structures have eluded me. In short, the structural and argumentative pattern described here is pervasive in the *Laozi*.

It will be noted that I have only rarely adduced Wang Bi's *commentary* for establishing the links here. Although Wang Bi operates on the assumption that the *Laozi* used the forms of IPS and occasionally points them out, the presence of this pattern does not hinge on Wang Bi's authority but survives, as I hope to have shown, a scholarly test at falsification. What to the bright young philosophers of the Zhengshi era (240–49) was a shared knowledge concerning the *Laozi* reappears as a modern scholarly discovery.

There is a theoretical possibility that the *Laozi* has been streamlined at some moment to fit this stylistic pattern. The plausibility of such a hypothesis is low because only part of the *Laozi* shows this pattern. The two finds in Guodian and Mawangdui allow us to empirically falsify this hypothesis. Both finds contain the full range of interlocking parallel style in both the open and closed forms as well as *pars pro toto* constructions. For the Mawangdui texts this is easily verified through a comparison with the examples given here. But the Guodian *Laozi* also contain besides many elements of the open form such as [twice] the segment in *Laozi* 64 analyzed in the beginning of this chapter also *zhang* 9 and 44 and in closed IPS studied above. The pattern is even maintained when the sequence of the phrases is different from the received texts including the Mawangdui. But we might argue that third-century scribes and editors might have proceeded to some streamlining within the existing texts to fit the structural logic. An example is *zhang* 56 in Guodian *Laozi* A. The phrase 挫其銳解其紛 in the Wang Bi text has an equivalent here in 劃其畚解其紛; it is placed after 和其光同其塵 while the received text puts it before. As it is part of a parallel staircase construction with two sets of three phrases the position of the items in the sequence cannot be changed as it can in the *abba* variant of binary constructs. Consequently, the phrase 劃其畚解其紛 has to match up with the phrase 不可得而貴亦不可得而疏 instead of the 不可得而利亦不可得而害 to which the structure of the received text links it. It is imaginable that in view of the two parallel sets of three an editor would have felt free to rearrange the sequence so as to make a better fit, and even to adjust some of the terms used to that purpose. The stability of the Guodian find suggests, however, a textual status of the *Laozi* materials (none of the three segments contains a reference to the person Laozi) already high enough to narrowly limit editorial discretion on this point.

Interlocking Parallel Style in Early Texts Outside the *Laozi*

The pattern of interlocking parallel style was already common in pre-Han Chinese texts. I shall not try to arrive at a quantitative, historical, geographical, or linguistic description of the genesis and spread of this pattern. This would demand an analysis of practically all classical literature and might not provide insights worth the effort. The only proof I shall try to arrive at is that this stylistic pattern is extant in other early texts and is not peculiar to the *Laozi*. The presence of IPS patterns in texts beginning with those more or less contemporary to the *Laozi* would support the plausibility of my proposition.

I shall cite passages from the the *Guanzi* 管子, the *Li ji* 禮記 and *Hanfeizi* 韓非子, the *Xiao jing* 孝經, the *Mozi* 墨子, and the Wings of the *Zhouyi* 周易; these are far from representative and they are the product of casual reading rather than systematic search. Eventually, however, I hope that the use of IPS and the forms in which it is being applied might also help with the dating of texts.

In the *Neiye* 內業 chapter of the *Guanzi* a passage reads—and I will present it directly in structural writing:

1a 一物能化謂之神   2b 一事能變謂之智
3a 化不易氣   4b 變不易智
    5c 唯執一之君子能為此乎
       執一不失能君萬物 [37]

The passage is written in open IPS with explicit links between phrases 1 and 3 through 化 and between phrases 2 and 4 through 變. A translation may run:

1a That which is able to transform in unison with other entities I call 'Spirit.'

2b That which is able to change in unison with [government] affairs I call 'Wisdom.'

3a In this transformation not to alter [the Spirit's] breath of life—

4b In this change not to alter [Wisdom's] knowledge—

5c only a *Junzi* who holds on to the One is able to manage this! Holding on to the One and not letting go he is able to rule over the ten thousand kinds of entities. [38]

In *Li ji* 17 it is said—and I will present the text immediately in structural writing: [39]

1a 禮節民心   2b 樂和民聲
    3c 政以行之
    4c 刑以防之
    5c 禮樂刑政四達而不悖
       則王道備矣
           6b 樂者為同

7a 禮者為異   8b 同則相親
9a 異則相敬   10b 樂勝則流
11a 禮勝則離
                    12b 合情
13a 飾貌
          14c 者
     禮   樂
          之事也

The passage is in open IPS. The binary construction based on *li* 禮
and *yue* 樂 continues beyond this.

A translation may run:

1a Rites regulated the   2b Music harmonized the
   people's hearts,   people's voices,
          3c Government policies served to execute (rites and
             music),
          4c Punishments served to prevent (their abuse).
          5c When there was no rebellion against these four
             means of rites, music, government policies and
             punishments, the way of the kings was flourishing.
                                6b Music established
                                   similarities.
7a Rites established the   8b Similarity brought about
   differences.   affection.
9a Differences brought about 10b When music prevailed there
   respect.   resulted interflow.
11a When rites prevailed   12b To bring sentiments together
    there resulted separation.   and
13a differentiate between the
    outer appearances
          14c is what
     rites   and   music
          have to achieve.

This presents many of the elements of IPS defined above, including an *a b b a* sequence when the new series of the a/b parallels in
phrase 6 starts with a *b* phrase. The pattern contains an "impurity"
in 5c, lumping ritual and music together with government measures
and punishments into "four means," although the "government meas-
ures/punishments" pair is not taken up in the further discussion.

There are many passages with interlocking parallel style in the
Zhongyong 中庸 chapter of the *Li ji*, such as this example:[40]

1a 喜怒哀樂之未發謂之中　　2b 發而皆中節謂之和
3a 中也者天下之大本也　　　4b 和也者天下之達道也
　　　　　　5c 致
中　　　　　　　　　　和
　　天地位焉萬物育焉

In translation:

1a [The situation] before
   liking, hatred, sadness
   and happiness have
   arisen is called "middle."
3a "Middle" is the big root
   of All Under Heaven.

2b When they have arisen but
   are regulated from the "mid
   dle" [the situation] is called
   "harmony."
4b "Harmony" is the way through
   which things under Heaven
   are achieved.

　　　　5c When
"middle"　　and　　"harmony"
have come about, Heaven and Earth are in their
position, and the ten thousand kinds of beings are
nourished thereby.

The sequence does not need explanation. Whether the last two
phrases in 5c concerning Heaven/Earth and the ten thousand kinds
of beings should and could be associated with the existing strains
will remain open here.

There are frequent passages in the *Li ji* with interlocking parallel style but lacking *c*-phrases. It may be assumed that this often
described pattern of parallel prose belongs to the same stylistic type
but does not share the philosophical content the *a b a b c* structure
presents.

An example:[41]

　　　　　1c 子曰君子
2a 道人以言 而　　　3b 禁人以行
　　　　7c 故
5a 言必慮其所終　而　6b 行必稽其所敝
　　　　7c 則民
8a 謹於言　　　而　　9b 慎於行
　　　　10c 詩云
11a 慎爾出話　　　　12b 敬爾威儀
　　　　13c 大雅曰
14a 穆穆文王　　　　15b 於緝熙敬止

A translation may run:

1c The master says: The Junzi

2a leads others with words   and   3b controls others with deeds

4c Therefore,

5a when speaking, he has to consider where his   and,   6b when acting, he words has end up   to find out what may be unworthy in his acts.

7c As a consequence, people will

8a be watchful with words and   9b circumspect with deeds.

10c The *Shi* says:

11a Circumspect when uttering words and   12b respectful in majestic attitude.

13c The *Da ya* says:

14a Solemn indeed was King Wen;   15b he constantly made efforts to fulfil his duties.

This passage again presents a mixture of open and closed interlocking parallel style; pairs 2/3, 5/6, and 8/9 open in repeating the key words "words" and "deeds," so that their sequence is *a b a b a b.* Since the dialectics of words and deeds are a constant theme in Chinese philosophy and political poetry, the text then takes up two quotations from the classics based on these two in order to give some classical polish to the argument. These quotations, however, do not explicitly use the key terms; in the *Shi* 詩 quotation the coherence is easily established with reference to *hua* 話, "speech," clearly referring to the "words" above, and *yi* 儀 referring to "deeds." The *Da ya* quotation denotes with the *mu mu* 穆穆 a "virtue" associated with the field of the words *yan* 言 and *hua* 話, while the second part seems to refer to deeds and activities. We get an overall sequence of *c a b c a b c a b c a b c a b.*

This passage may give some clue to the genesis of IPS; the *c* phrases, even in the *Laozi,* frequently contain explicit elements of the *a* and *b* series. I think that, in the first stages of interlocking parallel style, the last phrases came to fulfill more and more the function of a summary, and gradually developed into a phrase containing elements of both series, yet breaking away from parallelism until it finally became a separate conclusion. The classical quotations inserted into the grid of the text are clearly different in character from the preceding lines and may represent a step in that direction.

The *Li ji* also contains a number of passages where the discussion of more than two elements is presented in open interlocking parallel style. Thus, in its *Liyun* 禮運 chapter, there is an open triple construction around the terms *ming* 明 (or *ze* 則), *yang* 養, and *shi* 事, which I will quote here without detailed discussion.[42]

故

君者所明也非明人者也

　君者所養也非養人者也

　　君者所事也非事人者也

故君

明人則有過

　養人則不足

　　事人則失位

故百姓

則君以自治也

　養君以自安也

　　事君自顯也

In the third round, a 則 appears where a *ming* 明 would have been expected. Some commentators have read this *ze* as a *ming*, others such as Sun Xidan (1736–84) have done the inverse, and have transformed the previous three *ming* into *ze*.[43] For our structural analysis it suffices to say that these commentators are right in understanding the prevalence of the information coming from structure over that coming from textual transmission here. Either way, a change has to be made. A translation may run:

That is why
a ruler is someone to whom information is provided, not someone who provides information to others. Or: a ruler is someone whom [others] will take as their model, not someone who will take others as his model;
　a ruler is someone to whom provisions are provided, not someone who provides provisions to others;
　　a ruler is someone whom other serve, not someone who serves others.

That is why if a ruler

provides information to others (or: takes others as his model)
he will commit transgressions;

    provides provisions for others, there will not be enough
    [for all of them];

        serves others he will lose his position [as a ruler].

        That is why the Hundred Clans will
give information to the ruler (or: take the ruler as their model)
by way of bringing order to themselves;

    provide provisions to the ruler by way of finding peace for
    themselves;

        serve the ruler by way of finding distinction for
        themselves.

The *Hanfeizi* 韓非子 opens with a statement in interlocking parallel
style:

        1c 臣聞

2a 不知而言不智   3b 知而不言不忠

        4c 為人臣

          5b 不忠當死

6a 言而不當亦當死

       7c 雖然臣願悉言所聞唯大王裁其罪

    1c Being a minister
2a to know nothing but talk
    anyhow, means being   3b to know but not to talk means
    ignorant;   being disloyal.
        4c To be a minister

          5b but to be disloyal deserves
          death;

6a to talk without its being
    true equally deserves death.

        6c Nonetheless I want to say all I have heard. May
        the Great King fix my guilt for it.[44]

A long interlocking parallel passage further down in another
chapter describes the dialectics between remuneration and
punishment.[45]

The *Mozi* 墨子 also opens with a passage in interlocking parallel
style, spelling out the two main strategies of attracting qualified
people. It argues:[46]

1a 入國而不存其士則亡國矣   2b 見賢而不急則緩其君
                              3b 非賢無急
4a 非士無與慮國   5b 緩賢
6a 忘士
        7c 而能以其國存者未曾有也

The parallelism is not too rigorous in the numbers of characters
and it contains an inversion in the beginning, *a b b a*. The irregulari-
ties in the numbers of characters might be due to textual corruption.
This opening section is written in open IPS with a repetition of the
key words *xian* 賢 and *shi* 士.

In translation:

1a If upon entering a state,
    [a ruler] does not secure
    its scholars, he ruins   2b If upon seeing a worthy no
    that state.   haste is made [to attract him
                                       to the court], one puts off one's
                                       prince.
                                   3b That the worthies are rejected
                                       and there is no urgent effort
                                       [to recruit them],
4a that the scholars are
    rejected and there is no
    deliberating with them about
    the state,
        [in other words that]   5b the worthies are put off and
6a the scholars are forgotten,
        7c but that one should be capable of making one's state
            endure—this has never happened!

In the *Xiao jing* 孝經, there are several passages in interlocking
parallel style, unrecognized by translators. In one case the commentary by Zheng Xuan 鄭玄 gives a hint concerning the linkages within
a set of phrases in *Xiao jing* 17.[47] The passage runs:

        1c 子曰君子之事上也
2a 進思盡忠   3b 退思補過
4a 將順其美   5b 匡救其惡
        6c 故上下能相親也

1c The Master said: In serving the ruler,
  the *Junzi* will,

2a when being promoted
[to serve in the court], be
concerned [only] with
maximizing [his] loyalty.

3b when withdrawing [from]
service, be concerned [only]
with amending [his] mistakes.

Because of his
4a making efforts to be in
accordance with the
beauty of [loyalty]   and

5b striving to make up for the
evil of [his mistakes]

6c the ruler and [his] subordinates cannot
but be close to each other.

It might not seem difficult to find the linkages in this regular
little piece of closed IPS, because the notions of 惡 and 過 on the one
hand and 美 and 忠 on the other clearly proclaim that they are
connected. Zheng Xuan obliges further by directly joining the 惡
from phrase 5 and the 過 from phrase 3 into a single expression,
commenting 5b with the words "if the gentleman has transgressions
and blemishes 君子有過惡 he will correct and stop them."

The *Xici* appended to the *Zhouyi* have become a foundation text
for early Xuanxue scholars matched only by the *Laozi*. In the first
zhang already, a long section is written in open IPS.

1a 乾道成男	2b 坤道成女
3a 乾知大始	4b 坤作成物
5a 乾以易知	6b 坤以簡能
7a 易則易知	8b 簡則易從
9a 易知則有親	10b 易從則有功
11a 有親則可久	12b 有功則可大
13a 可久則賢人之德	14b 可大則賢人之業

15c

易   簡

而天下之理得矣
天下之理得而成位乎其中矣[48]

A translation read through the commentary by Han Kangbo may
run:

1a The Dao of Qian forms
the male

3a Qian is knowledgeable
about the Great
Beginning.

5a Qian is knowledgeable
through ease.

7a As [Qian] is easy, it is
easy to know.

9a Being easy to know it
has kindred [spirits]

11a Having kindred [spirits]
it is able to endure.

13a Being able to endure,
it is what [is visible] in
the virtue of the worthy.

2b The Dao of Kun forms the
female.

4b Kun acts to bring beings to
completion.

6b Kun is capable through simplicity.

8b As [Kun] is simple, it is easy
to follow.

10b Being easy to follow it has
achievements.

12b Having achievements it is
able to be great.

14b Being able to be great, it is
what [is visible] in the
enterprise of the worthy.

15c [Due to] this
    ease   and   simplicity
[of the worthy] all [particular] features [of
beings] under Heaven are grasped [by him].
As all [particular] features [of beings] under
Heaven are grasped, he completes the
positions [of the images of the hexagrams]
between them [e.g. Heaven and Earth].

The examples cited here and in some of the notes are but a
general indication of the presence of interlocking parallel style in
material that is likely to be prior to the Han. I think it can be safely
stated that IPS is a frequent pattern in early Chinese texts. From a
cursory analysis it seems to have evolved out of a "zipper" construction of interlocking parallel prose, of which the last pair gradually
was used to assume the functions of a general conclusion. This
qualitative difference called for formally differentiating the *c*
phrases from the paired phrases.

Interlocking Parallel Style in Wang Bi's Time

During the second and third centuries, the *Laozi*, the *Zhouyi*, and
the *Lunyu* became the foundation texts for several generations of

scholars and philosophers looking for a way out of what they deemed
the prison of the *zhangju* 章句 commentaries. Discussions about the
capability or inability of language to deal with ultimate philosophical questions and the insights of the Sages, especially Confucius
himself, focused the attention on the linguistic devices used in texts
presumably written or edited by those Sages of former times. Yang
Xiong pioneered the idea of using, in his own works, the communication forms of Confucius. In this manner he imitated the complex
structures of the *Zhouyi*, the *Laozi*'s discourses on the last things,
and the *Lunyu*'s oral and often unfathomable utterances as his
model.

Since the generation of Wang Bi and well into the fourth century
at least, a distinct stylistic feature of the *Laozi*, IPS, became the
standard form for philosophical writing. In oral communication
other forms closer to the *Lunyu* style were preferred.

Wang Bi's essays display in a highly systematized IPS far beyond the short pieces available from earlier texts. As we have seen,
little attention has been paid to this feature in *Laozi* scholarship,
and the same is true for scholars working on Wang Bi, He Yan, or
even Shi Daoan 釋道安 and other early Chinese Buddhists who
had grown up in the "Learning of the Dark," Xuanxue, tradition.
Since some of the relevant texts by Wang Bi, such as the *Laozi*
weizhi lüeli 老子微指略例, will be presented in full translation in
another part of this project to be separately published, I shall be
brief with the documentation here.[49] This text is a model of fully
developed IPS, originally extracted from the *Laozi*, then developed
into a prose style even for long pieces. The words and phrases
in quotation marks are terms imported from the *Laozi*. The text
begins:

1c 夫	
2a 物之所以生	3b 功之所以成
4c 必	
5a 生乎無形	6b 由乎無名
7a 無形	8b 無名
9c 者，萬物之宗也。	
10a 不溫不涼	11b 不宮不商
	12b 聽之不可得而聞
13a 視之不可得而彰	
14a 體之不可得而知	15b 味之不可得而嘗

16c 故其

17a 為物也則混成為象也則無形   18b 為音也則希聲為味也則無呈

19c 故能為品物之

20b 宗

21a 主

22c 包通天地，靡使不經也 。⁵⁰

1c It is generally true:

2a That by which things are
created—

3b That by which achievements
are brought about—

4c necessarily

5a [things] are created out
of the "featureless."

6b [achievements] are based on
the "nameless."

7a The featureless   and

8b the nameless

9c is [what the *Laozi* calls] the "ancestor of
the ten thousand kinds of entities."

10a [Being featureless,] it
neither warms nor cools.

11b [Being nameless,] it neither
[lets sound forth the notes]
gong or *shang*.

12b [Even when] "listening
for it," one is [still] unable to
hear [it]."

13a [Even when] "looking for
it," one is [still] unable
to perceive [it].

14a [Even when] groping for
it, one is [still] unable to
identify it.

15b [Even when] going after
its taste, one is [still] unable
to get its flavor.

16c That is why

17a "as a thing" it "completes
out of the diffuse," as an
"image" it is "without
form,"

18b as a "sound" it "has
an inaudible tone," as a
"taste" it is without flavor.

19c That is why it is able to be

20b the "principle" and

21a the "master"

22c of all [different] categories of entities,
to embrace and permeate Heaven
and Earth so that there is nothing
that it does not thread through.

Phrase 5 explicitly takes up *sheng* 生 from phrase 2, phrase 6 implicitly links up through *you* 由 with the *suoyi cheng* 所以成 of phrase 3. With "featureless" and "nameless," phrases 7 and 8, which grammatically are integrated into a *c* phrase, take up the key terms of the pair 5/6. This gives two strains 2/5/7 and 3/6/8 in a regular sequence. The attributes "cold" and "warm" belong to "things" and their "form," while musical sounds are pertinent to the "name" complex later taken up in the terms "listening" and "tasting," which integrates phrases 10 and 11 into the grid. Phrases 8–11 seem to form a series of 4 parallels, but are actually related to the two *a* and *b* strains. Phrase 12 refers with "listening" to the "name" series, that is, *b*; phrase 13 with "looking for it" to the "form" of "things," that is to *a*; phrase 14 refers to form as names cannot be "touched," and phrase 15 refers to "names" via the reference *Laozi* 35. The next block of four parallel phrases substantiates the argument brought forth earlier by quoting directly from *Laozi* texts and reveals itself as a "short exposition" of this text, trying to systematize its scattered contents. This group is unusual because it does not interlock individual statements but pairs. Again in phrase 17 *wu* 物 refers to "things" as much as the next phrase about *xiang* 象, while phrase 18 refers with both parts to the "names" block. The last phrase, 19 through 22, is actually a single *c* element spiked with elements from the two strains. The text goes on with the same binary construction and does not contain parts not written in IPS. By inserting the entire analysis of the *Laozi* (and, in another essay, of the *Zhouyi*) into the stylistic pattern of IPS, and by inserting ample quotations from the *Laozi* into these arguments, Wang Bi systematizes the *Laozi*'s often terse statements.

A passage from one of Wang Bi's commentaries to the *Laozi* will show that the same stylistic pattern is used both for his own writing and for elucidating the structure of passages from the *Laozi*.

Laozi 3.1 runs:

不尚賢	使民不爭
不貴難得之貨	使民不為盜
不見可欲	使民心不亂

Wang Bi's commentary runs in my reconstruction:

賢猶能也
尚者嘉之名也
貴者隆之稱也
唯能是任尚也曷為

唯用是施貴之曷為
尚賢顯名榮過其任下奔而競校能相射
貴貨過用貪者競趣穿窬探篋沒命而盜
故可欲不見則心無所亂也

It is immediately visible that neither in the *Laozi* text nor in Wang Bi's commentary is Schlegel's rule of parallelism strictly observed. Still, the parallelisms are open and the links explicit enough to consider the passage a serious candidate for IPS, even if the parallel pairs share only some general features but not the neat order of many other pieces. The passage translates:

1a "Worthy" is like "capable."
"To shower with honors" is a term for "to emulate."

2b "To overly appreciate" is an expression for "to exalt."

3a What is the purpose of showering [someone] with honors who is only capable of handling this [particular] assignment [and no others]?

4b Why should [something] be overly appreciated the use of which is only in this [particular] application [and in no others]?

5a If, in granting honors to worthies and glorifying the famous, the emulation exceeds their assignment, those below will rush forward to compete, compare their [own] capabilities [to those of those honored] and outdo each other.

6b If the appreciation of goods exceeds their use, the greedy will compete to rush for them. They will [as Kongzi says, *Lunyu* 17.10, comparing "small men to robbers who] "break through walls and search in chests," and will commit robbery without regard for their [own] life.

> 7c That is why [the text says] that, if [things] that
> might be craved for are not displayed [by those
> above], the hearts [of the people] have nothing to
> disturb them!

Apart from being written in IPS, the commentary also brings out the structure of the first three phrases of the *Laozi*, which otherwise might have been treated as three parallel phrases. The slight change in the second half of the third phrase from 民 of the first pair to 民心 indicates that the third phrase might have a separate status; the binary base model of IPS makes it improbable that there should be three parallels, and Wang Bi's commentary therefore suggests that the third phrase sums up the two previous ones and is a stand-alone *c* element. A translation of the *Laozi* segment would run:

1a Not to shower worthies
   with honors induces the
   people not to struggle.

2b Not to overly appreciate goods
   that are hard to get induces
   the people not to become
   robbers.

3c [In short,] not to display [things] that might be
   craved for induces the hearts of the people not to
   become prone to chaos.

In Wang Bi's reading, the implied actor for whom this strategy is developed is the ruler.

The use of IPS by Wang Bi and his contemporaries such as He Yan has not attracted the attention of scholars; the result is an increase in the fuzziness of their readings. Given the great prestige of the philosophers of the Zhengshi 正始 era in later decades and centuries, it is not surprising that authors of essays, prefaces, and commentaries of the third, fourth, and fifth centuries would continue to use this style as the basic model in their own writings. This includes such authors as Shi Daoan 釋道安 (312–85) and Shi Huiyuan 釋慧遠 (334–417).[51]

Conclusion

Interlocking parallel style began as part of a binary rhetoric. This rhetoric typically proceeds by juxtaposing complementary opposites such as Heaven and Earth, wealth and fame, rewards and punishments, Yin and Yang, pointing out their analogous structures through the parallelism in the statements about them and arriving at general conclusions. While mostly used in short, highly stylized segments such as the openings of books or chapters, or in prefaces, its prevalence in nearly half the *Laozi* chapters made it a stylistic model for the ontological argumentation developed in the middle of the third century.

Earlier commentaries, such as the two *Laozi* chapters in the *Hanfeizi* or the surviving elements from Zhuang Zun's, do not give sufficient information to allow an assessment of how they read the IPS sections in the *Laozi*. Given the general prevalence of elements of this style in a broad range of writings, however, it is likely that they proceeded from an understanding that there were IPS passages. However, with the revival of the pre-Han discussion about the capacity of language to deal with the "That-by-which" of the ten thousand kinds of entities, this stylistic feature in the *Laozi* was seen as one of many devices to enrich the capacity of language to deal with extremely complex structures like the cosmic order and with extremely simple structures like Being.

The *Zhouyi* and the *Lunyu* were seen as further attempts in this direction. In a qualitative change, the Xuanxue authors moved from tidbits and segments in IPS toward writing entire essays in this style. This would seem to presuppose a positive understanding of the rules of this style, which also guided the reading strategies for the more elusive parts of the *Laozi*.

While Wang Bi greatly stresses the sophistication of the *Laozi*'s *wen* 文, "textual composition," and does so in flourishing IPS, I do not find any explicit statement concerning this style in either third-century writings or in later Six Dynasties literary theory. This absence of an explicit discussion might be one of the reasons why a positive knowledge of IPS, still evident in Song-dynasty commentators, had faded so that modern scholars were reduced to reading texts of considerable literary and argumentative refinement and cohesiveness as a jumble of disconnected proverbs linked with an occasional "therefore" by some mad hatter from the Han dynasty. Still, the third-century changeover to long essays in IPS must have been based on a positive and fairly explicit understanding of its rules. Among surviving documents from this period, Wang Bi's structural analyses of the *Laozi* and the *Zhouyi*, the *Zhouyi lüeli*

周易略例 and the *Laozi weizhi lüeli* 老子微指略例 clearly are the longest, most elaborate examples of this style from the third century, and, in my personal assessment, the most important philosophical writings from this period.

While IPS proved of great advantage and economy for pursuits of the "necessary" features of that by which the entities are, passages in Wang Bi's own work reveal that the limits imposed by the binary arrangement encoded into IPS also could obstruct the development of his argument, producing occasional odd structures.[52]

Beyond the pragmatic advantages of understanding the rules of IPS for establishing the structural connections and hierarchies within a text and reducing textual fuzziness, this understanding opens an important though wordless source of philosophic and argumentative information contained in the text. Much as with the hexagrams of the *Zhouyi*, these structures become a silent text to be actualized. They set the parameters within which the written words operate and guide the strategies of the reader.

In his "Structure of the *Laozi*'s Subtle Pointers," Wang Bi deals explicitly with the philosophical bases of the *Laozi*'s argumentative style and its misunderstanding by different commentators. However, there is no explicit word on IPS to be found. From the presence of IPS elements in the few surviving fragments of the writings of He Yan, his senior by many years, we can assume that the fashion to use IPS had sprung up before Wang Bi, and we can assume that it was based on an understanding that this was the basic organizing form of many key sections of the *Laozi*, and emulated this practice of the revered text. Rather than having a discovery of an important stylistic feature by Wang Bi as a commentator, we seem to have a shared understanding among his peers about the IPS elements in the text. The few times where Wang Bi feels the necessity to explicitly mark the IPS connection in closed passaged or the long parallel staircases documented above, seem to be those segments where others have failed to understand the structure.

We thus conclude with three arguments, each one of them being valid independently:

1. Wang Bi and other early Xuanxue philosophers of the third century read sizeable parts of the *Laozi* as being written in IPS. Any study of their reading the *Laozi* will have to be based on this understanding of theirs.

2. In an emulation of the philosophical potential of this feature, they crafted their own writings on this model, with Wang Bi producing some of the most finely wrought and longest surviving essays in this style.

3. A close check of textual structures of the *Laozi* reveals that the consensus among Xuanxue scholars with regard to the use of both open and closed IPS elements in the *Laozi* is based on a highly plausible reading of this text. Their common interest in the ability of language to deal with ultimate things prompted their attention to the means of communication used in texts such as the *Laozi* and the *Zhouyi*. Such attention will not be found in commentators such as the Xiang Er, who, with a different agenda, largely disregard the rhetorical devices of the *Laozi*. The viability of the reading strategy used by Wang Bi is buttressed not only from a large array of pieces from the *Laozi* itself, but also from the presence of similar structures in a broad number of other early Chinese texts. In other words, their reading strategy transcends their particular interests in reading the *Laozi* and has the value of a scholarly insight.

The cultural transfer involved in translating and analyzing these texts will have to make the silent text encoded in the IPS structure explicit.

Deconstructing and Constructing Meaning

The Hidden Meaning

Wang Bi not only wrote commentaries on the *Laozi* and the *Zhouyi*, which have had a formative influence on the reading of these texts in later centuries down to the present; he is also the first commentator from whom texts are transmitted that outline the philosophic and methodological bases for his commentaries, namely the *Laozi weizhi lüeli* 老子微指略例 (*LZWZLL*) for the *Laozi* and the *Zhouyi lüeli* 周易略例 (*ZYLL*) for the *Zhouyi*. As evident from Liu Xie's *Wenxin diaolong*, the commentary of this period was subsumed under the genre of the essay, *lun* 論.[1] Its formal fragmentation into small items dealing with phrases of the main text did not prevent its being seen as presenting a full and cohesive argument on its own. As the *lun* used to a large extent the "classics" as the reality they were studying, the commentary and the essay are essentially based on the same kind of material and approach.

Wang Bi was writing during a time when many of the best and best-educated minds were focusing on the *Laozi*, *Lunyu*, and *Zhouyi* as their prime sources of philosophic insight. The fierce competition for intellectual excellence in this difficult field greatly contributed to enhancing the philological and philosophical quality of the commentaries written during that period. Wang Bi's construction of the *Laozi* thus presents a serious scholarly and philosophic challenge to a highly educated environment where the need for still another commentary certainly was not evident. This chapter will not deal with Wang Bi's philosophy, but with his craft. Oddly enough, the craft of Chinese commentators has received very little attention. Historians of philosophy have operated on the assumption that the commentators basically present their own philosophy in the guise of a humble comment on the classics, and they have therefore as a rule quoted passages from these commentators which looked relatively independent of the text on which they were commenting.

Studying Wang Bi's craft is also a means to check the assumption implied in this previous treatment, that Wang Bi's comments are basically impositions on the text with little or no respect for that work; and to find out whether his comments are based on a consistent and arguable methodology, and if so which?

Wang Bi's two "Structures" do not focus on giving short summaries of the main tenets of the *Laozi* and *Zhouyi* respectively, but try to spell out the silent formal structures of these texts. They try, moreover, to discover the philosophic implications of these structures to the reader. The following pages deal primarily with the *LZWZLL*. The *ZYLL* was written later and focuses on a different type of coding. I shall cite it only when and insofar it helps to highlight certain arguments implied in the *LZWZLL* but not fully developed there. Both essays start from the implied philosophic puzzle about the highly unusual means of communication used by these texts.

In fact, in the reading of Wang Bi and his contemporaries, the *Laozi* consists of a large number of short independent chapters, their sequence by and large serendipitous. Each *zhang* 章 starts anew, but the limits between the *zhang* seem fairly firm.

The *Laozi* uses a broad array of linguistic and rhetorical devices, ranging from onomatopoieia to similes, from quotations and stylistic parallelism to authoritative pronouncement or bald philosophical statement of fact without explanation; at the same time it constantly warns the reader that language, including its own, is an unreliable medium for communication about ultimate things: "A way that can be spoken of is not the eternal Way" (*Laozi* 1.1); "Forced, I give it the style, *zi* 字, 'Way'" (*Laozi* 25.5). The *Laozi* as a written book is thus an attempt to continue to use language for the philosophic inquiry into the ultimate things in the full knowledge that language as a defining instrument is, in the last analysis, insufficient. These and similar *Laozi* statements are taken up in the *LZWZLL*.

The *Zhouyi* establishes layers of superimposed explanations from the words in the verbalized explanations to the overall meaning of a hexagram, the image used and the individual lines, the *guaci* 卦辭, *xiangci* 象辭, and *tuanci* 彖辭, through the symbols occurring within them to the "meaning" encoded into the silent structure of the hexagram itself, and finally the *Xici* 繫辭 and other appended chapters theorizing about the relationship of words and meaning.[2] The authority for this reading goes back to a statement in the *Xici* traditionally attributed to Confucius:

> The Master said: "[Written] words 書 do not exhaust [spoken] language 言; [spoken] language does not exhaust meaning. Does this mean that it is impossible to perceive the meaning of the Sage?" The Master said: "The Sage[s] set up the images, *xiang* 象, to exhaustively [present their] meaning; they established the trigrams, *gua* 卦, in order to exhaustively [present] right and wrong; and they linked up the sayings in order to exhaustively [present] their words."[3]

According to this passage, the entire *Zhouyi* is constructed as an answer to the philosophic problem of the inability of language to fully express the meaning of the Sage by using symbolic, structural, and other forms of expression. The *ZYLL* focuses on this aspect of the *Zhouyi* and its philosophic implications.

Both the *Zhouyi* and the *Laozi*, accordingly, do not use these forms because they were part of an unquestioned tradition, or because they just happened to be available. From their explicit statements about the limited potential of language Wang Bi inferred that both texts are consciously constructed in this manner. Their recondite literary forms are thus an essential part of their philosophic content. As a consequence, the reader can enter the text properly only if he has understood this contradiction in the two texts between the actual use of language and the simultaneous insight into its insufficiency, and applies a reading strategy that keeps in mind that the texts are coded in a manner conscious of this contradiction. The double duty of the commentator then is to explain what philosophic problem the texts reacted to by having recourse to these seemingly cumbersome means of communication, and in the process help the reader to overcome traditional and inappropriate reading strategies and develop the strategy the two texts themselves require.

The essential unreliability of philososphic language does not prompt Wang Bi to adopt an attitude of negligence with regard to the actual rhetorical devices used in the *Laozi*. The opposite is the case. Wang Bi deals with the text as a model of philosophic rhetoric, stressing again the importance of its literary craft and the necessity of understanding it in order to grasp the text's elusive meaning. He writes:

> As for its literary form 其為文, [the individual arguments of the *Laozi*] take up the end in order to give evidence of the beginning, and they do not relate the beginning in order to fully exhaust the end. "They open up but do not go all the way," "they show the way but do not lead forward" [in accordance with the practice of the gentleman's teaching in the *Liji* 禮記 18.6/97.10ff.]. [Thus,] only after careful searching does one fully realize his meaning, and only after making inferences does one fully understand the principle [that] he [is pointing at].[4]

This discovery of the philosophic implications of the formal, literary, and rhetorical structure of these texts by Wang Bi coincides with Cao Pi's 曹丕 "discovery" just a few decades earlier of *wenqi* 文氣, the literary endowment of texts as a distinct feature carrying philosophic implications worthy of scholarly consideration.[5] The revolution brought about through the literature of the Jian'an 建安 (196–220) era during the transition from Han to the Three Kingdoms had installed the new poetry as a means of expressing both individual feeling and, potentially, philosophic insight. Poetry as a nonargumentative form of expression became a legitimate medium for dealing with the inexpressible, and eventually a form of philosophic discourse.[6] On a structural level, Cao Pi argued with "in literary texts, *qi* 氣 is the dominant thing" 文以氣為主, that the new poetry had the power to express what was intrinsically diffuse and hard to define. At the same time, as Zhou Jizhi 周繼旨 has argued, this broke with the theoretical assumption underlying earlier reading strategies. Based on Dong Zhongshu's theory of the correspondence between Heaven or Nature and society, this earlier reading strategy looked for clues decipherable in terms of Yin and Yang and the Five Elements.[7] The new theory assumed the core topic of philosophic and literary texts to be directly the Dao, and suggested a reading that looked for clues in this direction.

The *qi* corresponds to the personal endowment of the author, which is as hard to detect and to describe by means of language as the Dao itself. In a related argument, Kong Fan quotes the first phrases of Liu Shao's 劉邵 (fl. 224 CE) *Renwu zhi* 人物志 to illustrate this point:

> The fundamentals of a personality come from its feelings and nature, *qingxing* 情性, but the ordering principle, *li* 理, of these feelings and nature is verily subtle and abstruse.[8]

A poem contains and hides this particular endowment like a face or the pupil of the eye hide and give access to the *qi* 氣 with which a person is endowed. Deciphering the face in physiognomy, or looking into the person's inner being through the pupil of the eye, arts that occupied many of the most brilliant minds at the time, are thus efforts similar to that of grasping the *qi* of a poem or the ineffable of the *Laozi* text. The formulations used in the Conversations of the Pure Ones, *qingtan* 清談, of the period to characterize the personality, the poetry, and the philosophic statements of the famous scholars of the time consciously shirked the well-defined and flat moral vocabulary of Han evaluations contained, for example, in Ban Gu's "Tables of Personalities of Ancient and Recent Times," *Gujin renbiao* 古今人表, and used symbolic, metaphoric, and other means of expression.[9]

The *Laozi* was a text popular with the proponents of *qingtan* as well as with the Jian'an poets. Its use of literary and often poetic forms certainly was a driving force in the new value attributed to such forms of expression for philosophic inquiry. In turn, the rising fashion in the use of such forms also helped focus attention on the meanings of the *Laozi*'s choice of this particular form of expression.

Wang Bi's theoretical description and practical analysis of the literary and rhetorical devices of the *Laozi* as an essential part of his philosophizing in turn added great legitimacy to other experiments with nonlinear forms of philosophic discourse like poetry, and enhanced the theoretical understanding of literary texts.

As we are here primarily concerned with the particulars of the commentator's craft, and as philosophy and philosophy of language will have their day elsewhere,[10] I shall at this point simply name those elements in Wang Bi's philosophic inquiry of the *Laozi*'s language that are necessary for understanding the methodological underpinnings of his craft as a commentator, and not fully develop his philosophy of language.

The Implied Author and His Authority: Kongzi and Laozi

Wang Bi reads the *Laozi* as a text crafted and constructed by one person, Laozi. Wang Bi talks about "the text of Laozi" 老子之文[11] and "the book of Laozi" 老子之書,[12] which defines the author as an individual, and his product as a crafted text, *wen* 文. In the *LZWZLL*, Laozi appears as the subject in phrases describing him as crafting the text. Wang Bi and his contemporaries did not see the text as a loose collection of proverbs or other philosophic matter from different sources that, beyond certain thematic affinities, could not claim any philosophic consistency. The assumption of the *Laozi*'s being written by an author called Laozi is an assumption about the philosophic homogeneity of this text. As a first step, we thus define "Laozi" as the emblem of the *Laozi*'s homogeneity. From this it follows, in terms of reading strategy, that each section of the *Laozi* has to be read in the context of the whole, a context that defines the angle of approach.

Who is this Laozi for Wang Bi? In order to understand Wang Bi's strategy of constructing the *Laozi*, we have to reconstruct his assessment of this author. Evidently a text bequeathed by a god through a medium would require a different reading strategy than, for example, the babble of a village idiot.

In Wang Bi's time and circles, the stature of Laozi was mostly defined in relation to that of Confucius, then generally seen as the last of the Sages. For this purpose we have diffuse statements about and depictions of the encounters between the two men; words written and said, attributed to the two, in which, in Wang Bi's reading, they state their own opinions of their relative status; the development of various assessments of the two during the Han; statements by Wang Bi and others; and, finally, reports by later writers on the respective opinions of Wang Bi and others.

The question of the relative status of Laozi and Confucius was a matter of greatest concern at the time. It had religious importance in the spiritual and ethical competition between the Ru and the emerging Daoist church; it had a political importance insofar as it reflected which of the different approaches to ordering society was considered fundamental; and it had philosophic importance because it influenced the status of the different traditional texts and, more important, the strategies for their reading.

The various reports about encounters between Laozi and Confucius in pre-Han and Han texts have been studied for the purpose of establishing the life dates of Laozi.[13] The texts were written, however, for a different purpose, namely to talk about the relationship and hierarchy between the two masters. Michel Soymié seems to be alone in having dealt with this aspect in a fine study on the textual and pictorial evidence of these encounters.[14] Since the *Zhuangzi*, Confucius appears as Laozi's student[15] while being himself a "supreme man" 至人 in his own right who is even used in the *Zhuangzi* to expound his, Zhuangzi's, own teachings.[16] Confucius asks Laozi about the Dao, about the "basis of ritual and music"[17] and quotes a Lao Dan 老聃 as an authority in discussions about special ritual problems.[18] This feature has been incorporated without criticism in many texts such as the *Lüshi chunqiu* 呂氏春秋, *Hanfeizi* 韓非子, and the *Kongzi jiayu* 孔子家語.[19] There are many Han-dynasty reliefs that show the two men in discussion.[20] These anecdotes share the assumption that both men pursued a common goal, and that, accordingly, their insights and teachings supplemented each other rather than being mutually exclusive. As Confucius' teacher, Laozi ranks higher than his student.

Sima Tan's "Treatise on the Six Schools," which Sima Qian included in his autobiography, shares the assumption common during the early Western Han that Laozi was superior to Confucius. During these first decades of the Western Han, the *Laozi* as a text of political philosophy was much appreciated by the center.[21] Sima Tan does not base himself on the above-mentioned stories that make Laozi the teacher of Confucius in matters of ritual, but on the relationship of the philosophic views contained in the *Laozi* and in the statements attributed to Confucius. Sima Tan's treatment of the "schools" is hierarchical, with the most important coming last. This first place was given by him to the "Daoist" writings, which he said excelled in treating the "fundament" of things, while the teaching of the Ru, though slightly defective, was said to be better suited for the management of daily affairs.[22]

The state sponsorship of the Ru teaching of the classics since Han Wudi seems to have somewhat impaired the official standing of the *Laozi*.[23] Still, as Benjamin Wallacker has shown in his study of Han Confucianism, the "doctors of the Five Classics" at no moment enjoyed a doctrinal monopoly as sometimes suggested in statements about the official stature of Confucianism during the Han. A man like Yang Xiong would not find it odd to imitate in his writings the *Zhouyi*, the *Lunyu*, as well as the *Laozi*, and would state that:

> Some of the things Laozi said about *Dao* and *De* I accept, but as to [his] denigration of human kindness and justice as well as [his advocacy of] breaking off and demolishing ritual behavior and study, of this I accept nothing.[24]

Laozi reached his lowest ranking at the time on Ban Gu's (32–92) "Tables of Personalities of Ancient and Recent Times" in the *Hanshu*; these tables classify a very large number of historic personalities into a nine-tiered scheme beginning with top-top, *shang shang* 上上 through top-middle and top-low to the middle and lower sections with the same tripartite subdivision. The upper three and the lowest grade also have terms attached to them. The highest rank is the Sage, *shengren* 聖人, the second the person with human kindness, *ren ren* 仁人, and the third the knowledgeable, *zhi ren* 智人. The lowest rank is the fool, *yuren* 愚人.[25] As Wang Baoxuan has pointed out, the seemingly regular division into nine ranks in three groups hides a different tripartite division established by Confucius, according to the *Lunyu*, to which Ban Gu refers in the preface to the "Tables of Personalities":[26]

> With [people] above [the level] of those in the middle it is possible to talk about the ultimate. With [people] below [the level] of those in the middle it is not possible to talk about the ultimate.[27]

Ban Gu links this statement with another one from the same source: "Those of highest knowledge and those of lowest foolishness indeed do not change."[28] Those of the highest knowledge are the Sages who need no teaching and change; those of the lowest foolishness are the fools in Ban Gu's table and cannot be taught and changed for the better. Confucius himself defines those in the highest rank as being "born knowledgeable" and those in the lowest as being uneducable when he says that "he is the highest who is born knowledgeable ... but he who, although he makes efforts, does not become educated the people consider the lowest."[29] Both the Sage and the fool are born as what they are. The Sage is a world event, and the fool a world disaster. The Sages in Ban Gu's table are the Sage rulers who bring about great peace such as Yao, Shun, and the Duke of Zhou, and the fools are those evil rulers like Zhou, the last ruler of the Shang. Neither Sage nor fool is brought about by visible and calculable causes or efforts. The "people in the middle," however, the *zhongren* 中人, who occupy the ranks 2 through 8 in Ban Gu's scale, can change and can be taught. This is where typical human beings come in. The highest rank they can hope to achieve is the second, and they may fall as low as the eighth.

Well in tune with the assessment prevailing among some of the Ru at the time, Ban Gu downgrades Laozi to the fourth rank, to *zhongshang* 中上, while keeping Confucius as the last of the Sages in the top rank. This assessment, however, was not uncontroversial. A few decades after Ban Gu's death in 92 CE, leading scholars like Ma Rong 馬融 (79–166 CE) took up again the study of the *Laozi*, and within a different system of religious values, Laozi rose during the Later Han to become the highest god, with Confucius distinctly inferior.

The imperially sponsored "Laozi Inscription," *Laozi ming* 老子銘, of 165, with which the court might have tried to coopt some of the rising popular acclaim of Laozi for itself, sees Laozi as the highest god "coexisting with the primodial chaos" and explicitly takes to task Ban Gu for his assessment.[30] This did not necessarily imply a rejection of Confucius. The Xiang Er commentary attributed to one of the two fathers of the Taoist church, Zhang Lu 張魯 or Zhang Daoling 張道陵, writes in a commentary to *Laozi* 21.1 孔德之容唯道是從: "The Dao is truly great; it taught Confucius to let him know, but the later generations did not believe the Dao's writings and exalted only the books of Confucius, considering them unsurpassed. That is why the Dao [through the book *Laozi*] makes this clear [what is said in the above-quoted *Laozi* phrase] to tell it to later worthies." Extrapolating from this commentary, the *Laozi* phrase has to be translated: "What vast content of the virtue of

Confucius [himself] was just [the result] of his following [what] the Dao [had told him]."[31] Thus even this text assumes a basic agreement between the teachings of Confucius and the *Laozi*.

For Wang Bi and the other prominent members of the Scholarly Exploration of the Dark, Xuanxue, neither of the three options presented here, Laozi as a mediocre thinker, Laozi as the teacher of the Sage Confucius, and Laozi as the highest god dealt accurately with the historical facts.

Ban Gu's nine-tiered scheme received an important boost at the beginning of the Wei dynasty. When in 220 CE Chen Qun 陳群 designed the famous system of the Nine Grades of the Mean and Correct, *jiupin zhongzheng* 九品中正 for Cao Pi, which became the main instrument for the evaluation, selection, and promotion of officials until the Tang introduced the state examinations, he copied this system for the grading of the living directly from the one Ban Gu had developed for that of the dead.[32] Wang Bi and many others thus continued to operate within Ban Gu's ninefold scheme without sharing his particular assessments or copying his terminology. Ban Gu's term for the second level, *ren ren* 仁人, the Humane, they rarely used but instead used the Worthy, *xianren* 賢人, or the Second Degree Sage, *yasheng* 亞聖. Wang Baoxuan discovered a hitherto unknown piece of a Wang Bi notice to the *Xici* that deals with the difference between a Sage and a worthy. In the first section of the *Xici* there is a description of how, on the basis of an understanding of the universe through the hexagrams, the world can be ordered. The protagonist in this achievement, however, is not, as might be expected, the Sage, but the Worthy. Wang Bi comments on this fact:

不曰聖人者,聖人體無,不可以人名而名。故易簡之主,皆以賢人名之。然則以賢是聖之次,故寄賢以為名。窮易簡之理,盡乾坤之奧,必聖人乃能耳。

As to [the *Xici*'s] not saying "the Sage" [but the worthy]— the Sage embodies negativity; therefore he cannot be named by the name of a common human being. Therefore the protagonists for the "easy" [understanding] and the "simple" following [in action] [mentioned in the *Xici* here] are all defined by [the term] worthy. Thus it is because the worthy is second to the Sage that [the text] draws on the [term] worthy for a definition. [But] to fully penetrate "the principle" of the "easy and simple"

and get to the bottom of the mystery of *qian* 乾 and *kun* 坤 —
definitely a Sage only is able to do this.[33]

Wang Bi argues that the specific achievements that will come
about have to be assigned to someone in the range of "common men"
but not to a Sage, whose person and action defy definition. The *Xici*
then argues "from the Easy and the Simple, the principle of All
Under Heaven [can be] grasped" 易簡而天下之理得矣. Only the Sage is
able to achieve such a full grasp of the ordering principle of the
world.

For Wang Bi, the historical record supported neither Ban Gu's
evaluation nor the claims of those who saw Laozi as the highest god,
nor indeed the tradition that Confucius was the disciple of Laozi. As
these three assumptions, however, were present in the intellectual
climate of his time, Wang Bi's own assessment must be read against
this background, and they receive their particular flavor from their
critical rejection of these other assessments. Where, then, does
Wang Bi situate Laozi on the scale of history, and on what grounds
does he base his judgment?

There is no biography of Laozi in the surviving parts of Wang
Bi's *LZWZLL*, but Wang Bi gives Laozi a short biographical note in
his commentary to the *Lunyu*. Commenting on the name[s] Lao
Peng 老彭 in the *Lunyu*, Wang Bi writes:

"Lao" 老 is Lao Dan 老聃. "Peng" 彭 is Peng Zu 彭祖. Laozi is
a man from the village Quren 曲仁 in the *xiang* Lai 厲 in the
district Hu 苦 in Chu 楚. His family name is Lao 老. His *ming*
名 is Er 耳. His *zi* 字 is Boyang 伯陽. His posthumous honorific
is Dan 聃. He was an archivist under the Zhou.[34]

This note is mostly based on Sima Qian's biography of Laozi.[35]
With its sober dryness the note rejects the claims about the god
Laozi as "coexistent with the primordial breath" as given in the
Laozi ming, or statements like the one in the Xiang Er commentary to *Laozi* 10.1 that "the dispersed form of the One is *qi*,
while its concentrated form is the Lord Lao On High" 一 散形為氣，
聚形為太上老君.[36]

Wang Bi's note is a commentary to a statement in the *Lunyu*.
Extrapolating from Wang Bi's commentary, it has to be translated
as follows:

> The Master said: "In handing down [the teachings of old] and not creating [anything new], in being credible [myself] and in [still] loving antiquity, my humble self compares [well] to our Lao 老 and Peng 彭."

Wang Bi's *Solving the Doubtful Points in the Lunyu* takes the *Lunyu Commentary* to task that had been put together around 243 by He Yan and his colleagues. They read "Lao Peng" as the name of a single person by quoting the commentary by Bao Xian 包咸 (1st cent. CE):

> Lao Peng was a worthy and high official from the Yin dynasty. He loved transmitting old stories. "I [Confucius] am like Lao Peng" means that he [Confucius also] only transmits them [that is, old stories].[37]

Wang Bi follows Zheng Xuan, the first to suggest a reference here to Laozi and Pengzu.[38] The modest "my humble self compares . . ." means, in fact, that Confucius considered himself superior to Laozi and Pengzu in the respects mentioned. Seen together with the *Lunyu* phrase on which it comments, the note establishes that Confucius feels it proper to compare himself with Laozi; their status must be comparable, they must rank close enough to each other to make the statement meaningful. The note thus makes Confucius himself talk back to Ban Gu's low assessment of Laozi's caliber. At the same time, Confucius modestly claims that he is comparable but superior to Laozi. In Ban Gu's scale, this would put Laozi into a close second to the Sage, for which the term Second Degree Sage, *yasheng* 亞聖, had been coined during the later Han. It is a person so high in the second highest rank that he is nearly a Sage, while staying in the realm of accessibility.

Apart from the above statement by Confucius himself, Wang Bi has evidence from *Laozi*. In the *Laozi* there are many statements by an authorial "I." In a number of cases these are either explicitly or implicitly statements by the Sage talking about himself.[39] But in *Laozi* 70, the "I" talks about himself, and then there follows a statement about the Sage. The text in the translation as extrapolated from Wang's commentary and written in structural writing to make the IPS structures visible:

> My words [Laozi says, and ditto
> for my activities]

are very easy to understand   and   very easy to put into
practice.
But [still even] them of the others
no one is able to understand   and   no one is able to put into
practice.
[My] words have the principle.   [My] activities have the ruler.
It is [hence] a fact that only those
without any understanding will
therefore not understand me [and
ditto for practice].
[Consequently] the fewer there
are of those who understand me
the more I am honored. This is
why the Sage wears coarse cloth,
but carries a piece of jade in his
bosom.[40]

In the *LZWZLL*, Wang Bi quotes this statement in the following
context:

> The book of Laozi can almost [as Confucius said about the
> *Shijing*] "be summed up in one phrase," ah! Emulating the root
> [by way] of bringing to rest the stem and branches [growing
> from it]—that is all! In observing on what the [ten thousand
> kinds of entities] are based, and in investigating whereto [they]
> return, [Laozi's] "words" do not depart from the "principle" and
> [his] activities do not lose [sight] of the "ruler" [as Laozi says
> about himself in *Laozi* 70.2].[41]

Wang Bi thus identifies the "I" in *zhang* 70 as Laozi. It becomes clear
that, while Laozi's words are easy to understand, but hardly understood by anyone, the Sage is even further removed as he, according
to *Laozi* 2.2/3, "takes residence in management without interference
and practices teaching without words" so that there are neither
words to be understood nor activities to be put into practice. As
Arthur Waley observed, the *Laozi* is the first philosophical Chinese
text in which the author uses not his name but "I," *wu/wo* 吾／我 for
himself.[42] In *Laozi* 70 this "I" accordingly is comparable to the Sage
but slightly inferior to him.[43]

On the authority of Confucius and Laozi themselves, Wang Bi
thus situates Laozi directly below the Sage Confucius. His contemporary Ruan Ji 阮籍 (210–63), said to have agreed with him on the
issue, described Laozi as a superior worthy, *shang xian* 上賢, and a

second-degree Sage, *yasheng* 亞聖, the two ranks being the same.[44] A fourth-century tract by an author critical of Wang Bi and supportive of Ban Gu had the title "Lao Dan Is No Great Worthy," which implies that Wang Bi and his friends considered Laozi to be on the second rank in Ban Gu's scale.[45]

On the other hand, the authorial "I" of the *Laozi* ranks itself above the "vulgar men," *zhongren* 眾人. *Zhongren* is a polemical term. They are not the people, who are called *min* 民, or *baixing* 百姓 in the *Laozi*. These "vulgar men" "have too much,"[46] display their intelligence,[47] control people with a surveillance machinery,[48] have houses with terraces,[49] still have "ambitions,"[50] know much and have studied much,[51] are the ones who educate.[52] They belong to those above, to the ruling circles to whose behavior those below will respond.[53] The *Laozi* denounces them as *suren* 俗人, as vulgar people.[54] They are accordingly the vulgar scholars, people with the social standing of scholars but without the necessary understanding. That is why I have translated *zhongren* as "vulgar scholars." The authorial "I" establishes a clear difference between himself and these vulgar scholars because the "place abhorred by the vulgar scholars" is "close to the Way."[55] There is, however, no fundamental difference; the authorial "I" is still struggling to rise above the vulgar scholars; it "wants to be" different from them, saying: "I alone desire to be different from the others in that I honor the nourishing mother."[56] We conclude that the authorial "I" is far superior to the vulgar scholars and a close second to the Sage, but still moves in the same grand framework as the vulgar scholars.

Ranking, according to these self-definitions as Wang Bi read them, immediately below the Sage, *Laozi* operates on a level attainable by mortal "people from the middle," *zhongren* 中人. While this attainable status of the author might seem to promise the reader an easier access to the text, it in fact undermines the reliability of the author as a philosopher, and, as a consequence, of the text as a harbinger of truth. As a second-degree Sage, Laozi is an unreliable philosopher. Modern literature since Stendhal's *La Chartreuse de Parme* and Faulkner's *The Sound and the Fury* has played with the unconsciously unreliable narrator in an effort to highlight the fictional quality of reality and history. As we shall see, Laozi is a more complex case, because Wang Bi sees him as proceeding in full awareness of the unavoidable unreliability of his own statements.

In a famous exchange, Wang Bi himself explicitly defined the relationship between Confucius and Laozi. There are two versions of the statement, the first in He Shao's 何劭 "Biography of Wang Bi" written just a few decades after the event (He Shao died in 301). This anecdote is quoted in practically every article and book dealing with Xuanxue, and sadly enough in most cases, with the exception of Qian Mu, the punctuation is wrong so that the point is lost. Given the importance of the passage, I shall translate both versions and include the Chinese texts:

[Wang] Bi was, from his early youth on, intelligent and penetrating. When he was just beyond his 10th year, he was infatuated with Mr. Lao [Laozi]; he understood [Laozi's] arguments, and was capable of holding forth [about them]. When [his] father, [Wang] Ye 〔王〕業, was a Secretarial Court Gentleman, *shangshu lang* 上書郎, Pei Hui 裴徽 (fl. 230–49) had been a Court Gentleman at the Ministry of Personnel, *libu lang* 吏部郎 [that is, there was a connection between the two families]. Before [Wang] Bi had even been capped [and had completed his 20th year in 245], he [already] went to visit [Pei Hui who then was a high official]. [Pei] Hui considered him extraordinary at first sight, and asked [Wang] Bi: "Generally speaking, negativity is in fact that which forms the basis of the ten thousand kinds of entities, 夫無者誠萬物之所資也. The Sage [Confucius,] however, was absolutely unwilling to discourse about it [about negativity], while *Laozi* holds forth about it endlessly. Why [is that so]?" 然聖人莫肯致言，而老子申之無已者何. [Wang] Bi answered: "The Sage embodies negativity. Negativity, furthermore, cannot be elaborated upon, that is why [the Sage] does not speak [about it]. 聖人體無，無又不可以訓，故不説. Laozi [however] belongs to [the realm of specific] entities. 老子是有者也. In that sense [his] constant talking about negativity is [exactly his] deficiency" 故恆言無，所不足.[57]

The second version, transmitted in the *Shishuo xinyu*, is slightly different.

[Even] before Wang Fusi [Bi] had passed the capping ceremony [before he had completed his 20th year, that is, before 245 CE], he visited Pei Hui [who at the time was a senior official]. [Pei] Hui [who had already heard about the young man's philosophical acuity] asked him: "Generally spoken, negativity is in fact that which forms the basis of the ten thousand kinds of entities 夫無者誠萬物之所資. The Sage [Confucius], however, was absolutely unwilling to discourse about it [about negativity], while *Laozi* holds forth about it endlessly. Why [is that so]?" 然聖人莫肯致言，而老子申之無已，何邪. [Wang] Bi answered: "The Sage embodies negativity. Negativity furthermore cannot be elaborated upon. From this follows that words by necessity pertain to [specific] entities 聖人體無　無又不可以訓　故言必及有. Lao[zi] and Zhuang[zi, however,] have not escaped from [the realm of specific] entities [and thus their] constant talking [about negativity] is [exactly] their deficiency 老莊未免於有恆訓，其所不足.[58]

We have no exact knowledge about the process in which these oral exchanges were memorized and transmitted before they were written down. From the variations in the same story as well as from their occasional attribution to different people we can assume that different people who heard them or about them transmitted them independently. The fact that these statements were so carefully preserved and transmitted at all attests to the high store set at the time on such short spontaneous philosophical and other oral exchanges, which were in stark contrast to the extensive learned written digressions characteristic of Han scholarship.

The above exchange must have taken place in 244 or 245, three or four years before Wang Bi wrote his *Commentary on the Laozi*, which he did in 248.[59] While from the sources quoted hitherto we cannot be sure that Wang Bi did not change his opinion on the matter later on, later sources unanimously refer to this statement as the most precise expression of Wang Bi's thinking about the person of Laozi in relation to Confucius. Given the actual influence of Wang Bi's position, a change in attitude would probably have been sensational enough to be reported. Still, the statement in its extreme terseness of the Sage's "embodying negativity" leaves out his entire and very complex relationship with other people, and his own emotions, dealt with in more detail in other sections of Wang's work.

Pei Hui's question again presupposes the comparability of Confucius and Laozi, that the differences between Confucius and Laozi were so small that their relative rank was hard to distinguish. This must have been a shared view among proponents of Xuanxue at the time; the question does not deal with comparability, but with the small differences between them.

Pei Hui's question, however, not only presupposes the comparability of Confucius and Laozi but also the compatibility of their philosophic views. Both are assumed to deal with the same philosophic subject matter, namely with "negativity" as "that which in fact forms the basis of the ten thousand kinds of entities," that is with the relationship of this "That-by-which" and the ten thousand kinds of entities. For Laozi, this would be relatively easy to establish because the Laozi deals with the issue. For Confucius the opposite is true. There is no statement attributed to him that explicitly takes up the notion of "negativity."

However, there had been an assumption prevalent since the beginning of the Later Han and documented in statements by Yang Xiong and Huan Tan that the term *yuan* 元 which is the very first word of the *Chunqiu*, as well as the term *taiji* 太極 in the *Xici* were merely other appelations for what the *Laozi* calls Dao[60] and that, accordingly, the classics edited by Confucius were dealing with the same issue as the *Laozi*. The Sage as well as Laozi, who is only minutely different from him, both deal with this single relevant philosophical problem. Wang Bi and Pei Hui share this basic assumption, and Wang Bi now establishes the differences within this commonality. This assumption has important consequences for Wang Bi's construction of the *Laozi* and of the *Zhouyi*, supposed to be the product of a succession of certified Sages with Confucius adding the last layers.

The reading of any text presupposes a general assumption about its nature, which establishes the context for the entire text. If, for example, a text is assumed to be a coded message, the reading strategy will be completely different from a text assumed to be a straight communication. If a text is assumed to contain the insights of the Sage, the reading strategy will be radically different from that applied to a text assumed to be written by the village idiot; the insights of the Sage are accepted as truths that only wait to be understood, while the babble of the idiot is read under the assumption that any truths in there result from random accident. The familiar role of the wise fool, however, undermines even the realiability of these general contexts.

The exchange between Pei Hui and Wang Bi helps us determine the two basic assumptions guiding Wang Bi's reading strategy. First, it shows the caliber of Confucius and Laozi as Sages or near-Sages; second, it shows that Sages and near-Sages essentially deal with a single issue, namely the relationship of *wu* 無 to the ten thousand kinds of entities. As this is the core issue of these texts, the commentaries to the *Laozi*, *Zhouyi*, and *Lunyu* have to read each individual section as a part of this overall endeavor. Wang Bi thus begins his *LZWZLL* not with a statement about *Laozi* or anyone else, but with a statement about the "That-by-which" in its relationship to the ten thousand kinds of entities, and about the impossibility of defining the "That-by-which" but the possibility of recognizing aspects of it as "shining forth" in the specific ten thousand kinds of entities.[61]

The expected caliber of the text is thus determined by the status of the author; the expected core issue of the texts is determined by the fact that, as Sages and near-Sages they deal with a single issue, the only true object of philosophy; and the homogeneity of the texts' individual parts is, therefore, to be constructed on the basis of these two assumptions.

The consequences of these three parameters guiding the construction of the text through the commentary are clear and straightforward for the *Laozi*. The question of Pei Hui, however, does not deal with *Laozi*; he has few problems reading this text. He is laboring over the problem that, although, as all agree, the Sage Confucius in fact deals with the same core issue, he never seems to mention it. As opposed to the *Laozi*, the textual surface of the Confucius texts, such as the *Zhouyi*, does not provide evident clues about his thinking on the core issue.

Wang Bi's answer to Pei Hui now holds the status of the author/editor against the actual textual surface. From the sageliness of the author/editor Confucius it is clear what must be and can only be the core issue of the Confucius texts, whatever the textual surface might say. The main new contribution his statement makes is thus to establish a reading strategy for the Confucius texts, namely that they have to be read as essentially dealing with the relationship of the "That-by-which" with the ten thousand kinds of entities even if the textual surface might suggest otherwise. It will be the duty of Wang Bi's commentaries to the *Lunyu* and the *Zhouyi* to bring out this well-hidden thought.

Wang Bi's answer deals with the problem that Confucius never seems to be talking about negativity or such things, but he does not question the legitimacy of Pei Hui's bringing up the point. Since Sima Tan's "Treatise on the Six Schools," it had become customary to group thinkers according to the schools to which they presumably belonged. Even the Imperial Library was organized in this manner, and so was, as a consequence, the book catalogue in the *Hanshu*. The proponents of Xuanxue, however, among whom Pei Hui ranked high, followed and developed a tradition outlined elsewhere in this study which attempted to overcome these petty school differences and return to serious philosophic inquiry. They rejected the philosophic validity of such terms as "Ru" and "Daojia." In their view, it is a misunderstanding that Confucius was the founder of a doctrine of human and social relations of some practical value for the ordering of society as claimed by Sima Tan, and it is equally a misunderstanding that *Laozi* was having a cheap shot at the core tenets of Confucius when he advocated "discontinuing ritual, and discarding study." At the same time, they did not share the assumptions about the divine nature of either Confucius or Laozi which developed during the Later Han.[62]

In fact, they assumed, both were philosophers who loathed the shallow and socially dangerous babble of vulgar scholars. As a consequence, Wang Bi read works traditionally associated with mutually incompatible traditions of the Ru and the Daoists like the *Zhouyi* and *Lunyu* on the one side and the *Laozi* and *Zhuangzi* on the other as being part of the same philosophical endeavor, so that he was entitled to supplement his *Commentary on the Laozi* with elements from the *Lunyu, Zhouyi*, and *Zhuangzi* and his *Commentary on the Zhouyi* with elements from the *Laozi* and *Zhuangzi*.[63] His mentor He Yan seems to have made the point quite explicitly in one of his essays. The *Wenzhang xulu* 文章敍錄 is quoted in Liu Xiaobiao's *Commentary to the Shishuo xinyu*:

> Since the tracts of the Ru held that Laozi rejected the Sage [Confucius] and [advocated] discontinuing the ritual and discarding study, [He] Yan claimed that [Laozi in fact] was in agreement with the Sage [Confucius]. The essay he published

[on this issue] circulates widely. 自儒者論以老子非聖人絕禮棄
學，晏説與聖人同，著論行於世也。[64]

The author of the *Laozi*, consequently, is not a Daoist as opposed
to advocates of the other schools, but a philosopher pursuing the
elusive "That by which the ten thousand kinds of entities come
about." In terms of reading strategy, there is no reason to see him
set against the Sage Confucius as his implied opponent. On the
contrary, both are in fundamental agreement, although their level
of understanding might vary. As to the *Laozi*, it has to be read as a
text in fundamental agreement with the purpose of Confucius' philosophizing (which does not mean in agreement with the tenets of
the Ru who claimed to continue Confucius' tradition).

Wang Bi's conversation with Pei Hui establishes a further important interpretive principle. As the Sage was fully aware that
"That which forms the basis of the ten thousand kinds of entities"
and which he "embodied" could not be talked about, he did not.
The absence of any statements about such arcane subjects as *wu* 無,
"negativity," in the writings presumably edited by the Sage and
his predecessors is thus not a sign of their lack of interest or understanding of the ultimate things; just the opposite, their silence on
the subject is the highest proof for their embodying its essence.

Confucius' nonwriting of a book becomes the ultimate proof of
his insight. The Sage's acta, gesta, and verba, as recorded for example in the *Lunyu* and the *Zhouyi* have to be read as dark messages
implying some unspeakable point, all their seeming triviality notwithstanding. They deal, by implication, with the very same issues
the *Laozi* is trying to tackle head-on. The life of the Sage, including
his nonwriting of a book, becomes a living performance of that which
he embodies, namely negativity as the basis of the ten thousand
kinds of entities.[65] By inversion, *Laozi*'s search for verbal forms of
communication about the very same negativity "which forms the
basis of the ten thousand kinds of entities" shows him to belong, in
Wang Bi's terms as quoted by He Shao, "to [the realm of] entities."
The pleasant fact that we have a book *Laozi* as opposed to the Sage's
non-book, is a sign and a proof of Laozi's inferiority to the Sage.
Since the reader also belongs to this realm, and as Laozi, all his
closeness to the Sage notwithstanding, still ranks at the very top of
the scale of ordinary scholars, the inferiority of Laozi to the Sage
also assures his accessibility to us.

Wang Bi, then, is writing a commentary on the very efforts of the Laozi decribed above as being his deficiency, but there is no word in either his commentary to the *Laozi* nor his *LZWZLL* indicating a critical or even hostile approach to the text. This position, however, was held by some in Wang Bi's time. Xun Can 荀粲 (ca. 212–40 CE) argued that, since words were not able fully to express meanings, all the writings attributed to the Sage were unreliable to the extent of being but "the dregs of the Sage," worthless chatter without much content. From this follows that they neither deserved to be studied nor commented upon.[66] It is not reported whether he made the same argument for the *Laozi*, but, given the accepted hierarchy between Kongzi and Laozi at the time, if it was true for the former, it was definitely true for the latter. Wang Bi did not share this radical position, but implicitly argued against it theoretically in his theory of language and practically in his commentaries. The argumentative stress from Xun Can's position is felt in both realms as Wang Bi accepts the existence of the problem and deals with it quite extensively, as documented elsewhere.[67]

From the comparison made in Wang Bi's discussion with Pei Hui it might further be argued that the *Laozi* is an unreliable text due to *Laozi*'s relative lack of insight. This is not Wang Bi's argument. The Sage and *Laozi* are obviously so close to each other that the difference between them can be discovered only at a point not evident to the beholder. This minimal difference is in their treatment of language, not in their level of understanding negativity. In fact, Confucius does not talk about negativity, and the *Laozi* does talk about it. As we shall see, however, Wang Bi sees Laozi as fully aware of the inability of language to deal with that which is not specific, and of the ensuing unreliability of language as an instrument of philosophy. The *Laozi* contains truth enough, and this is enough obscured by misunderstanding to both deserve and need a commentary.

Following the *Laozi*'s own indications, a reading strategy has to be developed that remains fully aware of the infirmity, unreliability, and tentativeness of language's dealings with negativity, but which at the same time makes the best of this limited potential of communication. The *Zhouyi*, in contrast, uses a much more elaborate structure of multi-tiered communication in order to establish a structure which, while "embodying" negativity, is never forced into unreliable statements about it. As far as reading the *Laozi* is concerned, we are prompted to assume that the text does have a reliable understanding of that by which the ten thousand entities are, but that the language it uses to talk about it is tentative and unreliable, and consciously so.

One difference, however, remains between the two texts. The *Zhouyi* is seen by Wang Bi and his contemporaries as a book set up by Confucius and his Sage predecessors who "embodied negativity" in order to overcome these iniquities of language. It is a performance by these Sages that manages to talk the philosophy of Being without ever mentioning it. This arcane and esoteric structure makes it much harder for ordinary scholars to penetrate its depths. The *Laozi* is an accessible but terminologically unreliable book, not by a complete Sage but by a slightly inferior "second-degree Sage" about that by which the ten thousand kinds of entities are, and about him who embodies it, the Sage.

This assessment of *Laozi* was shared by other proponents of Xuanxue such as Ruan Ji and He Yan. Lu Xisheng 陸希聲, who himself ranked Laozi highest, writes in a critical note about Wang Bi that Ruan Ji had followed Wang's assessment:

> Wang Bi was of the opinion that the Sage [Confucius] is united in substance with the Dao 王弼以謂聖人與道合體, but that Mr. Lao was incapable of embodying the Dao 老氏未能體道. This is why, when Ruan Ji described him [*Laozi*] as a superior worthy and second-degree Sage, he was in agreement with [Wang] Fusi [Bi] 故阮籍謂之上賢亞聖之人，蓋同於輔嗣.[68]

The Buddhist master Shi Daoan (312–85) claims that "He Yan and Wang Bi both said that Lao[zi] does not attain [the level] of the Sage [Confucius]" 老未及聖, which was repeated by the southern author Zhou Yong (fifth century CE).[69] Wang Baoxuan has assembled good evidence that Zhuangzi was rated like Laozi among Xuanxue proponents including He Yan and Guo Xiang.[70]

This assessment of Laozi and Confucius has remained the trademark of the students of Xuanxue during the following centuries, setting them off against both the Daoists and the Ru 儒, who each claimed exclusive superiority for their respective founder.[71]

Wang Bi's assessment of *Laozi* thus rejects three options available in his time as well as the interpretation strategies based on them. His *Laozi* book is neither revealed by the highest deity, nor written by the Sage's teacher, nor concocted by a mediocre thinker. And it is not Daoist as opposed to the Ruist teachings of Confucius. Wang Bi joins the tradition of those who see the *Laozi* as the work of a philosopher who, like the Sage, is engaged in philosophy and not in setting up some "school," the work of a man, however, who, while having achieved the highest level to which a common mortal might aspire,[72] remains inferior to the Sage himself. This inferiority makes for his willingness to use a necessarily unreliable and tentative medium, definitory language, in his inquiry, a medium which at the same time makes discursive philosophy possible and leads into the deserts of schoolish doxography.

A last question has to be asked. If, indeed, the relative status of Laozi and Confucius was as important as we have claimed, why is there no extensive statement about either Laozi or the Sage in the *LZWZLL*? The answer might be in the transmission of this text. As shown elsewhere, the *LZWZLL* consists of a series of selections from an orginally larger text.[73] Two such selections exist, one shorter than the other and entirely contained therein. Both selections have been transmitted without an author's name in the Daoist canon, one as an independent text, the other as part of the Song dynasty compendium *Yunji qijian* 雲笈七籤.[74] It seems highly unlikely that the Daoist canon, although it carried works such as the *Mozi* and the *Hanfeizi*, would transmit statements from an author that fundamentally deviate from one of the Daoist core beliefs, namely the superiority of *Laozi* to all other beings. As we shall see, in Wang Bi's polemics against the various "schools," no one is exempted from criticism save the Daojia 道家, although there is nothing in Wang Bi's personal or scholarly record suggesting that he might have considered himself a supporter of the Daojia. This absence of criticism of the Daojia, therefore, again might suggest editorial interference. As a further piece of evidence, it might be pointed out that, regardless of the enormous importance of the Sage in the *Laozi*, the surviving selections of the *LZWZLL* hardly refer to him, and, if they do, then only in the most general terms. It is probable, though, that more statements on the Sage were contained in the *LZWZLL*. If, however, the Sage was referred to in the *LZWZLL* in a manner otherwise reserved for Laozi, it would be understandable that the Daozang selections would have left out such passages. I have to admit, however, that there is no hard evidence for either point.

We now extrapolate some first parameters guiding Wang Bi's reading of the *Laozi*, determining his methodology, and giving his criteria for legitimate and illegitimate interpretive steps.

- The *Laozi* is a text written by Laozi. From this follows that it is sound to assume that the text strives for philosophic homogeneity. A commentary has to read the individual sections as parts of a homogeneous whole.

- The *Laozi* explores the only real philosophic problem, the features of That-by-which the ten thousand kinds of entities are in its relationship to the ten thousand kinds of entities. This assumption determines the general context of the entire *Laozi*.

- As this That-by-which must necessarily be unspecific in order to be the basis of all that is specific, it eludes definition, definition being tied to specificity.

- At the same time, the That-by-which is present in the ten thousand kinds of entities as that by which they are. This relationship is replicated in certain structures prevailing between entities which makes it possible to use as pointers and signs the linguistic material describing them.

- Laozi operates with a conscious understanding of this linguistic structure. His text therefore does not contain definite and reliable terms, *ming* 名, but only makeshift heuristic devices.

- The strategy of reading the individual sections of the *Laozi* has to be determined on the basis of a correct understanding of the basic purport of this text, as well as of the consequences it has for the language used. The failure in the first respect leads to a failure in the second, and consequently to a complete failure to understand this text.

- The reader intent on understanding the *Laozi*'s philosophic inquiry, therefore, is not to focus on those aspects of the *Laozi*'s necessarily unreliable, makeshift, and particular statements that are unrelated to their purpose of pointing away from themselves at the That-by-which, but he is to focus on their common but abstruse center.

The Status of the *Laozi* and the Texts Ascribed to Confucius

If the above assessment of the relationship between the Sage and Laozi carries weight, it would have to be evident in Wang Bi's handling of their respective texts. Statements attributed to Confucius could be expected to figure as statements of higher authority than those of Laozi himself. The bulk of implicit but identifiable quotations from and clear allusions to other texts in the *Commentary on the Laozi*, namely 11 out of 21 referring to a total of 6 different texts, comes from the *Zhouyi*. Within the *Zhouyi*, 8 out of these 11 quotations come from the philosophical parts of the *Zhouyi*, namely the *Xici* 繫辭, and two from the *wenyan* 文言. Both these texts are ascribed to the "Master," who was commonly identified in Wang Bi's time as Confucius.[75] This is in accordance with the emphasis on statements by Confucius in Wang Bi's quotations from the *Lunyu* and the *Xiaojing*. One single quotation comes from the *tuan* 彖 and the *xiang* 象 for the hexagram *fu* 復, which in Wang Bi's *Commentary to the Zhouyi* is interpreted as the centerpiece of his political philosophy. The *tuan* and *xiang* were again assumed to have been inserted by Confucius himself. These texts are quoted as self-evident truths in line with the *Laozi*'s project. *Laozi* 5 begins, according to Wang Bi: "Heaven and Earth are not kindly. For them, the ten thousand entities are like straw and dogs. The Sage is not kindly. For him, the Hundred Families are like straw and dogs." On this second statement, Wang Bi comments:

> The Sage, "harmonizing [as the *Zhouyi* says of the "Great Man"] his capacity/receipt 德 with [that of] Heaven and Earth" likens the Hundred Families to straw and dogs.

The statement "harmonizes his capacity with that of Heaven and Earth" is made about the Great Man, *daren* 大人, in the *wenyan* section of hexagram 1 of the *Zhouyi*. Wang Bi follows the *wenyan* itself, which identifies this great man with the Sage. The *Laozi* does not explain why the Sage would do the same as Heaven and Earth. Wang Bi again replaces an explanation with the insertion of the quotation. The statements by Confucius in the *Zhouyi* thus come in not only as an authoritative source of unquestionable truth for Wang Bi's *Commentary* and its implied reader, but also for the *Laozi* itself. In Wang Bi's reading, the statement of the *Laozi* makes sense only on the basis of the *wenyan* statement. We shall thus have to check the hypothesis that the relationship between Confucius as the Sage and Laozi as a second-degree Sage is reflected in the relationship between the statements believed to be those of the Sage and the *Laozi* in the sense that the former are the basis of the latter.

Laozi 47 makes the famous statement that

[Only when] not going out of doors [into All Under Heaven one has something] by means of which to recognize All Under Heaven;

[only when] not peeping out of the window [to Heavenly phenomena one has some thing] by means of which to recognize the Way of Heaven;

Wang Bi's commentary runs:

As processes have a principle and as things have a master,
    [as Confucius says in the *Xici*: "What is (everyone)
    in All Under Heaven thinking about and
    cogitating about?! In All Under Heaven"]
although the "roads [of thinking]" are "manifold," "what they lead to" is the "same [end]";

although the "thoughts" are "hundredfold," "what they are directed to" is "one."[76]

The two phrases beginning with "although" nearly verbatim repeat a statement by the "Master" from the *Xici*. Again this statement is not argued out, but rather cited as an authority. The *Laozi*'s statement is only true and meaningful on the basis of the truth of Confucius' statement that there is only one single philosophic issue to which all thoughts therefore have to converge. As a consequence it does not matter which "process" or "material thing" one ponders as one will by necessity end up at their "principle" or "master."

In his commentary to *Laozi* 49.4 and 49.5, where the Sage establishes social order by being himself unspecifiable and diffuse so that "the Hundred Families all make the best of their eyes and ears [while I, the] Sage make all of them into infants," Wang Bi comes in with a lengthy quotation from the *Xici*. There it is said that Heaven and Earth establish the positions of the entities, and that the Sage then completes their capabilities with the effect that each gets his proper place. Again the *Laozi* statement seems to be made on the basis of the *Xici* statement, in the light of which it indeed becomes meaningful. The *Xici* quotation in Wang Bi on *Laozi* 70.4 again implies that the *Laozi* statement only makes sense on the basis of a *Xici* definition.

Wang's commentary on *Laozi* 73.8, where the Sage is said to "be at ease but still good at taking precautions," cites two phrases from the *Xici* and one from another section of the *Laozi*. These together obviously form the implicit bases of the *Laozi*'s present argument, because the commentary concludes, after quoting this evidence, "that is why [the *Laozi* text] says 'be at ease but still good at taking precautions.'"

In one case, Wang Bi goes a step further by introducing them with a "that is why it is said," *gu yue* 故曰, without mentioning the place where this might be stated. Normally he uses this formula at the end of a commentary; having explained the underlying argument, he then concludes "that is why [the *Laozi*] says. . . ." In this case, however, the text following *gu yue* is not from the *Laozi* but from the *Zhouyi*.[77] In a further case, he sees the *Laozi* itself as directly referring to the *Xici*.[78]

On the basis of these quotations, we conclude

- In Wang Bi's view, the *Laozi* and the *Zhouyi*, especially the philosophic parts ascribed to Confucius, are philosophically fully compatible.

- In this view, many of the philosophic statements of the *Laozi* rest on premises established by the Sage in the *Zhouyi* and are only understandable against this background.

- The *Zhouyi* or the parts referred to can thus claim a certain philosophic superiority over the *Laozi*, which reflects the small, but significant difference between the Sage Confucius and Laozi.

The Implied Reader and His Education

Having defined the author, the theme, and the language to treat it, we now proceed to study that imaginary being who is the victim of an author's whim, the addressee of his diatribes and the receptacle of his insights, the implied reader. He is no white sheet of paper onto which anything might be written. He is a specific historic being with memory, knowledge, intellectual habits and prejudices, and a potentially critical and even hostile attitude toward the author, quite apart from his inalienable and therefore unassailable rights to misunderstand, to select, to disapprove, and to get bored. The implied reader is a possible relation of the real reader contemporary with Wang Bi. While being a fiction of Wang Bi's, he still might be considered a fictionalized abstraction of actual contemporary readers, and we are therefore entitled to treat the information about actual readers from historical sources and that about the implied reader from Wang Bi's text as being, to a certain degree, supplements to each other.

Neither of the two readers makes an appearance in Wang Bi's *Commentary* (or the *Laozi* itself). But from certain proceedings of the *Commentary* and the *LZWZLL*, as well as from certain signs of stress within these texts, some of the features of this implied reader can be reconstructed, which in turn will help in outlining the intentions of Wang Bi's endeavor, since evidently he is trying to tell something to his historically specific implied reader.

Before considering the level of knowledge of the *Laozi* Wang Bi imputed to his implied reader, I shall map out this fictional being's basic education. Wang Bi's *Commentary to the Laozi* contains unidentified verbatim quotations from the *Zhouyi*, the *Lunyu*, the *Zuozhuan*, the *Xiaojing*, the *Zhuangzi*, and the *Huainanzi*. There might be more from other texts that have not been identified. These quotations differ in character because of different reader expectations. For the implied reader it might be less shocking to see that the *Laozi* agrees on certain issues with the *Zhuangzi* or *Huainanzi* than the assumption that the "Confucian classics" share the *Laozi*'s political philosophy.

As we have seen, the context in which the quotations are used tells something about the status of the respective texts in a textual hierarchy. If a quotation is cited as an authority on which an argument rests, its status is obviously higher than if some formula or comparison is used which also occurs elsewhere, but which is understandable without having to call up the original context as well as the status of the text in which it occurs.

Some quotations in the *Commentary*, such as those from the *Huainanzi* and the *Zhuangzi*, are fully understandable without any knowledge that a phrase or a statement from the respective text is used. In his commentary on *Laozi* 49.5, Wang Bi says:

> It is a fact [as the *Huainanzi* 14.138.9 says] that,
> "if [I] were to

rely on [my] knowledge, the others would litigate against [me]."	rely on [my] physical strength, the others would fight against [me]."

The *Huainanzi* language is fully integrated into Wang Bi's argument. The proof for the statement's truth comes from the logic of the argument, not from the authority of the *Huainanzi* called up from the treasure house of memory. In his commentary on *Laozi* 20.1, Wang Bi takes up a statement from *Zhuangzi* 8, which again has its logic and thus authority without the reader being in need of any knowledge of the source. The same is true for the verbatim use of a figure of speech in his commentary on *Laozi* 49.5. The quotability of these texts in the *Laozi Commentary* is based on the assumption that they share the *Laozi*'s basic orientation.

Wang Bi's implicit reference to the *Zuozhuan* 左傳 in his commentary on *Laozi* 24.2 has a different character. Wang Bi writes:

> Analyzed with regard to the Way, [the attitudes] are like

	the actions of Xi Zhi,
a leftover of rich food. Although the [food] basically is delicious, [the leftovers] may rot.	Although [Xi Zhi] basically had merits, he bragged about them himself and that was excessive and "superfluous" [and brought about his death].

First, this reference to Xi Zhi presupposes, in order to be understood, a full knowledge of the story Wang Bi alludes to. The reader has to know the *Zuozhuan* [and with it the *Chunqiu*] more or less by heart. Second, in the *Zuozhuan* story alluded to, the *Shangshu* is quoted with "How could one [deal with] resentment only when it is [already] apparent! Before it is visible it has to be dealt with." The contents of the story and of this maxim fit that of the *Laozi* text the commentary to which quotes them. The *Shangshu* and the *Zuozhuan*, accordingly, are used as part of a authoritative body of texts seen as sharing the same philosophy and as mutually illustrating each other. The allusion to the *Shangshu* quotation illustrates and proves that the *Laozi* and the "Confucian classics" are but explorations of the same philosophic issues. The second implicit reference to the *Zuozhuan* in Wang Bi on *Laozi* 32.3 deals with the counterproductive effects of using social regulations to control society.[79] This reference again presupposes a common philosophy underlying the *Laozi* and the *Zuozhuan*, which makes a similar point.

The unannounced quotation from the *Xiaojing* 孝經 in Wang Bi on *Laozi* 25.9 presupposes a knowledge that it is the Sage, Confucius himself, who makes the statement, "Among the natures [bequeathed to the ten thousand entities] by Heaven and Earth, the human being is the most exalted." The implied reader has to know the *Xiaojing* by heart. The statement receives its authority from its author, not from its logic. Technically it is used to explain why the highest of human beings, the king, could be mentioned in the *Laozi* among the four Great Ones together with Dao, Heaven, and Earth. The quotation proceeds again on the basis that a text like the *Xiaojing* and the *Laozi* share a common philosophy.

Wang Bi on *Laozi* 49.5 explains a statement in the *Laozi* that the Sage is "All Under Heaven's diffuse heart" by implicitly referring to a *Lunyu* statement by Confucius about the gentleman, *junzi*, being "in his relationship with All Under Heaven without preferences, and without disdain."[80] The commentary makes sense only if the reader identifies the allusion from the two terms "preference" and "disdain." The implied reader knows the *Lunyu* by heart. Again it is understood that Confucius and the *Laozi* share the same philosophy. The identification of the Sage and the *junzi* through this commentary is not further justified, but presupposed. Curiously, it rests on the fact that the two terms are interchangeably used in a third text, namely the *Wenyan* Commentary to the first hexagram of the *Zhouyi*.[81]

As has been said, the bulk of the identifiable quotations comes from the *Zhouyi*, cited as a source of authoritative truth in Wang Bi's *Commentary*. The identification of the quotations and their context is essential for the understanding of Wang Bi's interpretation. The implied reader knows the *Zhouyi* by heart and considers it the philosophically authoritative statement by the Sage.

From the biographies of contemporaries we know that the *Laozi* and the *Zhouyi* together were the basis of philosophical education during the 230s and 240s in Wei.[82] The *Zhuangzi* is not mentioned in this context, probably because of its very limited availability. To my knowledge, the only quotations from the *Zhuangzi* down to the end of the *zhengshi* era (249) are to be found in Wang Bi and He Yan.[83]

To conclude, Wang Bi's implied reader knows the *Zhouyi*, the *Lunyu*, the *Xiaojing*, and the *Zuozhuan* by heart, but is not required to have an encyclopedic knowledge. In contrast, the implied reader in Ge Hong's 葛洪 *Baopuzi* 抱樸子, a text written two generations after Wang Bi in the south by a scholar trained in the tradition of Han scholarship, is endowed with a complete recall of nearly the entire body of surviving pre-Han and Han literature if he is to have any hope of making sense of the "External chapters" 外篇 of the *Baopuzi*. Wang Bi's reader is pursuing philosophy; Wang challenges the reader's ability to think, not his education. Wang Bi's implied reader is the precocious genius and philosopher who pursues an understanding of the basis of the ten thousand entities and of social order by perusing the writings of the Sage and his close second, Laozi. He is not a polymath interested in acquiring a broad knowledge of the tenets of the various philosophical schools.

We now turn from the *Commentary*'s references to other more or less canonical texts to its cross-references to other sections of the *Laozi* itself, which occur in nearly each of the *zhang*. Wang Bi's commentaries to the individual phrases of the *Laozi* frequently use expressions and entire phrases from the *Laozi* that occur only much further down in the text and would thus technically be unrecognizable to a first reader. In his commentaries to *zhang* 10 alone, an extreme case, there are six such unmarked quotations from later

zhang.[84] Typically these would go as follows (the translation of the *Laozi* passage extrapolated from the commentary):
Laozi 10.1:

[For a ruler] to keep to the camp, to hold on to the[ir] One, and be able not to be separated from it—ah!

Commentary
"To keep to" is like "to stay in." "Camp" is the abode of eternal sojourn of human beings.
The "One" is the true [nature] of [the other] human beings.
    [The sentence] means: If a human being would be able to stay in [his] abode of eternal sojourn, "hold on to the One," and purify [his] spirit [so that] he would be able to be permanently "not separated" from [the abode and the One]—ah, then [indeed] "the ten thousand kinds of entities [would] submit [to him] on their own accord as guests" [as the *Laozi* 32.1 says] 則萬物自賓也.

    In the commentary, the entire statement following the "ah" is a verbatim unmarked quotation from *Laozi* 32.1. The text there runs:

The Eternal of the Way is namelessness. Even though the Unadorned may be small, no one in All Under Heaven is able to put [it] to service. If only the dukes and kings were able to keep to it [the Unadorned], the ten thousand kinds of entities would submit [to them] of their own accord as guests. 候王若能守之，萬物將自賓.

    Wang Bi's interpretation of the empty space opened by the exclamation "ah!" would appear utterly frivolous if the reader did not recognize that it is taken verbatim from another *zhang* of the *Laozi*, and that the sentence preceding it there is very similar in content to the sentences preceding the "ah!" here.
    Laozi 10.1 does not indicate who the subject of the sentence is. The commentary inserts a "human being," *ren* 人. The sentence, however, cannot hold true for any human being, but only for those who are in a position in which potentially the ten thousand

entities might gather as their guests. This sentence traditionally occurs in political arguments where a ruler is advised to honor the worthy with the consequence that All Under Heaven will render him their allegiance and gather around his court. The actual subject of *Laozi* 10.1 is, in fact, silently imported by Wang Bi from the first half of the phrase quoted verbatim from *zhang* 32.1, where it is the "dukes and kings" around whom the ten thousand entities will gather. I have inserted this into the translation of *Laozi* 10.1 by putting the subject "ruler" in brackets. This operation is confirmed as being legitimate by Wang Bi's quotation in the commentary to *Laozi* 10.6 from *Laozi* 37.1–3. There, the quotation includes "dukes and kings."

How is the reader to grasp "ah!" as meaning that it would be wonderful if the "dukes and kings" were able to "keep to the camp and hold on to the One," but that all too few of them manage to do it? In order to understand the critical and desperate undertone of this phrase, he has to keep another phrase from a later *zhang* in mind, namely *Laozi* 22.6, where it is said that "the Sage holds on to the One." For him this is his natural way of acting, while for the dukes and kings this is only a rare achievement, to be discussed with a hypothetical "if" or even "if only" indicating the uniqueness or even unreality of this option.

For a simple understanding of Wang Bi's construction of our example, *Laozi* 10.1, the reader has to be able to recognize unmarked quotations and the unstated context of these quotations, and to take other *Laozi* statements about the same issues into consideration. Without this level of textual command over the *Laozi*, he will not be able to follow Wang Bi's argument, whose credibility relies heavily on the fact that it uses the *Laozi* itself for explaining the *Laozi* and thus manages to achieve a homogeneous reading of the entire text.

A second example, *Laozi* 33.4 runs:

> 強行者有志也.
> He who powerfully practices, will have his will.

Wang Bi's commentary runs:

> 勤能行者，其志必獲．故曰強行者有志.
> "If he practices to the best of his capacities, he will by necessity have his will satisfied." That is why [the

Laozi] says: "He who powerfully practices, will have his will."

In order to identify the object of this practice, the reader will have to recognize that the formula 勤能行 in the commentary that explains the 強行 of the text is a quotation from *Laozi* 41.1 (further down than *zhang* 33), where the text runs:

上士聞道，勤能行之.
If a topmost scholar hears about the Way, he will practice it to the best of his capacities.

Through this indirect reference to *Laozi* 41.1 the commentary will supply him with three crucial pieces of information for *Laozi* 33.4. It will tell him that the meaning of 強 is not "violent," but "to the best of one's capacities," *qin neng* 勤能; it will tell him who is doing the 強行, namely the "topmost scholar," *shang shi* 上士, who seems to be identified with the Sage in that *zhang*; and it will tell him what this topmost scholar is practicing so eagerly, namely the Way. In this construction, *Laozi* 33.4 thus means:

He who powerfully practices [the Way, that is, a topmost scholar or Sage,] will have his will.

The reader will be required to remember *Laozi* 33.4 in reading 41.1. In 41.1 it is not clear what the result of the topmost scholar's practicing the Way might be. Wang Bi supplements this result there by way of a simple unmarked quotation from *Laozi* 33.4, namely 有志, "he will have his will." In some cases the quotations are made explicit, as in the commentary on *Laozi* 20.1, where Wang Bi begins "In the second *pian* 篇 of the *Laozi* it says," which is followed by a verbatim quotation.[85]

The implied reader knows the *Laozi* by heart. Wang Bi's *Commentary* thus does not assume he is reading the text for the first time and is eager for guidance. In a sense there cannot be a first reading of the *Laozi* for a third-century intellectual. The thoughts and many of the terms and expressions of the text had already become part of the background noise of the culture, even for those who might never have set eyes on the *Laozi*; some of them might have become part of proverbial lore as it the case with many modern "fixed sayings," *chengyu*, in the first place. As an authoritative, quotable text, the *Laozi* had been used at least since the third century BCE. There is a pyramid of textual constructions from the understandings and misunderstandings of the individual reader to certain readings commonly accepted in certain circles; to the constructions implied in quoting the *Laozi* in an argument, constructions that again presuppose a common understanding of the passage in question; to the oral explanation of the entire text by a teacher; to the written commentary; and finally to the analytical essay about the "basic meaning of the *Laozi*." All of these forms were present simultaneously in the third century CE. By understanding that the commentary is but the tip of the pyramid of the manifold genres that might construct this text, our eyes are also alerted to other sources for reconstructing the understanding of this text at a given time in a given philosophical, political, and social context. The political speeches and memorials in the dynastic histories, the well-developed genre of the essay, and even the commentaries to poems or historical works that might quote a passage from the *Laozi* are all potential but largely unused sources for a history of the construction of the *Laozi*. The young men in Wei had thus much more than commentaries of the *Laozi* to go by for learning about this text.

The biographies of young men of good families who grew up since the 190s, like He Yan, Zhong Hui, or Wang Bi himself, regularly mention a very early reading of the *Laozi*, often before they were ten. Often they would be able to outshine their older peers with their understanding of the text.[86] The reading would include the memorizing of all or substantial parts of the text. In the famous discussions about the *Laozi* between He Yan and Wang Bi, the two are not said to have held manuscripts in their hands, and the other guests, who relished young Wang Bi's triumph, most definitely had no texts at hand. Wang Bi and He Yan were discussing the meaning of certain passages of the *Laozi*; the discussion would not have made sense to anyone who did not know the entire text by heart, because otherwise he could not have checked on how far the two combatants were in accordance with the terminology and tenets of the text as a whole when they discussed one passage.[87] This evidence suggests that the implied reader is a relation to Wang Bi's real readers in terms of his utter familiarity with the *Laozi*.

The simultaneous presence of the entire *Laozi* in the minds of the reader has consequences for the perception of the time structure of the *Laozi*. Reading being an activity on the time axis, a hitherto unknown text unfolds successively in terms of time, space, and argument. In many literary and philosophic works, this time structure of the reading process is used by the author to gradually build up an argument, to tell a story with all the elements of suspense, and to play with the reader's anticipation of what is to come. Wang Bi's assumption that the implied reader knows the text by heart eliminates this part of the time structure and suggests a simultaneous presence of the entire text at any moment of part of it being read. We shall come back to this point.[88]

The Countertexts

Every text, an axiom first articulated by the Russian structuralist Victor Shklovskij goes, is written against the background of one or several others. These I will call countertexts. The young men of the third century had studied the text, we may presume, under the guidance of a teacher or their parents. Zhong Hui's mother personally instructed him, and probably used for the *Laozi* and the *Zhouyi* the commentaries written by his father, Zhong Yu 鍾繇.[89] The question is, did the young men know just the *Laozi* text or the text with one or several commentaries attached to it? Is Wang Bi talking back to an implied reader who already has a text in mind constructed by a previous commentator, or who even has a variety of such constructs stored in his memory? Is Wang Bi talking back to countertexts stored in the minds of his implied and real reader?

Laozi text manuscripts at the time could be without a commentary. The Suo Dan 索紞 manuscript fragment of the *Laozi* dated 270 CE is one such, although its grand title *Classic on Dao and De of the Grand Supreme Dark Recondite, Taishang xuanyuan daode jing* 太上玄元道德經, indicates that it was read in a particular tradition that Jao Tsung-i has identified as that of Zhang Daoling's Heavenly Master lineage.[90] Such a blank text, however, might at the time already have been an exception living on in provincial Wu, from which the manuscript takes the era name for its date, or in faraway Dunhuang, where Suo Dan made his living as an oneiromancer. According to Kong Yingda 孔穎達 (574–648), writing many centuries later, the Han-dynasty commentaries were typically appended to the main text as a separate unit. Ma Rong 馬融 (79–166) is credited by Kong Yingda with having been the first to insert his own commentary directly into the text.[91] The great change, however, seems to have come with the rearrangement of the *Zhouyi* by Wang Bi and, a few decades later, the *Chunqiu* and *Zuozhuan* by Du Yu. Wang Bi read the *Zhouyi* as a self-commenting text; he cut apart the commentaries contained in some of the "wings" and inserted them into the main text.[92] Du Yu 杜預 (222–84) constructed the *Zuozhuan* as a commentary to the *Chunqiu*, and interlaced the matching sections from the two texts.[93] This rearrangement seems to have been part of an overall rearrangement of the text/commentary relationship at the time with the commentary becoming an ever more integral part of the text's structure.[94] In fact, some of the most important commentary techniques applied by Wang Bi to the *Laozi* are based on self-interpreting techniques contained in the *Laozi* itself. We will return to this point.

So far as I know, we have no manuscript evidence of the general arrangement of text and commentary in Wang Bi's time. There is, however, some indirect information. When Fu Yi 傅奕 (554–639) wrote the history of the "old" *Laozi* manuscripts that had come to his attention, he proceeded chronologically. As the oldest MS he mentions a "manuscript of Xiang Yu's 項羽 concubine." This manuscript from the late third century BCE is named after its owner. The next manuscript is the "Wang An qiu zhi MS" 望安丘之本. Wang An qiu zhi might be identical with Wuqiu Wang (zhi) 毋丘望 (之), a first-century BCE commentator of the *Laozi*.[95] If so, this would be the first *Laozi* text in his list identified by the Commentary with which is was transmitted. All further MSS in the list, the Heshang zhangren 河上丈人, Wang Bi, and Heshang gong 河上公 texts, are identified by their commentator.[96] Fu Yi is only dealing with "old" manuscripts. This means that there were hardly any "old" texts around at his time that did not come with a commentary. This indirect evidence suggests that both the implied and the real reader of Wang Bi's *Commentary* at the time had not only read and memorized the *Laozi*, but knew the *Laozi* as constructed by one or several commentators.

The implied as well as the real reader might not have felt a great need for a *Laozi* commentary by a fairly pompous twenty-two-year-old from a highly placed family, given the availability of probably dozens of such commentaries by famous intellectuals in the local copy shop—if indeed this was the way commentaries were made available to a wider public at the time. They might have heard of Wang Bi's famous discussion with He Yan, but competition was strong, and we have to assume that the implied reader approached the text with a mixture of interest and scepticism, willing to ridicule it at the first signs of inadequacy.

In the process of reading Wang Bi's analysis, the historic readers would thus be required to temporarily sever the linkage between the *Laozi* text and the commentary or commentaries that they had read and hypothetically enter Wang Bi's construction of the text; they would then have to compare his construction with the others and decide which seemed most convincing, a decision that would involve the establishment of criteria for the quality of a commentary. And, finally, they would have to deconstruct the text as constructed by those other commentators (or by Wang Bi) in an effort to understand precisely where, in terms of basic method and particular phrase, the others or Wang Bi had gone wrong.

In this comparison, Wang Bi's *Commentary* and the *LZWZLL* cannot be disinterested bystanders. We have to assume that they provided help in the deconstruction of their competitors in order to tear the reader away from his habitual reading strategy which, in Wang Bi's eyes, would eternally block him from understanding the "purport [or thrust] of the *Laozi*'s pointers." Even if the dearth of historical sources available to us should not permit us to read the Wang Bi *Commentary* throughout as an implied dialogue with other constructions of the *Laozi*, and even if our lack of analytical sophistication should lead us overlook many signs of stress in Wang Bi's *Commentary* stemming from this contention, we can confidently state that this dialogue takes place, though the partners have vanished, and that these signs are there, though our eyes might fail to spot them. After this caveat, we may proceed to identify as many of such dialogical and contentious structures as we are able to find.

Of the numerous *Laozi* commentaries available at Wang Bi's time, and thus potentially in his readers' minds, precariously little has survived, and this has hardly been studied. Some studies have been done on the Heshang gong and the Xiang Er commentaries.[97] However, in view of the intellectual environment in which Wang Bi moved and the specific textual evidence, they seem to be his least likely candidates for either argument or dialogue, quite apart from the question of the date of the Heshang gong *Commentary*.[98]

Apart from self-commentaries contained for example in *Laozi* 13.1 with the phrase "what does. . . . mean," the oldest surviving explanations of sections of the *Laozi* are in the *Wenzi* 文子, which a Former Han dynasty manuscript find has by and large confirmed as an authentic early and probably pre-Han text,[99] and, more importantly in the *Hanfeizi*, whose author died in 233 BCE. Little is known about the role of the *Wenzi* during the Han dynasty beyond its close parallels in the *Huainanzi*. Given the strong "legalist" leanings of the Wei Court, the statement in the *Wei shu* 魏書 "The scholars of today take Shang [Yang] and Han[feizi] as their master and emulate legalist devices"[100] is credible. The *Hanfeizi* was thus read extensively in Wei and was part of the repertoire in the implied reader's mind. This is all the more probable since Wang Bi's *LZWZLL*, as well as his *Commentary*, take issue with legalist textual and political strategies.[101]

The bibliographic section of the *Han shu* lists four works explaining the *Laozi*. The first three, called *[Explanation of the] Classic Laozi Handed Down by Mr. Lin*, *Explanation of the Classic Laozi by Mr. Fu*, and *Explanation of the Classic Laozi by Mr. Xu*, were probably explanations of the entire text appended at the end or copied separately. The fourth, Liu Xiang's *Explanation of the Laozi* 劉向說老子, might have contained his reordering of the *Laozi* as well as some commentary.[102] Nothing is known about the contents and no quotations survive. Given the importance of the *Laozi* during the first decades of the Han, it is possible that these explanations were in tune with the strongly Legalist reading of the text at the time which is also evident in the textual stresses and the textual environment of the Mawangdui MSS.

Zhuang Zun, the first century BCE teacher of Yang Xiong (53 BCE–18 CE), is the next clearly dated author of specialized writings on the *Laozi* of which parts remain. He wrote a *Commentary to the Laozi*, *Laozi zhu* 老子註 in 2 *juan*, mentioned in the *Sui shu* catalogue and the *Jingdian shiwen* 經典釋文 but not afterwards; Shima Kuniō has therefore argued that it was lost by the time of the Tang dynasty.[103] Zhuang Zun also wrote an extensive *Purport of the Laozi*, *Laozi zhigui* 老子指歸," which the *Sui shu* catalogue lists with 11 *juan*, and later catalogues with 13 and 14 *juan* respectively. A long fragment of *juan* 7ff. of a work by this name is preserved in the Daozang covering the latter half of the *Laozi*, and Meng Wentong has compiled a record of the surviving quotations from the first half from various commentary collections of the Tang and Song.[104] Shima Kuniō has saved the material from charges of being a Song-dynasty fake by pointing to the closeness of many of its textual readings to other early quotations from the *Laozi*.[105] This argument has been strengthened by the close relationship of the Zhuang Zun text with the Mawangdui MSS. The relationship between Yang Xiong and Yan Zun provides a further link to Wang Bi, as Wang Bi took up the tradition of the late-Han Jingzhou 荊州 Academy under Liu Biao 劉表, where Yang Xiong was much in vogue.[106] At least one patron of Wang Bi's text in the Song, Chao Yuezhi 晁説之, claimed that Wang Bi's *Commentary* was philosophically built on the premises developed by Zhuang Zun that "humaneness, righteousness, and ritual behavior cannot be used on their own but [. . .] one has to make use of them by relying on the Way," and that "Heaven, Earth, and the ten thousand things are all grasped in the One," and thus was "in the tradition of Yan (Zhuang) Junping [= Zun]."[107]

I have not seen quotations surviving from the *Laozi* commentary by Anqiu Wangzhi 安丘望之, or Wang'an Qiuzhi 望安丘之, or Wuqiu Wang zhi 毋丘望之 probably from the first century BCE.[108] A manuscript of this text and commentary was among the materials studied by Fu Yi for his *Daodejing guben* 道德經古本. During the latter part of the Eastern Han period, when scholars of the Old Text school began to break through the tradition of specializing in only one classic and wrote on the common meaning of all, some like Ma Rong 馬融 (99–165) also wrote commentaries on the *Laozi*.[109] This text, however, is entirely lost. There is an anonymous *Laozi jiejie* 老子節解 of which sizable parts survive in quotations in commentary collections of the Song and possibly even the Tang period, but these might come from the work of a later author with a similar name.[110]

In Liu Biao's famous Jingzhou Academy the *Laozi* was much studied. The leading Jingzhou scholar, Song Zhong 宋衷, with whom Wang Bi's grandfather Wang Can 王粲 was closely associated, wrote a (lost) *Commentary to the Laozi* as well as to the other text most intensely studied in Jingzhou, Yang Xiong's *Taixuan jing*.[111] As the Jingzhou scholars surviving the Wei Feng 魏諷 rebellion against Cao Cao, in which many had been involved,[112] were absorbed into Wei, their texts exerted considerable influence there.

It is not known what role the *Laozi* commentaries associated with the emerging Daoist church played in Wei. Again, the surviving leaders of the Yellow Turban rebellion, as well as those of the Five Pecks of Rice rebellion, were absorbed by Cao Cao. Cao Cao himself as well as Cao Pi liked Daoist books.[113] Thus it is probable that the late-Han Xiang Er *Commentary*, alternately ascribed to Zhang Lu 張魯 (Rao Zongyi)[114] and Zhang Daoling 張道陵 (Tang Xuanzong 唐玄宗, Du Guangting 杜光庭),[115] and, according to later sources, among the main teaching material for Daoist adepts, was known in Wei.[116] It survives in a Dunhuang MS and a few external quotations.[117] The Heshang gong 河上公 *Commentary*, the date of which has been under discussion since the Tang dynasty, but which might date from the Eastern Han, belongs to the same category.

During the decades after the end of the Han, commentaries on the *Laozi* were popular in all three states. In Wu, Yu Fan 虞翻 (183–233) came out with a (now lost) *Commentary*,[118] Given the fame in Wei of Wu scholars like Yu Fan it is likely that copies of some of these works made it north. Finally, Fan Wang 範望, who also wrote a *Commentary on the Taixuan jing*, wrote a *Commentary to the Laozi*.[119]

In Wei itself, a number of *Laozi* commentaries preceded Wang Bi's. Sources mention a *Laozi* commentary by the recluse Sun Deng 孫登 (209–41) of which fragments survive;[120] by Zhong Yu 鍾繇, one of the Wei dynasty's highest officials who also wrote on the *Zhouyi*;[121] by Zhang Yi 張揖 (d. 239);[122] and by many young men of Wang Bi's age like Zhong Yu's son Zhong Hui 鐘會 (225–64)[123] and Xun Rong 荀融 (233–63),[124] both of whom were disputation partners of Wang Bi's;[125] by Dong Yu 董遇 (227–64);[126] and Meng Kang 孟康 (227–64),[127] not to mention the essays on the *Laozi* by He Yan 何晏 and later Ruan Ji 阮籍.[128] Alone from Zhong Hui's commentary fairly extensive quotations survive.

Writing a new *Commentary to the Laozi* meant that Wang Bi entered a field densely packed with some of the best and most innovative minds of the century, who either had written on the *Laozi* themselves or knew other writings about the *Laozi*, and who had formed definite opinions. The social and intellectual conditions for convincing his implied and his actual readers had greatly changed when compared to the preceding decades.

The Han-dynasty commentators had as a rule been teachers. They transmitted their readings to their students, and the first written commentaries might have evolved out of teacher or student notes. The commentator's authority as a teacher was in some cases enhanced by his authority as an officially appointed Doctor of [a] Classic. Under these conditions, the commentator would have to establish his fame and credibility primarily in competition with other commentators, but not with his students. They were there to learn, to receive the teacher's wisdom, and to hand it down.[129] Consequently, the teacher's commentary and approach, which in the scholarly literature is referred to as the "teacher's method," *shifa* 師法, would be guaranteed a certain authority, distribution, and continuity of distribution. The last came about as families at the time developed intellectual traditions referred to as "family approach," *jiafa* 家法," associating them with particular teachings over generations.[130] The number of such students under a single teacher could go as high as ten thousand, teaching in these cases being done via senior students.[131]

All this had changed with the collapse of the Han dynasty. The court's unsuccessful attempts at establishing some form of orthodoxy through the state university ended altogether when the court eunuchs after Hedi 和帝 (r. 89–105 CE) refused to recognize the classics as the basis for deliberations on state policy. Furthermore, the institution of the private teacher with his own crowds of students, which in itself signaled some diversity of opinion, all but disappeared in Wei in the north with the end of the Han. Wang Bi had neither been a student of some famous man, nor did he ever become a teacher. His *Commentary* had to gain acceptance through entirely different mechanisms.

First, with the collapse of the schools, the structure of the intellectual sphere changed greatly. Intellectual grouping no longer occurred according to teacher affiliation; a competitive market arose, where intellectuals would read and discuss various propositions about the same topic, and choose sides according to what they saw as the most brilliant and convincing arguments. A man like He Yan would, at the height of his own intellectual fame and political power, trash his *Commentary to the Laozi* because he felt young Wang Bi's was superior—and this gesture more than any other made him famous and made it into the *Shishuo xinyu*.[132] A man like Zhong Hui would let himself be convinced by an opinion of He Yan and proceed to promote He's argument through his own writings.[133] There were lively public debates in speech and writing on issues like the particular features of the Sage, the meaning of a core passage in the *Xici*, or the political strategies to be pursued to create long-term political stability after the demise of the Han. The oral debates in particular were eagerly noted down for posterity by participants so that we have some of them preserved in texts like the *Shishuo xinyu*, but also in the biographies of famous intellectuals of the time. In short, the social process through which arguments or commentaries would establish themselves had changed; they had to survive in a fierce intellectual competition within an elitist marketplace of ideas and could not rely on teacher-student transmission.

The collapse of the state university and the private schools—and of their interpretive authority within the body of their students—also meant that the meanings of the relevant texts were again open for discussion. As detailed earlier, there was a widely held assumption that the previous commentaries had not only missed the meaning of this or that phrase, but had missed the "basic meaning" of these texts altogether; and that, owing to this failure to understand their underlying purport, they were forced into using ever more cumbersome devices to fit the specific phrases to their overall assumptions. As a consequence of failing to understand the basic meaning, the commentaries thus lacked economy and elegance.[134] The flood of new commentaries to the *Laozi* coming with the end of the Han is thus part of the competition at the time for establishing a new intellectual hegemony over the classical texts without the traditional "schools" of thought playing a dominant role.

Long before coming out with his *Commentary on the Laozi* in 248, Wang Bi had already gained fame and notoriety among potential readers for his understanding of the text. Due to his elevated social position and the intellectual tradition of his family, he was, when still a minor, in contact with some of the most brilliant intellectuals of the time. The fame of his promise had spread far as early as 244 when he was eighteen years old and was consulted by a man of Pei Hui's stature as an authority on a question as important as the relative standing of Confucius and Laozi.[135] When his *Commentary* finally became available, there was already some expectation; this might have predisposed potential readers to give this particular commentary a chance. Wang Bi's *Commentary*, the youth and arrogance of its author notwithstanding, might thus have met with relatively favorable intellectual as well as social conditions to predispose an audience to give his construct a try.

The few reactions of contemporaries to Wang Bi's commentary evince their general admiration for the intellectual quality of his work, but we have no specific comments explaining the standards by which it was judged. Was it that Wang Bi provided the *Laozi*'s hallowed authority for opinions they themselves long held without their being in the least interested in the capacity of the *Commentary* to explain the *Laozi* itself? Was it that they agreed with the basic premise under which Wang Bi read the *Laozi*—as a work of political philosophy rather than as the work by a god on the prolongation of life—which convinced them? Or did they feel that he surpassed all others in the elegance and economy with which he explained the text as a homogeneous whole, even if the outcome might not have fitted the philosophical predilections of all of them?

Left in the doubt by the actual readers, we must consult Wang Bi's fictional counterpart of them, the implied reader. Wang Bi does not explicitly argue with his creature. The technique of his commenting, however, implies the general acceptance of certain standards of verifying the viability and plausibility of a commentary reading. These standards with which Wang Bi tried to convince his implied reader were those he assumed to be the standards by which the actual readers themselves would assess his work.

Our own reading of Wang Bi's *Commentary* is infinitely poorer than that of his implied and real reader, mostly because of the eventual success of Wang Bi's own *Commentary* and the absence of scholarship on the surviving fragments of other commentaries. However, while it remains desirable to read Wang Bi's *Commentary* line by line against the surviving fragments to discern the implicit dialogue and polemics, we are fortunate that Wang Bi used his *LZWZLL* in the same manner as his *Zhouyi lüeli* for an explicit polemics against other commentators and readers, thus setting his own *Commentary* into the context of an ongoing contest for the proper interpretation of the *Laozi*. This proves that he was familiar with other commentaries and expected that his readers were too.

This polemics are also a clear reflection of the renewed vigor of many of the pre-Qin schools of thought after the end of the Han. Wang Bi writes after having pointed out what he considered the *Laozi*'s "key points" in a fine parallel staircase sequence of IPS:

But
the Legalists promote equality and egality, and then apply punishment to supervise them [the people];
   the Name school promotes the fixation of the true, and then

uses terms to rectify them [the people];
    the Ru school promotes complete love, and then uses praise
    to drive them [the people] on;
        the Mohists promote parsimony and simplicity, and then
        use constraint to fixate them [the people] on this;
            the Eclectics promote all sorts of treats and use a
            variety [of means] to let [the people] act accordingly.[136]

Wang Bi follows this with the argument, specified for each school, that this extreme emphasis on one specific measure inevitably produces the very negative phenomenon it seeks to avoid; in short, "All these schools make use of the offspring but discard the mother." He criticizes them, in other words, primarily on their analytic methodology, and only on this basis does he dispute points of values and government strategies. These misguided political strategies appear in this context as the product of misguided philological and philosophic methodology. He continues:

However, [to paraphrase the *Xici*, in the *Laozi*]
the destination [of the various
arguments] is the same,
though the ways thither differ,   [the various arguments']
                                                    meanings coincide, but
                                                    the approaches vary,
            but the scholars [from the different schools]
are bewildered as to their [the
arguments' common] destination.   are befuddled as to their
                                    [the arguments' common]
                                    amount.[137]

Failing to grasp the basic thrust of the *Laozi*'s arguments, their strategy for reading the *Laozi* is dominated by the core concept of their school. The entire text is then buffeted by them into fitting this purpose. Wang Bi writes:

When they observe them [some of the arguments in the *Laozi*
advocating] equalizing, they style him [*Laozi*] Legalist;
    when they perceive them [some of the arguments in the *Laozi*
    advocating] delineating the true, they style him [*Laozi*] a
    member of the Name school;

when they observe them [some of the *Laozi*'s arguments advocating] pure love, they style him [*Laozi*] a Ruist;
  when they perceive them [some of the arguments in the *Laozi* advocating] parsimony and simplicity, they style him a Mohist;
    when they see them [some of the arguments in the *Laozi* advocating] unsystematic [tenets], they style him an Eclecticist.

According to what their eyes happen to perceive, they assign the name; depending on what they like, they cling to that meaning. That there are confused and faulty exegeses and struggles between different tendencies and interpretations is caused by this [faulty methodology of other scholars].[138]

From the existing record and present knowledge it is difficult if not impossible to pin down the unnamed commentators taken to task in this critique. They are referred to only as members of the various philosophical schools trying to appropriate the *Laozi*.

In this list of schools, Wang Bi is again indebted to Sima Tan's *Treatise on the Six Schools*. We learn that, by the middle of the third century CE, the *Laozi* was seen as a philosophic classic used, studied, and commented upon equally by all the schools, the Mohists and Ru included. The Mohists, for one school, had all but diappeared by the third century CE. Wang Bi included them into his criticism not because there actually was a commentary on the market that neded rebuttal. The purpose of his criticism here must be to reject any possible doctrinaire and schoolish interpretation of the *Laozi*, to refute a certain faulty methodology applied by all possible schools as long as they were just that, namely schools.[139]

The polemic translated above is surprising first because of an absence. The most important of the schools mentioned by Sima Tan, the Daoist school, Daojia 道家, is missing in all three sections that refer to the schools. Does this mean that Wang Bi by implication attacks the other schools from a Daojia perspective?

In Sima Tan's list, there is a hierarchy of schools. As they deal with the fundamentals, the Daojia come out highest, and all the rest including the Ru are measured against this high standard, and found deficient. Wang Bi does not share this high evaluation of the Daojia, ranking, as he does, Confucius above *Laozi*. Had he wanted to align himself with the Daojia, the above polemic would have been the place to do so. With the development of the Daoist religion and its social organizations toward the end of the Han, the status of the Daojia as a philosophic school of independent standing became diffuse if it ever had an existence outside of Sima Tan's tract. The only commentary that might be associated with the Daojia is that by Zhuang Zun, said to have been "an amateur of *Laozi* and *Zhuangzi*,"[140] who wrote long before Daoism became an organized religion. In the framework of this newly developing Daoist religion, however, some commentaries like the Xiang Er were written, which Wang Bi was unaware of, disregarded, or saw as unknown and irrelevant to his readers.

Both fragments of the *Laozi weizhi lüeli* have been transmitted in the Daoist canon, and it is unlikely that passages supportive of the Daojia would have been cut; still it might be as unlikely that passages openly critical of the Daojia would have been left in the text. There is thus a possibility that Wang Bi's critique of the Daoist commentaries on the *Laozi* had been cut from the excerpt at hand. On the other hand, it would have taken some editorial sophistication to cut out not one but three passages in the consecutive series within the *LZWZLL*, of which only the first explicitly mentioned the names of the schools. Only then would the reference to the Daojia disappear without trace. The problem is exacerbated by the fact that commentaries from the Daoist church tradition like the Xiang Er might very well be accused of reading the *Laozi* according to a limited set of preconceived notions (many having to do with longevity techniques) and bending the text to this religious purpose. By not following their line of argument, it might be said that Wang Bi engaged at least in an implicit polemic with these commentaries. The quest for longevity is entirely absent from his reading of the *Laozi*.

While we thus have no hard evidence to prove that Wang Bi included the Daojia or the religious current now called Daojiao in his criticism, the absence of polemics against the Daojia or Daojiao in no way implies that he accepted their strategy of interpreting the *Laozi* and attacked the other schools from a Daoist perspective. The fact that Wang Bi rated Confucius as the Sage above Laozi does not prevent his attacking the methodology of the Ru in this diatribe. It thus can be presumed that nothing would have prevented his attacking the commenting strategies of the Daoists even while writing a commentary on their hallowed classic.

Wang Bi's critique is not written from the perspective of one particular school; he attacks the common methodological mistake all the schools make in commenting the *Laozi*. In the introduction to the polemics quoted above, Wang Bi writes:

> Thus he who imposes discursive analysis upon the [particular] textual patterns of the *Laozi* will miss what he points at; and he who wishes to put the weight on the [particular] term [under consideration] will deviate from [the *Laozi*'s overall] meaning. 然則老子之文，欲辯而詰者則失其旨也，欲名而責者則違其義也.

The core error of the schools is to fasten onto the particular arguments and terms used by *Laozi*. Instead of basing their analysis on the underlying but common argumentative thrust of the different *zhang*, that is on the context provided by the entire text, they attach themselves to individual words; and once they have identified certain tenets that agree with those of their own school, they turn these passages and terms into the text's core, declare the *Laozi* to be in agreement with their own school tenets and use these elements as the basis for their interpretation of the entire remaining text. As a consequence, Wang Bi says after his attacks on the schools, we have "confused and faulty exegeses and struggles between different tendencies and interpretations" 紛紜憒錯之論，殊趣辯折之爭. The mistake of the schools is to read *Laozi*'s work not as that of a philosopher pursuing an elusive truth, but as a classic of high authority that could be appropriated and used to enhance the standing of this or that school. Thus a text which, if read correctly, would provide a strategy for establishing order in society becomes part of a strategy that cannot but produce the very opposite of what it intends to achieve.

As we have seen, Wang Bi argued in the introduction of the *LZWZLL* that reading the *Laozi* presupposes an understanding of the basic thrust of the entire text to provide the angle from which and the context in which to read individual passages. Wang Bi argues that the *Laozi* is pursuing one single philosophic goal throughout all the *zhang*, namely to elucidate the relationship of the That-by-which of the ten thousand kinds of entities to those ten thousand kinds of entities, and to extract from this the laws that should be followed in regulating society. Wang Bi's philosophical argument for the inability of language to define its elusive object will be studied in more detail elsewhere.[141] This inability forces the *Laozi* to examine a wide variety of phenomena to find structures that point at the topic under discussion.

This philosophic problem, however, makes the surface of the text highly unreliable, since the words, symbols, and metaphors are only signs pointing away from themselves and having no other function but to disappear in the fulfilment of this purpose.

The discursive mode of the schools consists in focusing on this highly unreliable, transitory, and makeshift material which the *Laozi* uses in its exploration; they are to those who "wish to impose discursive analysis upon the [particular] textual patterns of the *Laozi*, and thus miss what he points at" 欲辯而詰者則失其旨, and who "wish to put the weight on the [particular] term [under consideration] and thus deviate from [the *Laozi*'s] overall meaning" 欲名而責者則敗其性, as Wang Bi says in the introducution to the treatment of the schools. They construct the overall meaning from individual terms instead of reading the particular terms in the framework of the overall context.

Wang Bi here attacks a strategy of commenting familiar from the commentaries of the Han, including those already critical of the *zhangju* 章句 commentaries like Zheng Xuan 鄭玄. Against this style of commenting, Wang Bi argued in the parallel to the *LZWZLL*, the *Zhouyi lüeli*. As his *Zhouyi Commentary* is later than the *Laozi Commentary*, the argument there is more developed. In the famous *Ming xiang* 明象 section of the *Zhouyi lüeli* he develops a hierarchy governing the meaning of a hexagram, *yi* 意, the symbols used for it, *xiang* 象, and the words, *yan* 言, used in turn to describe the symbols. The "meaning" refers to the overall idea of a hexagram. For the first hexagram, *qian* 乾, this would be *jian* 健 and *gang* 剛, "vigor," and would be expressed through symbols, in this case "Heaven," *tian* 天, the "Dragon," *long* 龍 and the "horse," *ma* 馬, elaborated upon in the trigrams and the lines, while the "words" are in the *guaci* 卦辭, the *yaoci* 爻辭, the *tuanzhuan* 彖傳, the *xiangzhuan* 象傳, and the *wenyan* 文言. In the interpretation of this material, the same mistake is made.

As the words are born of the images, it is possible to explore the words in order to see the images. As the images are born of the meaning, it is possible to explore the images to see the meaning.

Understanding, accordingly, is possible. So is a commentary to help in this process. However, the purpose of the images and words is purely instrumental, and only he who understands this instrumentality will be able to use them properly. Beyond providing access to the next higher level they have no other purpose and do not merit any attention. The signifier has no other purpose but to point at the signified, and to disappear into this function. Only if all matter in the signifier extraneous to this function is disregarded can its purpose be fulfilled. The term used by Wang Bi for discarding and disregarding the instruments used to achieve a more abstract understanding is taken from the *Zhuangzi*. It is *wang* 忘, "to forget."

The Image is that by which a meaning is arrested. Once the meaning is reached, the image is forgotten.

He, however, who attaches himself to the instrument will not be able to achieve the end of getting the image or the meaning.

Therefore, he who clings to the words 存言者 will not reach the image; he who clings to the image will not reach the meaning. The image is born of the meaning, but if one clings to the image, then that which one is clinging to is not the image *thereof.* The words are born of the image but if one clings to the words, then that which one is clinging to are not the words *about it.* Accordingly it is he [alone] who forgets the image who gets the meaning, and it is he [alone] who forgets the words who gets the image.

And in a final radicalization of this argument, Wang Bi concludes:

Getting the meaning consists in forgetting the image; getting the image consists in forgetting the words[142] 得意在忘象得象在忘言.

Those who handle the *Zhouyi* improperly identify certain images with the meanings. As Wang Bi explains in his commentary to the first hexagram, which takes up the same argument:

As to that from which the images are born—they are born from the meanings.[143] First there is this [particular] meaning, and then [only] will it be illustrated with that [particular] object. Therefore *qian* 乾 is laid out by means of the [image of] the dragon, and *kun* 坤 is elucidated by means of the [image of] the horse; [but only] in accordance with the meaning of the situation will the image be adduced. Thus [in the first hexagram] the dragon's capacity, *long de* 龍德, in the first and second unbroken lines [from below] corresponds to the meaning of these [lines], and therefore it is possible to talk about the dragon in order to elucidate them [these lines]. As to the [expression] "vigorously active [till the] evening full of cares" 乾乾夕惕 [for the third line] this is not [characteristic of] the dragon's capacity, and to illustrate this [line] it is appropriate to take the image of the gentleman, *junzi*, [as the *Zhouyi* text in fact does by writing "the gentleman is all day long vigorously active and till the evening full of cares"].

The erroneous reduction of the much broader meaning to the narrow confines of the image leads to a strategy of commenting that needs ever more bizarre constructs to establish some homogeneity of meaning.

There are some who define the [image of the] horse as qian 乾. They put pressure on the text, *an wen* 案文, and burden the trigrams, *ze gua* 責卦, and, if there [is in the *Zhouyi* text] a horse, but no *qian* 乾, they come up with such a turbid overflow of manufactured explanations that one is hard put [even] to list them. If [the construct] of the interlocked trigrams 互體 does not suffice [which was pioneered by Zheng Xuan who posited two more trigrams inside each hexagram consisting of lines two through four and three through five thus opening additional options of interpretation], they then proceed to the "transformation of hexagrams," *gua bian* 卦變 [where a hexagram is transformed into another by switching the trigrams or by changing a line], and, if that still is not enough, they push things as far as [making use of the theory of] the Five Elements, *wu xing* 五行 [identifying the images with these elements and interpreting them in accordance with their relationships]. Once the basis, *yuan* 原, of it [that is, the understanding of the text's basic structure] is missed, the bizarre constructs get ever more numerous.[144]

Although the *Zhouyi* and the *Laozi* operate with different linguistic and symbolic devices to treat their elusive subjects, they both proceed from the assumption that straight terms and definitions are structurally unable to say what they want to say. In both cases the "meaning," *yi* 意 or *yi* 義 and the "purport," *zhi* 旨 or *zhi* 指, are at the origin and center of the texts, and only "thereafter," *ranhou* 然後, will various symbolic, metaphoric, and linguistic devices be used in an attempt to communicate to the reader this meaning and purport.

Since, however, the reader is confronted only with such devices, and as the meaning and purport are structurally elusive, these devices gain an importance of their own to the point that they themselves seem to be the subject matter of the text. The fallacies of the schools described by Wang Bi are thus not a product of dull wits or uneducated minds; the contrary is true. The scholars he criticizes by implication in the ZYLL, such as Zheng Xuan, certainly count among the most open-minded, brightest, and best educated in the century preceding Wang Bi. These fallacies have their origin in the complex structure of communication used by the *Zhouyi* and the *Laozi* that are in turn conditioned by the particular structure of language. Once this structure is forgotten, attempts to extract meaning from these hallowed texts must have recourse to ever more outlandish and complicated techniques of interpretation, with a resulting plethora of competing readings that all share one common origin—a misunderstanding of the texts' communication and a resulting wrong methodology.

The general attack on the schools on methodical grounds does not mean that there are no differences among them. Each has its particular way of bringing about chaos with the best of intentions of establishing order. What, then, does their sequence in Wang Bi's list signify? Wang Bi changed the order in which the schools are mentioned. Sima Tan's tract has three series of sequences; the first,

Yinyang jia 陰陽家, Ru, Mohists 墨家, Mingjia 名家, Legalists, and Daodejia 道德家 (later in the text called Daojia 道家), argues that they all "strive for good government," but in different ways, and that some are more penetrating than others. The second series describes the particular emphasis of each school, and switches positions for the Legalists and the Mingjia; at the end come the Daoists. Their characterization begins an evaluative argument: The Daoists combine all the strong points of the various schools; a similar claim made for the Ru is rejected. The third series follows the sequence of the second. The qualitative difference is between the Daojia on the one side and the five remaining schools on the other. Chinese rhetorics use both sequences, one with the most important (positive or negative) element at the end, and one with the most important element at the beginning, but I do not recall having ever seen a random sequence. The sequence with the most important element at the beginning is the more common.

Wang Bi goes beyond Sima Tan, inverts his sequence, and changes its meaning. Like Sima Tan, he characterizes each school through its focus on one particular feature, but originally might have included the Daojia. But while Sima Tan focused on the graded positive contribution of each school, all of which were eventually absorbed into the Daojia, Wang Bi focuses on the common methodological flaw and grades them according to their influence and the level of their negative social consequences. According to Wang Bi, the political strategies of all the schools are not just uncomprehensive, but strictly counterproductive, and the same is true for their strategies of reading the *Laozi*. Wang Bi eliminates the Yinyang jia altogether. Of great importance at Sima Tan's time, when its position in his sequence of schools indicated that it surpassed even the Ru, it had lost all respectability in Wang Bi's eyes and is not even mentioned among the schools. In the *ZYLL*, he refers to the theory of the "Five Elements" 五行, which forms an essential part of Yinyang school doctrine, only as an example for the absurdity scholars might resort to to make sense out of the *Zhouyi* ("and if that still is not enough, they push things as far as [making use of the theory of] the Five Elements, *wu xing*!" 五行).[145] Within the schools, Wang Bi rearranges Sima Tan's sequence. The intention of the sequence is evident from the fact that Wang Bi leaves the Zajia 雜家, the Eclectics, at the end. In Wang Bi's sequence, the Legalists come out most important in terms of influence and damage, to be followed by the Name-school, the Ru, the Mohists, and the Eclectics.

From this we infer that Wang Bi's implied reader is most negatively affected by Legalist thinking, and secondly by Name-school influences, with the Ru third. This assessment of the implied reader ties in with independent information from other contemporary sources which speak of the pervading influence of Legalism and the Mingjia at the Cao Wei Court. Wang Bi's implied and explicit polemics in his *Commentary* primarily target those trends of thought high on the above list. At the same time, he does not deny that elements from all these schools might be found on the *Laozi*'s textual surface. By not associating his own approach with any of these schools, he also confronted them all with one single new approach, which one might call that of philosophy. In recognition of this, the doxography of the ensuing decades and the university establishments of the southern dynasties in the ensuing centuries have not subsumed Wang Bi's project under any of the schools such as Daojia, but gave it an entirely new name, Xuanxue 玄學, the Scholarly Exploration of That-which-is-Dark.

The polemics against the schools also say something about the implied reader the *Commentary* addresses. In his summary of the purport of the *Laozi*, Wang Bi links two elements, the ontological dealing with the relationship of the "That-by-which" and the ten thousand entities, and the politological dealing with the ruler's strategies for ordering society. As we see from Wang Bi's list of the "essential points" of the *Laozi* quoted above, a practical application of the philosophic insights is at the center of attention.

From this we conclude that Wang Bi's implied reader is, in fact, the ruler himself. This does not mean that only the ruler alone was supposed to read the *Commentary*; in the generation of political strategies to be used by the ruler a large segment of the upper officials as well as of those qualifying for higher appointments were involved. In theory, the strategies eventually chosen were those of the ruler, even if in fact they were developed and executed by officials. The officials in turn would replicate the basic relationship between the one ruler and the Hundred Families on a lower level in the relationship between themselves and the regions or offices under their control, where the same mechanics prevailed. The identification of the implied reader as the leadership is confirmed by Wang Bi's construction of the *Laozi*, where the human actors responsible for the fate of society are the ideal ruler who brings about order, that is the Sage, or the actual ruler who creates chaos, and needs the insights contained in the *Laozi* to prevent the collapse of society and the ruin of his own position. The implied reader and addressee is thus this latter type of defective leader in need of instruction and informed by the counterproductive strategies spread by the different schools.

Wang Bi's implied reader, we conclude,

- Might be tempted by an argument that the ultimate things were beyond language, and that texts therefore were perfectly unreliable and futile products.

- Knew the *Laozi* by heart.

- Agreed that, if it was to be taken seriously, the text was in need of a commentary.

- Knew other commentaries to it.

- Did not define his intellectual leanings in terms of a teacher or his teaching.

- Assumed that the *Laozi* contained great insights that might have been forgotten or submerged by the rattle of commentators.

- Assumed that the *Laozi* and the Confucius texts essentially dealt with the same issue so that they could mutually elucidate each other.

- Was willing to have himself convinced by argument (not by authority) to follow a different reading of the *Laozi*.

- Was strongly influenced by the teaching of the various schools, primarily the Legalist and Name schools, in terms of his political thinking and reading strategies for the *Laozi*.

- Was the actual contemporary leadership defined as defective in understanding and consequently responsible for what was seen as the prevailing social chaos, and in urgent need of instruction.

The *Commentary* thus has to generally help the reader in constantly rediscovering this common aim of the various *zhang* by inserting them into the homogeneous overall purport and constructing the homogeneity of the text; in this manner it will prevent the reader from falling into the trap of reading the text in a discursive manner, and ending up with all the traps but neither fish nor hare. Wang Bi's *Commentary* has, at the same time, the specific burden of undoing a reading strategy both well established and prevalent that attaches itself to the textual surface and bends the text to the purposes of particular schools. Only in this manner will the true meaning of the *Laozi* be discovered with the ensuing sociopolitical blessings.

In tune with the purpose of the *Commentary* to deconstruct the implied reader's previous construction of the entire text and of each passage, an accurate and fully informed rendering of one of Wang Bi's comments would make the implied countertext or countertexts explicit. It would have to begin with an extensive bracket detailing how the reading of the passage in question by common opinion and/ or the commentators X, Y, and Z lacked elegance and economy and erred due to their particular misconstruction of the basic purport of the *Laozi* as well as of its particular use of language, while the commentators A, B, and C, while getting the basic purport right, failed to understand the implications of the rhetorical figures, grammatical features, or metaphoric constructs employed by the *Laozi* and therefore failed to get the particular meaning of a passage. Evidently, at the present stage of research on the fragments of other commentaries, such a bracket can only be a general threat to the reader of this study, which can be made true only to a very limited extent.

The Homogeneity Hypothesis

Wang Bi assumed that the *Laozi* had been written by a single historical person, a librarian at the Zhou court called Laozi. The story of the *Laozi* being written by a unified single person called Laozi is a story about the homogeneity of the text. There were other options. The *Shijing* was always assumed to be composed by a variety of authors; the story of Confucius selecting from a larger group of songs those that might fit a common moral purpose established a framework for a methodologically homogeneous interpretation of the whole through commentaries. Multiple authorship was also assumed for the *Shujing* and the *Zhouyi*. Both (and the latter text claims this explicitly in the *Xici*) were said to have been composed and put together by a succession of Sages over a long period of time, ending with Confucius. The homogeneity of these texts, then, was postulated against the evidence available from the textual surface. They were seen as homogeneous in terms of their values, and their various parts would require a similar method of interpretation to get at their hidden common message.

In the case of the *Laozi*, the postulate of homogeneity is not evident from the surface of the text. The *Laozi* consists of a fair number, in Wang Bi's reading of 80 or 81 short *zhang* (for *Laozi* 31 no commentary exists and while it is quoted by Wang Bi on *Laozi* 30.5, there is a tradition that Wang Bi assumed that it did not belong into the text),[146] each counting between 21 (*zhang* 40) and 131 (*zhang* 38) Chinese characters. Their language is highly metaphoric, and the particular object under consideration is often not stated, so that neither in terms of linkage among the *zhang* nor in terms of terminology is there evident homogeneity. Many statements contained in the *Laozi* are attributed to other authors in sources available to Wang Bi.[147] On the other hand, the different *zhang* might be said to share certain key terms like *dao* 道, *de* 德, and *xuan* 玄; certain key metaphors like the water or the baby; certain key problems like the behavior of the Sage in relation to the general patterns of nature or the relation of the ten thousand kinds of things to their common existential base; certain general philosophic attitudes concerning the proper running of the state. They furthermore share a number of rhetorical features like the use of interlocking parallel style, the structuring of the arguments in two parts, both of which argue along parallel lines, and the presence of rhymed passages.

When Wang Bi claimed in the *LZWZLL* that the "book of Laozi can almost be summed up in one phrase," he showed how aware he was of the problem of the text's homogeneity. He took this phrase from the *Lunyu* 2.2, where Confucius deals with the problem of the *Shijing*'s homogeneity, saying: "[True,] the *Shi*[*jing*] has three hundred poems, [but] they can be summed up in one phrase: Do not think anything decadent."[148] Wang Bi continued:

In observing on what [the ten thousand kinds of entities] are based, and in investigating whereto [they] return, [Laozi's] "words" do not depart from "the principle," and [his] activities do not lose [sight] of "the ruler" [as Laozi says about himself in *Laozi* 70.2]. Although the [*Laozi*] text has five thousand characters, what "threads through them" is the "One" [as is the case for the Dao of Confucius according to his statement in *Lunyu* 4.15]. Although [its] ideas are broad and far-flung, in their multitude they are of the same kind. Once it is understood that it can be "summed up in one phrase" there is nothing recondite that is not discerned; but when each theme is [interpreted] as having a [separate] meaning, then, analytic skill notwithstanding, the delusions will only increase.[149]

Wang Bi is thus quite conscious of the importance of the homogeneity hypothesis for the reading of the *Laozi*; a strategy of reading each section as having its own meaning as determined by the textual surface will only lead to increased misunderstanding of the text's actual meaning. The construction of the *Laozi*'s meaning hinges on the construction of its homogeneity, and the latter again hinges on a viable understanding of the fundamental problem the *Laozi* deals with. For Wang Bi, a grasp of the philosophic issue confronted by *Laozi* will also provide an understanding of his use of language, and consequently of the proper strategy for reading the *Laozi*.

Wang Bi's assumption of homogeneity is a hypothesis to be verified in the process of his commenting on the text. It legitimates certain operations like defining a term through the context in which it appears elsewhere, but the results have to prove their own worth and come in as tests on the validity of the hypothesis.

Homogeneity, however, is established by integrating the different parts of a text into a common framework, which, as a rule, is not spelled out in the text itself. It therefore must be a construct of the interpreter, who has to prove its validity by being able to guide the reading of these different parts so that a homogeneous text will result. It is in this process, however, that anomalies might appear. Guided by the general hypothesis about the overall purport of the text, some individual parts might have to be bent and twisted to fit into this framework. Wang Bi's criticism of the schools claimed that the actual text rebelled against their general hypotheses to a degree that it forced them to come up with bizarre constructions of individual passages to make them fit.

In contrast to their proceedings, Wang Bi establishes a highly innovative and original way of developing his own strategies of reading the *Laozi*: In an early anticipation of one of the characteristic procedures of modern hermeneutics, he extracts the strategies for reading the *Laozi* from the indications about the nature of the text given in the *Laozi* itself. In terms of developing commentary strategies, this was a decisive and very influential step. It rejected the legitimacy of any reading strategy based on material or thought imposed from outside, and established the notion of the text as a basically self-illuminating unit where the primary material for explanation and interpretation had to be taken from the text itself. While other traditions of reading continued to exist especially in religious Daoist circles and in the ongoing handling of the *chan-wei* texts even after their official and repeated ban, Wang Bi's commentary strategy marks a turning point in mainstream Chinese commenting on texts ranging from the Chinese classics to the Hundred Schools to Buddhist sutras and shastras not only through the particular strategies he was developing but through the methodology with which he was doing this. Installing the text as the main authority in matters of itself, the commentator becomes the humble tool articulating the text's self-explanation. By strictly limiting the legitimate material to draw on for the interpretation of a given passage and by restricting the commentator to a supportive role, the commentary submits to very high standards of falsifiability. Its incapacity to explain a passage with the tools so legitimized cannot anymore lead to the development of a tool unsupported by the text to eliminate the anomaly, and threatens to falsify the credibility of the entire enterprise. Other commentators will then have a rational and scholarly basis to offer a new reading based on hypotheses about the purpose and structure of the text that are better supported by the available material.

While this humble role of the commentator as the tool of the text's self-explanation seems modest enough, its claim to present an authentic reading of the insight of the Sages of old implies a proud and blunt rejection of earlier efforts as methodologically ill-guided and practically desastrous as we see it in Wang Bi's curt dismissal of the totality of the existing "schools."

In this hermeneutic enterprise, Wang Bi acts the philosopher, not the historian. Neither he nor other Xuanxue commentators of his time or after try to reconstruct the historical horizon and environment of their author in order to read his text in this context. As the example of commentaries to the *Chunqiu* or the *Shi* shows most clearly, this historization did not necessarily imply the reduction of the text to a cultural product relevant and meaningful at its time and place but not anymore in the present. From both of these texts commentators were able to extract general norms through the very technique of historically respecifying their implied object of praise or criticism. In contrast to this procedure, the Xuanxue commentators highlight their texts' ongoing relevance for their own and any other time by translating and conflating the texts' metaphorical or anecdotal statements into a newly created Xuanxue language of ontology and political philosophy. In this translated and systematized form the texts present philosophical insights that can be further developed or taken to task by later philosophers, most of all the commentators themselves. Wang Bi himself is a very fine example for the creative new options of philosophic thinking opened by this seemingly passive approach.

The first of these indications taken from the text itself is the implication of homogeneity in the identity of an author talking of himself as "I." For Wang Bi, the assumption of philosophical homogeneity of the text thus informs his reading of its individual *zhang*, and the core hypotheses on which this homogeneity rests are tested in the confrontation with the individual *zhang*. In this confrontation, a new criterion of the accuracy of the *Commentary* appears, economy or elegance. This seems to be an utterly unscholarly measure, but it is used with great seriousness in Western mathematics as a criterion of truth and quality. The more easily the *Commentary* manages to fit the entirety of the actual text into the framework, the more solid its claim to having properly understood its purpose. The more often auxiliary constructs are necessary to link the two, the lower the credibility of the *Commentary*.

While Wang Bi's motive for studying the *Laozi* certainly was that of a philosopher, his method as a commentator was that of a philologist bound by rather strict rules of exegesis extracted from the text itself. It is probable that the methodological principle underlying these rules had been in the making before he wrote his commentaries. The methodology used by the *Gongyang zhuan* for the interpretation of the *Chunqiu* is clearly derived from an analysis of the writing practice of the *Chunqiu;* Zhao Qi's commentary of the *Mengzi* claims to apply to the *Mengzi* the reading strategy used by

Mengzi for the *Shi*; Bi Zhi's lost commentary on the *Zhouyi* used the Wings of the *Zhouyi* as his guide to the understanding of this text. The particular problem in the case of the *Laozi* was the necessary unreliability of the surface text that was due to the structure of the problem it was dealing with. To handle this problem which again was indicated by the text's own statements, strategies had to be developed that had to be infinitely more sophisticated than the relatively simple formula\deviation model of the *Gongyang* or the overall meaning\particular term or phrase model of Zhao Qi. Only by beating his opponents in handling the *Laozi* more economically within rules of exegesis whose derivation was falsifiable could Wang Bi's *Commentary* and the philosophy it carried win the day. This open competition did much to enhance the quality of Wang Bi's *Commentary*. Commentators who could rely on an existing school or religious community, where the authority of the teacher or the religious guide would be able to impose a reading without much competition, were less inclined to go by rigorous rules of exegesis, and could claim special dispensations from these rules on the basis of divine inspiration or of traditions handed down to them from some hallowed authority. With a similar procedure a man in Wang Bi's position would have gone under in the merciless laughter of his contemporaries.

The homogeneity hypothesis and the argument about the necessary unreliability of language increase the leeway and bargaining power of both text and commentary. While legitimating certain analytical operations of textual enrichment and transformation through the recourse to other passages in other *zhang*, that is, through a thickening of the context, it also enhances the capacity of the text to insist on itself. An individual *zhang* or fragment thereof can do little to ward off frivolous impositions of meaning or violent distortions; there is not enough context. Once the homogeneity hypothesis is established, however, the commentator has to come up with a homogeneous interpretation of the entire text. While the text has no way of directly challenging the commentator's assumptions about the specific content of the homogeneity, it is able, through its sheer length and diversity, to challenge the validity, economy, and elegance of each specific comment, creating enough glaring non sequiturs and forcing him to disregard unexplainable matter. This allows the reader to dissociate himself from the commentator, and demand or create another reading, in which the assumptions about the specific basis of the text's homogeneity are better borne out by comments on individual passages.

This still means that, in a text such as the *Laozi* with its absent subjects, diffuse grammar, and implicit links, it is the commentator who constructs the text. But he is not free in his construction. He operates within the constraints imposed by the homogeneity hypothesis and the openness offered by a text with unreliable wording, and he has to negotiate his way around the obstacles the individual phrases and sections put in his way with the help of interpretive techniques accepted as legitimate by his own—and very demanding—intellectual environment.

The Potentiality of the Text: Comparing Different Commentary Constructions of the Laozi

In the conversation with Pei Hui, Wang Bi had spelled out the common theme of the Sage and Laozi, the relationship of "negativity," *wu* 無, with the ten thousand kinds of entities. In the *LZWZLL*, Wang Bi claims that "the book of Laozi can almost [as Confucius said about the *Shijing*] 'be summed up in one phrase,' ah: Emulating the root [by way] of bringing to rest the stem and branches [growing from it]—that is all!" 崇本息末而已矣.[150] In another section of the *LZWZLL*, he specifies this further:

- To respond to and not to act upon.

- To adapt and not to initiate.

- To emulate the root by way of bringing to rest its [the root's] outgrowth.

- To keep to the mother by way of maintaining [her] offspring.

- To hold lightly indeed skill and arts [of government as a means to control the people].

- "Act [on dangers to one's life and position as a ruler]" while "they have not now come about."

- Not to "put the blame on others" but necessarily to seek all [mistakes] in oneself [as the lord]

  - These are its [i.e., the *Laozi* text's] key points.[151]

We are not inquiring here whether Wang Bi's construction of the *Laozi* reconstructs the "original meaning," if ever there was such a thing. This section will treat the above quoted conclusion about the basic purport of the *Laozi* as hypothesis and will study the interpretive devices used by Wang Bi to verify and specify this hypothesis. The result should be a catalogue of indentifiable devices formulated as a set of rules of interpretation, the validity of which was accepted even by commentators disagreeing with Wang Bi on important philosophical points such as Zhong Hui.

The analysis will proceed in three steps. First, some *zhang* are analyzed in their entirety against the background of other commentaries so as to provide an introduction to the particularity of Wang Bi's commentary as well as the complex interaction of the different devices of commenting used by Wang Bi. Second, the various devices will be documented and analyzed one by one. Third, I shall try to draw general conclusions from Wang Bi's strategies of commenting with regard to his own construction of the text, the shared assumptions about legitimate commenting strategies, and with regard to the nature of what is called "text." The Wang Bi *Laozi* text as well as the Wang Bi *Commentary* text used below are based on my critical edition in *Wang Bi: The Structure of the Laozi's Pointers and Commentary on the Laozi: Critical Edition of the Text, Translation and Commentary.*

Example 1: *Laozi* 17.1

Text:
大上下知有之

Commentary:
大上謂大人也　大人在上　故曰大上　大人在上　居無為之事
行不言之教　萬物作焉而不為始　故下知有之而已

The *Laozi* sentence is far from clear in terms of both grammar and content. That many different options for its grammatical as well as content construction existed will be shown later after the analysis of Wang Bi's construction.

Wang Bi first proceeds to establish the subject of the first half of the *Laozi*'s phrase, *da shang* 大上. Most current texts read *tai* 太 for *da* 大. *Tai* is an adnoun modifying a noun, and if Wang Bi's text had this character, reading it as a noun "the Great [Man]" would have been ungrammatical and lacking in elegance. That Wang Bi's *Laozi* text read *da* 大 is confirmed by Lu Deming, and, even more important, substantiated as a relevant early reading by both Mawangdui MSS as well as Guodian C. Reading *da* 大 as a noun "something/someone great" is possible. Wang Bi identifies the *da* 大 in *dashang* 大上 as the "Great Man," *daren* 大人. This Great Man is a prominent character in the first hexagram of the *Zhouyi*, which provides internal evidence for the fact that Wang's text read *da* 大.

There remains the problem, however, of directly linking the Great Man with the other protagonists of the *Laozi*. The *Zhouyi* refers to the Great Man through the symbol of the dragon, and with the term gentleman, *junzi*. The *wenyan* 文言 commentary (attributed to Confucius) to the fifth position further identifies this dragon/Great Man/*junzi* as the Sage, *shengren* 聖人, a character familiar from other parts of the *Laozi*. The identification of the Great Man of hexagram 1 of the *Zhouyi* with the Sage in the *Laozi* is repeated by Wang Bi in his commentary on *Laozi* 5.2. Commenting on the second part of the *Laozi* statement that "Heaven and Earth are not kindly; for them the ten thousand kinds of entities are like straw and dogs. The Sage is not kindly; for him the Hundred Families are like straw and dogs," Wang Bi explains this juxtaposition of the Sage with Heaven and Earth by saying "the Sage harmonizes his capacity/receipt with [that of] Heaven and Earth"; from "harmonizes" to the end, this statement repeats a statement of the *wenyan* to hexagram 1 of the *Zhouyi*, where the subject of the phrase, however, is not the Sage, but the Great Man. In his commentary on *Laozi* 17.1, Wang Bi also establishes a direct link between the Great [Man] and the Sage. He writes "If the Great Man is at the top, he takes residence in management without interference and practices teaching without words [so that] the ten thousand entities come about but he does not initiate them." The entire passage from "he takes residence" to the end is a quotation from *Laozi* 2.2 and 2.3. Wang Bi relies on the fact that the reader will remember that the subject of the statement in *Laozi* 2.2 and 2.3 is the Sage.

In the *wenyan* commentary to this hexagram the result of the Great Man's occupation of the fifth position is social harmony. "Once the Sage is going about [in the highly visible position of the ruler being as high in the fifth position as if he were 'in the Heavens,'] the ten thousand kinds of entities perceive him [with the consequence that] those rooted in Heaven will associate with things above, those rooted in Earth will associate with things below so that each follows its own kind."[152] The commentary does not claim what the Sage, once arrived in the ruler's position, will busy himself about. Evidently he neither acts nor teaches, but his sheer presence in this position ensures the self-regulating interaction of the ten thousand kinds of entities. This *wenyan* commentary thus restates the core points of the *Laozi* quotation adduced by Wang Bi, confirming the compatibility of the *da* 大, the *daren* 大人, and the *shengren* 聖人. In terms of commentary strategy, Wang Bi thus verifies the plausibility of identifying one term with another by looking at parallelisms in the context in which the two texts occur. In this construction, the *Laozi* phrase thus does have (which is not always the case) a subject, the Great/Great Man/*junzi*/Sage. The Great [Man] in *Laozi* 17.1 is linked up with other statements in the *Laozi* and elsewhere about the Sage's ordering society.

This identification, which has nothing violent about it, is part of a strategy of textual implosion. The individual terms are not taken at face value but read under the assumption that they are ever new attempts to use the means of language to point at something beyond language's reach. They are therefore read from the point of view of their common denominator, not from the perspective of their surface variety. This implosive commenting can, as in the present case, cross textual borderlines if the texts in question deal with the same fundamental issues. This identification of the *da* 大 of our *Laozi* text with the *daren* 大人 of the *Zhouyi*, who there is identified with the *junzi* and the Sage, now opens the way for Wang Bi to see whether there are statements about the Sage in the *Laozi* which could help elucidate the remainder of *Laozi* 17.1. As for the reader, he will take this identification as a hypothesis to be verified by the construction of the remainder of the phrase and the *zhang*.

From Wang Bi's procedure, we define a first rule guiding him in his commenting and establishing an intersubjective basis of verification:

All surface variety of terminology notwithstanding, the philosophical texts like the *Laozi*, the *Zhouyi*, and the *Lunyu* deal with the same few core issues, among them the Sage. They are written by Sages or their close seconds such as Laozi. The truth these Sages embody is one, and so is their teaching, whatever material or form of communication they might use for exemplification. It is thus a legitimate and rational procedure to identify the core notions across terminological variety and textual borders on the basis of context similarity. On this basis it is then legitimate to use the less ambiguous statement concerning term y (for example *da ren* 大人 in the *Zhouyi*) to help construct the meaning of a more ambiguous statement about a term x identified with it (for example *da* 大 in) *Laozi* 17.1).

This rule thus supports the following procedures:

- Implosion of the surface text variety into subtext commonality on the basis of context.

- Usage, for the construction of the meaning of statements concerning subject x, of statements from elsewhere within the text or from other legitimized texts concerning other subjects that are identical with or have been identified with subject x. The procedure will be called context enrichment. The availability of such parallel texts also enhances the plausibility of the interpretation of the statement about subject x.

At the same time this rule dismisses the following procedures as illegitimate:

- Random identification of surface text items with materials extraneous to the text or with structures different from the text at hand.

- Random claims for identity of the meaning of terms on the basis of identical wording. In the present case, other uses of *da* 大 in the *Laozi* are irrelevant.

- Random use of text-internal or extraneous materials for the construction of meaning without prior verification that these other materials in fact pertain to the same subject.

In identifying the subject of the *Laozi*'s sentence, Wang Bi at the same time eliminates a potential second part of the subject, *shang* 上. Other commentators have in fact constructed *tai shang* 太上 as a binomial. By writing 大上謂大人也 (*da shang* refers to the Great Man) and not writing 大上大人也 (*da shang* is the Great Man), he left the option for 上 to be a verb. In his next phrase, he spells this out by saying 大人在上，故曰大上, "the Great Man rests in the topmost [position]; that is why [the *Laozi*] says: '[If] the Great [Man] is at the top.'" The translation of 在 as "rests" is based on Wang Bi's commentary to the parallel in the *Zhouyi*, where the fifth line of the first hexagram has the note 飛龍在天. Wang Bi's comment focuses on the expression 在. He says: "As [the dragon] neither acts [in the manner he does in the third position] nor wavers [in the manner he does in the fourth position, because both are only transitional on his way to the supreme fifth position], but [simply] 'rests in Heaven' 在天, how else should he do this but by 'being aflight.' That is why [the *Zhouyi*] says: 'Aflight the dragon [rests in the Heavens]'."[153]

This construction has to do two things: first, to be viable in terms of the grammatical and content potential of 上, which it is; second, to become part of the verification for the hypothesis that the *da* 大 in fact refers to the Great Man.

In the *Zhouyi* hexagram 1, the Great Man can be in very different positions, from being hidden in the first position to being on the throne in the fifth to being arrogant in the sixth. Within the *Zhouyi* hexagrams, the highest position, that of the ruler, is the fifth, not the sixth. The line statement for the fifth position reads "aflight the dragon rests in the Heavens. [They] have the benefit of seeing the Great Man." The *wenyan* commentary identifies those who have this advantage. In its notes for this fifth line, the "Master" [Confucius] is quoted as saying that this means 聖人作而萬物睹, that "once the Sage is going about [in the highly visible position of the ruler, being as high as if he were 'in the Heavens'], the ten thousand kinds of entities perceive [him, that is, have 'the benefit of seeing the Great Man']."[154] The context of the expression "Great Man" in the *Zhouyi* thus supports the plausibility of Wang Bi's construction of *shang* 上 as a verb with the meaning "being in the topmost [position]."

Extrapolating from Wang's commentary, we have to translate the first two characters as "the" "Great [Man] is in the topmost [position]." Only the rest of the phrase will give us enough context to determine the modality of this statement, which might be factual (the Great [Man] is in the topmost [position]), conditional (if or once the Great [Man] is . . .), or hypothetical (if the Great [Man] were . . .).

Is a *Laozi* statement about the Great Man/Sage in the ruler's position a plausible construct? The *Laozi* does not explicitly speak of the Sage as ruler, and, while the Sages in Ban Gu's "Tables of Personalities from Ancient and Recent Times" were mostly rulers, at least the last of them, Confucius, was not, so that there was a faint possibility to read the Sage as a term for a unique and especially endowed being, but not necessarily one in charge of society as a whole.

The *Laozi*'s statements about the Sage, however, are mostly such that they make sense only under the condition that the Sage is indeed in a ruler's position, where each of his actions or inactions would affect all the Hundred Families or even ten thousand kinds of entities. In the standard construction (*Laozi* 5, 7, 77) the Sage imitates Heaven and Earth or the Dao so that his attitude and action, as theirs, has a bearing on the ten thousand kinds of entities. In other constructions (*Laozi* 2, 3, 12, 19, 22, 26 [where the *junzi* appears as an equivalent of the Sage], 27, 28, 29, 49, 57, 58, 60, 63, 64, 71, 72, 78), the Sage is said to practice the correct way of governing a state and holding on to his position as a ruler, which again presupposes him to be in that position. While none of these parallels prove Wang Bi's reading of *da shang* 大上, they enrich the context enough to substantiate its plausibility.

Wang Bi's reading of 大 as "Great [Man]" is further bolstered by the immediate context. The subsequent three *Laozi* phrases all begin with "the one after [this one]," 其次. This formula would normally presuppose that "the one before [this one]" is some human being, which ties in with the Great [Man]. The 次 suggests a hierarchy, with the Great [Man] being superior to those mentioned in the following sentences. In Wang Bi's reading, the first and the three following phrases of *Laozi* 17 describe a series of rulers of ever lower quality, beginning with the Great Man and ending with a ruler who is "not [even] taken seriously" by the lower orders.

For this construct Wang Bi finds an echo in *Laozi* 38. There, Wang Bi reads the *Laozi* as describing various techniques of government. He establishes a qualitative difference between the noninterference of the ruler who has the "highest receipt/capacity"

上德, and all others who do interfere and thus are of "inferior receipt/capacity," *xia de* 下德. These latter again are graded from the one who makes use of "kindliness," *ren* 仁, to the one who makes use of "foresight," *qianzhi* 前智, which is "the beginning of inanity." *Laozi* 17.2ff. does not define the governmental strategies of the series following the Great Man. But in his commentary, Wang Bi supplements them from *Laozi* 38.

The Great Man himself is not directly defined in terms of *zhang* 38, but the logical slot would be that of the ruler described there as having "highest receipt/capacity" 上德. That Wang Bi thought so is evident from his commentary to the fifth line of the first hexagram, where he says of the Great Man that "by means of his supreme capacity 至德 he rests in the grandest position." The two terms 至德 and 上德 are used in the same sense.

In *Laozi* 38, the first after the Great Man uses "kindliness" 仁, as does the next to the highest in *Laozi* 17.2ff.; the next makes use of authority, *wei quan* 威權, and the last of "intelligence," *zhi* 智, the term that Wang Bi translates as "foresight" in his commentary to *Laozi* 38. The list in *Laozi* 17 is shorter than in *Laozi* 38; Wang Bi identified the highest and the lowest in both series. The term *wei quan* 威權 is not used in either text of or commentary to *Laozi* 38, but it must stand as a summary term for the devices "justice" and "ritual," *yi* 義 and *li* 禮, mentioned there. The parallel hierarchies of governmental devices in *Laozi* 17 and *Laozi* 38 are cited by Wang Bi through implicit references as proof of the plausibility of his reading of *Laozi* 17. The construction of the reading of 大上 also settles that of the rest of the first phrase as meaning "those below know that He [the Great Man] exists."

Wang Bi "translates" this phrase by adding to the *Laozi*'s 下知有之 the characters 而已, forcing a translation of the *Laozi* 17.1 as

If the Great [Man] is at the top, those below know [only] that He exists [and nothing more].

This reading can claim internal logic. As the Sage brings about the social harmony of the Hundred Families without interfering with action or laying down the line with words, there are no acts or words through which they could define him. They are as unable to define him as it is impossible to define the Way itself, which the

Sage embodies, a theme frequently repeated in the *Laozi*.[155] Language and cognition thus do have the same problem with the Dao as with the Sage; they are both undefinable, although the existence of the ten thousand kinds of entities depends on the former, and the order among the people on the latter. From this existence and order, one single firm conclusion is possible, that there is something like a Dao or a Sage, but beyond this vague notion language fails. In terms of internal consistency of the first phrase, the reading constructed by Wang Bi thus makes sense.

In terms of the overall context of the *zhang*, the identification of *xia* 下 as "those below" is confirmed by the occurrence of *baixing* 百姓, the "Hundred Families," in the last *Laozi* phrase, 17.6, to which we shall turn shortly.

The next three phrases in the *Laozi* share more or less one single pattern. They run:

其次親而譽之
其次畏之
其次侮之

It must be defined to whom the different *qi* 其 refer, who is the subject of the verbs 親而譽, 畏, and 侮, and to whom or what the different 之 at the end refer.

The *qi* 其 must refer to some subject in the previous phrase. For the first phrase quoted here, the candidates would either be the "Great Man" or "those below." The same grammatical ambivalence prevails for the remaining two terms to be identified. The meaning of these phrases cannot be constructed in an unequivocal manner independent of a fairly bold decision linking the open elements with the defined elements of the previous phrase, and determining the grammar on this basis.

Wang Bi constructs these phrases in analogy with the first phrase of this *zhang*. He is supported in this by the parallelism of the first four phrases, each of which end with a 之 after a verb. In his commentary to 其次親而譽之, Wang Bi inserts the subject "those below" 下 for 親而譽之 when he writes 使下得親而譽之也. From this it follows that 其次 in this sentence refers to someone second in quality to the Great Man, but who is also 上, in the ruler's position. This requires a translation:

If one second to him [the Great Man] is [at the top], [those below] will be close to him and praise him.

This sets the agenda for the next phrase:

If one second to him [who is second to the Great Man] is [at the top], [those below] will fear him.

and for the last phrase in this series:

If one second to him [who is second to him who is second to the Great Man] is [at the top], [those below] do not take him seriously.

The compatibility of this descending order of instruments of government especially with *Laozi* 38 has been mentioned. From these procedures we extract a further rule:

The merger of different terms depends for verification of its plausibility on the parallelism in the argumentative structure in which the different terms are embedded, and on the viability of the grammatical construction necessary to establish this parallelism.

The next phrase in the *Laozi* runs:

信不足焉，有不信。

This phrase breaks the parallelism of the previous phrase and Wang Bi therefore reads it as a summary statement concerning the descending hierarchy in those previous phrases. There are several cases in the *Laozi* where the same construction prevails. Once this decision is made, the sentence must give the reason why the attitude of "those below" towards their superiors deteriorates the lower the quality of these superiors. This decision about the probable meaning defines the different subjects for the first and second halves in accordance with those of the previous sentences, forcing a first translation:

If the *xin* 信 [of the ruler] is insufficient, there will be absence of *xin* 信 [among those below].

The consecutive sequence between the two halves is established by Wang Bi's insertion of *ze* 則 between the two when he writes 信不足焉，則有不信. Wang Bi's commentary runs:

> This means they [those below] follow those above. If one is reining in the body but misses [its original] nature, virulent diseases will spring up. If one is supporting entities but misses [their] true [essence], then transgressions will occur [committed by them]. It is the Way of That-which-is-of-itself-what-it-is that if credibility [of those above] is not sufficient, there will be a lack of credibility [among those below]. That which in one's [a ruler's] own position is insufficient[ly regulated] cannot be regulated through intelligence.

Xin 信 is interpreted here as remaining true to the "[original] nature," *xing* 性, or "true [nature]," *zhen* 真. In this reading of the term, Wang Bi finds support in *Laozi* 21.5, where he reads *xin* as the "credible evidence" present in the ten thousand kinds of entities if they "relate back" to their abstruse origin. In the same manner, Confucius claims superiority over Laozi in terms of *xin* 信.[156] Wang Bi's reading thus finds support in other authenticated texts. Wang Bi constructs the *Laozi* 17.5 phrase in the following manner:

> [In short,] as credibility [of those at the top who are of lower calibre than the Great Man] is lacking, there is, [as a consequence] absence of credibility [among the people below].

Remains the last phrase of this *zhang*, which runs:

猶兮其貴言也功成事遂而百姓皆曰我自然

The *qi* 其 in the first part again refers to an unnamed subject, which has to be constructed. The term *baixing* 百姓, "Hundred Families," links up with "those below" in the first phrase (and from there in the subsequent phrases). The consequences of the attitude of the Great Man of *Laozi* 17.1 are that "achievements are completed and processes followed through" 功成事遂, and are therefore fundamentally different from the chaotic developments following the government strategies of the rulers of lower caliber. Wang Bi therefore identifies the Great Man as the only remaining actor fitting the requirements of this *qi* 其. He does this by repeating, in his commentary, the phrase characterizing the Great Man in the commentary on *Laozi* 17.1, that "he takes residence in management without interference and practices teaching without words." As a consequence of this, he argues, the text speaks of "achievements completed and processes followed through."

Wang Bi comments on the words 猶兮, saying "being undecided 猶兮 means that it is impossible to make out any clues in his [the Great Man's expression] and that it is impossible to discern his [the Great Man's] intentions." The impossibility, however, of discerning the specifics of his meaning has the consequence that "his words are being respected [by those below]." Extrapolating from these comments, *Laozi* 17.6 has to be translated:

> Undecided he is [the Great Man, if at the top]! [But] his words are being respected [by those below]!

As a consequence of his being "undecided" it is impossible for the Hundred Families to define in any precise terms the actions and intentions of the Great Man at the top. The result of his diffuseness is that, as Wang Bi says in the commentary, no one "can alter his words" and thus "by necessity they will be followed." In this way the Great Man is responsible for maintaining the self-regulative process of society, a point just stated by Wang Bi as a general consensus. From this follows the paradox that, although the entire social order with the people's "achievements completed and processes followed through" is in the last count due to the Great Man's being in the ruler's position, as they come about without his interfering in any manner, the Hundred Families are bound to assume that this regulation will ensue from the interrelated regulation of the structure of their own natures. The translation of the subsequent part thus runs:

> [If in this manner the Hundred Families'] achievements are completed and processes followed through, the Hundred Families all say "we are like this [that is, have this bountiful life] spontaneously."

This reading of the last phrase reinforces the reading of the first phrase of this *zhang*. It has the same cast, the Great Man and the

Hundred Families, and restates and specifies some of the propositions of the first sentence. "Those below" in the first phrase who, if a Great Man is at the top, "know only that he exists" but are unable to spell out his particular features and contributions, return in the last phrase as the Hundred Families who conclude from the undefinability of the Great Man at the top that regulated order springs from the preset harmony of their own natures.

In this context, Wang Bi had to make a decision whose achievements and processes the text was talking about. The immediate context suggests either that they are the Sage's, because he is the focus of the sentence where the statement is made, or the Hundred Families', because otherwise it would not make sense that they attribute them to their own natures. From the *Lunyu* parallel quoted below, a thick context suggests the second variant, for which Wang Bi also opted. These parallels help support the internal consistency of Wang Bi's construction of this *zhang*.

Proceeding in the now familiar way of verification, we can check the plausibility of Wang Bi's clarification of this obscure passage by looking for other statements in the *Laozi* and other authenticated texts such as the *Zhouyi* and the *Lunyu* that might claim that, if a Sage is ruling society, the people will at best know that he exists, but will be unable to define him.

Laozi 15.1 says "those in antiquity who were well versed in the Way were recondite and abstruse, so deep that they could not be discerned 古之善為道者，微妙玄通，深不可識. As they are undiscernable, [I] say when forced to give a sketch of them: Hesitant [they are] as if crossing a [frozen] river in winter." In his commentary to *Laozi* 15.2, Wang Bi identifies "those in antiquity who were well-versed in the Way" as "persons of highest receipt/capacity" 上德之人, a term from *zhang* 38 already familiar as being identified with the Great Man and the Sage. This parallel clearly enhances the probability of the reading of Wang Bi's *Laozi* 17.1. The expression "forced to give a sketch of them" 強為之容 closely resembles a similar statement in *Laozi* 25.4ff. about the "thing" from 21.1 "that completes out of the diffuse. It is born before Heaven and Earth." About this entity the *Laozi* writes "I do not know its name. Therefore, forced, [I] give it the style 字 'Way.' And when forced to make up a name for it, I would say '[it is] great.'" As the Sage is "well-versed in the Way," they share many of the same features.

The impossibility of specifically defining the Way thus matches the impossibility of specifically defining the Sage, and further strengthens Wang Bi's case. In *Laozi* 70, the authorial "I" compares itself with the Sage. The "I" claims that his "words are very easy to understand and [his activities] very easy to put into practice." Still, "of the others, no one is able to understand them [my words] and put them [my activities] into practice." The *zhang* ends with the statement that the Sage is even harder to discern. "This is why the Sage wears coarse cloth, but carries a piece of jade in his bosom." Wang Bi reads the coarse cloth as meaning that "he joins in the same dust with them [the other entities]" like the wise ruler in *Laozi* 56.6. That "he carries a piece of jade in his bosom" is read to mean that "he is treasuring his true [nature]." Wang Bi thus concludes: "The reason why the Sage is hard to discern is [in fact] that he 'joins in the same dust [with the others],' but does not stand out, that he 'carries a piece of jade in his bosom' but does not let it show forth." Within the *Laozi* itself, Wang Bi thus finds good support for the probability of his reading of 17.1.

There is even stronger support from none other than Confucius himself. In *Lunyu* 8.19 for which a commentary by Wang Bi survives, Confucius says:

> Great indeed was Yao being the ruler! Immeasurable he was! Only Heaven is great, and only Yao was a match for it. So boundless was he [Yao], that the people were unable to define him. 大哉堯之為君也 巍巍乎 唯天為大唯堯則之 蕩蕩乎 民無能名焉

Wang Bi's commentary runs:

> The Sage [alone] has the capacity of imitating Heaven. That is why, when the [text] says "only Yao imitated it," it means that only Yao at this time fully imitated Heaven's Way. "Immeasurable," *weiwei* 巍巍, is a designation for being without shape and definition. Generally speaking, what a definition defines arises out of goodness [of the object] having something [specific] in which it "manifests" itself [as the next phrase of the *Lunyu* says] and kindness [of the object] having something [particular] to which it attaches itself. Goodness and evil [,however], hinge on each other so that the particulars of definitions take shape [that is, once there is goodness, there is

also evil]. But if there is [,as in a true Sage,] great love without any personal preference, where would [particular] kindness find a place [with him]? The highest goodness [read *shan* 善 for *mei* 美] [like that of the Sage] has no one-sidedness; where then should a [necessarily particular] definition [of this goodness] arise? That is why [Yao] in his imitation of Heaven and completion of the transformation [of the people] was identical in [his] Way with That-which-is-of-itself-what-it-is, and neither preferred his own sons [for the succession], nor lorded it over his ministers. [As a consequence,] the wicked ones were automatically punished [without the Sage's intervention] and the good ones automatically "achieved" 功 but, while [the good ones] "completed" [their] "achievements," 功成 [in accordance with the next sentence of the *Lunyu*, which runs 巍巍乎其有成功也 "immeasurable indeed is the way in which he manages the completion of achievements"] it was not he [the Sage] who established their renown, and, while punishment was inflicted [on the wicked], it was not he [the Sage] who used physical punishment on them. [Thus] "the Hundred Families make daily use of him but do not know" by what means [these results] come about [as the *Xici* 7.3.8 says about the Way]. How, then could they have a definition for him?[157]

Confucius himself thus confirms for the Sage in the ruling position what the *Laozi* claims, namely that "those below" or the "Hundred Families," who are called here the "people," 民 "know [only] that he exists," but that he is so vast and all-encompassing that they have no way of defining him; yet in the last count the social process in which the good ones complete their achievements and the evil ones get punished all hinge on him.[158] The quotation from the *Xici* inserted into the *Lunyu* commentary again links the Sage to what he embodies, the Way itself. In fact, Wang Bi takes the basic structure of the statement here in the *Laozi* from a series of statements about the Way. Their standard form appears in the commentary to *Laozi* 1.2: "The Way begins and completes the ten thousand kinds of entities by means of [its] featurelessness and namelessness. That the ten thousand kinds of entities are begun and completed by it [the Way] but that they do not know that by which these [two, their beginning and completion] come to be as they are is [its aspect of being] Dark-and-Dark-Again."

The parallel with the *Lunyu* phrase "immeasurable indeed is the way in which he manages the completion of achievements" allows Wang Bi to save himself another description of the way in which a Sage manages to have the people's "achievements completed and processes followed through." The argument is too well known. The beneficiaries are the good ones, who will have their achievements completed [and the evil ones will have their punishment meted out], but this self-regulation of society comes about through the fuzzy noninterference of the Sage in the ruler's position.

Wang Bi's interpretation of *gui yan* 貴言 is modeled after the *guishen* 貴身 in *Laozi* 13.5, where *gui* also is read as meaning "to be respected" in the sense that "no other entity can change him." Wang Bi thus manages to construct a text that gives a consistent reading to the *zhang* in question: which is viable in terms of its grammar; which is confirmed in the plausibility of its key propositions by a sizable number of other passages in the *Laozi* itself in Wang Bi's interpretation of them, and by very close parallels in other authenticated classical texts such as the *Lunyu* and the *Zhouyi*; and the identifications of which (especially with regard to the *da shang* 大上 the Great Man at the top and the *xia* 下 as "those below," the people) is well confirmed by significant textual parallels. The material on which his analysis of the argument of the *zhang* rests is taken mostly from the *zhang* itself and from parallels in the *Laozi*, not introduced at random on the basis of a religious or ideological belief.

Wang Bi's construction does not contain, at the present level of our reading, polemics against other commentators. Where we do not have the real countertexts, its character as a construction set against others becomes evident only when actually confronted with other potential constructions, a confrontation we shall now undertake. Ideally, we would insert here comments from texts we could identify as Wang Bi's countertexts. Apart from Zhuang Zun, to whom there probably is a link of tradition, there is no visible trace of Wang Bi talking back to surviving commentaries which are or might be earlier than his. However, the constructions presented by these other commentators will allow us to measure the range of the potentiality of the *Laozi* text, and thus to gauge the difficulties and challenges Wang Bi was facing when writing his own commentary. At the same time, this allows us to highlight his method of commenting by confronting it with other options. Last but not least, it will show the enormous historical range of content and grammatically accepted constructs the *Laozi* had by then developed and thus contribute to our understanding of the complex and highly interactive relationship between text and reading.

Zhuang Zun's reading of this *zhang* prefigured that by Wang Bi. His commentary to the first sentence does not survive. The second sentence, however, which in the textual family to which Zhuang Zun's text according to Shima Kuniō belonged read 其次親之譽之, Zhuang Zun comments: "The others rejoice in [him] being the lord and call him 'emperor'" 人樂為主曰帝. This means that Zhuang Zun identified the *xia* 下 of the first *Laozi* sentence as 人, "the others," more specifically the people, and that he identified the *tai shang* 太上 (for this is how this textual tradition read Wang Bi's 大上) of the first phrase with someone still higher than the "emperor," *di* 帝. It is possible but not probable that Zhuang (like Wang Bi) read 上 as a verb "being at the top," because it would make *tai* 太 into an awkward noun. It is probable that he read *taishang* 太上 as a compound, "the Great Supreme," in the grammatical function of an object preceding the verb for emphasis, "as to the Great Supreme, those below know [only] that he exists." The difference is not too important, however, because in Zhuang Zun's reading, too, the person spoken of in the expression 太上 is in the ruler's position, is the ruler of the highest caliber, and the text deals with the perception of the various types of rulers among the lower orders. The second phrase thus was read by Zhuang Zun: "The one after him [who is the ruler of highest caliber] [they, those below,] were close to and praised."

This basic congruity between the two commentaries is confirmed by Zhuang Zun's comment on the next *Laozi* phrase, which in his textual family read 其次畏之侮之, a reading that reduces from four to three the types of rulers discussed. Zhuang Zun writes 嗟之嘆之，故謂之王: "They sigh about him and lament about him, therefore they speak of him [only as] 'king'." The two terms "sigh" and "lament" comment on the terms 畏 and 侮 respectively. Rather than being read as a "translation" of these terms into synonyms, they must be seen as consequences of the terms used in the *Laozi*.[159]

For the explanation of these terms, however, Zhuang Zun does not cite other material from the *Laozi*; his commentary does not

provide the proof of the plausibility of his construction. The explanatory terms used in his comment do not appear elsewhere in the
Laozi, the hierarchy of the appellations of the various types of rulers
does not appear elsewhere in the *Laozi*, and the reason why the
succeeding kinds of rulers cause such reactions among their subjects
is not explained. Extrapolating from Zhuang Zun, the *Laozi* thus
read: "The one after this one [who is second in caliber to the highest]
[they, those below] dread and loathe." No further comments by
Zhuang Zun on this *zhang* survive; thus we ignore his construction
of the rest.

Wang Bi's reading followed or coincided with Zhuang Zun's
construction for the first two phrases. His method of proceeding,
however, is quite different. By enriching the context with parallels,
he manages to establish the plausibility of his construction in the
framework of the *Laozi* and other authenticated texts, making what
in Zhuang Zun was a stated belief into an argued construct, the
internal logic of which is translucent.

Going back further to the *Hanfeizi*, we do not have an interpretation of this *zhang* in his chapter on the *Laozi*, but in chapter 16,
Nan san 難三, inserted into a critical analysis of the advice concerning policy, *zheng* 政, given by Confucius to three different princes,
the first phrase of *Laozi* 17 is quoted as 太上下智有之. In each case
the advice given was different, and Zigong asked the master for
the reason. The problems they were facing were different is the
answer. The answer to Prince Gao of Ye was: "[Correct] policy
consists in cherishing those close by and attracting those far off"
悦近而來遠. The *Hanfeizi* goes on to quote "someone," *huo* 或 as
saying that:

> the answers of Confucius are words that will bring down a
> state 亡國之言也. The people of Ye are insubordinate in their
> hearts, and to tell [the prince] to benefit those who are close by
> and attract those far away is to teach people to cherish favors.
> But a policy of giving favors means that those who have no
> merit will get emoluments, while those who have committed
> a crime get away with it. That is the way to demolish
> the laws!

The text then continues to point out how Yao and Shun proceeded
and ends:

An enlightened prince will spot small treachery in its minute [beginnings] and consequently there will be no big conspiracy among the people; he will mete out small punishments in the initial stages, and consequently there will be no great rebellion among the people. This is called [in *Laozi* 63] "make provisions for difficulties while they still are easy [to be handled], act on great [problems] while they are still small." Now those who have merits definitely have to get their reward; those rewarded are not obliged to the prince as [their rewards] are brought about by [their] efforts. Those who have committed crimes definitely have to get punished, but those punished will not resent the authorities, since [their punishment] is generated by their crimes. The people know 知 that punishment and rewards (賞 for 罰) both originate in their own [behavior] and therefore they will exert themselves to gain merit and profit in the [state] enterprise, but will not receive presents from their prince.

Here follows the passage 太上下智有之　此言太上之下民無説〔＝悦〕也安取懷惠之民上　君之民無利害説以悦近來遠亦可舍己. It starts with the *Laozi* quotation 太上下智有之 and then proceeds to give an explanation. I have given it first without spacing. The "commentary" begins 此言太上之下民無説（＝悦）也. The break can be either 此言太上之下　民無説（＝悦）也 or 此言太上之下民　無説（＝悦）也. The former, "under an optimal ruler, the people will . . ." is more likely, but the difference to the latter, "the lowly people under an optimal ruler will . . .," is marginal for our purposes. Under both readings it is evident that this text "translates" the *Laozi*'s 太上下 into 太上之下 or 太上之下民, which means it makes the break after 下 to form a 太上下　智有之 (as opposed to Wang Bi's 太上　下智有之).[160] The translation now is without problems:

[As the *Laozi* says] "Under an optimal [ruler] [the people] know [why] they [= rewards and punishments] are there [that is, they are a consequence of their own action]."[161] This means: As under an optimal [kind of ruler] the people do not cherish [any particular dispensations from their ruler], where would one get people cherishing favors? The people of the highest [kinds] of prince are without benefits or damages [from their prince,] which means that [the policy] of cherishing those close by and attracting those far away may also be discarded.[162]

The argument here is that a supreme kind of ruler will set up things in a way that people know their fortune depends on the evaluation of their action by abstract and anonymous laws, not on the favors or disfavors of the ruler. We can surmise from this context that the *Hanfeizi* read the next passages of the *Laozi* much like Zhuang (Yan) Zun and Wang Bi as describing the people's reactions to rulers of lower quality. The *Wenzi* 文子, large parts of which antedate the *Hanfeizi*, might in fact be the background for the *Hanfeizi* statement. It is disturbing that a long *Wenzi* text on bamboo strips discovered in 1973 in the Han dynasty tomb no. 40 in Dingxian 定縣 in Hebei should have to wait until December 1995 for its publication.[163] This find seems to prove, however, that the surviving text by and large consists of pre-Han material. The age of the section used here is confirmed by the fact that it reappears verbatim with minor variants in the *Huainanzi* 淮南子.[164] The first phrase of *Laozi* 17.1 appears here in a long paragraph detailing the deterioration of rulers' policies from the "emperors," *di* 帝, over the "kings," *wang* 王, to the "hegemons," *ba* 霸. The section confronts the government technique of the Sage who "with regard to other entities is without any [particular activity]" 於物無有 with rulers of the lower order who "put emphasis on favors or on violent suppression" 重為慧（＝惠）重為暴. The consequences are the same as in the *Hanfeizi*: once favors are distributed, "those without merits are richly rewarded, those without efforts to show receive high emoluments," and, once a ruler exerts violent suppression, "he will punish at random so that those without crime will go to their death, and those who practice the Dao will receive physical punishment."

Thus [the ruler] who goes in for favors in this very act generates cunningness, and [the ruler] who exerts violent suppression in this very act produces chaos, and the mentality of cunning and chaos is the mode of a doomed state. Thus, if there are punishments in the state and the ruler is without [personal] rage, if there are rewards at the court and the prince is not the one who gives them, those who are being punished will not resent the prince, because [the punishment] it apportioned by the crime; and those who are being rewarded are not grateful to their lord because it is brought about by their merit. The people know[165] that the arrival of rewards and punishments is throughout brought about by their own [actions]. Consequently they make efforts to gain merit and take care of their duties and do not receive gratuities from others. As a consequence the courts are deserted and there are no traces from feet, while the fields are being opened and there are no weeds.

Next comes the decisive phrase 故太上下知有之 or 故太上下知而有之. This is followed by a lengthy description of the ruler correctly practicing the Way of the king so that society regulates itself "without anything emanating from him" 莫出於己. The text has to be interpunctuated in the same manner as I have suggested for the *Hanfeizi* text, namely 太上下 知有之, and translated "Under an optimal [ruler] [the people] know [why] they [= rewards and punishments] are there."[166]

The *Wenzi*, *Hanfeizi*, and *Huainanzi* agree in their contextualization of the first phrase of *Laozi* 17.1, and in their grammatical treatment of it. It cannot be proved that they saw this text as a part of the *Laozi*, but they all quote other elements from other parts of the *Laozi* in the immediate vicinity of the phrase under consideration here and have dealt with the *Laozi* extensively. The three texts are very closely linked with two of them, the *Wenzi* and *Huainanzi* being by and large identical, and the *Hanfeizi* inserting the whole into an argument supported with a statement of Confucius. While the three texts insert the text into a sequence of ever-lower quality rulers as does Wang Bi, all three differ from him by assigning a different grammatical construction and particular meaning to the phrase. The reading is not exactly elegant, because it is at some distance from the spontaneous reading. The 知 (智) 有之 or 知而有之 is "translated" in fact by the phrase 民知賞誅之來皆生於身 or 民知賞誅之 皆起於身也 (*Hanfeizi*): "The people know that the arrival of rewards and punishments is throughout brought about by their own [actions]." This translation provides the subject (民), the object (賞誅), and translates the opaque 有 into a notion of "why [it] is there" with terms such as 來, 生 and 起.

The late Later Han Xiang Er 想爾 commentary presents a completely different construction. For the first *Laozi* phrase, its text has 太上 instead of 大上. The commentary runs:

知道上知也知（也）惡事下知也雖有上知當具識惡事改之不敢為也。

This commentary survives in a single manuscript and contains many mistakes. In the present case, 也 after 知 in the second phrase is, I believe, a scribal error due to the mechanical repetition of the 知也 immediately preceding.[167] The commentary thus translates:

To understand the Way is supreme knowledge. To understand evil affairs is lower knowledge. Even if one has supreme knowledge, one should [also] be completely familiar with evil affairs [so that one might] reeducate them [who perpetrate evil affairs] and [thus manage it that they] will not dare to perpetrate them.

The Xiang Er commentary reads the *taishang* 太上 of *Laozi* 17.1 as an abbreviated form of "someone who has supreme knowledge," interpolating the term "knowledge." The legitimation for this fairly radical step comes from the contrast with *xiazhi* 下知, lower knowledge. Grammatically, the *taishang* with his supreme knowledge is the subject of the phrase, 下知 is a prepositioned object of 有, and the 之 refers back to this object. The Xiang Er reads this 有之 in a very rare turn as an imperative by translating it into *dang* 當 "should be."[168] This "should be" signals that Xiang Er reads the *Laozi* as a direct guide to action for the Daoist adept, not as a series of analytic philosophical statements. Extrapolating from this commentary, we are to read *Laozi* 17.1 instead of Wang Bi's "if the Great Man is at the top those below know [only] that he exists:"

[Having] the grand and supreme [knowledge] [also] is to have lower knowledge.

The "translation" of *xiazhi* 下知, lower knowledge into being "completely familiar with evil affairs" 具識惡事 does not claim further textual corroboration. There is no other *Laozi* text in Xiang Er's interpretation taking up the issue of having to have both higher and lower knowledge that could confirm the plausibility of this reading. The next *Laozi* phrase reads in the Xiang Er edition, as it probably did in Zhuang Zun's, 其次親之譽之. The commentary runs:

見求善之人學曉道意可親也見學善之人懃懃者可
就譽也復教勸之勉力助道宣教 。¹⁶⁹

This commentary translates as:

> Seeing a person who is striving after the good awakening to the
> meaning of the Way, he [the man with supreme knowledge]
> might befriend [this person].
>   Seeing a person who is studying to be good being very
> diligent [in his studies,] he [the man with supreme knowledge]
> might well praise [this person].
>   He will furthermore teach and encourage them [these per-
> sons to exert their strength to assist the Dao in propagating
> the teaching.

Xiang Er relates the two 之 after 親 and 譽 respectively to two
different persons. 其次 therefore has to be translated in the plural,
encompassing both persons addressed in the two 之. The 可 indicates that the 親之譽之 has again to be read as an imperative. Xiang
Er thus constructs the second *Laozi* phrase as:

> Those below [you, the one with the highest knowledge], [either]
> befriend [or] praise!

The addressee being the person with the highest knowledge,
that is, the Daoist adept with knowledge about the Way, is thus
admonished in the proper way of behaviour toward those of lesser
caliber. In this way, the point of reference for 其次 still is 太上, but
while *taishang* is the subject of the first phrase, 其次 here is an
object preceding the verb for purposes of stress. While this is grammatically possible, the shift in the subject is decidedly less elegant
than the Zhuang Zun/Wang Bi construct.
    Xiang Er gets into more trouble with the next sentence, where
his text reads:

其次畏之

Xiang Er again splits the phrase into two. The transmitted text
has him comment on this part first, and then add a separate
comment on the succeeding element 侮之. The first commentary
reads:

見惡人誠為説善 [170] 其人聞義則服
可教改也。就申道誠示之畏以天威令自改也。

This translates:

> Seeing an evil person, he [you with the highest knowledge] admonishes [that person] and explains to [that person how to do] good; if that person, once he hears sense, submits, he can be taught and reformed. That is, point out the Way, admonish and direct him [this person], strike fear [into him] by means of Heaven's majesty, and get [him] to reform himself.

This commentary requires a translation of the *Laozi* text as:

> Into those below [=those mentioned in the preceding phrase] [either] strike fear,

Then comes the second part of this *Laozi* phrase, 侮之. Xiang Er comments on this:

為惡人説善不化而甫 （笑） 之者此即芻苟 （＝芻狗） 之徒耳非人也可欺
侮 [171] 之，勿與語也。

This translates as:

> If [he with the highest knowledge] explains to an evil person [how to do] good, and [that person] does not reform but even ridicules him, then that person belongs to the category of "straw dogs" [mentioned in *Laozi* 5.1 and described there as "vulgar people" 庸庸之人, "whose spirit cannot communicate with Heaven"], and is no human being. [This person] may be mistreated, but [he with the highest knowledge] should definitely not talk with this [person].

We thus have a second change in the grammatical role of the first two characters. In the first sentence, they were the subject, in the second an object preceding the verb defined by its relationship to the preceding subject; in the third sentence, they are an object preceding the verb defined by its relationship to the object preceding the verb in the previous sentence. These ever-changing constructs for each new phrase are distinctly inferior to the more elegant solution of Zhuang Zun/Wang Bi. The *Laozi* phrase 侮之 thus reads:

[or] treat them with disdain!"

This latter treatment would be reserved for those who prove resistant to education and should be, as the Xiang Er writes on *Laozi* 5.1, "wiped out," *sha* 煞.

The Xiang Er text has the next *Laozi* phrase without the two 焉 as 信不足，有不信. The commentary runs 芧苟（＝芻狗）之徒 內信不足 故不信善之言也, which translates as, "As the inner faith of those who belong to the category of straw dogs is insufficient, they don't have faith in the words of good people." The Xiang Er commentary had constructed the preceding two groups of two verbs, each referring to a descending scale of four types of people. The structure of these two phrases was parallel, and their internal structure again repetitive. The phrase presently discussed breaks the parallelism. Wang Bi follows the rhetorical rule that such a phrase must be a general statement pertaining to the entire preceding set of parallel phrases, (or begin a new topic). Xiang Er's solution disregards this rhetorical feature and relates the phrase only to the second part of that immediately preceding, namely to those of the straw dog category. Consequently, the phrase has to be supplemented with a logical link and translated as "[The reason why they may only be mistreated but not spoken to is that], as [their] inner faith as [people] who belong to the category of straw dogs is insufficient, they don't have faith in the words of good people." Since no comparable phrase is offered on the other three types, this reading breaks the parallelism without any support within the text. Extrapolating from this category the *Laozi* phrase reads:

> As the faith [in Daoist truths of those who should be mistreated] is insufficient, it happens that they lack faith [in the words of those who teach these truths].

The Xiang Er *Laozi* text continues:

猶其貴言，成功事遂

for which the commentary runs:

道之所言無一可棄者得仙之士但貴道言故輒成功事遂也。

This commentary translates as:

There is not one of the words [uttered] by the Way that may be discarded. The adept who has achieved immortality will just hold [all] the Way's words in honor, and thus it is that at once he will "complete [his] achievement, and [his] affair will go through [that is, he will achieve immortality]."

Like Wang Bi, Xiang Er assumes that this last phrase again refers to the person addressed with the terms *taishang* or *da shang* in the very first phrase of this *zhang*. Xiang Er here refers to this person with the "grand and supreme [knowledge]" as "the adept who has achieved immortality." To explain the diffuse grammatical structure of this *Laozi* phrase, Xiang Er "translates" it, rendering 猶 as 但, inserting, on the basis of *Laozi* 35.5 道出言, "the words brought forth by the Way," 道 for 其, and adding with 故 a logical link between the two sections. Extrapolating from this translation, he constructed the *Laozi* phrase as:

[By] always holding its [the Way's] words in honor, he [with the grand and superior knowledge mentioned in the first phrase] completes [his] achievement and [sees his] affair go through.

The crucial insertion of 道 has no basis in the context here but can claim that the *Laozi* speaks in *zhang* 35 of the "words uttered by the Way." The last *Laozi* sentence of this *zhang* reads:

百姓謂我自然

for which Xiang Er's commentary runs:

我，仙士也。百姓不學我有貴信道言[172]以致此功而意我自然，當示不肯企及效我也。

This translates as:

"My [in 'my nature']" refers to the immortal. The Hundred Families have not learned that it is through my honoring and believing the words of the Way that [I] complete this achievement [of attaining immortality], but think this [success] came about [just] because of my nature, which is to show why they are not willing to eagerly imitate me.(?)

The person with the superior knowledge has not spoken as "I" in this *zhang*. The introduction of this "I" here is crucial for Xiang Er's reading of the phrase, but is unsupported by other textual evidence. While the insertion of 道 in the previous phrase and the identification of 我 in this phrase, might not rest on a solid textual basis, it manages to provide a logical link for the two phrases and the entire *zhang*. It is by honoring the words of the Way that the person with superior knowledge, who is also addressed as the "good man" in the commentary to this *zhang*, will achieve his success, immortality. This the Hundred Families ignore and, thinking that reaching immortality is due to the superior man's nature, and cannot be achieved through religious practice and good deeds, they refuse to emulate the immortal (if I translate the last phrase correctly).

Extrapolating from this commentary, the last phrase in *Laozi* 17 must be translated as:

> [But] the Hundred Families [the nonbelievers] [simply] attribute this [attainment of immortality] to my nature [and not to my honoring the words of the Way].

On the basis of this *zhang*, we can say that Xiang Er constructs a logically viable text, which loosely fits his construction of the overall meaning of the text. He proceeds from the assumption that the *Laozi* contains the "words uttered by the Way," a text completely prescribing the rules for the believer to follow. Grammatical forms which, if under duress, might be constructed as imperatives, are thus read in this way. Although the Xiang Er does on occasion implicitly refer to other sections of the *Laozi* by way of deciphering a cryptic passage (or to his own commentary by way of avoiding repetition), he is not bound by the more textual rules of rhetorical structure, grammatical probability, content plausibility, or economy and elegance. With a firm belief that the ultimate purpose of the *Laozi* is known to him, he feels free to bend the patterns of the textual surface to this purpose. All key terms on which the meaning of this *zhang* in this reading hinge, are inserted without direct textual or contextual basis. The delicate balance between providing a plausible and elegant reading of a passage and linking this passage with the presumed overall thrust of the text is clearly tilted in favor of the latter.

Unlike Wang Bi, Xiang Er does not seem to treat the reader as a sophisticated and well-informed competitor in the struggle for the meaning of this text but as an adept who learns the hidden meaning from a person endowed with religious authority and who, through this text and commentary is being told how to behave in order to achieve the status of an immortal. Such advice is even given to those who already have the "superior knowledge"; in the very first commentary to *Laozi* 17 they are told that they "should" also equip themselves with the "lower knowledge." Still, we have to learn to live with the fact that, like Schroedinger's cat, the *Laozi* has many simultaneous lives, well shielded from each other, sometimes even within the same head.

As a fourth example, we will now take the Heshang gong commentary. In this text, the first *Laozi* phrase reads

太上下知有之

The Heshang gong comments on this phrase:

太上謂太古無名號之君。下知有之者下知上有君而不臣事質樸淳也。
若不知者沒而無。謚法者號之曰皇。

This translates:

"Taishang" refers to the princes in highest antiquity, who were without personal name or appellation [such as Fu Xi, Huangdi, Yao, and Shun].[173] "Xia zhi you zhi" 下知有之 means those below know that up there is a prince, but do not minister and serve him [as he is] unadorned and pure in [his] disposition [so that they do not have his personal name]. Had [those below, on the other hand,] not [at all] known [about them], they would be completely nonexistent [in the historical records] [and we would not even have their family names and posthumous names]. The "Rules for Posthumous Names" calls them August, *huang*.[174]

On this basis, the Heshang gong read the *Laozi* text:

About [those who in] highest antiquity [were rulers], those below knew [only] that they existed [but as they did not serve them they did not know their personal names].

This puts him into the same reading strategy with Zhuang Zun and Wang Bi in terms of defining the subjects and objects of the two parts of this statement. Still, with the *tai* 太 instead of Wang Bi's *da* 大, the Heshang gong's solution uses the 太上 for "in highest antiquity," which is confirmed by the later commentary formula in this *zhang*, which writes 太上之君 instead of the 太古之君 here, but now has to supplement the core noun, "prince," *jun* 君, in this and the subsequent phrases. True, the Heshang gong's reading of 下 in the second half supports an assumption that the first half might deal with the ruler, but he has used his textual capital to construct "in high antiquity," and has to supplement the ruler without having a word left. Wang Bi's construction managed, with careful textual enrichment, to get a better documented reading out of these two characters.

The emphasis in Heshang gong is not on the incapacity of language to define the characteristics of this kind of ruler, but on the lack of familiarity with the rulers in highest antiquity, since they were so modest and simple in their character that they did not have people serving them and thus being familiar with them beyond the basic understanding that they existed. To interpret the "those below know [only] that he exists" in this manner is quite ingenious as it coincides with the stories told about them in historic times and with the *Laozi*'s own assumption of their being simple and unadorned, *pu* 樸. It also has some contextual support: The subsequent *Laozi* phrases all describe an attitude of the lower orders toward their princes.

The Heshang gong text reads the next phrase

其次親而譽之，

on which it comments

其德可見，恩惠可稱，故親愛而譽之。

This translates:

The capacity of this one may be perceived, and [his] favors and kindnesses may be praised; that is why [those below] are close to him, love him, and glorify him.

The *Laozi* phrase thus runs:

> Those inferior to/after them [who in highest antiquity were above] they [those below] are close to and they glorify them.

Like Zhuang Zun and Wang Bi, the Heshang gong keeps "those below" as the subject for the second half of the subsequent phrases.

On the next *Laozi* phrase 其次畏之, the Heshang gong comments 設刑法以治之: "He sets up punishments and laws in order to bring them [those below] to order." From this comment we infer that he read the *Laozi* phrase as

> Those [rulers] inferior to/after those [whom they are close to and glorify] they [those below] fear.

The next *Laozi* phrase 其次侮之 is commented on thus: 禁多令煩 不可歸誠，故欺侮之: "[As to this one], although [his] prohibitions are multiplied and [his] orders profuse, [those below] cannot be brought back to honesty, that is why they cheat and deceive him." The Heshang gong's construction for this *Laozi* sentence thus reads:

> Those [rulers] inferior to/after those [whom they fear], they [those below] deceive.

In the sequence given in this reading, the particular measures used by the various types of rulers can be inferred only from the reactions of those below. Like Wang Bi, the Heshang gong commentary reads this sequence as a parallel to the sequence in *Laozi* 18 and 38, and uses much of the same vocabulary to specify the types of rule. There is no explicit time frame here. The mentioning, however, of the "highest antiquity" in the first commentary might suggest that these subsequent princes were both later in time and inferior in quality. Shima Kuniō has concluded from this implied time sequence that the Heshang gong here follows Gu Huan's 顧歡 commentary from the Southern Qi at the end of the fifth century, which explicitly links the types of rulers to the different ages.[175]

As opposed to the Heshang gong, Wang Bi makes it a necessary sequence in both time and caliber by showing how the ruler's inability to handle the government technique of the previous phrase by necessity leads to his adoption of the next technique.[176]

The *Laozi* text 信不足焉 is commented on as 君信不足於下
下有巧詐之民也 "If the prince's credibility is insufficient among those
below, there will be cunning and deceiving people below." We infer
that the *Laozi* text was constructed as:

[This last relationship between ruler and subjects is owing to
the fact that as this last type of prince] is lacking in credibility.

The next *Laozi* phrase, 有不信焉 is given a separate commentary
that reads 下則應之，以不信欺其君也. "Then those below will respond
to him [the prince who is lacking in credibility] by deceiving their
prince with unfaithfulness." The *Laozi* phrase thus reads:

those below [too] have unfaithfulness!

The Heshang gong thus agrees with Xiang Er in linking this
phrase or these two phrases only with the last of the sequence,
where the people cheat and deceive their ruler. The weakness of this
commentary is that it imputes to the text the redundancy of stating
the same thing twice, and of breaking the rules of parallelism by
directly associating these two elements with only the last of a series
of parallel statements.

The next *Laozi* phrase, 猶兮其貴言, has the commentary 說太上
之君舉事猶猶　然貴重於言　恐離道　失自然也. "This means that, when
the princes of high antiquity undertook something, they were meticulous in their planning; thus, that they 'paid great attention [to
their] words' means that they were afraid that they might depart
from the Way and lose That-which-is-of-itself-what-it-is."[177] This
forces a translation of the *Laozi* phrase as:

Meticulous in [their] planning they [the princes of high antiq-
uity] were, and paid attention to [their] words.

There is some echo in *Laozi* 56, "He who knows does not speak,"
which the Heshang gong comments: "He who knows cherishes actions not words." The Heshang gong joins the Xiang Er and Wang Bi
in linking this phrase to the person mentioned in the first phrase.

Again in tune with Wang Bi, the Heshang gong links the next
Laozi statement, 成功事遂, not with the preceding but with the
following phrase. He comments 謂天下太平: "This refers to Great
Peace in All Under Heaven," which gives a construction for the
Laozi phrase:

when [they thus] complete achievements and when processes are followed through. . . .

The last *Laozi* phrase, 百姓皆謂我自然, is commented on 百姓不知君上之德淳厚　反以為己自當然也. "The Hundred Families do not recognize the purity and honesty of the capacity of the ruler above [as the cause]; to the contrary, they assume this to be so [that is, Great Peace to prevail] due to they themselves being so." The construction is similar to that by Wang Bi; the princes of antiquity brought about Great Peace, but, as they did not actively interfere, the people failed to recognize their contribution and thought it was due to their own nature or actions. In this translation the shocking personalization of 自然 in 我自然 is avoided, and in fact 自然 is not treated as a compound noun at all. Heshang gong "translates" 我自然 as 己自當然. The 然 is translated 當然, which leaves 己自 as a translation of 我自 and consequently splits the wording not between 我 and 自然, but between 我自 and 然! This requires a translation of this *Laozi* phrase as:

The Hundred Families say: "We ourselves happen to be like this."[178]

The potentiality of this *zhang* is not only one of different content interpretations but includes substantially diverging options of grammatical structure as well as assignment of implicit subjects and objects. To demonstrate the range of the text's potentiality, I shall juxtapose the various translations extrapolated from the commentaries.

Zhuang Zun

As to the Great Supreme, those below know [only] that He exists.

The one after him [who is the ruler of highest caliber] [they, those below] are close to and praise him.
The one after this one [who is second in caliber to the

Wang Bi

If the Great [Man] is at the top, those below know [only] that he exists [and nothing more].

If one second to him [the Great Man] is [at the top], [those below] will be close to him and praise him.
If one second to him [who is second to the Great Man]

highest] [they, those below] dread and loathe.
(No more commentary available for extrapolation.)

is [at the top], [those below] will fear him.
If one second to him [who is second to him who is second to the Great Man] is [at the top], [those below] do not take him seriously. [In short,] as credibility [of those at the top who are of lower calibre than the Great Man] is lacking, there is [,as a consequence,] absence of credibility [among the people below].
Undecided he is [the Great Man if at the top]! [But] his words are respected by those below!
[If in this manner the Hundred Families'] achievements are completed and processes followed through, the Hundred Families all say "we are like this [that is, have this bountiful life] spontaneously."

Wenzi, Hanfeizi, Huainanzi

Under an optimal [ruler] [the people] know [why] they [=rewards and punishments] are there.

Xiang Er
[Having] the grand and supreme [knowledge] [also] is to have lower knowledge!

Heshang gong
About [those who in] highest antiquity [were rulers], those below knew [only] that they existed [but as they did not serve them they did not know their personal names]

Those below [you, the one with the highest knowledge] either befriend [or praise]!

Into those below [those mentioned in the preceding phrase] [either] strike fear or treat them with disdain!

As the faith [in Daoist truths of those who should be mistreated] is insufficient, it happens that they lack faith [in the words of those who teach these truths].

[By] always holding its [the Way's] words in honor, he [with the grand and superior knowledge mentioned in the first phrase] completes [his] achievement and [sees his] affair go through, [but] the Hundred Families [the non believers] [just] say: "We ourselves happen to be like this."

Those inferior to/after them [who in highest antiquity were above] they [those below] are close to and they glorify them.
Those inferior to/after these [whom they are close to and glorify], they [those below] fear.
Those inferior to/after those [whom they fear], they [those below] deceive.
[This last relationship between ruler and subjects is due to the fact that as this last type of prince] is lacking in credibility, those below [too] have unfaithfulness.
Meticulous in [their] planning they [the princes of high antiquity] were, and paid attention to [their] words. When [they thus] complete achievements and when processes are followed through the Hundred Families all [mistakenly] attribute this [attainment of immortality] to my nature [and not to my honoring the words of the Way].

Example 2: Laozi 6

Wang Bi gives the entire *Laozi* text of this *zhang* and then comments on it in its entirety. For analytical purposes we shall here

match the individual pieces of text and commentary. Wang Bi's
Laozi text begins:

谷神不死是謂玄牝。

Wang Bi proceeds to translate the metaphoric concepts of the *Laozi*
into straight philosophic language. His commentary runs:

谷神谷中央無谷也無形無影無逆無違處卑不動守靜不衰。谷以之成而不見
其形此至物也。處卑而不可得名故謂之玄牝。

The "spirit of the valley" is the non-valley in the middle of the
valley. It [this spirit] is without form and contour, without
contrariness and deviation, it resides in a lowly position [that
is, in the valley] and does not move; it keeps the calm and does
not deteriorate. The valley is constituted by it, but it does not
show its form. This is the highest entity. Its lowly position
[notwithstanding], there is no way to define it. That is why
[Laozi only] "calls it" Dark Female Animal [but does not "define" it as such].

The core elements of the first two *Laozi* sentences, the notion of
the "spirit of the valley," the claim that "it does not die," and the fact
that it "is called the Dark Female Animal" are taken up one after the
other. Wang Bi stays close to the spontaneous reading of these first
sentences.[179] A translation extrapolated from Wang Bi's commentary is:

The spirit of the valley does not die. [I] call it "Dark Female."

Wang Bi's commentary does not reinterpret characters to mean
something entirely different from what they normally mean; nor
does he introduce a new term or concept from outside as the guiding
notion to understanding the text. His reading makes possible if not
full sense without any knowledge of the rest of the *Laozi* or of other
texts. In this respect it is economical.

In fact, however, Wang Bi's reading of this passage is constructed on the basis of an extensive network of implicit and explicit
links to other sections of the *Laozi*. The term *shen* 神, "spirit,"
appears in *Laozi* 29.2, where the *Laozi* says 夫天下神器也. "It is a fact
that All Under Heaven is a vessel of [something] spiritual," on which

Wang Bi comments: "[Things] spiritual are 'without shape [as the *Laozi* says about the Great Image in 41.14]' and 'without corners' [as the *Xici* says of the spirit in 7.3.b2] 神無形無方也. 'Vessel' is something completed through combination [with something else that fills it] 器合成也. As [in the case of All Under Heaven,] it is combined with something shapeless, [the text] calls it [=All Under Heaven] 'a vessel of something spiritual.'"

The definitions for the spirit are thus taken from another part of the *Laozi* and from the *Zhouyi*, which also gives further definitions. The *Xici* say "That which is unfathomable [by means] of Yin and Yang is called 'spirit.'"[180] The "spirit" is defined as something invisible and immaterial, which nonetheless gives life. The *Zhouyi, Shuogua* 5, describes the spirit as "that which is spoken of as being more subtle than the ten thousand kinds of entities" 妙萬物而為言者也 and then proceeds to map out how the "spirit" provides the underlying order of all the ten thousand kinds of entitities.[181] Wang Bi's metaphoric interpretation of "spirit" is thus reinforced by similar statements in authenticated texts. Wang Bi reads the "spirit of the valley" as the nonvalley, the nothingness in the middle of it, which indeed makes the valley a valley. This nothingness is in itself without form or shape, and does not lean in any direction, is "without contrariness and deviation" toward anything that might come to reside in the valley. Against the possible reading of *shen* 神 as a god or spirit, Wang Bi constructs it as a metaphoric expression.

The valley is taken at face value as an empty space able to accommodate a great variety of things in the same manner as the "vessel" that is All Under Heaven. This relationship between valley and spirit, which also is that between the vessel and the spirit quoted above, is further detailed in the important *Laozi* 11 to be studied later in this chapter.

Wang Bi also interprets the valley as a low-lying place, so that the spirit, being "in the midst of the valley," "resides in a lowly position." This ties in with the immediate context because it prefigures the symbolism implied in the gender of the "Dark Female," since the position of the female is "low" like that of earth compared to the "high" position of man and Heaven. Again, there are echoes from other chapters of the *Laozi*. *Laozi* 66, for which there is no Wang Bi commentary, argues that "that which enables the rivers and oceans to be kings over the hundred gullies [so that they all flow into them] is that they are good at lowering themselves below them [the gullies]," a statement taken up in *Laozi* 32.4. There, *Laozi* says: "[I] compare the [role] of the Way in All-Under-Heaven to the [relationship] of rivers and the sea to rivulets and streams," a teaching instantly applied to the king who has "to lower himself below the people if he wants to be on top of them." This statement is repeated in different words in *Laozi* 28.1, where the Sage "knows that as its [All Under Heaven's] cock he [has to] keep to [being] its hen, [and then he] will be All Under Heaven's valley." In the commentary to this passage, Wang Bi adds that "a valley does not yearn for other entities; the other entities render themselves to it on their own."

The spirit of the valley does not move and interfere, but stays in complete inaction and "keeps the calm"; this nonvalley in the middle of the valley is no part of the process of generation and decay of all specific entities. It "does not die," and is not created. Still, while this nonvalley is itself undefinable, the valley is "made up by it." While a valley is a limited and therefore specific space, it is unspecific as to the entities that might find a place in it. What Wang Bi calls the "usability" of the valley is due to this absence of specificity. In the same manner the hub in *Laozi* 11 is able to absorb all the thirty spokes of a wheel because it lacks any specificity with regard to any one of these spokes. The valley is not completely devoid of all specifics; it remains a specific valley of a specific place and size. Its particular and limited absence of specificity, which enables it to accommodate a great variety of entities is thus a particular manifestation of that which, by being devoid of all specificity, is able to be the basis of all the ten thousand kinds of entities. The spirit of the valley is thus a particular and linguistically more accessible manifestation of this "That-by-which." In this sense "the valley is made up by it." This prefigures the second aspect of the symbolism of the "Female," namely generation.

That by which the ten thousand kinds of entities are is characterized by two features: first, that it is that by which they are, an aspect otherwise expressed in the term *dao* 道; and second, that it is, and for this very reason, not discernible, an aspect for which the standard term is *xuan* 玄, dark. In the *LZWZLL*, Wang Bi himself sums up his various commentaries on *dao* 道: "Dao is taken for [its aspect] of being that on which the ten thousand kinds of entities are based" 道也者取乎萬物之所由也.[182] The term "dark" 玄 appears in eight of the *Laozi*'s chapters. In his commentary to *Laozi* 1.5, Wang Bi says "the [term] 'dark' is taken for that [aspect of the ultimate principle] that it cannot be spoken of as being thus [and nothing else]" 取於不可得而謂之然也. In Wang Bi's reading, the metaphor "dark female" elegantly expresses both aspects.

The expression *wei* 謂, "is called," in the statement "It is called the Dark Female" is not innocent either. Wang Bi marks the importance of this expression by implicitly separating it from its counterpart, the definition, *ming* 名, when he says "that is why [*Laozi* only] 'calls it' Dark Female [but does not 'define' it as such]." As has been elaborated elsewhere, Wang Bi made the various statements about language in the *Laozi* into a philosophy of language, the core point being that language is an unavoidable but insufficient instrument of philosophy. The very structure of Being precludes any positive definition. *Laozi* thus operates with consciously unreliable terms, which he announces with words like the *wei* 謂, "is called," here, or *yiwei* 以為, "is taken for," and other terms elsewhere. This in turn asks of the reader and commentator to look for the intended meaning of the statement instead of the poor linguistic material that signifies it. The makeshift character of these terms also permits their identification with or replacement by other terms pointing in the same direction, as happens in the next phrase of the *Laozi* here.

Who then is doing the "calling"? No subject is given in the Chinese text and Wang Bi does not specify a subject. The option that *Laozi* and Wang Bi refer with the "Dark Female" to some generally familiar term finds no support in the available sources, as this term is not used anywhere else in surviving pre-Qin texts. The same is true for the next formula "is called the root of Heaven and Earth." In *Laozi* 25, the fabrication of these makeshift terms is done by the authorial "I." It says about the "thing that completes out of the diffuse" that "one might take it for the mother of All Under Heaven. I do not know its name. Therefore, forced, I give it the style 'Way.' And when forced to make up a name for it, I would say '[it is] great'." This would suggest that in Wang Bi's reading all these terms originate with the person Laozi himself. In order to bring out the subjective and makeshift character of these formulas, one therefore has to translate either "[I] call it the Dark Female" or "[one may] call it the Dark Female." The *Laozi* text continues:

玄牝之門是謂天地之根。

Wang Bi comments:

> 門玄牝之所由也。本其所由與太極同體。故謂之天地之根也。
>
> "Door" is that on which the Dark Female is based. Basically what it is based on has the same substance as the Taiji 太極, the Great Ultimate [of the *Xici* which "creates the two formations (Yin and Yang)"]. That is why [this door] "is spoken of" [in the text] as "the root of Heaven and Earth"!

The expression "root of Heaven and Earth" does not occur elsewhere in the *Laozi* or in other contemporary texts. The *Laozi* itself thus establishes an important interpretive principle, namely, the legitimacy of identifying various makeshift appellations for the Ultimate, in this case *men* 門, "door," and *tiandi zhi gen* 天地之根, the "root of Heaven and Earth." A similar procedure occurs in *Laozi* 52.1: "As All Under Heaven has a beginning, it may [also] be taken for All Under Heaven's mother," where the terms *shi* 始, "beginning," and *mu* 母, "mother," are equated. Wang Bi continues in this vein by again identifying this *men* 門, "door," with the *taiji* 太極, the "Great Ultimate" of the *Xici*, which "gives life to the two principles [Yin and Yang]," which in turn are at the basis of all specific entities.[183]

The term *men*, "door," is regularly identified in Wang Bi's commentary as that from which something emanates.[184] Thus we have the spirit of the valley called the Dark Female in its twofold aspect, and that from which the Dark Female emanates is called the root of Heaven and Earth. This philosophically complex construct would seem to require some parallel in the rest of the *Laozi* to prove its probability. The term *men*, "door," leads to the parallel in *Laozi* 1.5: "Both [the 'beginning' and the 'mother' mentioned previously] emerge from a common [origin] but they have different names. Their common [origin] is spoken of as the Dark, the Dark-and-Dark-Again. It is the door [from which] the many and the subtle [emerge]." The "many" here refers to the multitude of entities engendered by the "mother"; "subtle" is according to Wang's commentary to the previous sentence 始物之妙 "the entity-initating subtlety" and thus is linked to the "beginning." Both "beginning" and "mother" emanate in the last count from that which is "Dark-and-Dark-Again." This is not the place to go into the philosophical analysis of these passages. It is important, however, that the two aspects described in *Laozi* 6 with the terms *xuan* 玄, "dark," and *pin* 牝, "female animal," reappear in substance in the notions of beginning/ subtleness and mother/multitude, while the "door" that is the "Dark-and-Dark-Again" reappears in the "door" that is "the root of Heaven and Earth." Wang Bi thus constructs the present passage in the context of his construction of other statements of the *Laozi* in order to check the consistency of his construction with other statements. According to Wang Bi, this has to be translated as:

> The door [from] which the Dark Female [comes] [I] call the root of Heaven and Earth.

The end of the *Laozi* text runs:

綿綿若存用之不勤。

Wang Bi comments:

欲言存耶則不見其形欲言亡耶萬物以之生故曰綿綿若存也無物不成用而不勞也故曰用之不勤

If one wishes to state that it exists [the objection would be that] it does not show its form. If one wishes to state that it does not exist, [it still remains true] that the ten thousand kinds of entities are generated by means of it. That is why [the text says]: "Intangible it is, but still it exists!" There is no entity not completed [through it], but, while being used [in this extensive manner,] it does not labor [to have them completed]. That is why [the text] says: "Its being used does not exert it"!

Having followed the text in its broadening of the inquiry to the "root of Heaven and Earth," Wang Bi can now safely refer to other forms of expression about the Way itself to explain the rest of the text. The paradox: "If one wishes to state that it exists, [the objection would be that] one does not see its form; if one wishes to state that it does not exist, [it still remains true] that the ten thousand kinds of entities are generated by means of it" reoccurs nearly verbatim in Wang Bi on *Laozi* 14.2, where he comments on the One that the *Laozi* there "calls the shape of the shapeless, the appearance of the no-thing." In this manner the "root of Heaven and Earth" is further identified with the One. The *Laozi* phrase 綿綿若存, "Intangible it is but still persists," for which the above is the commentary, is taken up in a description of the Sage in Wang Bi on *Laozi* 23.3. There, the Sage who handles things in accordance with the Way, imitates its feature: "To complete and regulate the ten thousand kinds of entities by means of [its] being shapeless and without interference." He does so by making "noninterference his residence" and the "unspoken his teaching" so that, like the Way, he is "intangible but still existent," with the consequence that "the other entities [all] achieve their true [nature]." Apart from adding two more alternative ways of speaking to the list of door, root, and One, this reference adds further parallels to reinforce the reading of 綿綿若存 as describing the paradox of the That-by-which, which, intangible in itself, still is the basis of all that is tangible.

The construction of 用之不勤 as "its being used does not exert it" is reinforced by *Laozi* 45.1f. There, the *Laozi* talks about the Great Completion, the Great Filling, the Great Straightening, and so forth. Their greatness is seen as absolute and beyond the relative categories of great and small. The *Laozi* there says "[it is the mark of] the Great Filling to be as if empty. Its use does not exhaust it" 大盈若沖　其用不窮. In Wang Bi's construction, this refers to the same thought expressed in the last sentence of *Laozi* 6. The line from *Laozi* 45.2 is again taken up in Wang Bi's construction of *Laozi* 4.1: "The Way is made use of by pouring out and is also not filled up." Wang Bi comments on this line: "If [the Way] is 'made use of by pouring out' [as the text here says] this 'use indeed will not' be able to 'exhaust it' [as the *Laozi* says in 45.2]. If, however, it were filled up to create fullness, it would overflow once fullness had come."

The translation of the last phrase of *Laozi* 6 extrapolated from Wang Bi runs:

> Intangible it is, but still it exists. Its being used does not exert it.

Wang Bi's commentary on this *zhang* is a fine example of his interpretive skills. His point of departure is a flat and highly viable reading of the fairly straightforward grammar. He does not introduce new topics from outside as subjects for the individual phrase but keeps to the rule that a change in subject must either be explicit or must be very strongly suggested by context. He keeps to the standard meaning of the characters. His commentaries to characters like "door" keep to shared cultural assumptions. He establishes an argumentatively consistent reading of the *zhang* itself. He reinforces each element in his construction with parallels from other *zhang*; this establishes the compatibility of the arguments in this *zhang* with the rest of the *Laozi* in the context of an assumed homogeneity of the entire text to create a plausible reading. This is true not only for the substance of the argument but also for its form which he links to the *Laozi*'s theory of language. While there is no limit to the interpretive genius, Wang Bi again uses the same limited set of interpretive procedures and verification techniques found in the first example.

As we shall shortly see, however, the range in the potentiality of the text we found in the previous example with its grammatical openness is as great in a *zhang* like this with a fairly definite grammatical structure but an evidently metaphoric form of argument. Zhuang Zun comments the phrase "The spirit of the valley does not die" with the words:

> The Great Harmony is a subtle ether, a subtle thing like the spirit. Emptiness is its house, calm its eternal [state]. Leaving and entering it needs no crack [to get through], coming and going it needs no opening. When going into action there is nothing it does not get through; when resting there is nothing it does not complete. It transforms transformable [other things], but is not [itself] transformed. It creates created [things], but is not itself created.[185]

Zhuang Zun identifies the "spirit of the valley" with the *taihe* 太和, the Great Harmony. The term is probably taken from the *dahe* 大和 in the *tuan* to the first hexagram of the *Zhouyi*, but does not occur in the *Laozi*. In his commentary to *Laozi* 1, Zhuang Zun lists a series of symbols, saying, "Among the symbols for the Highest none is more elevated than *dao* and *de*. Among those for that which is second [to the Highest] none is greater than spiritual brightness, *shenming* 神明. Among those for that which is second to this, none is greater than *taihe* 太和." The list continues through *tiandi* 天地, *yinyang* 陰陽, and *dasheng* 大聖.[186] The "spirit" is interpreted as a metaphor for something without shape and form that moves without hindrance. In this commentary, which might be a fragment, Zhuang

Zun does not deal with the notion of the "valley." The spirit as the *taihe*, however, while generating and transforming all that is generated and transformed, is not in itself generated and transformed, which interprets the "does not die" of the *Laozi* text. Wang Bi inherits from Zhuang Zun the construction that this "spirit of the valley" is the basis of all entities and processes without being affected by their generation, change, and decay. In this commentary by Zhuang Zun, however, the core notions and interpretations are again stated and associated, not deduced. Even the possible parallels to the *Zhouyi* do not seem to be based on a detailed structural analysis.

Zhuang Zun comments on the sentence "It is called the Dark Female Animal":

> The "Female Animal," by having the softness of a female animal is capable of generating. "Dark" is like [=an expression for being] so abstruse and distant that one does not see [it]. Although the infant-entities [that is the ten thousand things] are like [their] mother, none of them sees her shape.[187]

This comment interprets the generative symbolism implied in the notion of the "Female Animal," and implies the link of the "darkness" of the Female Animal with the invisibility of the "spirit" in the previous phrase. The last sentence decodes the symbolism of the "Dark Female Animal" but, while stating the "darkness" and invisibility of the Female Animal for the other beings, it fails to give the philosophical basis for why this Female Animal should be imperceptible. Again Wang follows the drift of this interpretation, but, while reconstructing what basically is also Zhuang Zun's grammar, he stays closer to the text and links things up without extraneous matter.

Zhuang Zun has a different text for the next phrase. From his commentary we see that instead of 謂 in 玄牝之門　是謂天地之根, he probably had 為.[188] His commentary runs:

太和之所以生而不死始而不終開導神明
為天地之根元

That which causes the Great Harmony to generate but not to die, to initiate but not to end, and to open and guide the vital spirit, *shenming*, is the root and origin of Heaven and Earth.

We will leave out here the insertion of outside concepts like *shenming* and *taihe*, neither of which occurs in the *Laozi*. The "door" of the Dark Female Animal in the *Laozi* text is interpreted here as a very terse expression for "that which causes to generate but not to die, to initiate but not to end, to open and guide." Only the "to open," *kai* 開, may be linked to the notion of the door. In this commentary, the root and origin of Heaven and Earth are the agents operating what is expressed by "door." Zhuang Zun thus constructs this *Laozi* sentence as meaning:

> As to the [operating of] the door of the Dark Female Animal, this is [done by] the root of Heaven and Earth.

Wang Bi does not go along with either this text or this interpretation. He reads "[I] call it the root of Heaven and Earth," as another appellation for what is expressed by "door."

The consequences of Zhuang Zun's verbalization of the term "door" become evident in his commentary to the next phrase, "Intangible it is but still exists. Its being used does not exhaust it."

> In moving and resting, in its darkness and subtlety, it is [simultaneously] as if it did not exist and did exist; completing things and following through affairs there is nothing it does not bring about; illuminating it is, and does not go under. The reason why its "being used does not exhaust it" is that it lives a life that does not live, and embodies a form without form.[189]

What does the "it" refer to? In Wang Bi's construction, it refers to the "root of Heaven and Earth" of the immediately preceding sentence, which again is identified with the "door" of the Dark Female Animal. In Zhuang Zun, the imported expressions "moving and resting," "completing things and following through affairs" directly link up with the statement about the *taihe* in the commentary to the first sentence. The last sentence also is a restatement of the last sentence of this first commentary. The subject of the above phrases thus is not the "root," or the "door" of the Dark Female Animal, but the Dark Female Animal/spirit/*taihe* itself. According to Zhuang Zun, the last *Laozi* phrases have thus to be translated:

Intangible it [the Dark Female Animal/spirit] is as if persisting. Its being used does not exhaust it.

Again, this difference in subject notwithstanding, Wang Bi accepts much of Zhuang Zun's construction of the meaning of these phrases.

Zhuang Zun prefigures Wang Bi in staying fairly close to the surface meaning of the text. There are few grammatical or terminological constructs that radically alter this level of the text. They differ in their basic approaches, however. Zhuang Zun follows the Han tradition of liberally introducing concepts into the text for which there is no internal basis. At the same time, he does not seem concerned with the intrinsic homogeneity of the text. He hardly ever alludes to phrases or philosophic arguments in parts of the *Laozi* other than those he writes about, but links the various *zhang* through the application of his own unified terminology. Thus there is little effort to convince the reader through the closeness of the commentary to the text and the density of the commentarial texture. Zhuang Zun's commentary relies on its own authority, and thus has the marks of a school commentary. At the same time, it begins a movement of close analysis of the philosophic meaning of the text. It sees it as dealing with that by which the ten thousand kinds of entities are, that is as a philosophical text, and not as a guide book for acolytes. Zhuang Zun reads the *Laozi* as a book of philosophic analysis, not of practical advice. He therefore keeps to the *Laozi*'s analytic and descriptive grammar and does not introduce exhortations to the reader ("you must") from an overcharged context as do other commentaries like the Xiang Er and Heshang gong. Again, going back a bit earlier, we see two pieces of *Laozi* 6 interpreted in the *Wenzi*:

The Great Way is without interference; as being without interference, it is in possession of nothing; what is in possession of nothing does not reside [in a particular place]; what does not reside takes residence in the shapeless; what is shapeless does not move; what does not move is without words; what is without words is calm in its soundlessness and shapelessness; as to the soundless and shapeless, gazing at it, one does not see it, listening for it, one does not hear it; this is spoken of as the fine subtlety 微妙. This is referred to as the highest spirit 至神;

intangible it is, but still it exists 綿綿若存; it is called the root of Heaven and Earth 是謂天地之根.[190]

The "spirit of the valley" does not appear here, only the "highest spirit" 至神, whom Wang Bi would call "the Ultimate (or Highest) Entity" 至物. The emphasis here is only on the fact that the elusiveness of the Dao to the human senses notwithstanding, this Dao, this "highest spirit," "is intangible, but still it exists," 綿綿若存, which is taken from *Laozi* 6. Other parts of the *Wenzi* have explored the generative aspect of the Dao so that the second quotation from *Laozi* 6, "It is called the root of Heaven and Earth," does not come as a surprise. There is reason to assume that the *Wenzi* was aware of the entirety of *Laozi* 6 and quoted elements from it: The statement "Intangible it is, but still it exists" interprets the first phrase of *Laozi* 6, "the spirit of the valley does not die" which also stressed the ongoing existence of this elusive spirit. The piece translated above gives us some indications at to the *Wenzi*'s reading of *Laozi* 6. By quoting "It is called the root of Heaven and Earth" after 綿綿若存 (in all known texts the sequence is the other way around), it makes clear that 是 in 是謂天地之根 refers to the "spirit" and not to the noun immediately preceding this element in the other texts, namely "door," *men* 門, as in Wang Bi. In this construction 玄牝之門 cannot be accommodated. I do not see any possibility than to assume that the *Wenzi*'s text did not have the reduplication of 玄牝, but read 谷神不死　是謂玄牝之門　綿綿若存　是謂天地之根（用之不勤）. This gives an extrapolated translation of:

> The spirit of the valley does not die. It is called the door of the dark female animal. Intangible it [this spirit] is, but still it exists. It is called the root of Heaven and Earth.

This reading of the quoted passages clearly prefigures that by Wang Bi, while it does away with what Wang Bi sees as *Laozi*'s discovery of the "That-by-which" beyond the Dao itself.

While the examples given above show that Wang Bi can justly be said to be in the tradition of Zhuang Zun in terms of some of his textual constructions, if not in the purpose and method of his commenting, the Xiang Er commentary again takes a completely different approach, reading the *zhang* as a guide to sexual practices for male acolytes that include withholding ejaculation so as to preserve the semen, which can then be guided upwards to replenish the spirit. It begins with a blunt claim 谷者欲也, verbatim "'valley' means 'desire.'" At first sight this might prompt a flashy translation of the first phrase of *Laozi* 6 as "the spirit of desire does not die," but, sadly enough, Xiang Er only makes either one of two philological arguments. Option A is that the difference between the two characters 谷 and 欲 is the radical 欠. The Xiang Er statement suggests that in the Qin/Han reforms of the script, when many homophone loan characters were formally separated by having radicals attached to them,[191] the "transcribers" failed to notice that 谷 in the old text should actually be transcribed as 欲. This option is preserved in Guodian A while in other pre-Qin texts, the character 欲 was already written in this form. The Mawangdui MSS point to a second, phonetic option. They write 浴 instead of 谷 for the later standard character 欲, a form that signals the later 谷 in Guodian A. In this manner, they confirm that there was no current character 欲 here. However, the pronounciation of 浴 is *yu* and thus the same as for 欲. While the Xiang Er *Laozi* text does write 谷 and not 浴, the fluidity of the characters and the pronunciation is sufficient to make the assumption that 谷 should be read as 欲 by no means frivolous. Whatever the philological strength of the argument, the Xiang Er's gloss simply identifies the character 谷 as being the character 欲. Replacing 谷 by 欲, we get a first *Laozi* sentence with a different length and grammar. In the Wang Bi reading, 谷神不死 was a full sentence, and so was 是謂玄牝. In the Xiang Er reading, the two become one single phrase because the 欲 now acts as a verb. Before offering a translation, I shall translate the rest of the commentary to this first phrase. The Xiang Er commentary continues:

精結為神欲令神不死當結精自守牝者地也　性安女像之　故不擊　男欲結精心當像地似女勿為事先。

Semen becomes spirit through coagulation. If [you] desire to bring it about that [your] spirit does not die, [you] have to let [your] semen coagulate and conserve it in yourself. "Female Animal" refers to "earth" [according to the *tuan* to hexagram 2, *kun* 坤, of the *Zhouyi*, which says "the female horse belongs to the category of earth"]. The nature of its [earth's] substance is calmness. The woman imitates it [the Earth], therefore she does not play the lead [in sexual intercourse].[192] If a male wants to let [his] semen coagulate, [his] heart has to imitate the Earth and copy the woman['s behavior], and definitely should not push ahead [with ejaculating].[193]

The person addressed is the male Daoist acolyte, the issue is his sexual behavior and technique. The implied imperative in the translation of the *Laozi* phrase "this means [for you that you have to play the role of] the Dark Female Animal" is based on the Xiang Er's "if a male wants to let [his] semen coagulate, [his] heart has to imitate the earth and copy the woman['s behavior]." Extrapolating from this commentary, the Xiang Er read the first phrase in *Laozi* 6 as follows:

If [you] desire to have [your] spirit not die, this means [for you that you have to play the role of] the Dark Female Animal.

The Xiang Er reads the text as a guidebook for achieving long life. The factual statements in the *Laozi* are thus translated into advice and prescription for the adept. That context determines the reading strategies for the text and leaves it little leeway to insist upon itself. The violence of this imposition of the context upon the text is visible in deformations and elements left unexplained. A construction beginning with *yu* 欲, "if you want," and continuing with *shi wei* 是謂, "this is called," instead of an expression for "then you have to" is odd, and the commentator simply inserts the imperatives "has to," *dang* 當, and "definitely should not" *wu* 勿, on the strength of his contextual understanding. Before "Dark Female Animal," the Xiang Er's construction needs an expression for "to act as," which is not there and again is supplemented by the commentary advising the male to "imitate" the female. The dark color of the Female Animal is not explained.

For the next *Laozi* phrase, the Xiang Er text differs from the Wang Bi text. It reads:

玄牝門天地根。

The Xiang Er commentary runs:

牝地也女像之陰孔為門死生之官也　最要故名根男茶亦名根。
The "Female Animal" refers to the Earth.[194] The woman imitates it [the Earth]. The female orifice is the "door"; it is the

administrator/orifice of death and life.[195] It is the most impor-
tant [thing]; therefore [the text] calls it "root." The *membrum virile* is also called "root."[196]

The Xiang Er thus makes the argument that the imitation of the Female Animal of the first phrase is mandatory because its "door" is "the most important [thing]," which controls life and death. Extrapolating from this argument of Xiang Er, the above *Laozi* line has to be translated:

[This is because] the door of the Dark Female Animal is [even] the root of Heaven and Earth.

In this commentary, the Xiang Er opts for a grammatically uncontroversial construction and focuses on the symbolic interpretation of the "door" of the "Dark Female Animal." It is the "administrator of death and life" insofar as new human life is born from it, and, as we shall see, the male's "leakage" of semen into it is the cause of his death. The identification of the "door" as the orifice of the vagina puts the *Laozi* on record as elevating it to the rank of being "the root of Heaven and Earth." The Xiang Er is quick to react to this by adding a further quality, making it into the "administrator of death and life." The rule laid down in his reading of the first *Laozi* phrase thus fulfills its reason and importance.

The specific wording of the "Dark Female Animal" might suggest a search for an interpretation of the kind pursued by Xiang Er, especially so since the term "Dark Female Animal" had by Han times become associated with sexual practices.

The *Commentary to the Hou Han shu* quotes the biography of Rong Cheng 容成 from the *Liexian zhuan* 列仙傳 ascribed to Liu Xiang (77 BCE – 6 CE). Rong is supposed to be the teacher of Yellow Emperor, and a book on sexual practices is listed under his name:

容成公者能善補導之事。取精於玄牝，其要谷神不死守生養氣者也。髮白復黑，齒洛復生。御婦人之術，謂握固不泄，還精補腦也。

Master Rong Cheng was good at matters of supplementing [the brain with semen] and guiding [the semen to the brain through the spine]. He absorbed semen 精 (or vital essence) from the Dark Female Animal for the purpose of preventing

[his] spirit of the valley from dying, of preserving [his] life, and nurturing [his] *qi* 氣. [His] white hair turned black again; the teeth that had fallen out grew again. This art of having sexual intercourse with women[197] consists in restraining oneself and not ejaculating, and to return the semen to supplement one's brain.[198]

This reading, which largely predates the Xiang Er commentary, constructs—as does the Xiang Er—the "Dark Female Animal" as the vagina. Although it does not change the term "valley" but keeps the "spirit of the valley," it in fact does the same as the Xiang Er by adding a *yao* 要 before it so that he had "the purpose of preventing his spirit of the valley from dying," which corresponds to the Xiang Er's *yu* 欲, "if you wish . . ." The male student of immortality is advised here to "absorb," *qu* 取, the female seminal fluid and guide it, together with his own semen, to his brain.

While going along with the basic construction of the first phrase, the Xiang Er takes strong exception to this technique. In the commentary to *Laozi* 9.1 it writes: "The Dao instructs men to coagulate the semen and make it into spirit. Nowadays people falsely call artificial tricks 'Daoist.' They base themselves on the texts by Huang Di, the Dark Woman 玄女, Gongzi 龔子, and Rong Cheng and teach each other to follow the woman and not to ejaculate, intending [thus] to make the semen return and supplement the brain."[199] The surviving parts of the Xiang Er are not very clear about this *jiejing* 結精, "coagulating the semen." Their technique, however, must be close enough to that attributed to Rong Cheng and others to cause the confusion. The main point of difference seems to be that, in the Xiang Er's view, coagulating the semen is more than a purely sexual technique. In an elaborate comparison of the semen in the body with water in a pond contained in this commentary on *Laozi* 21.6, Xiang Er spells out his teaching more in detail. Further up in the commentary to *Laozi* 21.4 and .5, he states first:

有道精分之與萬物萬物精共一本生死之官也精其真當寶之也。

There is a semen of the Dao 道精 which it distributes to the ten thousand beings. [Thus] the the semen of the ten thousand beings has one common basis. It is the administrator of life and death. As [this] semen is their true [nature] they have to treasure it.

And second in his comments on *Laozi* 21.6:

古仙士寶精，以生；今人失精，以死；大信也。今但結精，便可得生乎。
The immortals of old treasured semen and thereby lived [on].
Men today lose [their] semen and therefore die. This is the
grand faith. Now it is only through coagulating [one's] semen
that [long] life can be achieved? No! All the practices have to be
completed!

In the end comes the comparison:

精並喻像泄水身為池堤封善行為水源若斯三備池乃全堅心不專善無堤封水
必去行善不積源不通水必燥干決水漑野渠如溪江雖堤在源流泄必亦空 XX
燥炘裂，百病並生，斯三不慎，池為空坑也。[200]
Semen is like pond water. The body is the dike of the pond.
Good deeds are the water source. Once these three are well
prepared, the pond is kept whole and firm. If the heart is not
thoroughly keen on being good, there is no dike, and the water
will inevitably leak out. If the goodness of the actions does not
pile up, the source is not open and the water will by necessity
dry up. If the water bursts open and soaks the open fields
[instead of running into the pond] so that the gutters become
like rivers, the source will run out even if the dikes are still
there and the pond will also be necessarily empty. The bed (of
the pond) will dry and crack; the hundred diseases will simultaneously arise. If one does not guard against these three
[dangers, of the heart's being insufficiently good, the action's
being insufficiently good, and the water spilling over outside
the pond,] the pond will be an empty pit.

The main problem is to prevent the loss of semen or vital essence, *jing* 精, the water in the simile, but the Xiang Er makes sure
that this can only be done through a proper moral rather than
simply a sexual practice. If the water is lost, blocked, or spilled, the
body will be an empty pit, things dry up, and the hundred diseases
arise. Three dangers threaten the body as a tight pond for the
semen: a mind not bent on good, which undermines the body's
function as a dike; a course of action not set to do good, which blocks
the steady flow of fresh vital essence; and something described not
in moral but in natural terms, a "bursting open" of the channel of the

vital essence that leads into the dike of the body so that it is leaked into the open fields. The meaning of this last item is not spelled out. It looks as if it refers to loss of semen through sexual intercourse or other procedures. This is precisely the topic of *Laozi* 6 which we are still dealing with here, namely the regulation of this "natural" loss of vital essence for the purposes of prolonging life.

Neither grammar nor content of the next *Laozi* phrase in *Laozi* 6, 綿綿若存, can be called self-evident. Both have to be constructed from scratch. The Xiang Er comments:

陰陽之道以若合ᵃ精為生年以知命當令ᵇ自止年少之時雖有當閑省之綿綿者微也從其微少若少年則長存矣今此乃為大害道造之何道重繼祠種類不絕欲令合精產生故教之年少微省不絕不教之勤力也勤力之計出愚人之心耳豈可怨道乎上德之人志操堅彊能不戀合ᶜ產出少時便絕又善神早成言此者道精也故令天地無祠龍無子仙人無妻ᵈ玉女無夫其大信也。

As in the Way of Yin and Yang [= sexual intercourse] mixing of the seminal fluids means creating life, once you have reached the age [of 50] where [as Confucius said in *Lunyu* 2.4] you "know what has been ordained [for you by Heaven]," you have to bring [this form of intercourse] to a halt. When in younger years, while you [might still] have it [sexual intercourse of this kind], you have to reduce and curtail it. The 綿綿 means "small," that is, to follow [this rule] from small on. If you do this on from the time when you are young, you will exist long. Now if the great mishap should come about [of one's not having male offspring], how could the Dao have brought it about? The Dao[ists?] consider[s] it important that the ancestral sacrifices be continued and that the different species be not discontinued, and it wishes to let [the adepts] mix [their] seminal fluids and have offspring. That is why it teaches them to minimalize and curtail [procreative sexual intercourse] while still young in years, but not to break it off [altogether], and it does not teach them to force [themselves] to it 勤力 [the reduction of sexual intercourse]. The strategy of forcing [oneself] comes out of the heart of stupid people, how can one resent the Dao for it? [Only] people with "highest capacity" [of whom *Laozi* 38 says they are "without interference and without concerns"] are so strong in their will and firm in their resolution that they are able not to have a craving to mix [the seminal fluids] and procreate. They [alone] will completely break off [procreative sexual intercourse] while they are still young. Furthermore, they are good at the early perfection of the spirit (?). This is what is referred to as "the semen of the Way," *dao jing* 道精. Thus, what prompts Heaven and Earth to be without ancestral sacrifices [that is, offspring], the dragon to be without children, the immortals without wifes and the jade maidens without husbands is their great faith [in the Way].

This commentary in fact provides a "translation" of the *Laozi* text 綿綿若存 on which it comments, namely 若少年則長存矣, "If you do this on from the time when you are young, you will exist long." He thus constructs the *Laozi* phrase which Wang Bi rendered "intangible it is, but still it exists" with the "root of Heaven and Earth" as its subject, as:

If [you already] while [you] are small [act as stated in the first phrase], [you] will [continue to] exist [for long].

The rendering of the *Laozi*'s *ruo* 若 as *ze* 則 in the sense of *nai* 乃 is a legitimate possibility. More difficult is the change in subject without direct textual authority. In the Xiang Er construction, however, the previous sentence "[this is because] the door of the Dark Female Animal is [even] the root of Heaven and Earth" acts as a gloss to the first sentence; and therefore a reading which carries over the implied addressee, "you," of the first sentence into the third is tolerable.

The last line of this *zhang*, 用之不勤, carries the commentary:

能用此道應得仙壽男女之事不勤ᵉ也。
If [you] are able to make use of this way [described in phrases 1 and 3], [you] will definitely achieve immortality. In the affairs of man and woman [sexual matters] [you] should not force yourself [to break off sexual intercourse altogether at a young age].[201]

This construction keeps the old addressee as well as the prescriptive stance. It breaks the four characters into two separate admonitions. By saying "make use of this way," it inserts *dao* 道 for the *zhi* 之 in *yongzhi* 用之. The term 道 does not occur in this *zhang*, and this identification strongly deviates from the surface meaning without other supporting evidence than the necessity to establish an overall meaning for this *zhang* and the fact that the *Laozi* does use the term *yong* 用 with *dao* 道 in *zhang* 4 and 40. The first half of the last *Laozi* phrase, *yongzhi* 用之, has thus to be read:

Make use of this [method]!

For the second half, *bu qin* 不勤, the commentary gives 不可不勤也 as a "translation." The duplication of the negatives inverts any possible meaning here, and I therefore have followed Shima Kuniō in eliminating the second 不 as a scribal error. This statement in fact takes up the polemics of the previous comment, where 勤, however, is written 懃. There must have been a debate in which the emerging Daoist communities were accused of encouraging young people to force themselves to abandon sexual intercourse completely with the result that they were prevented from having male offspring for the ancestral rites. The term for "forcing oneself" in this debate must have been 懃力. Within the *Laozi*, the term 勤 does occur elsewhere (*zhang* 41 and 53), but the Xiang Er commentaries to these passages have not survived, and from their context they do not seem to fit the needs of the present passage. The Xiang Er commentary inserts the meaning of the term from this outside debate into the second part of the *Laozi* phrase, which shows that it read the *Laozi* as a text containing advice even with regard to particular events and debates occurring much after it had been composed, which in turn gave the commentator the freedom to link the dark passages with these events. Taken together, the Xiang Er constructs the last phrase of the *zhang* as meaning:

Make use of this [method], but don't force [yourself to break off sexual intercourse completely while still young]!

Xiang Er, accordingly, follows a line of reading the *Laozi* as a prescriptive guide to prolonging life, including sexual practices that by his time had become well established. He did not, and he did not have to, create this interpretive context, but operated within it in a polemical debate with other "Daoist" interpretations. This reading has its own rhyme and logic, and operates within assumptions shared widely by the audience of these texts. Other commentaries like the Heshang gong operate largely within the same context.

The purpose of comparing these commentaries was to specify the importance and meaning of the concept of textual construction by highlighting the extremely broad spectrum of potential rational options left open by the uncommented on text as a potentiality. I shall end this comparison by again juxtaposing the four translations of *Laozi* 6 extrapolated here from *Wenzi*, Zhuang Zun, Xiang Er, and Wang Bi.

Wenzi

The spirit of the valley does not die. It is called the door of the Dark Female

Intangible it [this spirit] is, but still it exists. It is called the root of Heaven and Earth.

Zhuang Zun

The spirit of the valley does not die. It is called the Dark Female Animal. As to the [operating of] the door of the Dark Female Animal, this is [done by] the root of Heaven and Earth.

Intangible it [the Dark Female Animal/spirit] is but it still exists. Its being used, does not exhaust it.

Xiang Er

If [you] desire to have [your] spirit not die, this means [that you have to play the role of] the Dark Female Animal.
[This is because] the door of the Dark Female Animal [I] call the root of Heaven and Earth.
If [you already] while [you] are small [act as stated in the first phrase], [you] will [continue to] exist [for long]. Make use of this [method], but don't force [yourself to break off sexual intercourse completely while still young]!

Wang Bi

The spirit of the valley does not die. [I] call it "Dark Female."

The door [from] which the Dark Female [comes] is [even]the root of Heaven and Earth.
Intangible it is, but still it exists

Its being used does not exert it.

Example 3: Laozi 11

This third example will not begin with Wang Bi but follow the chronological order insofar as it can be established. There are two passages in the *Wenzi* that deal with the topic of the the first phrase of *Laozi* 11.

> The hub is empty but from the center sets up the thirty spokes [to form a wheel], each of which exerts its energy to the utmost. But if one of them alone gets into it [the hub], all the spokes may be discarded, and one hardly will get anywhere [with the carriage], be it near or far.[202]

The wheel here becomes a simile for the relationship between the emperor and his ministers, the emperor being the empty center, the ministers each going about his particular business. The same argument is proffered in the second reference:

> Thirty spokes come together in one hub; each fits into one slot and they are not to get into each other's way, this is like ministers each keeping to his assigned duty.[203]

The material at hand does not seem to permit a reconstruction of the *Wenzi*'s reading of the entire *Laozi* 11, and I will therefore leave this text aside. We begin the investigation with Zhuang Zun. On *Laozi* 11.1,

三十輻共一轂當其無有車之用，

Zhuang Zun's comment runs:

> In olden times the Sages taught the people to adapt to what Heaven did, and not to busy themselves about their knowledge and skill. When drinking [they were to] use a gourd, when eating, their hands. [As a consequence] the ten thousand beings were all equal; there was no high and low. When the [time] came when there were kings, the Hundred Families, because of the heavy taxes and ponderous levies, were extremely exhausted. The demands by the ruler were relentless, and tributes [requested] from ever greater distances. Men and women bore these loads and could not manage them anymore.

Therefore the Intelligent made pushcarts 推轂, harnessed horses [to carriages] and subdued oxen so that they would carry heavy loads over long distances and relieve the people of their labor. Later generations handed [these inventions] down, and skills and craft flourished. They carved colored hubs and red wheels, embellished them with gold and silver, and attached blue pearls to them. The money wasted on a single carriage was enough to impoverish the [entire] people. This is why Laozi was concerned that this creative activity would damage the Dao and the De, and made clear [in this chapter] how doing good creates trouble and chaos. Thus in order to hand down a warning he took up the three issues of the carriages, the vessels, and the palaces to explain how having and not having [of intended] advantage and [intended] function depend on each other.[204]

The second *Laozi* phrase in this *zhang* runs:

挺埴以為器當其無有器之用

Zhuang Zun's comment:

At a time when the Dao and the De were deteriorating, sorrows and sufferings attacked from within, and Yin and Yang caused injury from without. The common folk were feeble and weak, emaciated and full of diseases. Therefore fire and water rose at the same time; the five tastes all formed [at the same time]; no difference was made between the raw and the cooked, and the dry and moist were not kept apart. Thus the Intelligent formed clay into vessels in order to cook the sour and salty. But, as a consequence hunting, extravagance, and villainy came about, and everybody slit open bellies [of female animals to get the unborn as a delicacy?] and broke eggshells to please the heart of their master. They carved stones and cut jade to make them into plates, so that the "Uncarved dispersed and was made into vessels" [as *Laozi* says in 28.6] and went straight to such an extreme.

The third *Laozi* phrase runs:

鑿戶牖以為室當其無有室之用

Zhuang Zun comments:

The heart of people had already changed, the ten thousand beings were full of hatred, insects and snakes rose, poisonous insects were growing, wild animals harmed people. As a consequence caves were not sufficient anymore to ward of calamities and preserve life intact so that life could be lived to the end. Thus the Intelligent created residential quarters with a ridgepole on top and a shelter below. They cut windows to [have lookouts], fortified the gates, and secured the doors; opening and closing [them] went fast. The advantage was that wasps and insects could not get in, wild beasts were unable to get at them; but as a consequence there arose palaces with ornamented towers, lofty terraces, and pillared rooms, and only big gates secured safety, and only city walls were [considered] safe. [As a consequence] officers and common soldiers were worn out and emaciated, and countless was the number of people who died. However, if the olden times are considered to have been well ordered, while the later times are considered to be in chaos, this only [proves] that the evil of mutual dependency of having and not having [of intended] advantage and [intended] function [respectively] depends on men![205]

Sadly, no commentary survives on what is, in Wang Bi's reading, the last sentence of this *zhang*.[206] The general argument, already stated in the commentary on *Laozi* 28.1, is that the good intentions of the Intelligent to bring some advantage to the suffering people end up by triggering developments that make people's lives even more miserable, in short how "doing good creates trouble and chaos" 為善之生禍亂. Because in the last sentence of *Laozi* 28, 有之以為利無之以為用, the 有 is linked with 利, and 無 with 用, I have read Zhuang Zun's formula 有無利用相資 in the first commentary and 有無利用相因 as interlocked constructions "the having of [the intended] advantage and the not-having of the [intended] function condition each other." This ties in with Zhuang Zun's argument that the carts, vessels, and houses indeed had the intended advantages (利) for transport, eating, and shelter but, due to developments that ensued, they did not have the intended function of improving people's lives permanently.

In my understanding, Zhuang Zun constructed *Laozi* 28 as follows:

[The Intelligent] joined thirty spokes for a cart,[207] but [although it had the intended advantage of helping with transport] it did not have the [intended] function of a carriage [to permanently alleviate the burden of the people].

[They] formed clay and made vessels from it, but [although these had the intended advantage of improving people's cooking and eating] they did not have the [intended] function [of permanently improving people's livelihood].

[They] cut doors and windows and made houses out of it,[208] but [although the houses had the intended advantage of providing shelter] they did not have the [intended] function [of securing people's lives].

There is no commentary for the last phrase

故有之以為利無之以為用，

but I would suggest the following extrapolation:

Thus [while] what one has is the [intended] advantage; what one does not have is the [intended] function.

Zhuang Zun's commentary establishes a logical context by linking the basic argument to the series in *Laozi* 2.1 有無相生，難易相成, and so forth, and an argumentative context by linking this *zhang* to others in the *Laozi* that deal with the historical deterioration that set in since olden times with the development of technology, like *Laozi* 28, which it quotes, *Laozi* 57, 80 and the chapters chronicling the moral deterioration like *Laozi* 17, 18, and 38. Zhuang Zun assumes that the *Laozi* has a "warning" to give to later generations, and that the examples selected are a part of a cultural criticism directed against the Intelligent who are not Sages enough to see that the very instruments they develop to alleviate the people's burden end up in increasing it. This reading is unique in having the *Laozi* react to particular *historical* circumstances. This construction fulfils the requirement of consistency with other parts of the *Laozi*, and of textual viability. It creates a meaningful argument, and operates with a single notion imported from outside this *zhang*, namely the Intelligent, zhizhe 智者. There is much criticism against these Intelligent in *Laozi* 18.2, 19.1, 65.3. It can be considered a shared cultural knowledge that these technical things were made by cultural heroes as described in the *Xici*.[209] As a consequence, their import into the text as the makers of these devices is not forced. We get a rationally argued relatively close reading of this *zhang*.

As in the examples already given, the Xiang Er commentary engages in polemics against other commentaries. The first *Laozi* phrase is commented upon here:

In olden times before there were carriages, the Dao, without much ado, had [Yu's director of chariots] Xi Zhong make them. When the stupid get hold of a carriage they crave only for profit 利 and neither think of practising the Dao, nor are aware of the Dao's spirit [in this carriage]. When a worthy sees this, he will indeed recognize the Dao's favor, and silently steel himself and put the emphasis on keeping to the true [nature] of the Dao.

For the next two technical inventions, the Xiang Er only notes that that the same explanation applies to them. For the last sentence of this *zhang*,

故有之以為利無之以為用，

the Xiang Er gives the following explanation:

These three things [carriage, vessel, and house] are indeed hard to manufacture, and without the Dao they cannot be completed. [But] when the stupid get them, they crave only for the profit [to be had by] them, and do not know of their origin [in the Dao]. When a worthy sees this, he in turn will keep to [that which causes] their functionality and makes making use of the Dao the basis [of his actions]. The hearts of the worthy and the stupid are like south and north, completely apart. This in fact is the meaning of these three [examples]. Nowadays, however, the fabricated "True text on causes and effects" 因緣真文 comes up with a fake concoction, saying [about this *zhang*]: "The Dao has a Heavenly hub, and the human body has a hub." "Concentrating qi 氣," it is "soft" [as the *Laozi* says in 10.2]. The "spokes" refer to the physical shape [of man] being a hub[?]." Furthermore [this text says], "The nourishing of the embryo and the tempering of the body must be as when earth is made into a brick." Furthermore, it says, "The Dao has a door and window in the human body." All this is heretic false-hood and cannot be used. Those who make use of it commit a colossal error.

The Xiang Er constructs the text as a polemic against wrong behavior, and a handbook for correct behavior, and conducts a run-ning battle against other readings of the *Laozi* that obviously were popular among its potential audience.

Both Xiang Er comments quoted here share the same argumen-tative baseline. The problem with extrapolating the Xiang Er's read-ing of the *Laozi* text lies in the role of the worthy. There are two options: Either the second half of the three examples starting with 當其無有 refers to the worthy; or the entire text is a polemic against the stupid from which the proper attitude of the worthy is abstracted only as an implied counterpoint. As the commentary says that the 車之用 is based on the Dao, the worthy should be aware of it. However, there seems to be no way to construct the phrase 當其無有車之用 in a manner to allow for a reading, "He should have/ hold onto/keep in mind [that which causes] the functionality of the carriage." Consequently, all the statements about the worthy must be verbalizitions of what is implied in the criticism of the stupid. We thus extrapolate a translation:

[The stupid take] thirty spokes combined [for] a carriage, but they do not have [consciousness of that which causes] the functionality of the carriage [that is, the Dao]. [You, reader and adept, must do the opposite.]

The last *Laozi* phrase sums up these three arguments:

Thus, what they [the stupid] hold on to is the profit [brought by these contraptions]; what they do not hold on to is [that which causes] the[ir] functionality.

As in the previous examples, the Xiang Er is most secure in the institutional parameters of its interpretation, which is does not have to justify by appeals to reason. The expression *yong* 用 appears nowhere either in the rest of the Xiang Er or in its construction of the *Laozi* in the meaning given here. The confrontation of the stupid with the worthy does appear in the *Laozi*, but there is no visible indicator in this *zhang* to suggest its application. The value of this comment as a religious and philosophical text is of course not influenced by such considerations. Obviously, its attitude concerning the technical innovations of society is fundamentally different from that of Zhuang Zun. Here in the Xiang Er, they are engineered by order of the Dao itself, and the worthy will not disdain their use; but while rejecting the blind craving of the stupid for the advantages involved, he will use them in the consciousness that they are "silent favors" bestowed by the Way.

The polemics quoted in the end suggest still another construction of our text. From the few notes, it seems possible to determine at least the outline of the reading of *Laozi* 11 suggested by the "True Text on Causes and Effects:"

Thirty spokes all unite in the single hub, but it does not have the function of a carriage.

This commentary seems to read this text as a riddle: "[What is this:] Thirty spokes all unite in the single hub, but it does not have the function of a carriage?" This reading is no exception. There are other commentaries which suggest that the thirty spokes refer to a ritual wheel mentioned in the *Zhouli* 周禮, built in imitation of the moon where one month has thirty days, and which "does not have the function of a carriage."[210] The commentary solves the riddle by pointing out that the spokes refer to the parts of the body, which are all linked to and dependent on the "hub" of the Dao in it. The pun lies in the fact that the Dao has a *tian gu* 天轂, a heavenly hub, and one in the human body, although I have not been able to verify this implication. In fact, the result does not have the function of a carriage. The next phrase would then run:

[What is it:] Clay is formed to make a vessel, but it does not have the function of a vessel.

Here the riddle is in the unmentioned firing of the clay. The nourishing of the embryo and the tempering of the body is compared to the firing of clay. The pun is more successful here, because a "vessel," *qi* 器, is often also used to designate a human being.[211] The third example would translate:

[What is it:] Doors and windows are drilled to make a room, but it does not have the function of a room.

Here, this text claims the pun is in a reference to the Dao's having doors and windows by which to get into the human body. The construction of the last line is difficult, since we have no further quotation. It probably read:

Thus, while [these three] are there as an advantage, there is nothing [practical] they can be used for.

With all the basic differences of approach separating Zhuang Zun from the two subsequent constructions, they share a basic grammatical construction, most important the linkage between *wu* 無 and *you* 有 in the three phrases of the type 當其無有X之用. Within the *zhang* itself, however, the last phrase uses these two terms separately, and it is this point on which Wang Bi capitalizes to make the *zhang* a cornerstone of his construction of *Laozi*'s philosophy.

As a reminder, I shall repeat Wang Bi's text for the first three phrases of *Laozi* 11:

三十輻共一轂當其無有車之用
挺埴以為器當其無有器之用
鑿戶牖以為室當其無有室之用

The text begins with three examples, which are stylistically parallel. For Wang Bi as for all earlier commentators, the parallelism indicates that all three argue the same problem. Wang Bi comments on the first phrase:

轂所以能統三十輻者無也。以其無能受物之故故能以寡統眾也。

That by which a [= one] hub is capable of holding together thirty [different] spokes is its negativity [vis-à-vis their specific features]. Because of this negativity [the hub] is capable of taking in the points of origin of [many different] entities. That is why [the hub] is capable, being itself the minimum, to control the many [spokes].

Wang Bi elevates the 無 of the main text here into a separate term, "negativity," and thus eliminates the possible joining of 無有 in the sense of "does not have." This is justified by *Laozi* 40.3, 天下之物生於有有生於無, "the entities of All Under Heaven live from Entity, [but] Entity lives from negativity," where *wu* 無 appears as a separate noun.

The application of the verb *yong* 用 to negativity does not occur elsewhere in the *Laozi*, but the term *yong* 用 is frequently applied to *dao* 道 and other terms seen as equivalent to *wu* 無 (*Laozi* 4.1, 6.1, 40.2, 45.1–2). With this construction, the *zhang* links up with a great many others dealing with the features of that by which the ten thousand entities are. *Laozi* 11, however, contributes a new feature to these *zhang*. While it is often stated in Wang Bi's construction of the *Laozi* that that by which the ten thousand entities are is "negativity" or "without shape and name," this *zhang* makes a philosophic argument that only through this negativity vis-à-vis the spokes is the hub able to accommodate and control all of them. As the language in *Laozi* 11 is relatively unambiguous, the statement here is used to enrich and specify the context of statements seen as related as the beginning of *Laozi* 40.

Extrapolated from Wang's commentary, the three lines from *Laozi* 11 have to be translated as:

Thirty spokes share one hub. But it is the [latter's] negativity [vis-à-vis the specificity of the spokes] that is [the basis] for the usability of the existing carriage. One kneads clay in order to make a vessel. But its negativity [that is, the fact that inside the vessel there is no clay so that many different things can be put into it] makes for the usability of the existing vessel. One cuts out doors and windows to make a room. But it is their [the doors' and windows'] negativity [vis-à-vis the wall] which makes for the usability of the existing room.

While this construction manages to handle the term 無, and to insert the statement into the context of other tenets of the *Laozi*, the

construction of 有 in the combinations 有車, 有器, and 有室 is unique
in this *zhang*. Its justification comes from the last phrase of the
Laozi in this *zhang*:

故有之以為利無之以無用.

Wang Bi comments:

木埴壁所以成三者而皆以無為用也
言有之所以為利皆賴無以為用.

The three [spokes, vessels, rooms] are made from wood, clay
and mortar respectively, but all [depend] on negativity for
their usability. This means all entities in order to be beneficial
depend on negativity for their usability.

This commentary forces a translation of the *Laozi* text as:

Therefore that [they are specific] entities makes for [their]
being beneficial, while negativity makes for [their] usability.

In slightly different forms, Wang Bi reiterates this last formula
in his commentaries on *Laozi* 14 and 40.1. The "therefore" links this
last sentence to the preceding three and makes it into a summary
statement. Two terms from these preceding three statements
are taken up by the summary—*you* 有 and *wu* 無. Wang Bi gets
his justification for the unusual reading of 有車, 有器, and 有室 as
meaning "existing carriage," "existing vessel," and "existing room"
from the meaning of *you* 有 in the summary statement. It should be
kept in mind that, in view of the *Laozi*'s constant warnings about
the unreliability of its language, its frequent use of metaphors and
similes, his often forced and diffuse grammar and content, as well as
his blunt creation of new terms, the creation of new philosophical
uses for familiar colloquial terms and forms of expression cannot
have shocked Wang Bi, who shared the *Laozi*'s quandary.

We next take up the commentary by Wang Bi's contemporary
and friend Zhong Hui 鐘會, whose education looked very similar to
Wang Bi's. His father, Zhong Yu 鍾繇, also had written a *Commentary on the Laozi*, of which, however, nothing survives. The historical record does not tell us whether Zhong Hui's commentary was
earlier or later than Wang Bi's; it is likely that is was later as it is

never mentioned in the context of the anecdotes surrounding Wang Bi's finishing his *Commentary*. As we are at this stage investigating the range of the *Laozi*'s potentiality and do not really focus on the difficult problems of the historical sequence of the different commentaries, the date is of no primary importance.

The Zhong Hui commentary seems to have enjoyed a reasonable popularity: Li Shan's *Commentary to the Wen Xuan* quotes from it; and Li Lin's 李霖 (fl. 1172) *Daode zhen jing qushan ji* 道德真經取善集 quotes from it at length.[212]

Commenting on the last phrase of *Laozi* 11,

故有之以為利無之以為用,

Zhong Hui writes:

[The *Laozi*] takes up the above three cases [of the hub of the wheel, of the vessel, and of the room] to elucidate the mutual dependency of *you* 有 and *wu* 無. [Only by being] together can neither possibly go under.
舉上三事明有無相資俱不可廢。

That is why

that which is [,namely the wood, the clay and the mortar] is considered to be [= provide] the usefulness *li* 利, and this usefulness lies in the physical substance, *ti* 體;	that which is not [,namely that all three, the hub, the vessel, and the room have "nothing" inside] is considered to be [= provide] the usability *yong* 用, and this usability lies in [the hub's, the vessel's and the room's] emptiness, *kong* 空.

故

有之以為利利在於體	無之以為用用在於空。

Thus

the physical substance is the outside and the usefulness *li* 利 [provided by it] depends on the usability *yong* 用 [provided by] the emptiness [of hub,	The emptiness is the inside, and the usability, *yong* 用, [provided by it] relies on the usefulness *li* 利 [provided by] the physical substance in order to

vessel, and room] in order   come about.
to achieve completion.
　　故
體為外利資空用以得成   空為內用籍體利以得就。
Thus, only if usefulness and usability depend
on each other, can both not come to naught.
That which is not depends on that which is for
usefulness, and that which is depends on that
which is not for usability. The two categories
endow each other.
但利用相籍咸不可亡也。無賴有為利有籍無為用。二法
相假。[213]

Zhong Hui's construction follows the radical innovation introduced by Wang Bi, namely the treatment of both *you* 有 and *wu* 無
in this last sentence as nouns based on the same nouns in the second
halves of the three examples. However, Zhong Hui remains strictly
within the boundaries of *zhang* 11. Neither *you* nor *wu* are linked up
with other *Laozi* passages where they appear as independent philosophic terms. *You* 有 remains the specific physical matter providing
the "outside" of the hub, the vessel, and the room. *Wu* 無 remains
the specific absence of matter "inside" these physical bodies. By
stressing the interdependence of *you* and *wu* with the formula
有無相資, Zhong Hui, like Zhuang Zun, links this *zhang* to *Laozi*
2.1 有無相生, which he restates. The *Laozi* phrase in 2.1 is part of a
series of antonyms together with "difficult and easy," "long and
short," and "high and low." Both parts in these pairs operate on the
same level. While for Wang Bi *wu* 無 clearly is the basis of ordered
regularity of the realm of *you* 有, Zhong Hui extracts from the
basically same construction of the text a mutual dependency of the
two realms. Thus, even while operating within the same context
used by Zhuang Zun, Zhong Hui constructs a new meaning. By
accepting the basic premise of Wang Bi's commentary to this *zhang*,
that it deals with the relationship of the material and immaterial
realms, Zhong Hui's commentary ipso facto becomes a discussion
with that of Wang Bi. Wang Bi constructs the last phrase of the
Laozi 11 with its new concept of *li* 利 on the basis of the three
statements about the carriage, vessel, and house. In his construction of these three statements, the *wu* 無 clearly is the basis for the
functionality of *you* 有. Zhong Hui bases his analysis on the grammatical parallelism and implied equality between 有 and 無 in the

last phrase, and reads the statements about the carriage, vessel, and room in this light.

From the commentary translated above, it is clear that Zhong Hui constructed the last phrase in *Laozi* 11 differently from Wang Bi:

> Therefore
> that which is is taken for
> [that which provides]
> usefulness [to that which
> is not]   while   that which is not is taken
>   for [that which provides]
>   usability [to that which
>   is].

This construction has the practical advantage of respecting the strict formal parallel between the two parts, while Wang Bi weaves them into a single sentence with a grammatical division of labor. Zhong Hui's construction has the disadvantage, that the term *li* 利 appears for the first time in this *zhang* in this phrase and does not seem to have either focus or status comparable to the *wu* 無. The term *li* 利 in Zhong Hui here indicates the actual usefulness: Although both hub and vessel are empty inside, their particular use is determined by the specific matter surrounding this emptiness. The term *yong* 用 indicates usability: Only because the hub, vessel, and room are "negative" and hollow inside is the general possibility of their particular use established.[214]

Extrapolating from this last commentary, we might even be able to reconstruct Zhong Hui's reading of the entire *zhang* 11:

> Thirty spokes share one hub. But it is that of it [the hub] which is not which constitutes the usability of the carriage which is. One kneads clay in order to make a vessel. But it is that of it [the vessel] which is not which constitutes the usability of the vessel that is. One cuts out doors and windows in order to make a room. But it is that of it [the room] which is not that constitutes the usability of the room that is.

Both Wang Bi and Zhong Hui share a commitment to stay very close to the text, to base the commentary on rational extrapolation with as little extraneous material as possible, and both read the

Laozi as the work of a philosopher, and not a Daoist god or teacher advising adepts in proper ways to reach immortality. Zhong Hui's theory of the "mutual dependency" of *you* and *wu*, however, marks a fundamental rift in the two men's world views. From this little passage we might presume that Zhong Hui was a key figure in the transition from what scholars have described as the "cherishing the *wu*," *guiwu* 貴無, of Wang Bi to the "cherishing of the *you*," *guiyou* 貴有, of such texts as the *Liezi*, and Guo Xiang/Xiang Xiu's *Commentary on the Zhuangzi* a few decades after Wang Bi's death.[215] Zhong Hui's commentary shows that, even within the same philosophical tradition, Wang Bi's solutions were still being contested, but with an approach that accepted the stern rules of exegesis Wang Bi had established.

A fair number of fragments have survived from the *Daode zhen jing jiejie* 道德真經節解. The dates of this commentary are unclear; Lu Deming writes that some claim that *Laozi* himself had written it, and others that Heshang gong was the author. A commentary by this name is mentioned for the later Han. Modern scholars like Yan Lingfeng have assumed that it was written by Ge Hong, and Kusuyama Haruki 楠山春樹, who has done the most intensive work on it, assumes that it is linked to what he calls the remaking of the Heshang gong commentary.[216] We shall bypass this issue and try to read it as another option for constructing *Laozi* 11, which coexisted for many centuries with that presented by Wang Bi.

A fragment survives that deals with the following statement in *Laozi* 11 (with the first character different from Wang Bi's text):

埏埴以為器當其無有器之用

The *Jiejie Commentary* comments as follows:

謂古人為土器不燒鍊得水則敗為不成器也。子欲為道
不入室依時鍊形者則為俗人必死也。

This means: when people of old made clay vessels they did not fire and temper them. When water got into them, they would disintegrate, and become incomplete vessels. If you wish to pursue the Way but fail to deeply "delve into the house" [that is, pursue the studies to unravel the mystery] and to temper [your] body for the prescribed time, then you are [just] a vulgar person and you are sure to die.[217]

This requires that we translate the preceding *Laozi* text as:

> If [only] from clay the vessel is made [and it is not properly fired], it will not have a vessel's use. If [only by] drilling doors and windows the house [= the body] is made [but you do not properly delve into it and temper your spirit and body], it will not have a house's use [of providing shelter for immortality].

This commentator links the 無 and 有 in the section 當其無有器之用 in the way the Xiang Er commentary did, and reads the entire piece as a single grammatically linked sentence. The comments on the two other examples are not transmitted, but there are short notes on the very last *Laozi* phrase in this *zhang*:

> 故有之以為利無之以為用

About the term *you* 有 in the first half, the *Jiejie* writes 謂有道也 "[the '*you* 有'] means 'having the Way.'" The location of this commentary after 有之以為利 indicates that it was read as a separate sentence. Extrapolating from this commentary, we translate:

> therefore having it [the Way] is considered an advantage.

The next commentary provides us with the subject of both sentences. It runs:

> 謂聖人守一行自然無所用
> This means that the Sage holds on to the One and practices [his] nature and is in need of nothing [else].

Accordingly we get a reading of this entire *Laozi* sentence as follows:

> Therefore [the Sage] takes having it [the Way] as a blessing [so that] there is nothing [else] he needs.

From the comment on the phrase about the vessel, we know that the *Jiejie* read the three examples of the *Laozi* as negative teachings. If someone pursuing the Way is not tempering his spirit and body, he might look like a long-lasting vessel, but as an unfired clay vessel will disintegrate with water, his body will disintegrate and die.

For the last phrase, the *Jiejie* introduces a completely new subject, the Sage, and an equally new object, the Way. The two additions in this sentence are in fact one; once the *zhi* 之 is referred to the Way, the Sage comes in automatically as the subject, because it is he who "has" the Way. The Way itself is not simply invented as an object. In the *Jiejie*'s reading, the first three examples in the *zhang* are negative material; they describe what one should not do and the consequences of this wrong approach. Thus a possible rational reading can assume that after a "therefore" will come the positive conclusion, confronting the Sage's attitude with that of the "vulgar person." The operations of the *Jiejie* are far more violent than those of Wang Bi; by presenting the theme of the *zhang* as being the necessary self-tempering of the acolyte and introducing the core notions for understanding the *zhang* from outside, the *Jiejie* still manages to fulfil the ultimate goal of the commentator, to construct a cohesive and meaningful text and situate it in a homogeneous whole.

We shall again juxtapose the different translations in a tentative chronological order with the tradition established by Zhuang Zun on the left, and the "Daoist" tradition on the right.

Zhuang Zun

[The Intelligent] joined thirty spokes for a cart but [although it had the intended advantage of helping with transport,] it did not have the [intended] function of a carriage [to permanently alleviate the burden of the people].
[They] formed clay and made vessels from it, but [although these had the intended advantage of improving people's cooking and eating] they did not have the [intended] function [of permanently improving people's livelihood].

Xiang Er

[The stupid take] thirty spokes combined [for] a carriage, but they do not have [consciousness of that which causes] the functionality of the carriage [that is, the Dao]. [You, reader and adept, must do the opposite.]

[They] cut doors and windows
and made houses out of it,
but [although the houses
had the intended advantage
of providing shelter] they
did not have the [intended]
function [of securing
people's lives].
Thus [while] what one has is
the [intended] advantage;
what one does not [have is
the intended] function.

Thus what they [the stupid]
hold on to is the profit
[brought by these
contraptions]; what they do
not hold on to is [that
which causes] the[ir]
functionality.

The True Text on Causes and Effects

[What is it:] Thirty spokes all
unite in the single hub, but
it does not have the
function of a carriage.
[What is it:] Clay is formed to
make a vessel, but it does
not have the function of a
vessel.
[What is it:] Doors and
windows are drilled to
make a room, but it does
not have the function of a
room.
Thus, while [these three] are
there as an advantage,
there is nothing [practical]
they can be used for.

Wang Bi

Thirty spokes share one hub.
But is is the [latter's]
negativity [vis-à-vis the

specificity of the spokes]
that is [the basis] for the
usability of the existing
carriage.
One kneads clay in order to
make a vessel. But its
negativity [that is, the fact
that inside the vessel there
is no clay so that many
different things can be put
into it] makes for the
usability of the existing
vessel.
One cuts out doors and
windows to make a room.
But it is their [the doors' and
windows'] negativity
[vis-à-vis the wall] that
makes for the usability of
the existing room.
Therefore that [they are
specific] entities makes for
[their] being beneficial,
while negativity makes for
[their] usability.

Zhong Hui

Daode zhen jing jiejie

Thirty spokes share one hub.
But it is that of it [the hub]
which is not which
constitutes the usability of
the carriage which is.

One kneads clay in order to
make a vessel. But it is
that of it [the vessel] that is
not that constitutes the
usability of the vessel that
is.

If [only] from clay the vessel
is made [and it is not
properly fired], it will not
have a vessel's use.

One cuts out doors and
windows in order to make a

If [only by] drilling doors and
windows the house [= the

room. But it is that of it [the room] that is not that constitutes the usability of the room that is.

Therefore that which is is taken for [that which provides] usefulness [to that which is not], while that which is not is taken for [that which provides usability (to that which is).

body] is made [but you do not properly delve into it and temper your spirit and body], it will not have a house's use [of providing shelter for immortality]. Therefore [the Sage] takes having it [the Way] as a blessing [so that] there is nothing [else] he needs.

Conclusions

For highly influential and exceedingly well-educated readers/ commentators of the *Laozi* around the middle of the third century at one of the intellectually most vibrant times in Chinese intellectual history, the various grammatical options presented above were considered rational and acceptable constructions of the same text, their extreme differences notwithstanding. A claim that history has made its selection by having Wang Bi survive largely intact cannot be substantiated. As shown elsewhere, this line of transmission nearly broke off during the middle and late Tang, when the Heshang gong and Xuan Zong's imperial commentary reigned supreme.[218] The conditions for textual transmission were also different for the three commentaries. The patronage for the Xiang Er depended on the vagaries of the particular brand of Daoism it propounded, and the fate of Zhuang Zun's commentary on the changing status of Han scholarship in later centuries.

What causes the wide differences among the different authors in constructing the same text? Two conditions are present. First, the structure of the text's grammar, logical links, and terminology is fairly open so that different legitimate constructs are possible. This condition is important, but it does not seem essential because there always is the possibility of constructing a text on the basis of a metalevel of communication that will alter all elements of the surface text. Second, there is the context, the horizon of expectations against which the text is perceived. Since Frege's pathbreaking study, the determining influence of context for the meaning of an individual word in a sentence has been recognized.[219] We are dealing here, however, with a much broader context, which determines the character of the text a priori without much inference from the surface wording. I shall concentrate here on the Xiang Er and Wang Bi commentaries.

Wherever the Xiang Er speaks of the text, it simply calls it *dao* 道. The text consists of "that which is said by the Dao" 道之所言 (commentary on *Laozi* 17), a formula going back to the *Laozi* phrase about the "words uttered by the Way" 道出言 in *zhang* 35. In the commentary to *Laozi* 21.1, the Xiang Er writes: "The Dao is truly great. It taught Confucius to become knowledgeable, but later generations did not believe in the text of the Dao anymore 後世不信道文, but only exalted the books of Confucius and considered them insuperable. That is why the Dao makes this clear [that Confucius was taught by the Dao through the phrase in the *Laozi* to which this is the commentary, namely 孔德之容唯道是從, which has to be rendered "the appearance of Confucius' capacity is only [due to his] following the Dao"] and tells it to later worthies." The text is thus the Way's own verbalization, coming as a polemic against the Confucian books as well as false "Daoist" teachings. This depiction coincides with the extremely high position given to Laozi in the single surviving reference to him. In the commentary to *Laozi* 10.1, the Xiang Er defines the "One" mentioned there as the Dao, 一者道也.

The One is beyond Heaven and Earth, and enters into the sphere between Heaven and Earth, but when it goes back and forth in the human body it is all over under the skin, not [as some fake Daoists claim] just in one place. The One, when it disperses its form is the ether, *qi* 氣, and when it assembles its form, is the Great Supreme Lord Lao 太上老君.[220]

In this sense, *Laozi* is identical with the Dao by being the concentrated form of the One that is the Way. The text thus has the highest possible authority from what by the late second century was for some circles the highest god. This god, as depicted in the imperially ordered inscription for him, the *Laozi ming* 老子銘, was coeternal with the primeval chaos, and embodied himself into an endless series of historical personages down to the present. The "words uttered by the Way" in the form of the *Laozi* thus have the highest authority of truth for the Xiang Er commentary, while in Wang Bi they are the groping—and in terms of their language essentially unreliable—attempts at philosophizing by a philosopher slightly inferior to Confucius.

In the tradition followed by Xiang Er, Laozi had discovered the secret of longevity; his book contained, whatever its surface might seem to say to the uninitiated, the prescriptions for attaining it, which were then formulated into a guidebook of religious discipline which also has Xiang Er as its author. The *Laozi* is not one of a body of texts of equal value here but the one and only important source of truth. In the tradition leading up to Wang Bi on the other hand, the *Laozi* dealt with the same topic many of the other "classics"—in his view—dealt with, namely "that by which the ten thousand kinds of entities are." It is an attempt at understanding the truth someone else, Confucius, embodied and performed in his words and actions. The *Laozi* here operates on the same philosophic and linguistic level as books like the *Lunyu* or the *Zhouyi*, and has to be read with them.

If the attribution of the Xiang Er to one of the Daoist church fathers is correct, it would explain the very authoritative language of this commentary. It is not an argumentative commentary trying to rationally convince the audience by explaining the difficult passages of the text in the light of those that seem clearer; rather it is a commentary that claims either religious authority by direct inspiration (not made explicit in the commentary) or teacher authority in a teacher/student relationship, or both. The Xiang Er's (as well as Zhuang Zun's) main instrument of explanation is the import of concepts from outside the *Laozi*. The implied reader of the Xiang Er is a student, an acolyte, someone under the religious and academic authority of a teacher. The Xiang Er does not seem to assume that the students had read other commentaries, but it did assume that they had heard, and were influenced by, other Daoist teachings. Wang Bi had to assume that his readers had read other commentaries to the *Laozi* and that the survival of his own hinged on its scholarly quality to be proved in a "free market" competition. His main strategy is to explain the text in its own terms by linking the terms and arguments in the different *zhang* with each other.

The horizon of perception or the context thus turns out to be decisive for the strategies of constructing the text and reducing the enormous range of its potentiality to a verifiable level of definiteness. The Xiang Er commentary is a fine example of the overwhelming importance of context because none of the key teachings it extracts from the *Laozi* are clearly delineated in the surface text. The Wang Bi *Commentary* is a fine example of a largely internalist reading. The two strategies reflect different intellectual and social environments; operate on different relationships between the author, the commentator, and the reader; and claim different types of authority for their exegesis. However, both are constructions of the text, lifting a potential to actuality. As constructions they have to be treated primarily as intellectual products of their times and traditions. The question of whether they found out the "true meaning" of the *Laozi* rests on assumptions that are not verifiable, if they are relevant.

In his criticism of the different schools, Wang Bi claimed that all had produced their particular *Laozi* constructions. While it is hard to associate the different schools directly with the available material and find, for example, a systematic Mohist or Ruist reading of the *Laozi*, the comparison of the available material confirms Wang Bi's claim that in his time many radically different textual constructions of the *Laozi* already existed. Wang Bi claims that these differences are all due to mistakes in the basic method of reading the *Laozi*. On this issue we do not have to take sides. The comparison of the different readings, however, yields a number of uncomfortable insights:

- For all commentators the necessity to comment on the *Laozi* was evident from the painful difference between the status of the text/person as well as the philosophical/religious importance associated with it and the range of actualized potential meanings extracted from it, which made the text practically unusable.

- There is no agreement among the different old commentators as to the grammatical and the logical structure of the different *zhang*. We can assume that the surviving commentaries managed to find enough patronage for either their reading strategies or the resulting philosophic statements or both to be handed down. It is highly likely that other commentaries with perhaps an even wider margin of diversity were written but not handed down. The Xiang Er commentary survives just in one Dunhuang MS, and it engages in battle with other "Daoist" readings of the *Laozi* of which we often know not more than what this single copy tells us.

- The text sustains as viable a variety of radically different constructions, if the factual acceptance of these constructions by distinct sets of readers is taken as an indicator of what was considered a viable reading.

- The commentators operated within intellectual traditions. Mostly within their traditions they studied each others' constructions and would absorb what seemed philologically convincing, and perhaps philosophically and politically acceptable. Wang Bi took a number of hints from Zhuang Zun as Zhong Hui did from Wang Bi. Much research in this respect still remains to be done.

- There is no reason to assume that there ever was a golden age where the text was unambiguous, and when the diversities in the construction were smaller. The available traditions like *Wenzi, Hanfeizi*, Zhuang Zun and Xiang Er have not invented their reading strategies, which go back much further. In fact, the concept of an "original" *Laozi* text with an intrinsically unambiguous meaning accessible to an audience that shared its philosophic, rhetorical, and cultural orientations, and was able to read it within the same context in which it had been written, might not be plausible; definitely it is not an operative concept, because it only adds one more commentator to the long list. Whatever the circumstances of the genesis of the *Laozi*, we have to treat it as an (unintentional) series of potentialities, of latent options, actualized by commentators, or modern scholars, to the best of their knowledge and understanding. The text does not subscribe to the modern notion of textual ambiguity, and neither do the commentators. The text goes as far as it can in reducing ambiguity of understanding concerning a very elusive object and structure, and the commentators do their share by translating the text into an optimally unambiguous homogeneous whole.

- All commentators share the assumption that the text in fact is unambiguous, and that it is their duty to rediscover the original meaning. We are not dealing merely with various interpretations of basically the same sentences with their grammatical and logical links as would be the case in studies of the Old and New Testaments or of Indian or Greek philosophers. We are dealing with different grammatical and logical constructs supported by the same Chinese text with a normal range of textual variants. The commentators did not develop a set of grammatical concepts to define the relationship of the words to each other. Still, they had to develop, and did develop, a way of telling their readers how the text was to be constructed, and how ambivalence was to be eliminated. They did this in a variety of ways, in many cases by means of translations. These translations would make explicit the grammatical and logical relationships they saw embedded in the *Laozi* statements. As a consequence, the problem of translating the *Laozi* is not in any way a problem first faced by the modern translator into the modern Chinese vernacular or foreign languages who is separated from the text by a huge cultural distance. It is a problem faced and handled by readers and commentators from the earliest times. The modern translators, however, have mostly failed to study closely the efforts of their predecessors.

• The impatient scorn of modern translators for the efforts of the earlier commentators is quite superficial. As the above comparisons show, even commentators like Xiang Er tried to arrive at a homogeneous reading of the text, and the commentaries altogether show a varying but generally high degree of textual sophistication in the solution of the many riddles in the *Laozi*.

• The above tentative analysis of sample commentaries suggests that the decisive step in determining the meaning of a text is not prompted by the verbiage of this text itself, but has been made earlier before it ever reached a reader. The fundamental difference between Xiang Er and Wang Bi is not in the particular construction of this or that phrase but in the general framework within which the *Laozi* was perceived. This general context determined the questions for which the answers were then extracted from the text. The second contextual ring within which the plausibility of a particular reading would be determined is the rest of the text as well as other texts assumed to belong to the same group. There one might find clearer statements of the same issue; the term that seems diffuse here is there associated with a subject or an object that could be imported; in short, this second ring becomes the quarry from which to mine the material for enriching the particular context of a passage enough to pin down its meaning. Only then comes the third ring, namely the immediate context of the phrase or the *zhang*, with its terminology, rhetoric, grammar, and logic. The diversity in the outcome of the constructions given above shows to what degree the outer contextual rings— here the assumption of the *Laozi* as a text dealing with prolonging life, there the assumption of it as a philosophical text dealing with that by which the ten thousand entities are—determine the inner, and to what extent the *Laozi* as a linguistic and rhetorical structure was molded by such influences. The range of potentiality of the textual surface differs in different texts, even among different parts of the same text. The range of the textual surface of the *Chunqiu* or the *Zuozhan* is infinitely smaller than that of the *Laozi*, while that of the *Zhouyi* is similar. The Han constructions of the *Chunqiu* widely differ in the meaning of its statements and omissions, but they differ little in grammar and logic.

Having outlined the problem Wang Bi faced—the extreme range of potentiality and ambivalence of the *Laozi* as seen from the existing commentaries—we shall now study in systematic detail his techniques for establishing an unambiguous, homogeneous meaning for the *Laozi* as a part of a group of authoritative texts that included the *Zhouyi*, and the *Lunyu*.

The Craft of Wang Bi's Commentary

Introduction

The general strategy of Wang Bi's commenting is to reduce to a minimum the ambivalence of the individual passages and terms of the text. This ambivalence was in practical fact evident in the coexistence of wildly varying readings of the very same words by different commentators as we have documented above; and it was a theoretical fact in that many of the *Laozi*'s phrases do not have an explicit subject; many of its metaphors and comparisons are difficult to grasp; and its terminology sometimes does not seem consistent.

Wang Bi's general technique of reducing ambivalence consists in linking the obscure section with a section that deals with the same issue in less diffuse terms, and of explaining the diffuse section in the light of the clearer one. The result of this merger is a dramatic shrinking of the number of issues Wang Bi's *Laozi* is thought to deal with. Wang Bi's statement on the single core issue of the *Laozi* has been quoted above, and the analysis of his *Laozi* indeed yields a finite and small number of tightly interlocked issues that flow out of one single core thought. A detailed study of their philosophic content will be presented elsewhere.[1]

Wang Bi's commenting takes on many specific forms. He explains individual words, metaphors, or similes. He makes explicit certain implied consequences of the *Laozi*'s statements. He indicates subjects, objects, logical and grammatical links, wherever they seem presupposed by the text but are in danger of being missed by the reader. And he points out structural parallels with other sections of the text.

Integration of Commentary and Text

Wang Bi's *Laozi Commentary* is transmitted in 81 *zhang*. For *zhang* 31 and 66 there is no commentary. For *zhang* 31 a tradition reported in Song texts says that Wang Bi considered that *zhang* spurious. For *zhang* 66, no other cause for the absence of a commentary is discernible except the lack of ambivalence in the text, which seems to make a commentary of Wang Bi's type superfluous. We do not know whether sections of Wang Bi's *Commentary* were lost. The agreement between early quotations from the *Commentary* and the transmitted text is extremely high, and thus the probability of major losses small.[2]

In all forms in which it has come down to us, the *Commentary* is inserted into the text in the manner that must have become popular during the last decades of the second century. We have, however, no manuscript evidence of the exact way in which text and commentary were interlaced. There is reason to assume that the single source claiming that Ma Rong pioneered the insertion of the commentary into the text—namely Kong Yingda—may be correct. Wang Bi himself interlaced what up to his time were separate "wings" of the *Zhouyi* with the text directly attached to the hexagrams; this elevated these commentaries to the hexagrams and their lines to the level of the main text and made them an organic part of it. A few decades after Wang Bi, Du Yu did the same for the *Zuozhuan* by making this originally independent text into a commentary to the *Chunqiu* with an authority status akin to the *Chunqiu* itself. He did not, however, proceed by inserting the respective *Zuozhuan* section under each day, month, or event, but by cutting the *Chunqiu* record into years and inserting the *Zuozhuan* section for the entire year after the entire *Chunqiu* section on that year.[3] His own commentary, however, seems to have been inserted straight under the respective texts to which they referred. Transferred to Wang Bi's *Laozi Commentary*, this would give two attested options for the way in which Wang Bi originally wrote it. He could have added his complete commentary for each *zhang* at the end of that *zhang*, or he could have inserted his commentary notes directly under its respective parts.

In the texts handed down, Wang Bi intersects the remaining 79 *zhang* of the *Laozi* with a total of about 403 commentary statements. While this gives roughly five comments per *zhang*, there are some extremes on both ends in terms of number and length. Some (16, 20, 25, 41) are broken into rather small items resulting in up to fifteen comments per *zhang* (20). Five *zhang* (4, 6, 19, 75, and 78) have only one comment; with the exception of *zhang* 78, they first give the entire *Laozi* text of the *zhang*, and then go through the details in the commentary en bloc. *Zhang* 38 stands out for its extreme length, and it might in fact be a *zhang* with a single commentary because the second item is attested only in one source. Since these *zhang* with a single commentary survive in today's editions we have to check whether they are not the remains of the original organization. This would mean that originally all *zhang* were commented upon in this manner, and that later compilers cut the commentary blocks and distributed the pieces to their appropriate places.

The hypothesis seems to find support in a curious feature of Wang Bi's *Commentary*. In no less than 146 places, Wang Bi repeats verbatim the *Laozi* phrase or a segment thereof to which the commentary pertains with the formula "that is why [the Laozi] says," 故, 故曰, 故云 or 故謂.

Laozi 7.2 might serve as an example:

Text:
>This [pattern of Heaven and Earthmentioned before]
>is the reason why the Sage

puts his own person in the background and [manages it in this way] that his own person comes to the fore.

disregards his own person and [manages it in this way] that his own person will last.

>Indeed is it not because of the absence of private interests in him that he is able to accomplish his private interest?

Wang Bi obviously considers the beginning half self-evident and comments only on the last phrase:

"Absence of private interest" means that
he does not act with regard to his own person.
It is because [in this manner]
his "person will excel"   and   his "person will last"
that [the text] says "he is able to accomplish his private interests."

It might be argued that this uneconomical repetition of a phrase available in immediate proximity would make sense if the entire commentary for a *zhang* had been appended to the end of each *zhang*. The same repetition of sections of the main text occurs in Wang Bi's *Zhouyi Commentary*. Should it turn out that Wang Bi appended his entire commentary to each *zhang* of the *Laozi*, it would follow that he also appended his entire commentary to each hexagram of the *Zhouyi*. Given the extreme shortness of the *zhang* of the *Laozi*, however, the argument that it was necessary to repeat the text to remind the reader of it is not convincing.

A closer look at the references to the main text in the *Laozi* after *gu* 故 in the commentary shows that they are part of a wider argumentative structure. In the example above, the quotation at the end is clearly integrated into an argument. Besides the 146 direct and verbatim quotations from the main text there are another 30 that take up the core vocabulary but add explanatory material into the text itself. An example is *Laozi* 18.2.

Once knowledge and insight have appeared [in the ruler's actions], there will be great deceit [among his subjects].
智慧出焉有大偽

Wang Bi comments:

If he practices tricks and applies his intelligence to spy out cunning and deceit, his interests become apparent and his shape becomes visible [and as a consequence] the other beings will know how to evade him. That is why [according to the *Laozi*] once knowledge and insight have appeared [in the ruler's actions,] great deceit [among the subjects] is born.
故智慧出則大偽生也

The logical link between the two halves of the *Laozi* phrase is not spelled out there, nor are the dynamics underlying this logic. Wang Bi deals with the latter first, and then provides an umambiguous translation of the *Laozi* phrase. He reads *yan* 焉 as a particle indicating a completed action, so that, once knowledge and insight have appeared, great deceit will be the consequence. To highlight this, he translates *yan* 焉 with *ze* 則. In this construction 有 has to mean "there will be." In order to bring out the aspect that the application of knowledge by the ruler in fact "will bring about" deceit among the people, he translates *you* 有 with *sheng* 生. At the same time, Wang Bi retains the structure of the original. The final repetition is not a reminder of the passage that is being treated—a reminder that would make sense only in the beginning of a piece of commentary (as in Wang Bi on *Laozi* 7.2 above)—but a return to reread the original after the close analysis, either in the full original or with some logical additions in the light of the explanations just given.

A further feature of Wang Bi's commentary adds weight to this argument. In eighteen *zhang* (3, 22, 24, 27, 37, 44, 46, 55, 59, 63, 64, 65, 67, 68, 72, 73, 78, 79) Wang Bi does not comment on the last sentence of the *zhang*. All these *Laozi* sentences can be read as summaries or conclusions of the *zhang* of which they form the end. It is very unlikely that these comments were lost. Sometimes, as in *Laozi* 7.2, a *zhang* has two arguments. In this case the first argument about Heaven and Earth ends with the conclusion, "That is why [Heaven and Earth] are able to excel and persist." Although it ends the argument of 7.1, it stands after the commentary for 7.1 at the beginning of 7.2 which then deals with the Sage. The commentary for 7.2 does not deal with this phrase about Heaven and Earth. We have here exactly the same structure as in the case of the uncommented upon last sentences, only this time in the middle of a *zhang*. A similar case is *Laozi* 56.7. We have thus to look for another explanation for this feature as well as for the inordinate amount of verbatim quotations from the immediately preceding *Laozi* text. Perhaps the analysis of this structure will also help in deciding the question of the original arrangement of Wang Bi's *Laozi Commentary*. *Laozi* 24 will serve as an example:

The first *Laozi* phrase, 企者不立, is commented on by Wang Bi:

物尚進則失安故曰企者不立

The other entities [that is, his subjects] will [as a consequence of his example] think much of [their own] advancement, and consequently make [him] lose [his] security. That is why [the text] says: "[A ruler] who takes a high stand, will not stand [firmly]."

This commentary settles the question of the identity of the implied actors, namely for the first part a ruler who acts wrongly, and for the second his subjects who react to his posture. It also settles the question of the logical link between the two halves. If the ruler stresses his exalted position and behaves pompously, his underlings will also strive for status advancement, and, as a consequence of this, his own status will be threatened. Having received this guidance from the commentary, the reader may now handle the remaining phrases in this series at his own discretion. They are

跨者不行, 自見者不明, 自是者不彰, 自伐者無功, 自矜者不長.

Following this guidance, we translate

[A ruler] who makes great strides will not make headway. [A ruler] who shows himself does not become enlightened. [A ruler] who is self-righteous will not have [his being right] shine forth. [A ruler] who brags will not have [his] achievements [uncontested]. [A ruler] who praises himself will not have [his virtue] grow.

The brackets come from the context of these sentences as they are quoted in the commentary on *Laozi* 22. The next *Laozi* sentence, 其於道也曰餘食贅行, again needs a commentary, as it is highly ambivalent. The commentary runs:

其唯於道而論之若郤至之行盛饌之餘也 本雖美更可藏也本雖有功而自伐之故更為疣贅也

Analyzed with regard to the Way [these attitudes of the ruler] are like the actions of Xi Zhi, like a leftover in rich food. Although [the food] is basically delicious, [the leftovers] may rot. Although [Xi Zhi] basically had merits, he bragged about them himself, and that was excessive and "superfluous" [and brought about his death].

The Xi Zhi story from the *Zuozhuan* nicely illustrates this *zhang*. He bragged about his unquestionable merits, and someone observed that this would evoke the resentment of his superiors, that in this bragging his impending doom could already be discerned. Extrapolating from this commentary, the *Laozi* text has to be translated

> With regard to the Way, [I] call these [attitudes] "leftover food" and "superfluous actions."

The commentary thus inserts itself into the rhetorical structure of the text guiding the reading of the individual sentences and leaving the reader to his own devices for those passages that follow from the interpretive framework. Wang Bi also did this with the long series of statements, and does so again now by not giving a comment on the last *Laozi* phrase which runs:

物或惡之故有道者不處.

Like the implied reader we surmise that the negative results outlined above come about because the resentment and envy of others is provoked by these actions.

> [The mechanism through which the above-mentioned negative results come about is that] other entities might loathe him [who brags about himself in this manner.] That is why one who has the Way will not opt [for this course of action].

Obviously, Wang Bi's commentary sets out to make the entire argument of the *Laozi* so translucent that the conclusion would be so self-evident that the reader could be relied upon to decipher it with his own wits. The reader's capacity to decode the conclusion himself also offered superb and, for the reader, very satisfying proof of the validity of Wang Bi's approach.

The lively interplay between guidance by the commentator and free action by the reader in the framework set up by the commentary which this *zhang* and the other *zhang* presented earlier in this chapter show strongly suggests that the commentary was, as a rule, directly integrated into the text. Moreover, it inserted itself into the time sequence and procedural structure of reading, becoming an inalienable part of the text's rhetoric as well as the reading/constructing procedure of the reader, whom it provided with bridges, thoroughfares, and links in a text where he was in constant danger of getting lost, or of interpreting randomly.

Emphatic Rejection of Other Readings

We take up the second issue that needs elucidation—the large number of Wang Bi comments that end with the formulas 故, 故曰, 故謂, and so forth, followed by a verbatim quotation of the *Laozi* phrase that has been commented upon.

One might argue that this repetition of the main text served to stabilize the *Laozi* through repetition. Attempts in this direction can already be seen in the Mawangdui B *Laozi* manuscript, which lists the exact number of Chinese characters for each of the two parts of the text. In fact, these quotations have served to stabilize the text, because preserved in them are many of the readings in Wang Bi's *Laozi* main text that have long been superimposed by readings taken from the Heshang gong *Laozi* text.[4] Still, while this stabilization theory has some merit, it is not very convincing. Altogether, only a small part of the *Laozi* is thus repeated; and it is improbable that a commentator would anticipate that the status of his own commentary would become so high that copyists might superimpose another *Laozi* text but would keep his quotations from the *Laozi* in their original form. There must be another reason why the uneconomic repetition of the words of the main text at the end of a usually fairly short commentary occurs.

As stated in the introduction to this section, Wang Bi's implied reader knew the *Laozi* by heart, and knew it in one or more other commentarial constructions. His reading of the main text of some phrase would thus quite naturally proceed according to the construction of the commentary with which he had first read the text, or which he appreciated most. Wang Bi's *Commentary* thus serves the double function of demolishing the reader's previous construction of the passage in question, and convincing him of the plausibility and viability of the construction offered by his new commentary. At the end of this double-pronged procedure comes the 故, 故曰, or 故謂. In my opinion, it has a clear polemical tone: "that [and not because of the outlandish constructs suggested by the commentator whom you, dear reader, have previously read and followed] is why [the *Laozi*] says:" . . . The translation of the quotation then following must end with an exclamation mark!

Wang Bi does not give these verbatim quotations in all his comments, only in a sizable number. Although this cannot be verified because the commentaries against which his scorn was directed are no longer extant, I suggest that these reaffirmations of the true meaning of a passage come where he felt other commentators had most grievously misconstrued the *Laozi*. This would also explain Wang Bi's selection of certain passages for quotation while others do not receive such attention. Presenting an emphatic rejection of other constructions, these repetitions of passages from the *Laozi* text are thus archaeological evidence of one or several countertexts against whose presence in the minds of his readers Wang Bi was fighting. It would contribute both to the quality and the length of this study to follow this argument up with specific evidence. The scantiness of the still-available remains of these countertexts, however, and the doubtful dates of many commentaries, force me to abandon this endeavor. From the criticism he directs in the *LZWZLL* against manifold other interpretations, we can assume that Wang Bi was talking back not to one text but to a plethora.

These quotations from the *Laozi* also fulfil a second function. Assume that the reader approaches the *Laozi* text with a different construct in his head than that offered by Wang Bi. Then follows Wang Bi's commentary, which explains the *Laozi* passage both in terms of its surface structure and its philosophic meaning, sometimes including a translation of the passage into unambiguous and explicit contemporary language. At the end comes the quotation from the main text or a slightly supplemented translation. In this position it is an appeal to the reader to reread this original text in the light of the explanations given, to completely dissociate himself from the construct with which he began, and to latch onto the construction offered by Wang Bi.

The result of his comments is a text whose statements have no ambivalence for the implied (not necessarily the modern) reader, and are fully homogeneous. As Wang Bi's *Commentary* proceeds to construct the common philosophic bases out of which the different arguments of the *Laozi* grow, he presents the *Laozi* as not only a homogeneous text but as systematic philosophy.

Explaining Metaphors, Similes, Comparisons, and Symbols

In Wang Bi's construction, the *Laozi* makes use of a number of figures of speech, and the commentary attempts to decode their metaphoric values. The most famous certainly is the expression *chu gou* 芻狗 straw/dogs in *Laozi* 5:

> 天地不仁以萬物為芻狗
> Heaven and Earth are not kindly. For them, the ten thousand kinds of entities are like straw/dogs.

The interpretation chosen by some modern commentators in the tradition of the Heshang gong commentary—that this might refer to the "straw dogs" sacrificed then thrown away—has the advantage of linking the expression with a cultural artefact, which should facilitate decoding. However, the story always cited here from *Zhuangzi* 37.14.31f. tells of two stages in the straw dog's existence, first, it is adorned with great pomp, then it is thrown away and trampled on. No echo of this sequence can be found in *Laozi* 5. At best the second part of the scenario might work, that they are despised. In this case, however, it is not clear why this term should be used, since there are many others that would have been much more appropriate. The story about the origin of the straw dogs told in the Xiang Er commentary is different from the *Zhuangzi*'s, but runs into the same trouble.[5] Wang Bi thus tries to define the expression from the general context of his *Laozi* construction. He comments:

> Heaven and Earth do not produce grass for the benefit of cattle, but the cattle [still] eat the grass. They do not produce dogs for the benefit of men, but [still] men eat the dogs. As they do not interfere with the ten thousand kinds of entities, the ten thousand entities all fit into their use so that there is none that is not provided for.

In this manner, the statement becomes a metaphor for the self-regulatory order of nature, which provides for all without Heaven and Earth doing anyone favors, a statement that finds ample support in other sections of the *Laozi* as well as in the *Lunyu*.

Further down in *Laozi* 5, Wang Bi has to deal with an explicit comparison by the *Laozi*:

天地之間其猶橐籥乎虛而不屈動而愈出

The space between Heaven and Earth is like a
drum   or   flute,
        [that is],   hollow but inexhaustible
                                         [like the flute in the variety
                                         of sounds it can produce],
[and like the drum] the more
[it] is beaten, the more
[sound] comes out of it.

The *Laozi* interprets its own comparison in a very specific manner, without any philosophical vocabulary. Wang Bi's commentary reads both comparison and explanation in terms of the *Laozi*'s philosophic tenets. He writes:

Inside, the drum and flute are empty and hollow [respectively]. [The flute] has no feelings [of its own to prefer one sound over the other] and [the drum] has no activity [of its own to create this resonance rather than another]. That is why [as the text claims] [the flute] is hollow but is is impossible to exhaust it; [the drum], all the beating notwithstanding, is inexhaustible. In the [space] between Heaven and Earth That-which-is-of-itself-what-it-is is put grandly into effect; that is why [the space between Heaven and Earth] is inexhaustible "like a drum or a flute"!

Again the context establishes the reading strategy. According to the construction of the first part of this *zhang*, Heaven and Earth are not partial, show no particular concern for any one of the ten thousand entities. As a result, all of them can operate in accordance with their natures, which puts them into some "prestabilized harmony" with each other (to use a Leibniz expression). In some manner, the second part of the *zhang* will have to link up with the first. The "space between Heaven and Earth" is where the ten thousand entities are born. By being empty, it accommodates the ten thousand entities without any preferences. There are other similes and metaphors in the *Laozi* dealing with the unlimited potentiality of emptiness as a specific form of negativity.[6] In each case, their absence of specific preferences gives these emptinesses the possibility of absorbing or generating the greatest variety of entities. These other passages enrich the context of the present passage not only through being parallel in terms of content, but also through being much less ambivalent. The flute, being hollowed out, is "without feelings"; it has no preference for this sound or the other and therefore can play them all. Based on the immediate context as well as a number of similar comparisons in the *Laozi*, Wang Bi thus manages to construct a plausible meaning for this passage in terms of the immediate context of the *zhang*, and the broader context of the *Laozi*, viable in terms of grammar, vocabulary, and metaphor.

Another example is *Laozi* 28.1:

知其雄守其雌為天下谿

He who knows that as its [All Under Heaven's] cock he [has to] keep to being its hen, will be All Under Heaven's valley.

The statement operates with three metaphors, cock, hen, and valley. None are explained in the *Laozi* itself. Wang Bi comments:

A cock belongs to the category of those standing at the fore, a hen to the category of those standing in the background. He who knows how to be [the person] standing at the fore [in All Under Heaven] will by necessity keep in the background. That is why the Sage [as the *Laozi* says in 7.2] "puts his own person in the background and [manages it in this way] that his own person comes to the fore!"

The metaphors of cock and hen are thus explained as different expressions for the issues of *xian* 先 and *hou* 後 dealt with in *Laozi* 7.2. This parallel also provides the Sage as actor for this *zhang*, which has no subject for *zhi* 知. By introducing this parallel with its much smaller degree of grammatical and content ambivalence into the context of 28.1, Wang Bi manages to dramatically reduce the extreme grammatical and content ambivalence in this first phrase by reading it as a more diffuse restatement of the much clearer 7.2. The result again takes care of the immediate wording, the context of the *zhang*, and the larger context of the *Laozi*, and eventually constructs this *zhang* in a manner that makes the latter part of it into a core statement of the *Laozi*'s philosophy of history. We still have to deal with the last element of 28.1: "will be All Under Heaven's valley."

Wang defines the metaphorical valley:

谿不求物而物自歸之
A "valley" does not yearn for other entities, the other entities render themselves to it on their own.

The valley is lower than its environment. The 先/後 structure of the first half also implies a high/low 高下 hierarchy; in *Laozi* 6 the "spirit of the valley" is called a "Dark Female." The gender of this Female is seen there by Wang Bi as a metaphoric expression for the "lowly position" of the spirit of the valley. The valley in *Laozi* 28.1 thus fits the local "female animal," the hen. *Laozi* 6, however, which might look like the closest parallel to *Laozi* 28 because of the valley metaphor, deals with the undiscernable "root of Heaven and Earth." (The terms for "valley" in the two *zhang* differ; they are 谷 and 谿.) In Wang's construction, *Laozi* 28 deals with the Sage's treatment of society. Instead of going for the closest word, Wang Bi goes for the closest structure. This is provided by the relationship of rivers and seas to smaller waters. The smaller waters quite naturally run into the bigger ones because the latter "lower themselves" under them, which again is the cause why they can be so big. *Laozi* 32.4 says "[I] compare the [role] of the Way in All Under Heaven to the [relationship] of rivers and the sea to rivulets and streams." Wang Bi's comment is nearly the same as for the valley in 28.1:

川谷之不求江與海非江海召之 不召不求而自歸者也
The rivulets and streams are not striving [to flow into] the rivers and seas and [their running into them] is not caused by the rivers and the seas calling them; [thus] without either calling [by the latter] or striving [by the former] they render themselves [into the rivers and the seas] on their own.

Like *Laozi* 28, *Laozi* 32 deals with the role of the Sage in society. His policies in society will imitate the Way's relationship with All Under Heaven. This application is made immediately after the above quotation from *Laozi* 32.4. The model is actually provided by *Laozi* 66, for which there is no Wang Bi commentary. It begins:

That by which the rivers and seas are capable of being the lord over the hundred rivulets is that they are good at lowering themselves under them. . . . Therefore if one wants to stand above the people [as their lord] one has to lower oneself under them by means of one's words.

This argument is echoed in many other *Laozi* passages that deal with the necessity of the Sage ruler to adopt a lowly posture in *Laozi* 39.4 or 42.1. Wang Bi again defines the precise meaning of this metaphor by linking it to what he considers other articulations of the same issue that make their point more clearly.

Insertion of Subject

A sizable number of entire *zhang* of the *Laozi* lack a clear subject or actor. In an even larger number of individual phrases within the *zhang* reference is made, usually by means of the particle *qi* 其 to a preceding noun that is not clearly identified. In both cases, Wang Bi sets out to eliminate the ensuing confusion.

Twenty-three of the seventy-nine *zhang* of the *Laozi* in Wang Bi's construction are not explicit in identifying the actor to whom the *zhang* refers (3, 9, 10, 14, 18, 19, 22[?], 23, 24, 28, 32, 35, 36, 39, 52, 56, 57, 58, 59, 60, 63, 64, 71). *Zhang* 57, for example, begins 以正治國, "ruling the state by means of a standard." In this case it is easy to extrapolate the actor as being someone who rules a state. *Zhang* 3 不尚賢 使民不爭 "not to shower worthies with honors induces the people not to struggle," does not define the actor. Again the only one to have an influence on "the people" at large would be someone in a ruling position. Further down in 3.2, the *zhang* mentions the Sage enacting these principles. As "not struggling" clearly is an ideal attitude of the people in the *Laozi*, the actor of the phrase does things correctly. He thus must be both in a ruling position and a Sage, in short a Sage ruler.

In his commentary to a *Laozi* sentence in 27.5 about the Sage's "being good at saving other people," Wang Bi quotes the "not to shower worthies with honors" from *zhang* 3 with the Sage as the subject. We can thus safely assume that in Wang Bi's construction the implied actor of *Laozi* 3.1 is the Sage ruler.

Zhang 18 begins 大道廢焉有仁義, a phrase that seems to have a perfect actor and reads "once the Great Way has failed, there will be humaneness and justice." As is evident for Wang Bi from "humaneness and justice," however, the phrase deals with the history of society. The question of whether or not the Way prevails depends on the ruler. Wang Bi's commentary, "once he has lost the management without interference, he will in turn by means of the way of applying insight and establishing good [deeds] further the other beings," begins with a quotation from *Laozi* 2.2 according to which "the Sage takes residence in management without interference." The actual subject of *zhang* 18 is thus a ruler, and *Laozi* 18.1 has to be translated "once [a ruler] has abandoned the Great Way, there will be humaneness and justice [guiding his actions]."

Zhang 10 is more complicated. It begins 載營魄抱一 能無離乎, which, following Wang Bi's construction, reads "to keep to the camp, to hold on to the[ir] One, and be able not to be separated from it— ah!" It continues in the same manner without a hint as to whether the addressee is an ordinary human being, the Sage, or the ruler. Wang Bi provides no explicit answer, and, as he is otherwise ruthless in eliminating ambiguity, we must hypothesize that for him there could be no question who the addressee was. The result of this "keeping to the camp" and so forth is spelled out by Wang Bi's commentary: "then the ten thousand kinds of entities [would] submit of their own accord as guests." This formula occurs in *Laozi* 32.1: "If only the dukes and kings were able to keep to it [simplicity], the ten thousand kinds of entities would submit [to them] of their own accord as guests." We can thus introduce the "dukes and kings" from *zhang* 32 into the present *zhang* 10. The *zhang* itself confirms this procedure by speaking of "loving the people and governing the state" as the activities of the addressee. The dukes and kings should be Sages, but sadly enough they are not. Hence the desperate tone in *zhang* 10. In fact, according to *Laozi* 22.6, it is the Sage who is really able to do what the dukes and kings may at best aspire to, "hold on to the One." Since, in Wang Bi's construction, the *Laozi* is a text about the ontological bases of political rule, he proceeds from the assumption that the subject/actor in all but one (39) of these unassigned *zhang* is the ruler who either rules society by following the Way, and thus is a Sage, or who does not, and thus destroys himself and society. This assumption about one pervasive topic of the *Laozi* is so much engrained in Wang's commentary that in many cases he does not directly state the implicit subject, but operates on the basis that it is well known, as shown above.

Wang Bi thus proceeds from the assumption that all of the *zhang* in fact have proper if implicit actors, and that the seeming ambivalence of the text is but the result of a blurred and misinformed mind. At the same time, the lack of emphasis in Wang Bi's identification of these actors indicates that the countertext(s) against which his commentary was written shared Wang Bi's assumption about the core actors. The surviving commentaries quoted above in the confrontation of different commenting strategies do not share this feature with Wang Bi. From this we conclude that they do not really qualify as Wang Bi's countertexts.

The number of unspecified references among the 143 occurrences of 其 in 51 *zhang* is about 20 (in *zhang* 1, 21, 24, 27, 28, 52, 54, 56, 58, 59, 60, 64, 72, and 78) in Wang Bi's text and reading. The numbers in the other commentaries widely diverge, in part because these open references provided opportunities to enhance the homogeneity of the respective textual constructions by inserting references that would bring the text in line with the commentator's basic assumptions.[7]

Occasionally, Wang Bi will explicitly say what a *qi* 其 refers to, as in *Laozi* 78.1. In the commentary to this phrase, 天下莫柔弱於水 而攻堅強者莫之能先以其無以易之也, Wang Bi writes on the last section 以用也其謂水也 "the [term] 以 means here 'to make use.' [The word] 其 refers to water." This results in a translation: "Nothing in All Under Heaven is more supple and soft than water, and [thus the way a ruler can manage it] that no one is able to get ahead of him while attacking the firm and violently rigid is by his going about it by means of its [the water's characteristic] that there is nothing capable of altering it."

In most cases, he will just insert the term, as in *Laozi* 1.3 and 1.4. In these phrases, 故常無欲 以觀其妙 and 常有欲 以觀其徼, the point of reference for the 其 is not clear. Grammatically, there are four candidates in the preceding text (and infinitely more outside). The four are *dao* 道, *ming* 名, *wu ming* 無名 and *you ming* 有名. In Wang Bi's construction of *Laozi* 1.2, 無名 萬物之始 有名 萬物之母, the actual subject is neither 無名 nor 有名, but "it," which is defined in the commentary as *dao* 道 in the "translation" of the above phrases 言道以無形無名 始成萬物. The Dao assumes two functions at different moments of the ontological process described in the text with the nouns *shi* 始 and *mu* 母, and in the commentary with the verbs 始 and 成. While this cuts down the candidates by two, it also eliminates the *ming* 名 from *Laozi* 1.1, because it is not mentioned elsewhere in Wang's *Commentary*. Thus we are settled on Dao.

Laozi 21.2 道之為物 惟恍惟惚, "the Way as an entity is vague, ah, diffuse, ah," is followed by 恍兮惚兮 其中有物 惚兮恍兮 其中有象. The only previous noun to which this *qi* 其 could refer would be *dao* 道. This is the resulting translation: "The Way as an entity is vague, ah, diffuse, ah. Vague, ah, diffuse, ah, it is, [and] in it [in the Way] there is an entity; diffuse, ah, vague, ah, it is, [and] in it [in the Way] is an image." This does not make sense in the immediate context because in this way the "Way as an entity" would have "an entity in itself"; and no sense in the larger context because no echo exists in other sections of the *Laozi* in Wang Bi's construction. In this quandary, Wang Bi introduces a subject from "outside," namely the "ten thousand kinds of entities," *wan wu* 萬物, writing "by means of being shapeless [the Way] initiates the entities; by means of being unfettered [the Way] completes the entities. The ten thousand kinds of entities are [thus] initiated through it [the Way] and completed through it, but they do not know that through which this came about. That is why [the text] says:" Thus the Way is diffuse, but as that which initiates and completes the ten thousand kinds of entities it is present in them." In that sense "there is in them [in the ten thousand kinds of entities]" an entity or an image [of the Way], but due to its diffuseness, "it" remains undiscernable. This reading firmly sets the resulting text into the context of many similar statements in the *Laozi*. The end of this commentary also gives a fine example of the emphasis underlying the *gu yue* 故曰. Obviously there were other identifications of *qi* 其 that are emphatically rejected here.

A second source of high ambiguity in the *Laozi* is the *zhi* 之 after verbs. In many cases there has been a clear previous noun to which this refers, but there are cases where it remains open (as in *Laozi* 9.1, 9.2, 10.7ff., 54.4).

The 之 in *Laozi* 9.1 持而盈之 不若其已 does not have a previous noun to refer to. It might mean merely "something." In his commentary, Wang Bi says 持謂不失德也, "'to maintain' refers to 'not to let go of the receipt/capacity'." This second formula comes from *Laozi* 38.2, were it denotes the ruler of 'inferior capacity' 下德. In the search for a topic *Laozi* might refer to with this 之, Wang Bi cannot find another "to maintain," *chi* 持, in the *Laozi* from which to take an appropriate object. The two other occurrences of the term do not fit. He thus redefines "to maintain" as meaning "not to lose" 不失, which corresponds with the normal meaning of the word in the *Laozi*. For the "not to lose" there is a source in *Laozi* 38.2 which has a definite object, *de* 德. Wang Bi transfers this object here.

For the next phrase, *Laozi* 9.2 揣而梲之 不可常保, Wang Bi is not as lucky with finding elsewhere in the *Laozi* a proper insert for the 之. He therefore switches strategy and goes for an interpretation of the metaphor to decode the meaning. He comments, "If one has already polished the tip [of the sword] so that it becomes pointed, and grinds it in addition so that it becomes sharp, a situation [arises] where it is unavoidable that one will suffer a defeat. That is why [as the text says] 'One will be unable to protect [oneself] for long'." The actual noun "sword" is not included, because the meaning of the phrase is much broader. It refers, for example to a ruler who, while already in an honored position, then proceeds to grandly display his status, which will provoke others into competing with him, and eventually will result in his demise. For this reading, there are ample parallels in both the *Laozi* and the *Zhouyi*. So, in both cases, the 之 retains the general meaning of "something," and the phrases describe in general terms the social dynamics resulting from this style of action. However, by linking each of the two phrases to other statements in the *Laozi*, the ambivalence created by 之 is largely eliminated.

In *Laozi* 54.4, 修之身 其德乃真 修之家 其德乃有餘 as well as in the subsequent parallel phrases, the content of 之 is not defined. The term 修 does not occur elsewhere in the *Laozi*. Wang Bi solves the riddle by defining 之 as the content of the first two phrases of this *zhang*, which run: "He who is good at anchoring will not be uprooted. He who is good at holding on to [the One] will not be stripped [of anything]." In *Laozi* 54.3 these two phrases are said to be a *dao* 道, a "Way," and this is in fact the term that has to be inserted into the above quoted sentences, which translate: "If [I] strive after this [Way] as far as [my] person is concerned, [my] receipt/capacity from it [the Way] is the true essence. If [I] strive after this [Way] as far as [my] family is concerned, [my family's] receipt/capacity from it [the Way] is abundance."

In *Laozi* 10.7–8, the *Laozi* says 生之 畜之, and again there is no clear object this might refer to. Wang Bi refers to *Laozi* 51.1f., where, after a series beginning 道生之, 德畜之, the next sentence identifies 之 as the "ten thousand kinds of entities" 萬物 by saying 是以萬物莫不尊道 而貴德 "That is why there is none among the ten thousand kinds of entities that does not honor the Way and value the receipt/capacity." The same identification is transplanted into the phrase in 10.7, already written into the commentary on 10.6.

This last procedure is based on the assumption of a self-referentiality of the text that will not repeat explanations given elsewhere. At the same time it is based on the simultaneous presence of the entire text to the reader who knows it by heart, so that an explanation in *zhang* 51 is not "later" but just somewhere else than one given in *zhang* 10. The text has no time structure within which an argument could unfold and develop. Each *zhang* is at an equal distance from the common center of all *zhang*, a distance measured as that between language and the That-by-which.

As these examples show, Wang Bi was aware of the ambiguity of the *Laozi* for a reader. In his view, however, the text is not ambiguous and diffuse in itself. Wang Bi's solutions for the problems described above suggest that the *Laozi* is self-referencing and that passages might seem ambiguous only because they are not understood as shorthand references to other statements that spell out the same issue without or with less ambiguity.

Defining Terms through Equivalence

Wang Bi makes use of a commenting technique that had already become a widely used practice in the early commentaries to the *Chunqiu*, namely word definition through an equivalent. Xu Shen's 徐慎 (d. 120?) *Shuowen jiezi* 説文解字 absorbed many of these commentarial notes, and in turn became the source for later commentators looking for meanings of terms beyond their own whim. These glosses make commentarial work more scientific, more objective. Ruan Yuan's 阮元 *Jingji zuangu* 經籍纂故 is only the most systematic and well-documented handbook of this genre.[8]

The vocabulary of the *Laozi* is generally small and easy and does not need much technical commentary to explain the meaning of certain words. However, each term does have a spectrum of possible applications, and, if the core meaning of the term does not fit the context, diffuseness and ambivalence arises. In such cases, which Wang Bi sees as rare, he gives short dictionary definitions. They stand at the beginning of a commentary and usually consist of a simple synonym for that meaning in the spectrum of possible meanings that seems appropriate to him.

As a verb, *zai* 載 in the phrase 載營魄 in *Laozi* 10.1 intrinsically has a potential range of meaning "carrying," "containing," and, rarely, "being in or on" as in "being installed in a high office" 載高位 (Ban Gu), which Yan Shigu comments on as meaning 乘, "to ride on," "to be saddled in." Wang Bi's commentary seems linked to this rare meaning when he says it is "like staying in ..." 猶處也. Morohashi's *Dai kan wa jiten* (38309) lists only Wang Bi with this definition. In the next sentence the *Laozi*'s *zhuan* 專 in 專氣 again has a normal range of meaning "only," "special," but might also rarely function as a verb with the meaning "take exclusive control of" or "make exclusive use of." Wang Bi's commentary draws on this potential meaning when defining it as *ren* 任, "to put to use."

Translating the Text

Often combined with grammatical and content explanations of certain words, we find "translations" of a passage in question. In fact, to reduce the ambivalence of the text, Wang Bi has to translate it either implicitly or explicitly.

Translation does not necessarily mean to transpose into another language. A translation might transpose a text from one language period to another, like the Han-dynasty *Mengzi* "translation" by Zhao Qi studied by Dobson.[9] It might transpose the text from one language level to another, like the Qing dynasty translations of the *Shengyu* 聖喻 into the vernacular.[10] It might paraphrase with other, more easily understandable words the content of a given phrase, indicating the grammatical and logical links in the process and spelling out some of the implications, a technique used, for example in Wang Yi's 王逸 (89–158) commentary to the *Chuci* 楚辭.[11] And it might proceed by a straight translation that spells out implied grammatical and logical links as well as implied subjects and objects. Wang Bi uses the two last-mentioned procedures, and might in fact have pioneered the use of the last.

These translations might simply bring out the grammatical structure of an expression. An example occurs in *Laozi* 36.2 國之利器, "the useful instrument of the state," where it is not clear whether it is a useful instrument used by the state, or whether it is an instrument beneficial to the state. Wang Bi simply spells out the grammatical structure and cuts down the ambivalence by translating it into 利國之器也, "It is the instrument of benefit to the state." In other cases, translations establish both the grammar and the content, as in *Laozi* 21.7, where the expression 眾甫 is translated 物之始 "the beginning of the [ten thousand] entities," where 物 translates the 眾, 始 the 甫, and 之 shows the grammatical relation between the two.

In still other cases a subject is added to enhance precision. In the phrase in *Laozi* 16.3 吾以觀其復, which might mean "by means of XX I see their return," it is not clear, to what *yi* 以 might refer. The preceding text of the *Laozi* ran 致虛極也守靜篤也萬物並作, which Wang Bi read "to reach emptiness is [their] ultimate; to hold on to stillness is [their] blessing. [Even while] the ten thousand kinds of entities may all act at once." Wang Bi's commentary to the present phrase (吾以觀其復) runs 以虛靜觀其反復. He thus introduces from the previous *Laozi* text the terms *xu* 虛 and *jing* 靜 so that the *Laozi* phrase 吾以觀其復 has to be read "I [as opposed to others] by way of this [emptiness and stillness] perceive that to which they return." This small clarification has a substantial impact on the overall meaning. It becomes clear that the "simultaneous action" of all the ten thousand entities is in contrast to this emptiness and stillness. And, second, the emptiness and stillness of the entities is not immediately evident in their presence, but is perceived by the philosophical eye as their ultimate purport. With great economy and always staying close to the textual surface, Wang Bi's short comment reduces a textual construct of great potential range of grammar and meaning to a precise, definite statement.

Translations or paraphrases of entire sentences are usually introduced by Wang Bi with the word *yan* 言. I count 24 "translations"[12] and 17 paraphrases[13] in his *Commentary*.

An example of a "translation" may be *Laozi* 10.1. The text there runs 載營魄抱一 能無離乎. Wang Bi first proceeds to three definitions. The first, 載猶處也, has already been mentioned. It is technical and specifies the particular meaning from the spectrum covered by the applicable word here: "[The term] *zai* 載 is [to be understood as having a meaning] like *chu* 處, 'to stay in (or reside in)'." The second 營魄 occurs in the *Li Sao* of the *Chuci*, and is defined in Wang Yi's Han-dynasty commentary as *linghun* 靈魂, the "soul",[14] but here by Wang Bi as 人之常居處 "the abode of eternal sojourn of human beings." This is one of the few commentaries by Wang Bi that is not further substantiated. The third term to be defined is the *yi* 一, the "One," about which Wang Bi writes: 一 人之真也, "The One is the true [nature] of human beings." This definition is based on Wang Bi's reading of the term One in *Laozi* 39.1ff., and in effect merges the "abode of eternal sojourn" and the One. After having provided these definitions, Wang Bi proceeds to the translation:

言人能處常居之宅抱一清神能常無離乎則萬物自賓也

[The sentence] means, if a human being would be able to stay in [its] abode of eternal sojourn, "hold on to the One," and purify [its] spirit, [so that] it would be able to be permanently "not separated" from [the abode and the One]—ah, then [indeed] "the ten thousand kinds of entities [would] submit [to him] of their own accord as guests" [as the *Laozi* says in 32.1].

The "translation" replaces the original vocabulary with the new definitions, and makes the logical and grammatical links explicit. The insertion of *neng* 能, "to be able," reinforces the character of the particle *hu* 乎 at the end to form an exclamation mark instead of a question mark. The *ze* 則, "then," which introduces the last phrase, further enhances the putative character of the preceding lines in the sense of "if only." For the last phrase, 萬物自賓也, there is no visible textual basis here. Wang Bi suggests that in the exclamation translated here as "—ah!" a hidden statement is implied, and he proceeds to spell it out "then indeed the ten thousand kinds of entities would . . . ," which in fact is a quotation from another section of the *Laozi*, not a Wang Bi invention. For *Laozi* 30.4, 故善者果而已矣 不以取強矣, Wang Bi first defines *guo* 果, which has one possible meaning of "result," or, in a different grammatical mode, of "be done," with a rare option for a verbal use, "to complete." As the *zhang* is dealing with "someone who supports the lord of men by means of the Way," there is an expectation that the text will deal with his establishing order. From this context, Wang Bi says that the meaning of *guo* is "like" that of *ji* 濟, used in Wang's commentary with the meaning "to bring to order, to regulate." Wang then "translates" the phrase:

言善用師者趣以濟難而已矣　不以兵力取強於天下矣

This means: someone who is good at using troops will set his mind only on bringing troubles to order and that is it, but he will not by means of military force impose violent [rule] in All Under Heaven.

The insertion of 用師 after 善 is based on the preceding *Laozi* phrase, which speaks of the dreadful effects of using the military 師. The justification for the very elaborate "translation" of 不以取強 into 不以兵力取強於天下 is the statement in the first phrase of this *zhang* that "someone who supports the lord of men by means of the Way will not impose violent [rule] in All Under Heaven by means of soldiers" 不以兵強天下. Wang Bi reads 不以取強 as a short version of the 不以兵強天下. From the surface 不以取強 would translate "will not [proceed] by means of resorting to force" with 以 referring to the 取強, while this indeed very close parallel to the first phrase inserts the soldiers 兵 as the point of reference of 以 so that a reading "will not by means of [troops] impose violent [rule in All Under Heaven]" results. Comparing the *Laozi* text with the construction offered by this commentary and translation, we see a stunning reduction of ambivalence and diffuseness in this transition from potentiality to actuality.

The *Laozi* text does not tell us what the *shanzhe* 善者 is "good at"; the translation makes clear that he is "good at using troops" and thus fully aware of the potential noxious effects of this use mentioned in the preceding line. The *Laozi* does not tell us what is to be "done with" 果; the translation makes clear that he will "bring troubles to order"; the meaning of 而已 in the *Laozi* implies that nothing else but 果 is intended. The implied intention is made explicit by the addition of 趣, "setting one's mind on." Through this construction, the very diffuse 善者果而已 comes to mean that someone who understands the dangers of using the military because it is by means of the Way that he supports the lord of men will use troops only intermittently to quell some momentary trouble. In the second half, the *Laozi* does not spell out the object of *qiang* 強, but the commentary adds it as 天下. The *yi* 以 in the second half of the *Laozi* text is hard to understand if one accepts Wang Bi's reading of the first half. If military is used to quell troubles how could one say "it is not by means of resorting to violence"? By reading 以 in effect as 用之, and then inserting 兵力 for 之, Wang Bi manages a construction that leaves nothing murky, and is solidly based on context and other supporting evidence.

It turns out that the difference between a piecemeal commentary that explains the individual elements one by one and this kind of translation is not too great. As mentioned in the introduction, my own translation strategy follows the precedent of Wang Bi's translations for all those passages where he has not provided such explicit guidance. The *yan* 言 introducing these "translations" might in turn be translated in a more elaborate rendering as "translated into our contemporary language with all implicit grammatical and logical connections, subjects, and objects made explicit, this *Laozi* statement would read:"

A second type of presenting the content of an entire phrase or passage is the paraphrase that restates the purported content in other words. It also begins with *yan* 言. An example is *Laozi* 58.1:

其政悶悶.

Wang Bi comments:

言善治政者無形無名無事無正可舉 悶悶然卒至於大治故曰其政悶悶也
This means: [A ruler] who is good at regulating government will have neither shape, nor name, neither [government] activity nor standard that could be pointed out. [His government] is "hidden [from view]" [but] eventually will bring about the Great Order. That is why [the text says]: "He [a ruler] whose government is hidden [from view] . . ."

The paraphrase with the expressions 無事 and 無正 links the present passage to *Laozi* 57.1 以正治國 以奇用兵 以無事取天下, "[a ruler] who rules the state by means of standards will with cunning make use of the military. [Only a ruler who rules the state] by means of not busying himself [with government] activity will get hold of All Under Heaven." Needless to say, 無正 appears here only in its inverse form, 以正. The theme of the unfathomable ruler has already been mentioned in the analysis of *Laozi* 17. The paraphrase spells out what it sees as the implied consequence of this phrase in the words "eventually will bring about Great Order." The strategy of the paraphrase again consists in eliminating textual diffuseness through an enrichment of the context with material from other *zhang* of the *Laozi*; this would allow tying down the meaning of the crucial 悶悶 under the assumption that it is but another expression of a thought found in many parts of the *Laozi*. The passages cited here all stress the fact that this government cannot be discerned from manifest signs, which ties well with the metaphorical term 悶悶 "hidden."

Wang Bi's translations show that the problem with the *Laozi* the much-maligned modern Western language translator has is merely a variant of a very old Chinese problem. Translation into a different discourse always involves a dramatic reduction of textual ambivalence. The strategies to do this might differ as much as those among Xiang Er, Wang Bi, Duyvendak, Kimura Eiichi, Yan Lingfeng, D. C. Lau, or von Strauss. The quandary is always that the result is but one of several potential texts, which furthermore might be of major importance for a given place and time while being thoroughly irrelevant in terms of the text as a Chinese text from a given historical period, because it has never been constructed in that way.

Merging Terms and Structures

In Wang Bi's construction, the *Laozi* uses a great many terms for the That-by-which of the ten thousand entities. Some of them are metaphors that are still understood as such, like "root," "mother," "door," or "ancestor":

- "It is called the root 根 of Heaven and Earth" (6.1).

- "It is actually so that all of the entities, their diversity [notwithstanding], revert to their [common] root 歸其根" (16.2).

- "The mother 母 of the ten thousand kinds of entities" (1.2).

- "mother 母 of All Under Heaven" (25.3, 52.1f.).

- "the door 門 [from which] the many and the subtleness [emerge]" (1.5).

- "the door of the Dark Female" (6.1).

- "the ancestor 宗 of the ten thousand kinds of entities" (4.1).

Others are older metaphors that have already come to rest in that graveyard of dead metaphors that is language. Some abstract structures of the original metaphorical meaning still survive, but the speaker/writer will no longer notice a mixed metaphor. The best example is Dao, the "Way." This term was established as a philosophic word before the *Laozi*; thus it is not used as an instrument of definition, but appears rather as something that itself needs definition. Perhaps *shi* 始, "beginning," also belongs to this category of dead metaphor if the graph signals a reference to childbirth.

- "The Dao creates them [the ten thousand entities]" (51.1).

- "The Dao is what covers the ten thousand entities" (62.1).

Both examples show that Dao has already become an altogether abstract notion the particular metaphorical origin of which does not control its use anymore. Technically speaking, a "way" can neither "create" nor "cover."

- "The beginning 始 of Heaven and Earth" (1.2).

- "All Under Heaven has a beginning 始" (52.1).

Both examples retain a general reference to creation or childbirth, but the analogy has become too loose to help in specifying the exact process imagined in this "beginning."

Finally there are the two stunning new creations of the *Laozi*, *ziran* 自然, "That-which-is-of-itself-what-it-is," and, at least in Wang Bi's reading, *wu* 無, "negativity." They are technical philosophic terms that do not add philosophic depths to long-familiar words of great status like *dao* and *de*, but try to describe accurately a new philosophic insight by making use of nonloaded linguistic material. To my knowledge these are the first such creations of specific philosophic terms. Both terms try to articulate the inability of language to define the object of these new insights.[15]

- "the Ziran of the ten thousand entities" (64.9).

- "for entities to be beneficial, they rely on negativity 無 for their usability" (11.2).

The *Laozi* itself operates with three techniques to show that these terms are all makeshift devices to get a glimpse of something essentially beyond the reach of defining language.

The first technique consists in linking and identifying these terms and structures with each other:

- *Shi* 始 and *mu* 母: "All Under Heaven has a beginning; it may [also] be taken for All Under Heaven's mother" 天下有始可以為天下母 (52.1).

- *Dao* 道 and *zhong fu* 眾甫 (read as meaning "the beginning of the many) in *zhang* 21.

- *Men* 門 and gen 根: "The door [from] which the Dark Female [comes] is called the root of Heaven and Earth 玄牝之門是謂天地之根" (6.1).

- *Dao* 道 and *mu* 母: "There is a thing that completes out of the diffuse. It is born before Heaven and Earth. . . . One might take it for the mother 母 of All Under Heaven. I do not know its name. Therefore, forced, I give it the style 'dao' 道" (25.1ff.).

- *Dao* 道 and *zong* 宗: "The Way is made use of by pouring out [effusion] and is also not filled up—deep it is, resembling the ancestor 宗 of the ten thousand kinds of entities" (4.1).

From these identifications in the *Laozi* itself it is clear that the value of these terms is in their having a certain descriptive power, but that none qualify as definitions.

The second technique in fact provides the theoretical basis for the first. It consists in a flurry of expressions surrounding these core terms which signal their unreliability and makeshift character.

The examples given above provide some of the material. The beginning "may be taken for" 可以為 All Under Heaven's mother (52.1); the door "is called" 是謂 the root of Heaven and Earth (6.1); "one might take it" 可以為 for the mother of All-under-Heaven (25.3); I "give it the style" 字之曰 'dao' (25.5); it "resembles" 似 the ancestor of the ten thousand entities (4.1); the Great Dao "may be named among" 可名於 the small and "may be named among" the great (34.2f.); the common orgin of the "beginning" and the "mother" is "spoken of" 謂之 as the "Dark" (1.5). Of the 33 occurrences of the term *wei* 謂, "is spoken of as" or "is called," no less than twenty come with grand notions that defy definition (*zhang* 1, 6, 10, 14 (2), 16, 27 (2), 30, 36, 51, 56, 59 (2), 65, 68 (2), 69, 74, 78).

The third technique consists in stressing the makeshift character of the core terms by applying mutually exclusive attributes to them. "[The Great Dao] . . . dresses the ten thousand entities, but does not become [their] overlord. That is why . . . it may be named among the small; and, [insofar as] the ten thousand kinds of entities go back to it but do not know the[ir] lord, it [the Dao] may be named among the great" (34.2ff.). Here we have not only the two adnouns, "small" and "great," applied simultaneously to the same object, Dao, but a plethora of other statements. The Dao may simultaneously be called the greatest because it is that by which all entities exist, and the smallest, because its all-pervading presence notwithstanding it is not discernible. In *zhang* 6, Wang Bi constructs the phrase 綿綿若存 in a similar manner as meaning "intangible it [the root of Heaven and Earth] is, but still it exists." The first phrase of *Laozi* 25, "There is an entity that completes out of the diffuse," expresses the same thought that what "might be taken for the mother of All Under Heaven" "is," but remains undiscernible in its diffuseness. The next phrases continue with similar paradoxes. The same technique is extended to the Sage who consciously imitates the paradoxical nature of the Dao. [The Sage] is "he who knows that as its [All Under Heaven's] cock he [has to] keep to [being] its hen, [and thus he will] be All Under Heaven's valley . . . he who knows that as its whiteness he [has to] keep to [being] its blackness [and then he will] be the rule for All Under Heaven . . . he who knows that as its [most] glorified [person] he [has to] keep to being its [most] disgraced [person] [and then he will] be the gorge of All Under Heaven" (28.1ff.).

Wang Bi bases his own handling of the *Laozi* language on these procedures and indicators of the *Laozi* itself. The makeshift character of the terms, which becomes evident from their easy merger, does not imply that Wang Bi sees the *Laozi* as being inconsistent in its terminology. The *Laozi* might use different terms for the same object, but in Wang Bi's reading he does not use the same term for different issues.

For example, the metaphor of the baby or small child occurs in *Laozi* 10.2, 20.4, 28.1, 49.5, and 55.1 under the terms *yinger* 嬰兒, *haizi* 孩子, and *chizi* 赤子. The *Laozi* text itself says about it that "it does not now smile" 未咳 (20.4), and that it cannot be stung or seized by wild animals, has soft bones but a firm grip, is ignorant about the union of female and male, but grows up unscathed, and in that is "the culmination of the [true] essence," mutters all day but does not get hoarse, and in that is "the culmination of harmony" (55.1ff.). It is used as a comparison for "him who has the fullness of capacity in himself" (55.1) who is described by Wang Bi in terms of the Sage; as a metaphor for the ideal of becoming a Sage (10.2); as a comparison for the "I" of the *Laozi* (20.4); and, in 28.1 and 49.5, it is the ideal mental state to which the Sage ruler will bring back the people.

There are several problems. First, the most detailed description in *zhang* 55 operates with the term *chizi* 赤子 and not *yinger* 嬰兒; it

requires proof that these are two expressions with the same metaphoric value. The same is true for the relationship of *haizi* 孩子 to
the rest. Second, the *Laozi* does not spell out anything like a unified
metaphoric meaning in the different occurrences; in 28.1 and 49.5
there is no specification whatsoever. Third, from the available pre-
Han literature, the baby does not seem to be a standard metaphor
with a fixed meaning. And the diversity of the commentators in
deciphering this metaphor proves the extreme range of its potentiality. Strictly speaking, the baby needs a full construction to assume
a definite meaning at all.

There is a weak link between the expressions *chizi* and *yinger*.
Laozi 10.2, 專氣致柔 能若嬰兒乎, is constructed by Wang Bi as meaning "[For a ruler] to focus on the breath, to bring about softness, and
be able to be like a baby—ah!" From the parallels with the
neighboring statements it is legimate to establish a connection between the first and the second half of this statement so that "focusing on the breath" and "being able to bring about softness" is what
being a baby is all about, so that a translation might run "and [in
this] be able to be like a baby—ah!" In *Laozi* 55.2 the *chizi* is said to
骨弱筋柔, be "weak in the bones and soft in the sinews," which might
be linked to the "softness" mentioned in 10.2, and that "it mutters
all day but does not become hoarse" might be linked with "focusing
on the breath" in 10.2. Both are furthermore linked by the common
point of comparison.

While the *Laozi* does not spell out a unified metaphoric meaning
of the baby, Wang Bi does. Being a baby is "to be without desires"
無欲 (10.2, 55.1, 49.5). "Being ignorant" and not making use of
knowledge and intelligence is also mentioned in the *Laozi* text of
55.3, in another metaphor of the *Laozi* in the phrase following that
about the baby in 10.3, and in Wang Bi on 49.5, while it is the only
point in Wang Bi on 28.1.

What, then, is the source for Wang Bi's reading that the baby
metaphor means to be without desires and without knowledge? In
Laozi 28.1 and 49.5 the Sage sets out to transform the people into
such babies. According to *Laozi* 3.4, the Sage "makes permanently
sure that the people are without knowledge and desires"
常使民無知無欲. A similar statement occurs in *Laozi* 37.4. Wang Bi
merges the two statements and thus has a solid basis when constructing the phrase "[I] the Sage make all of them into infants" as
meaning "[I] get them all to be in harmony and without desires like

infants" and then proceeds to explain that they will not make use of their intelligence to compete with the ruler. The interpretation of the metaphoric statement is made dependent on an explicit statement elsewhere to eliminate ambivalence.

The metaphor of the baby, however, is used not only for the people in the *Laozi*, but also for the Sage himself. The Dao itself is "eternally without desires," (34.2), and the Sage, imitating it, "desires to have no desires" (64.7). His rejection of knowledge is equally well attested.

Once the meaning is unambiguously established, Wang Bi may turn around and use the metaphor in his own commentaries to eliminate ambiguity in other areas. In *Laozi* 50.1 we hear of someone who is so "good at holding on to life" 善攝生者 that neither beast nor arms can harm him. The only reason given is that he "is in a realm without death," which is a claim but no explanation. Wang first argues that the only person able to be invulnerable to the lances, horns, and claws is someone who "does not bind his person through desires." This eventually "makes it possible for him to imitate the infant." The argument supporting this link between the infant in 55.1 and him who "is good at holding on to life" here is that the *Laozi* claims invulnerability to humans and animals for either of them. "He who is good at holding on to life will neither encounter rhinoceros nor tiger when traveling over land nor suffer from [enemy] arms or weapons when going into battle" says the *Laozi* in 50.2. "He who has the fullness of capacity in himself is like an infant; wasps, scorpions, and vipers do not sting him; wild beasts and preying birds do not seize him," says the *Laozi* in 55.1. From this parallel it follows that "he who has the fullness of capacity" is identical with him "who is good at holding on to life," from which, again, it follows that the latter also must be like an infant, and that therefore the reason he can be invulnerable is his lack of desires.

The immediate context, however, retains control over the potential meaning of a term. It will have been noticed that, in the above analysis, the baby of *Laozi* 20.4 has been dropped. What happened to it? The *Laozi* there runs: "I am vacant, without clues 無兆 [for others to recognize me], like a baby that has not yet started to smile." Wang Bi comments: "This means 'I am vacant without a shape that could be named, without a clue that could be taken up, like a baby that is not yet capable of smiling'." Here, a specific context is given. This context links this statement to others about the inscrutability of the Sage, namely *Laozi* 15.1: "Those in antiquity who were well-versed in the Way were recondite and abstruse, so deep that they could not be discerned. As they were undiscernible, [I] say when forced to give a sketch of them: Hesitant they were—as if crossing a [frozen] river in winter. Undecided they were—as if fearing four neighbors." Wang Bi comments on this: "That in a person of 'highest receipt/capacity' it is impossible to perceive any clues [in] his [expression] and it is impossible to make out [his] intentions, is similar to these [two comparisons]." The core term in the baby metaphor, "clue," *zhao* 兆, is taken up in Wang Bi's commentary on 15.2. The comparison in 20.4 is not with a baby in its totality, but only with its blank face. While Wang Bi does construct a general metaphoric value for the babies, he does not proceed mechanically, but determines the applicability of the common metaphor on the basis of the immediate context.

The term *ming* 名, "name," might serve as a second example. It occurs twenty-four times in altogether ten *zhang* (1, 14, 21, 25, 32, 34, 37, 41, 44, 47). With the exception of the last two, all occurrences have to do with the Way. *Laozi* 41.15 says unambiguously "The Way is hidden and nameless" 道陰無名, confirmed by "the Eternal of the Way is namelessness" 道常無名 in *Laozi* 32.1, which, with the "Eternal," indicates this to be something unalterable. *Zhang* 25.4f. with its "I do not know its name; therefore, forced, I give it the style 'Way.' [Only if] forced to make up a name for it, I would say '[it is] great'," states that even someone like Laozi cannot overcome this obstacle to a definition of the Way. *Laozi* 14.2 describes the "One," which Wang Bi identifies with the Way as so "dim" that "it is impossible to name"; in the beginning of the same *zhang* the word *ming* 名 appears three more times: "That which [I] do not see if [I] look at it [I] call 'fine'" 名之曰夷, followed by similar statements about hearing and grasping. The definitions eventually used, like "fine," "inaudible," and "smooth," are all identified by Wang Bi as descriptions of undefinability. Thus the content of the *ming* 名 here is in fact summed up by *wu ming* 無名 further down. *Laozi* 1.1 claims that "a way that can be spoken of is not the eternal Way" and "a name that can be named is not the eternal name." In *zhang* 37, the sagely "I" imitates the Way in its rule and "quiets down" the people by means of his "simplicity of the nameless." There is thus a solid record in the *Laozi* describing the Way as "nameless."

This namelessness is confronted with a *you ming* 有名 in *zhang* 1; there is a time "when there are not now names" where the Way is the "beginning of the ten thousand kinds of entities" and a time "when there [already] are names" where it is the "mother of the ten thousand kinds of entities." This time frame is taken up again by the Sage in *Laozi* 32.3: "With the beginning of [my social] regulation, [I will] have names." The time of 有名, "when there are names," is thus the time when entities have become specific. The uses of the term in *zhang* 44 and 47 have different contexts, in *zhang* 44 ming means "fame" and is contrasted with *shen* 身, "one's own person"; in *zhang* 47 *ming* is a verb meaning "to define."

Wang Bi was thus stranded with a single troublesome case, namely 21.6. There, the "truthful essence," for which the same rules apply as for the Way, has a name. From Wang Bi's handling of this anomaly in the context of his assumptions we can see how conscious he was of his tacit premise of the *Laozi*'s terminological consistency. The text there runs: "From antiquity to the present its [the truthful essence's] name has not disappeared" 自古及今 其名不去. In Wang Bi's construction, the preceding lines in *Laozi* 21 have circumscribed the undefinability of the Way as such, beginning with 21.2: "The Way as a thing is vague, ah, diffuse, ah." Thus the context suggests that the term "name" might not be taken as meaning "definition." Still, Wang Bi has to cope with the phrase. He comments: "The ultimate of the absolutely true cannot [be determined by means of a] name. 'Namelessness' thus is its name" 至真之極 不可得名 無名則是其名也. By importing the very solid evidence from the rest of the *Laozi* that the Way is "nameless" Wang Bi manages to keep the consistency of the text by saying that "name" in this unique context of *zhang* 21.2 refers to the Way's negative definition of "namelessness." In this way *ming* 名 becomes a shorthand term for its opposite, *wuming* 無名.

A third example may be the terms *shi* 始, "beginning," and *mu* 母, "mother." *Laozi* 1.2 runs: "When there are not now names, it [the Way] is the beginning of the ten thousand kinds of entities 無名萬物之始, when there [already] are names, it is the mother of the ten thousand kinds of entities" 有名萬物之母. In this construction, the Dao is described as having two functions, formalized by the terms "beginning" and "mother." The function of "beginning" is also addressed with the term *sheng* 生. The phrase in *Laozi* 40.3, "Entity lives from negativity" 有生於無 refers with 有, "Entity," to the totality of specific entities and uses with *wu*, "negativity," a term considered by Wang Bi synonymous with Dao. The function of "mother" for the already specified entities is taken up in *Laozi* 25.1ff., where the Dao is described as "an entity that completes out of the diffuse" 有物混成, which "might be taken for the mother of Heaven and Earth" 可以為天地母. In this statement, the "mother" function is described with the term "to complete," *cheng* 成. The double function of the Way is taken up in *Laozi* 51.3: "The Way generates them [the ten thousand kinds of entities] and nourishes them." Wang Bi quotes this passage in his commentary on *Laozi* 1.2 and identifies the second function (nourishing) as that of the mother. The two functions are there formalized into the terms *shi* 始 and *cheng* 成. In a different terminology they reappear in Wang Bi's reading of *Laozi* 41.15: "In fact, it is only the Way that is good at providing as well as good at completing" 夫唯道善貸且善成. Again we have a terminological fixing of the difference between the *shi* 始 and *cheng* 成 functions of the Dao, which is well supported by other evidence in the *Laozi* using this as well as other terminologies. Again, however, Wang Bi has to deal with what for him must be an anomaly, an inconsistent use of the terms "beginning" and "mother" in which the two are in fact merged into one.

According to a first reading, the *Laozi* 52.1 says "All Under Heaven has a beginning; it may be taken for All Under Heaven's mother" 天下有始可以為天下母. This would merge the two functions carefully kept apart elsewhere. With the solid backing of the otherwise consistent *Laozi* construct of the two functions of the Dao and the terminology describing them, Wang Bi stresses the "may be taken for" 可以為 as the key to this phrase. He writes: "Being good at beginning it [All Under Heaven], it will consequently [also] be good at maintaining and nourishing it. That is why [the text says] 'As All Under Heaven has a beginning this [beginning],' as a consequence, 'may [also] be taken for All Under Heaven's mother!'" This forces a translation of the main text "[as] All Under Heaven has a beginning, this [beginning] may [also] be taken for All Under Heaven's mother." As we have seen, in Wang Bi's reading, the Way was indeed in charge of both aspects, beginning and completing. Thus Wang's reading of 52.1 makes use of the option offered by the "may be taken for" to impose the overall context of this thought in the *Laozi* on a particular sentence to eliminate an anomaly, which would have undermined the terminological consistency of the *Laozi*.

In Wang Bi's construction, the *Laozi* is thus communicating to his readers/commentators the proper strategy for reading, which is to assume consistency in the usage of the terms, but to merge the core notions on the basis of similar context.

On the basis of the *Laozi*'s own merger of his core notions, Wang Bi could claim theoretical and practical legitimacy for a commenting technique that radicalized the procedure used by the *Laozi* itself by merging, for example, all the terms for the That-by-which to form a pool of aspects of that which intrinsically defies definition. In this way he linked together for purposes of mutual illustration and explanation passages with different specific terms of similar philosophical meaning and structure as evident from their comparable argumentative context. The *Laozi* statements about the Way in 4.1, 8.1f., 14.4, 21.2f., 25.1ff., 34.1f., 37.1f., 40.1f., 41.15, 42.1, 51.1f., 62.1 all describe it as being something important with regard to all other entities, beginning them, generating them, covering them, or being in them. Through this merger, the immediate context, often quite diffuse by itself, could be greatly expanded and specified so that many statements that, taken alone, look blurred acquire a high degree of clarity and precision. This technique of context enrichment is of special importance for Wang Bi's efforts to reduce ambiguity.

Wang Bi continues the merging of core terms begun by the *Laozi*. After the *Laozi* identified 始 and 母 in 52.1, Wang Bi proceeds to identify the pair 母 and 子, "mother" and "son," with the pair 本 and 末. "The 'mother' [mentioned in the text] is the root; the 'offspring' [mentioned in the text] are the stem and branches" (52.2). This latter pair does not occur in the *Laozi*, but the term *ben* 本 appears in *Laozi* 26. Wang Bi probably takes the pair 本末 from the *Xici*. There it occurs in a description of the *Zhouyi* itself:

Its first [line at the bottom] is
hard to understand.

　　　　　　　　　　　　　　Its top [line] is easy to
　　　　　　　　　　　　　　understand.

　　They [correspond to]
root　　and　　　　　　　　　offspring
As to the beginning [line],
the statements [still]
deliberate about it.　　　　　As to the finish[ing, that is,

uppermost, line], it is the end of completion.

There is no commentary by Wang Bi, but Han Kangbo writes:

Generally [speaking],
processes

begin in the minutely small and "First" is the beginning of numbers. [The words concerning this first line] [still] deliberate on its features [those of the process depicted in the hexagram]. That is why they are "hard to understand."	then [only] do they get to become manifest. The top [line] is the end of the hexagram, the process has become entirely manifest. That is why it is "easy to understand."[16]

Wang Bi repeats the identification of the *Laozi*'s "mother" with 本 in the commentary on 20.15: "The 'nourishing mother' [mentioned in the text] is the root of life" 食母生之本也. However, the identification is based on structural parallels between mother and offspring on the one hand and root and "stem and branches" on the other. Once this parallelism is settled, Wang Bi uses it in his own language independent of terms in the text that have to be explained. Thus, at the end of his commentary to *Laozi* 38, Wang Bi speaks of "names" and "shapes" in parallel chains, using the two parallel relationships of mother/offspring and root/outgrowth, saying, for example:

By

discarding the root	and	rejecting the mother
and		
going along with the branches [growing out of the root]		adapting oneself to the offspring [of the mother]
there will. . . .		

Commenting on *Laozi* 39.3, "Once Heaven is not clear through [the One], it is in danger of being torn apart," Wang Bi merges the terms *yi* 一, *mu* 母, and *ben* 本: "Heaven makes use of the One and thus achieves clarity, but does not make use of [its intrinsic] clarity to achieve clarity. As long as it preserves the One, [its] clarity will not be lost, but, once it makes use of its clarity [to achieve clarity,] it is in danger of being torn apart. That is why the mother bringing about these achievements [of clarity, and so forth] is not to be discarded. That is why all [entities] that do not make use of her [the mother's] achievements [but of their own qualities] are in danger of losing their root."

In *Laozi* 41.11ff., four "great" things are mentioned, the "Great Squaring," the "Great Instrument," the "Great Sound," and the "Great Image." Wang Bi comments that "all these 'great' [things] are made up by the Way. Among the images [the Way] is the Great Image, but 'the Great Image is without form.'" The four "great" things thus become manifestations of the Way. In Wang Bi on *Laozi* 35.1, the Great Image is called the "mother of All Under Heaven" and is thus merged with the term "mother."

The term *chang* 常 is a frequent attribute accompanying the Way in the *Laozi* (1.1, 32.1, 37.1), but also occurs as a separate noun (16.5f., 52.9, 55.5). As a noun Wang Bi comments on it as the "eternal aspect" of the Way (1.1, 25.2, 47.1, 52.9), to which human beings are to "return" (59.2) because it is the "eternal aspect of their life-endowment" (16.5) associated with their common "root" (16.4) and therefore the basis of the "harmony" among the entities (55.5).

The term "the One" appears in the *Laozi* as a mature philosophic notion, and as an independent noun. The passages in the *Zhuangzi* where it appears in a similar form are in contexts where the ultimate "Oneness" or even harmony of the ten thousand kinds of entities is described. It remains a feature of the ten thousand entities.[17] In his commentary to the phrase "reduction results in attaining . . ." in *Laozi* 22.5, Wang Bi identifies it with *ben* 本: "The Way of That-which-is-of-itself-what-it-is resembles a tree. The more there is [of the tree] the farther away it is from its root. The less there is [of the tree] the [better] it attains its root." The next *Laozi* phrase, "This is why the Sage holds on to the One, and makes the empire [take it] as a model" is commented on: "The One is the absolute of reduction."

In the previous commentary the extreme of reduction gets to the "root" of the metaphoric tree. In the next example a entire chain of identifications occurs. Commenting on *Laozi* 28.6, "once the

Uncarved has dispersed [into particularities,] they [the entities] become instruments. Making use of them, the Sage makes officials and elders for them," Wang Bi writes: "The Uncarved is the True [nature] 樸真也. Once this True has dispersed [into particularities] 散, the hundred styles of action emerge, and the different categories are born. These are like '[specialized] instruments.' Responsive to [the fact] that their [the people's] allotments have dispersed, the Sage [does not cut and trim them but] purposely sets up officials and elders for them. 'Making the good ones into teachers' and 'the not good ones into the[ir] material' [as the *Laozi* 27.6–7 says], changing [in this manner] the[ir] habits and altering the[ir] customs is [his way] of 'returning [them] again to the' One [as the *Laozi* says in 28.5]."

The phrasing 復使歸於一也, "making [them] 'return again' to the One" at the end here summarizes the three uses of "return again" in this *zhang*, namely "he has them return again to being babies," "[he] has them return again to the unlimited," and "he has them return again to the Uncarved." The "One" here becomes the unifying term for the attitude of the baby, which, as Wang Bi says on 28.1, "makes no use of knowledge, but is in accord with the knowledge of That-which-is-of-itself-what-it-is," with the Unlimited 無極, and with the Uncarved. The One is thus read here as a term defining the unadulterated state of humans leading to a situation of social harmony, a reading clearly associated with the *Zhuangzi* passage referred to above.

In his commentary on *Laozi* 10.1, "[for a ruler] to keep to the camp, to hold on to the One and be able not be separated from it—ah!" Wang Bi bluntly defines this One as the "true [nature] of [the other] human beings" 一人之真也. The 真 again reappears in the present *zhang* 28 to define the "Uncarved," *pu* 樸.[18] The term "the Unlimited," *wuji* 無極, is interpreted by Wang Bi as "that which is inexhaustible" 不可窮也. This latter definition is used in the commentary to *Laozi* 4.1 for the Way. There the phrase "The Way is made use of by pouring out" is "translated" as "this use indeed will not be able to exhaust it." It is thus "inexhaustible," and consequently the Unlimited is read here again as another word for the Way. The term *pu* 樸, finally, is defined in Wang Bi on *Laozi* 32.1 as the parallel to the Way in terms of the Sage's behavior. "Simplicity as such," says Wang Bi, "has negativity as its heart" 樸之為物 以無為心, or "is close to not having [any specific feature at all]" 近於無有.

This term, "negativity," which has been developed in its first stages in the *Laozi*, is made into the core philosophic notion by Wang Bi. He does not simply merge the various notions concerning the That-by-which into a pool, but sets out to establish a stricter and more accurate philosophic vocabulary by reducing the great variety of terms to some core notions. The most radical of these is the term *wu* 無, here rendered as "negativity."

Commenting on *Laozi* 8.2, "That is why [water] is close to the Way" 故幾于道矣, Wang Bi writes: 道無水有 故曰幾也. "The Way is negativity; water is an entity. That is why [the text says that water is only] 'close to' [the Way, and not identical with it]." Here the term *wu* 無 is not used as a noun, but as a verb/adjective. In other places, however, Wang Bi establishes this identification of Dao and Wu explicitly. Commenting on Confucius' statement in *Lunyu* 7.6, "set your heart upon the Way" 志於道, Wang Bi writes: "As to 'Way,' it is a designation for negativity 道者無之稱也. There is nothing [negativity] does not penetrate, and there is nothing it does not provide the basis for; thus in a comparison it is called 'Way.' 'Vacant' it is [as the *Laozi* says in 25.20] and without substance [so that] it is impossible to form an image [of it.]" In *Laozi* 42.1 the sentence "The Dao generates the One" is commented on by Wang Bi: "On the basis of what is the One brought about? On the basis of negativity." Thus Dao 道 and 無 are merged here.

Wang Bi constructs *Laozi* 21 as a true arsenal of core terms: Basing himself on the *Laozi*'s identification of Dao 道 and the "beginning of the many," *zhong fu* 眾甫, Wang Bi then specifies that this is a "beginning of the ten thousand entities in negativity" 萬物之始於無.

Another case is the term *zhen* 真. In the *Laozi* it denotes a human being's "true nature." Wang Bi uses the term to define other statements. "[The Sage] permanently makes sure that the people are without knowledge and desires" (3.4) is commented on: "[That means he makes sure that the people] preserve their true [nature]" 守其真. Here, being "without knowledge and without desires" is characterized as "preserving one's true [nature]." In the commentary on *Laozi* 10.2, the "baby" mentioned there is identified as being "without anything that it desires." The same occurs in the commentary on *Laozi* 28.1: "[The Sage] has them [the other entities] return again to being babies," where Wang Bi says, "Babies make no use of knowledge, but are in accord with the knowledge of That-which-is-of-itself-what-it-is." This suggests that the terms 真 and 自然 are being made identical, which is confirmed by the commentary on *Laozi* 10.2.

This use of *ziran* again has a basis in *Laozi* 64.9, which speaks of the "That-which-is-of-itself-what-it-is of the ten thousand entities" 萬物之自然 as something propped up by redressing their *guo* 過, their "superfluities" and excesses. In his comment on *Laozi* 12.1 "the five colors let man's eyes go blind," and so forth, Wang Bi argues: "It is a fact that ears, eyes, mouth, and heart are all in accordance with [man's] nature 皆順其性也. If [in the above cases of exposing himself to the five colors, and so forth, man] is not [acting] by 'following the true nature' he will, on the contrary, [act] by hurting [his] That-which-is-of-itself-what-it-is. That is why [the text says] [they will let a man go] 'blind, deaf, numb, wild'." Here *xing* 性, "human nature," a term not used by the *Laozi* (but occurring in the *Zhuangzi* and other authors) is identified with *xingming* 性命, a term widely used in the *Zhuangzi* and also occurring in the *Zhouyi*. The formula *shun xingming* 順性命 in fact comes from the *Zhouyi*. The phrase "hurting [his] That-which-is-of-itself-what-it-is" simply restates the "not acting according to his nature" so that 性命 and 自然 are again linked. The pool from which the terminology material is taken again is the entire group of Confucius texts.

The *Laozi* does not explicitly link the various philosophic heroes who are able to follow the Dao. Based on the procedure of the *Laozi* mentioned above with regard to the That-by-which, Wang Bi establishes this link. As described above for *Laozi* 17.1, Wang Bi links the "Great [Man]," *da* 大, there with the Sage, 聖人, by quoting in the commentary to 17.1 a statement about the Sage made in *Laozi* 2.2f., and with the "great man," *daren* 大人, in hexagram 1 of the *Zhouyi*. In the commentary to a statement about the Great Man in *Laozi* 17.6, Wang Bi quotes his own statements about "those who in antiquity were well-versed in the Way" on *Laozi* 15.2. These again are defined in that commentary passage as "persons of supreme capacity" 上德之人, in a direct reference to him "who [possesses] the highest capacity" 上德 in *Laozi* 38.1, which therewith becomes another appellation for the same protagonist. He "who possesses the highest capacity" is referred to in the same chapter further down as the "Great Man," *da zhangfu* 大丈夫, a protagonist in turn identified as one of the "four Great Ones" mentioned in *Laozi* 25, and defined as the Sage through the application of a statement to him in the commentary that originally was applied to the Sage in the *Zhouyi*.

The "I" in *Laozi* 16.3 is identified with those in *Laozi* 50.2 "who are good at maintaining their lives" through the application of a phrase about them to the "I" in *Laozi* 16.3. Those "who are good at maintaining their lives" of *Laozi* 50.2 again are identified with him "who has the fullness of capacity in himself" and "compares to an infant" in *Laozi* 55.1. The "infant" is characterized as being "without desires" (commentary on 10.2), which is what is said of both him "who has the fullness of capacity in himself" (commentary on 55.1) and his counterpart in *Laozi* 50.2. The "gentleman of the highest [caliber]," *shang shi* 上士, in *Laozi* 41.1, who when "hearing of the Way will practice it to the utmost of his capacities," is identified in the commentary to 50.3 and 50.3 with the Sage through the use of descriptions for him from *Laozi* 58.10 and *Laozi* 7.2, which there pertain to the Sage. Through a quotation in the commentary on *Laozi* 41.1, he is furthermore identified with "him who powerfully practices [the Way]" in *Laozi* 33.4. In *Laozi* 33, it turns out that the powerful practice of the Way is only one of several features of a protagonist who is constructed by Wang Bi as the Sage, the other being his "seeing through himself," "vanquishing himself," "knowing how to have enough," and so forth. Those "of old who were good at being officers" and "who were good at fighting" in *Laozi* 68.1 and .2 are identified as further embodiments of the Sage through the application to them in the commentary on 68.2 of statements made about the Sage in *Laozi* 7.2 and Wang Bi's commentary on *Laozi* 10.5.

The same merger happens at the opposite end, where the various deficient modes of the Sage are grouped together in a descending typology the most systematic expression of which is *Laozi* 38; less elaborate ones will be found in *Laozi* 17, 18, and 19. The merger of terms is in fact only a subordinate form of the merger of structures, and is justified by the parallelism of those structures.

The mother/offspring 母/子 and root/outgrowth 本/末 pairs are an example. They are merely specific manifestations of a broader structure, namely negativity/specific entities 無/有 or negativity/ten thousand kinds of entities 無/萬物. In Wang Bi's construction of *Laozi* 11.1 and .2 and *Laozi* 42.3, *wu* 無 and *you* 有 appear as terms in this sense. The mother/offspring pair occurs in *Laozi* 52.2. In *Laozi* 4.1 and Wang Bi on *Laozi* 1.2 the pair reappears as Dao/ten thousand kinds of entities; in Wang Bi on 6.1 as root of Heaven and

Earth/ten thousand kinds of entities; in *Laozi* 14.2 as the One 一/ no-thing 無物/ shape-without-a-shape/appearance without an object 無狀之狀, 無物之象, defined by Wang Bi on *Laozi* 14.5 as "ancestor of the ten thousand entities" 萬物之宗; in *Laozi* 16.4 as root 根/entities in their diversity 物芸芸; in 21.7 as beginning 甫/ many 眾, identified in the commentary as *shi* 始/ten thousand kinds of entities, and so forth.

Wang Bi constructs the *Laozi* as defining the That-by-which by two interrelated aspects, namely that of being the basis of the ten thousand kinds of entities, in which capacity it is referred to as Dao, and that of being undiscernible, which is the aspect of Darkness, *xuan*. The twofold structure is explicitly established in *Laozi* 25, and is taken up in *LZWZLL*. The generative aspect is mentioned in *Laozi* 41.15: "The Way is hidden and nameless. In fact, only the Way is good at providing as well as good at completing." A second source is *Laozi* 25.1f.: "There is an entity that completes out of the diffuse. . . . One might take it for the mother of All Under Heaven." The undiscernibility is prepared by the "out of the diffuse," to be followed by the blunt statement "I do not know its name." Wang Bi comments on this: "A name is something to define the shape [of an object]. That which 'completes out of the diffuse,' and is 'without shape' [as the *Laozi* says about the Great Image in 41.14, which is described there by Wang Bi as one of the manifestations of the Dao] is impossible to define."

The generative aspect is formalized by Wang Bi through the terms "initiating," *shi* 始, and "completing," *cheng* 成. As a combination, the two terms come from the first section of the *Xici*, where *qian* 乾 and *kun* 坤 are defined: "The qian makes known the great beginning; the kun lets grow and perfects the entities."[19]

Once this structure has been established with fairly unambiguous material, Wang Bi uses it to specify the meaning of exceedingly diffuse passages. The terms 悦 and 惚 in *Laozi* 21.2, 道之為物惟悦惟惚, "The Way as a thing is vague, ah, diffuse, ah," both mean "vague," "diffuse," and have no clearly different meanings. Wang Bi, however, puts them into the already existing structure, and defines them as meaning 無形不繫, "without shape and unfettered." In the next commentary (21.3) he inserts these two categories into the familiar "initiating/perfecting" structure without further textual support: 以無形始物 不繫成物 "By means of being shapeless [the Way] initiates the entities; by means of being unfettered, [the Way] perfects the entities." The undiscernibility is expressed by the terms "vague" and "diffuse." Wang Bi brings out this quality in his commentary by continuing: "The ten thousand kinds of entities are [thus] initiated through [the Way] and perfected through it, but they do not know that through which this came to be." The numerous other passages denoting the diffuseness of the Dao and the Sage are treated in the same manner so as to create a unified structure amid some terminological diversity. As seen in the example just given, these structures are dynamic in character.

The negativity/ten thousand entities structure finds its replica in the Sage/people structure, which is conflated in similar manner. There is a deficient mode, the unenlightened ruler/people structure, where the dynamics which create order under the Sage engender chaos under this kind of ruler.

Conclusions

Wang Bi's craft of commenting is based on theoretical statements and practical procedures in the *Laozi* itself. In this way his proceedings are hermeneutic. His material to eliminate ambivalence comes for the greatest part from the *Laozi*, reinforced by parallels from texts associated with Confucius. Wang Bi thus subordinates himself in terms of methodology, of explanatory material, and of philosophic argument to the presumed author of the text. His technique of handling the *Zhouyi*, it might be added, is also based on the internal strategic guidance and commenting of the *Zhouyi* itself, especially of course the "wings." The authority of Laozi is due to his status as a *yasheng*. The status of Confucius being higher, the texts associated with him have a slightly higher level of authority.

The *Laozi* needs commenting. The commentators associated with the various schools, and under their guidance, their readers, have reduced the text to trivial supports for their respective tenets. The same has happened to texts like *Zhouyi* and *Lunyu*. In spite of the explicit warnings of the *Laozi* concerning its tentative use of language—warnings that are echoed in statements on language by Confucius and in the *Xici*—they have attached themselves to particular notions on the textual surface and construed the text on this basis. In the process, that to which the text—in ever renewed efforts—points, has been forgotten. Wang Bi's commentary rediscovers for the reader the pointers of the text, and thus restores it to its original function by inserting comments into its crevices to guide the reader and prevent him from relapsing into old errors.

Strictly speaking, the commentary performs three operations: the construction of the text into an understandable utterance; the explanation of the philosophic logic behind the text's statements; and the deconstruction of previous constructs enshrined in the mind of the reader. The three operations are linked but not identical. For the implied reader, the credibility of the textual construction is the primary concern; only on this basis can the commentary and its own philosophy claim the authority of the *Laozi*, and he will be willing to abandon the previous construction through which he read the text.

In Wang Bi's proceedings and theoretical statements, the two main standards for the validity of a specific commentary are plausibility and viability. Plausibility means that the particular construction fits the overall construction of Laozi as a philosopher interested in one particular fundamental topic, and of the *Laozi* text as a work holding forth in a homogeneous manner on a finite number of issues, all related to the core topic. Viability means that the particular construction of meaning is possible and economical within shared assumptions about grammatical constraints and the potential meaning of words and metaphors. Both are necessary conditions for a valid commentary; neither is sufficient alone. Still, they are not equal. The requirement of plausibility determines the range within which viable constructions may be made. There is not one passage in Wang's *Commentary* where a phrase was allowed to jar with the overall construct of homogeneity.

The implied reader of Wang Bi's *Commentary* is not a student or acolyte but a highly educated person familiar with the text, which he knows by heart, as well as with one or several commentaries that share the basic orientation of Wang Bi's philosophic reading. It is a critical and potentially hostile reader who approaches Wang's *Commentary* with a previous construction and reading routine in mind.

Wang Bi's *Commentary* is written against a series of lost countertexts present in the minds of his original reader. Much of the sensational impact his *Commentary* had according to contemporary sources, could only be reconstructed from a comparison with these countertexts. From the direction in which the visible relics of the arguments against the countertexts point, these countertexts shared Wang Bi's basic approach, and were not commentaries associated with the emerging Daoist communities.

The purpose of Wang Bi's *Commentary* is to reduce the ambiguity of the text, due to other commentators' mishandling of the textual surface, and in the process to undermine any claim they might have to a valid construction of its meaning. Diffuse expressions or statements in the text are mostly explained with the help of clearer statements on the same issue. In this manner, the text in all its complexity is imploded to a finite and small number of closely related issues which all hinge on one single relationship—that of the Dao to the ten thousand kinds of entities, and the replica of this relationship in that between the Sage [ruler] and the Hundred Families.

In this process, Wang Bi does not remain bound by the *Laozi*'s terminology. Making use of elements in the *Laozi*, the *Zhouyi*, and the *Lunyu*, Wang Bi attempts to develop a precise and abstract philosophic language. He inserts this language as core markers into his implosive commentaries. While the *Commentary's* construction of the text subordinates itself at every level under the text by adhering to the principles of plausibility and viability, it proceeds at the same time to reconstruct the text and to reformulate it so as to bring out what Wang Bi considers the systematic philosophy underlying the surface diversity of the *Laozi*. This is done with great economy, and often stunning interpretive genius, and it results in a completely unified text of high scholarly and philosophical caliber. While Wang Bi adheres to a basic rule of extracting his reading strategies and readings from indicators given by the text itself, his enterprise is not a historicist reconstruction of the rumblings of a dead thinker. He shared the basic assumption among his contemporaries of the *Laozi* being a foundational text of highest and direct relevance for the understanding of the dynamics of cosmic and social order. The freshness, power and ongoing persuasiveness of his *Laozi* reading derives from this enthralment with the relevant and even highly applicable insights to be discovered in this short text mediated by exceedingly high standards of interpretive plausibility that inherited much earlier art of interpretation, had to survive in a highly competitive context, and benefitted from the momentary leeway following the collapse of a centralized state authority with its encomium of orthodoxy.

Notes

Introduction

1. See R. Wagner, *Die Fragen Hui-yuan's an Kumarajiva*, 156–216.

2. The "four chapters" are Xinshu shang/xia 心術上下, Boxin 白心 and Neiye 內業. See Röllicke, *"Selbst-Erweisung." Der Ursprung des ziran Gedankens*, 164ff. See also Röllicke, "Hidden commentary in precanonical Chinese literature," pp. 15–24. Dr. Röllicke is a member of the Heidelberg research group "Text and Commentary."

3. "Wuxing," from the Guodian find (ca. 310 BCE), reproduced in *Guodian Chu mu zhujian*, 29–36, and transcribed there, 147–54. A very similar text from the early Western Han but with an inserted commentary is in Mawangdui Han mu boshu zhengli xiaozu, *Mawangdui Han mu boshu. Laozi chiaben ji juanhou gu yi shu* (n.p.).

4. Hebei sheng wenwu yanjiusuo Dingzhou Han jian zhengli xiaozu, "Dingzhou Xi Han Zhongshan Huai wang mu zhujian *Wenzi* shiwen," 27–34, provides a transcription of the Western Han bamboo strips found in Dingzhou that overlap with the *Wenzi* chapter 道德 in the received text or have close similarity with the *Wenzi*. The discussion between Wenzi and Laozi as reported in the received text in this chapter is transferred here to a discussion between King Ping of Chu and Wenzi. The verbatim *Laozi* quotations often ending a segment in the received text of this chapter, are mostly not in the bamboo strips. There is one notable exeption, namely the quotation from *Laozi* 29 on strip 0870 on p. 29 of this edition, cf. Li Dingshen and Xu Huijun (eds.), *Wenzi yaoquan*, 106. This quotation indicates together with a number of terms taken from the *Laozi* that the *Wenzi* was using *Laozi* material as authority and expanded on it. The name of

Laozi, however, is not mentioned in the bamboo strips. For a comparison of the bamboo strips with the received text see "Dingzhou Xi Han Zhongshan Huai wang mu zhujian *Wenzi* jiaokan ji," 35–37 and 40 from the same group that edited the text.

5. For a detailed study of the commentarial strategies of the *Gongyang zhuan* see the study by Joachim Gentz, University of Heidelberg, "Ritus und Praxis: Die *Chunqiu* Exegese des *Gongyang zhuan* von ihren Anfängen bis Dong Zhongshu." Mr. Gentz is a member of Heidelberg research group "Text and Commentary."

6. Wagner, "Twice Removed from the Truth: Fragment Collection in 18th and 19th Century China," 48ff.

7. Liang Kai, "Liuzu po jing tu," Ill. 37 in *Suiboku bijutsu taisei* vol. 4.

1. Wang Bi

1. Wang Bi never rose high enough in the official hierarchy to deserve a biography in the dynastic history. He Shao 何劭 wrote a *Wang Bi biezhuan* 王弼別傳, of which an excerpt survives in the commentary to Zhong Hui's biography in the *Sanguo zhi*. A few more anecdotes are transmitted in the *Shishuo xinyu*. The relevant material is gathered in an appendix to Lou Yulie, *Wang Bi ji jiaoshi*, 639–48. The most systematic biographical study hitherto is Wang Xiaoyi, *Wang Bi pingzhuan*.

2. R. Miao, *Early Medieval Chinese Poetry: The Life and Verse of Wang Ts'an (AD 177–217)*, has done some research on the family genealogy of Wang Can 王粲, but has not paid much attention to the family's social status. Wang Xiaoyi, "Wang Bi guli xintan." *Kong Meng xuebao* 75 (1998), gives much detail about the role and status of Shanyang during the Later Han.

3. Cf. the studies on this subject such as Nakamura Keiji, *Rikuchō kizokusei kenkyū*; D. Johnson, *The Medieval Chinese Oligarchy*; P. Ebrey, *The Aristocratic Families of Early Imperial China: A Case Study of the Po-ling Ts'ui Family*.

4. *Hou Han shu*, 46.1819.13.

5. Cf. He Changqun 賀昌群, *Wei Jin qingtan sixiang chulun* 魏晉清談思想初論; He Qimin 何啟民, *Wei Jin sixiang yu tanfeng* 魏晉思想與談風. Some of the best information on Guo Tai is given by Ge Hong in a polemical chapter of the "external chapter" of his *Baopu zi*, "Strictures on Guo [Tai]," *Zheng Guo* 正郭, 186ff.

6. *Sanguo zhi*, Wei, 21.597.10ff.

7. Fan Ye, *Hou Han shu*, 60B.1979. Huang-Lao thought refers to a philosophical and political doctrine much in prevalence during the early Han dynasty that stressed the self-regulatory forces of society as opposed to strict control from the center. It claims its descent from the doctrines of Huangdi and Laozi.

8. *Shishuo xinyu* 17.1, 635; Mather, *A New Account*, 323.

9. Zhang Hua, *Bowu zhi*, quoted in *Sanguo zhi*, *Wei*, 28.796.11.

10. Miyazaki Ichisada 科舉前史, *Kyūhin kanjinhō no kenkyū* 九品官人法 の研究 (The Mechanism of Aristocracy in China), 125.

11. Zhong Hui, Biography of his mother, quoted in Pei Songzhi, *Commentary to the Sanguo zhi*, *Wei*, 28.784.

12. He Shao, *Wang Bi biezhuan*, quoted in Pei Songzhi's *Commentary to the Sanguo zhi*, 28.795.

13. Ibid.

14. Ibid.

15. He Shao, *Wang Bi biezhuan*, quoted in Liu Xiaobiao's *Commentary to the Shishuo xinyu*, 2.6.

16. Cf. my "Lebensstil und Drogen," 87–108, for a more detailed analysis of these groupings, their lifestyle, and the political battles fought by and against them.

17. *Shishuo xinyu*, 4.6, 195f.; Mather, *A New Account*, 95.

18. Ibid. 4.7, 198; Mather, *A New Account*, 97. These essays are now lost, but some fragments remain that will be analyzed in detail in the volume dealing with Wang Bi's philosophy.

19. *Lunyu* 9.23.

20. He Shao, *Wang Bi biezhuan*, quoted in Pei Songzhi's commentary to *Sanguo zhi*, *Wei*, 28.795.

21. Cf. my "Lebensstil und Drogen," for a detailed description of the lifestyle of this generation. See also Morimitsu Kisaburō, "Gi Kin shidai ni ukeru ningen no hakken," *Tōyō bunka no mondai* 1 (1949): 122–201.

22. This argument has been first advanced by Wang Xiaoyi, *Zhongguo wenhua de qingliu*, 74f. It seems that the developments in the PRC during and after 1989 played a role in the formulation of the argument. This does not diminish its scholarly interest.

23. *Sanguo zhi*, *Wei*, 4.123.13f.

24. He Shao, *Wang Bi biezhuan*, quoted in Pei Songzhi's commentary to *Sanguo zhi, Wei*, 28.795.

25. *Wei shi chunqiu*, quoted in *Sanguo zhi, Wei*, 9.293. The *Jinshu* 2.25 takes up He Yan's praise for Sima Shi, who was posthumously elevated to the rank of emperor Jing of the Jin. The *Xici* quotation is in *Zhouyi yinde* 43 繫上 9. The translation follows the directions given by Han Kangbo's commentary, *Wang Bi ji jiaoshi*, 550f.

26. *Lunyu* 7.26.

27. Sima Guang, *Zizhi tongjian*, 75.2380: "He Yan . . . considered himself a genius of his age whom none other could match. He once gave an assessment of famous scholars [follows the quotation translated]. . . . With the 'spirit' he definitely wanted to compare himself."

28. He Shao, *Wang Bi biezhuan*, quoted in Liu Xiaobiao, commentary to the *Shishuo xinyu* 4.6, 196; Mather, 95. See also He Shao, *Wang Bi bie zhuan*, quoted in *Sanguo zhi, Wei*, 28.796.6.

29. Wang Bi, *Zhouyi lüeli*, 609.

30. Liu Yiqing, *Youming lu*, 20a.

31. He Shao, *Wang Bi bie zhuan*, quoted *in Sanguo zhi, Wei*, 28.796. Wang Xiaoyi, "Wang Bi guli xintan," 178, note 1.

32. This line of argument has been most extensively and rigorously explored in a book published in 1956 under the names of both Tang Yongtong and Ren Jiyu, but it seems that only older notes of Tang were used and the argumentation is entirely Ren Jiyu's. It has largely determined the way PRC scholars have dealt with Xuanxue until the mid-1980s. Ren Jiyu (and Tang Yongtong?), *Wei Jin xuanxue zhong de shehui zhengzhi sixiang*.

33. Zhang Zhan, *Liezi zhu*.

34. Cf. the chapter "The Language of the *Laozi* and *Lunyu*" in my *Language, Ontology, and Political Philosophy: Wang Bi's Scholarly Exploration of the Dark* (in press).

35. See Mather, *A New Account*, II.19 (40), II.50 (55), IV.23 (103), IV.38 (113), IV.85 (137), VIII.51 (226), VIII.98 (235), VIII.110 (237), for examples of this emulation of the Zhengshi era.

36. For Xun Rong, see He Shao, *Wang Bi biezhuan*, quoted in the commentary to *Sanguo zhi, Wei*, 28.759; for Ji Zhan, see *Jinshu* 68.1819f.

37. Cf. Wang Baoxuan, *Zhengshi xuanxue*, 412–25.

38. Ibid., 424.

39. Kong Yingda, "Preface," *Zhouyi zhengyi*, 1, line 8.

40. *Fozu tongji*, T. 1035, vol. 49.371a, last line. The dating there is not quite clear, but it can be inferred from the beginning of the chapter immediately following, which starts with the resumption of imperial duties by Zhongzong 中宗 in 705.

41. *Jinshu*, 75.1984f.

42. Sun Sheng, quoted in Pei Songzhi, commentary to the *Sanguo zhi*, *Wei*, 28.796. The quotation is probably from Sun's essay "Yi xiang miaoyu xianxing (The symbols of the *Yi* are more subtle than the visible shapes)."

43. Gu Yanwu, "Zhengshi," *Rizhi lu*, 13.5af. I am indebted to Robin Yates for the suggestion that Gu's views might have been influenced by events of his own time. Hou Wailu, *Zhongguo sixiang tongshi*, 3.34–38, has collected some more historical statements on Wang Bi and He Yan.

44. Zhu Yizun, "Wang Bi lun," *Pushuting ji*, 59.460a.

45. Qian Daxin, "He Yan lun," *Qianyantang ji*, 2.29–30.

2. The System of the Classics

1. He Shao, "Wang Bi biezhuan," in Pei Songzhi, *Sanguo zhi zhu*, 28:785.

2. Fragments of the *Jin yang qiu* survive in Pei Songzhi's *Sanguo zhi zhu* as well as in Liu Xiaobiao's *Shishuo xinyu zhu*.

3. The term translated here with "fitting and combining [arguments and terms from different places of the text]" is *fuhui*. The transmission of the Chinese characters for this expression is unstable. The Bonaben edition of the *Sanguo zhi* with Pei Songzhi's *Commentary*, based on two Song prints, 4601b.19, writes 賦會, the photomechanical reprint of the Wuyingdian 武英殿 edition of 1739, which is based on a Ming print, 1162b, writes 附會, while the Zhonghua Press edition, which is based on a comparision of these two and two more Ming editions as well as Qing scholarship, 796, decides in favor of 傅會. Zhan Ying, ed., Liu Xie, *Wenxin diaolong yizheng*, 1587–89, has assembled evidence showing that in fact the writings 附 and 傅 were both used. While it is clear that the expression 附會之辨 is meant polemically here, Tang Yongtong, "Wang Bi zhi *Zhouyi Lunyu* xinyi," 264–79, has pointed out that this term is not necessarily used in a negative sense. Cf. below, the text by Liu Xie.

4. Sun Sheng quoted in Pei Songzhi on *Sanguo zhi*, *Wei*, 796. This quotation does not name the work by Sun from which this passage is taken.

I assume it comes from Sun Sheng's lost "On the Symbols of the *[Zhou]yi* Being More Subtle Than Visible Forms," *Yi xiang miaoyu jianxing lun* 易象妙於見形論 mentioned in Sun's biography in *Jinshu*, 82:2147.

5. Liu Xie, *Wenxin diaolong yizheng,* 1589ff. Cf. Liu Hsieh, *The Literary Mind and the Carving of Dragons*, Vincent Shih, trans., 225f.

6. The expression is from the *Zhuangzi*, who says about "those of old who were regulating the Way" that the "principle of harmony emanated from their nature" 和理出其性 (*Zhuangzi yinde* 41.16.2). It is also used in Xi Kang, *Yangsheng lun*, which says of "those good at nourishing life" that they preserve [life] by means of the One, nourish it by means of harmony, [and thus their] principle of harmony increases daily and they are at one with the Great Conformity." Cf. D. Holzman, *La vie et la pensée de Hi K'ang* (223–62 Ap. J.-C.), p. 160 for the text, and p. 90 for a translation.

7. *He Shao, Wang Bi biezhuan*, 795.

8. The Mawangdui MS of the *Zhouyi* has a sequence different from that of the received text. It is reproduced in Fu Juyou et al., *Mawangdui Han mu wenwu*, 106–117.

9. Kong Yingda, *Zhouyi zhengyi*, treats Wang Bi's text this way, and so does the Tang-dynasty *Zhouyi* text in the "Forest of Stelae," *beilin*, kept in the in Xi'an museum.

10. Tang Yongtong, "Wang Bi zhi *Zhouyi Lunyu* xinyi," 264–79. The translation of this article by W. Liebenthal, "Wang Pi's New Interpretation of the I Ching and Lun-Yü," in *HJAS* 10 (1947):124–61, contains many mistakes. A supplement to Tang's argument is Wang Xiaoyi, "Jingzhou guanxue yu sanguo sixiang wenhua," in *Kongzi Yanjiu* 1 (1994):44–49.

11. Yu Yingshi, "Han Jin zhi jishi zhi xin zijue yu xin sichao" (The New Consciousness and New Trends in Thinking of the Scholars in the Transition from the Han to the Jin Dynasty), *Xinya xuebao* 41 (1959):25–144.

12. Cf. Gu Jiegang, *Handai xueshu shilüe* (An Outline of Han Learning), 81f. The discussion about the origin of the term *jing* 經 is described in Du Guoxiang, "Liang Han jing jingu wenxue zhi zhenglun" (The Discussion about the New and the Old Texts of the Classics during the Former and Later Han), 301–10. See also Hou Wailu et al., *Zhongguo sixiang tongshi*, II:313ff.

13. Wang Xianqian, *Shiming suzheng bu*, 6:12.

14. Cf. the biography of Yang Xiong 揚雄 in Ban Gu, *Han shu*, 57b:3577 line 14; *Sanguo zhi, Wei*, 4:136 line 5.

15. *Lunyu* 16.13.

16. *Lunyu* 17.17. For a detailed analysis of the development of the theory of philosophical language, see the first sections of the chapter "Discerning the That-by-which: The Language of the *Laozi* and the *Lunyu*" in my *Language, Ontology, and Political Philosophy* (In Press).

17. The term "lead classic" refers to the fact that, in most given periods, one classic was considered the core of this group. Since the Former Han, this classic was the *Chunqiu*, which was read as a text into which Confucius had written all the secrets of running society in accordance with the Way.

18. Cf. J. Gentz, *Ritus und Praxis*, 513; B. Wallacker, "The Spring and Autumn Annals as a Source of Law in Han China," 59–72; S. Queen, *From Chronicle to Canon: The Hermeneutics of the Spring and Autumn, according to Tung Chung-shu*, 127–81.

19. *Suishu*, 32:941.

20. Cf. Tjan Tjoe Som, *Po Hu T'ung: The Comprehensive Discussions in the White Tiger Hall*, I:90f.

21. The few surviving Eastern Han–dynasty commentaries carrying the title *zhangju*, such as Wang Yi's *Chuci zhangju* and Zhao Qi's *Mengzi zhangju*, fit neither in form nor in exegetical technique the caricature of *zhangju* commentaries and their exegetical techniques given by contemporary scholars. On Wang Yi's commentary Mr. Michael Schimmelpfennig, a member of the Heidelberg "Text and Commentary" reseach group, is about to finish a Ph.D. dissertation.

22. Cf. M. Nylan, "The Chin Wen/Ku Wen Controversy in Han Times," 117–29.

23. Cf. the poetic evaluations, *zan* 讚, at the end of the biographies of the Ru in Ban Gu, *Han shu*, 88:3620; cf. the *lun* 論 following Zheng Xuan's biography in Fan Ye, *Hou Han shu*, 35:1312; cf. T. Pokora, *Hsin lun (New Treatise) and Other Writings by Huan T'an*, 89.

24. I can find no textual evidence directly supporting M. Nylan's argument in "The Chin Wen/Ku Wen Controversy in Han Times," 112, that "Chang-chü were simply the textbooks used to teach 'official studies,' that is, interpretations of the Classics that, having received imperial approval, were taught at the Imperial Academy."

25. Kaga Eiji, "Gi Shin ni ukeru koten kaishaku no katachi—To Yo no 'Shunju kyōden shukai' ni tsuite" (The Interpretation of the Classics during the Wei and Jin Periods—On Tu Yu's Collected Explanations to the Text and the *Zhuan* of the *Chunqiu*), *Jinbun ronkyū* 13:15–24, 14:24–74, (1955) 15:32–58. The titles of the instalments vary slightly. See also his *Chugoku koten kaishaku shi, Gi Shin hen*.

26. Cf. the observations of Yu Fan 虞翻, a contemporary of Wang Bi, on the development of *Zhouyi* studies during the Later Han. *Yu Fan biezhuan* 虞翻別傳 in *Sanguo zhi, Wu*, 12:1322.

27. Michael Nylan, trans., Yang Hsiung, *The Canon of Supreme Mystery by Yang Hsiung.*

28. Zhuang's family name was the same as the personal name of the Han emperor Mingdi, Liu Zhuang, the use of which was taboo. Therefore Ban Hu's *Hanshu* used a character with a similar meaning, Yan, to replace it. Cf. Wang Deyou, *Laozi zhigui*, 3.

29. *Han shu*, 72:3056 line 11.

30. Zhuang (Yan) Zun, *Laozi zhu*, in Yan Lingfeng, ed., *Wuqiubeizhai Laozi jicheng*. Shima Kuniō, *Rōshi kōsei*, includes this text into his critical edition of the *Laozi*. I. Robinet, *Les commentaires du Tao Tö King jusqu'au VIIe siècle*, 210ff., gives an outline of the controversy over the different editions of this text. Cf. also Aat Vervoorn, "Zhuang Zun: A Daoist Philosopher of the Late First Century B.C.," *Monumenta Serica* 38 (1988–89): 69–94.

31. Zhuang (Yan) Zun, *Daode zhen jing zhigui*, ed. Zhengtong Taozang, *HY* 693. Cf. Shima Kuniō, *Rōshi kōsei*, 8ff., Wang Deyou, ed. and trans., *Laozi zhigui quanyi*. I use a different translation here for the title element 指歸 because Zhuang Zun does not operate with Wang Bi's analytic model of "pointers," although Wang Bi surely followed Zhuang Zun's precedent in choosing his title.

32. Cf. Michael A. N. Loewe, "Manuscripts Found Recently in China. A Preliminary Survey," *T'oung Pao* 63.1–2 (1977):99–136.

33. Cf. P. Demiéville, "Philosophy and Religion from Han to Sui," in D. Twitchett and J. K. Fairbank, eds., *The Cambridge History of China*, 1:810ff.

34. Cf. *Sanguo zhi, Shu*, 38:973, line 5, where it is said that Wang Shang 王商 sacrificed to Yan Junping 嚴君平 [Zun] and Li Hong 李弘. This Li Hong is not identical with the Li Hong from Mount Xin who early in the fourth century proclaimed himself to be the future king. Cf. A. Seidel, "The Image of the Perfect Ruler in Early Taoist Messianism: Lao-tzu and Li Hung," 231.

35. *Guan Lu biezhuan* 管輅別傳, quoted in Pei Songzhi's *Commentary to the Sanguo zhi*, in *Sanguo zhi, Wei*, 28:819 line 4. For more early sources on the fame and intellectual renown of Zhuang Zun, cf. Vervoorn, "Zhuang Zun," 72f.

36. Chao Yuezhi, *Fuzhi ji*, quoted in lieu of a preface to the *Ji Tang zi Laozi daode jing zhu*, 1. Chao's collected works contain a postface to a *Laozi* MS dated 1128, the *Ti xieben Laozi hou* 題寫本老子後, in which he deals with the deep understanding the *Laozi* evinces of the *Zhouyi*. Cf. *Songshan jingyu sheng ji.*

37. See pp. 177–248.

38. Yang Xiong, *Fayan zhu.*

39. Yang Xiong, *Taixuan jing.* Cf. Suzuki Yoshijirō, *Taigeneki no kenkyū.* and M. Nylan, trans., *The Canon of Supreme Mystery by Yang Hsiung.*

40. *Zhouli*, 24:6a.

41. Cf. M. Nylan, *The Canon of Supreme Mystery*, 29.

42. Yang Xiong, *Taixuan fu*, in Ban Gu, *Han shu*, 87b:3566.9 ff.

43. "The darkness of Heaven is its invisibility" 天以不見為玄, writes Yang Xiong in the *Xuangao* 玄告 section of the *Taixuan jing.* Cf. M. Nylan, *The Canon of Supreme Mystery*, 461.

44. *Han shu*, 57a:3514 line 9.

45. *Hou Han shu*, 40a:1330.

46. Wang Chong, *Lun heng*, 1028f.

47. *Hou Han shu*, 28a:955 line 4f.

48. T. Pokora, *Hsin-lun (New Treatise) and Other Writings by Huan T'an (43 B.C. – 28 A.D.).*

49. T. Pokora, *Hsin-lun*, xiv.

50. *Hou Han shu*, 28a:961 line 6f.; cf. Gu Jiegang, *Handai xueshu shilüe*, 185.

51. *Han shu*, 88:3602 line 6.

52. *Han shu*, 88:3602 line 11.

53. *Hou Han shu*, 62:2049 line 3f.

54. Ibid., 62:2050 line 4.

55. Ch'en Ch'i-yün, "A Confucian Magnate's Idea of Political Violence: Hsün Shuang's (128–190 A.D.) Interpretation of the Book of Changes," in *T'oung Pao* 54.1–3 (1978):91ff.

56. *Hou Han shu*, 62:2063 line 11. For more evidence of scholars being critical of the *zhangju*, see M. Nylan, "The Chin Wen/Ku Wen Controversy," 112–17. Nylan rightly points out that the borderlines between Old and New Text advocates were as blurred as between critics and authors of *zhangju* commentaries with some critics of *zhangju* authoring works with this element in the title.

57. Ibid., 64:2113.

58. Ibid., 60a:1965.

59. Ibid., 64:2113 line 6f.

60. Zheng Xuan wrote a commentary to such a text, the *Yi wei* 易緯, of which the book catalogue of the *Sui shu* lists an edition in 8j, *Suishu* 32.940.

61. Ibid., 35:1213 line 1f.

62. He Yan et al., *Lunyu jijie*.

63. *Hou Han shu*, 35:1209 line 15f.

64. Ibid., 79:2577.

65. Zheng Xuan, *Shipu xu*, in Ruan Yuan, ed., *Shisan jing zhushu*, 1:264.

66. *Hou Han shu*, 60b:1979.

67. Cf. A. Seidel, *La Divinisation du Lao Tseu dans le Taoisme des Han*, 39.

68. *Hou Han shu*, 60b: 1990. Cf. P. Pelliot, "Les classiques gravés sur pierre sous les Wei en 240–248," in *T'oung Pao* 23.1 (1924): 1f.

69. *Sanguo zhi, Wei*, 21:597.

70. *Hou Han shu*, 80b:2646.

71. *Sanguo zhi, Wei*, 21:599; see also the passage from the *Xian xian xingzhuang* 先賢行狀, *Deeds of Former Worthies*, quoted in the *Commentary* to this passage.

72. Xu Gan, *Zhonglun*, 1:10a.

73. Xie Cheng, *Hou Han shu* 後漢書, quoted in Pei Songzhi, commentary on *Sanguo zhi*, 6:211.

74. Cf. Hou Kang 侯康, *Bu Hou Han shu yiwen zhi* 2:2127a.

75. *Sanguo zhi, Shu*, 42:1027.

76. *Sanguo zhi, Wei*, 13:414.

77. *[Yu] Fan biezhuan* 翻別傳, quoted in Pei Songzhi, *Commentary to the Sanguo zhi*, 1323. Yu Fan also explicitly reset the hierarchy among the classics and claimed that, "in terms of greatness, none of the classics surpasses the *[Zhou]yi*" 經之大著莫過於易 Ibid.

78. Tang Yongtong, "Wang Bi zhi *Zhouyi Lunyu* xinyi," 265; R. P. Kramers, *K'ung Tzu Chia Yü*, 73ff.

79. *Sanguo zhi. Shu*, 42:1026.

80. Cf. Wang Can 王粲 (177–217), *Jingzhou wenxue jiguan zhi* 荆州文學記官志 (Report on the Literary Activities in Jingzhou), in Yan Kejun, *Quan shanggu sandai Qin Han sanguo liuchao wen, Quan Hou Han wen*, 91:5bf.

81. *Lunyu* 8.8.

82. Yu Yingshi, "Han Jin zhi ji shi zhi xin zijue yu xin sichao," *Xinya xuebao* 4.1 (1959):57f.

83. *San guo zhi, Shu*, 42:1027.

84. Wang Su, *Sheng zheng lun*, in Ma Guohan, ed., *Yu han shan fang ji yishu*, vol. III:2068a ff.

85. *Yu Fan biezhuan* 虞翻別傳, quoted in *San guo zhi, Wu*, 57:1322.

86. R. P. Kramers, *K'ung Tzu Chia Yu*, 79.

87. He Yan, preface to *Lunyu jijie*,1b.5.

88. Cf. Wang Su, ed., *Tang xieben Lunyu Zhengshi zhu ji qi yanjiu*.

89. Cf. pp. 19f.

90. Ji Yun et al., *Siku quanshu zongmu*, preface, 2b–3a, commenting on Wang Bi's *Commentary to the Zhouyi*.

91. Cf. *Nan Qi shu*, 39:684.

3. Technique and Philosophy of Structure

1. An earlier shorter version of this chapter has been published as "Interlocking Parallel Style: *Laozi* and Wang Bi" in *Études Asiatiques* 34.1 (1980):18–58. I am grateful to the editors for the permission to use sections of it verbatim. Wang Bi's philosophy of language will be dealt with in the chapter "Discerning the That-by-Which: The Language of the *Laozi* and the *Lunyu*" in my *Language, Ontology, and Political Philosophyy: Wang Bi's Scholarly Exploration of the Dark (Xuanxue)* (in press).

2. Wang Bi, Laozi weizhi lilüe, cf. my translation in "Wang Bi: 'The Structure of the *Laozi*'s Pointers' (Laozi weizhi lilüe)," *T'oung Pao* 72 (1986):92–129, at 112–14.

3. Zhao Qi, "Tici jie," *Mengzi zhushu*, 5.

4. Gustave Schlegel, *La loi du parallélisme en style chinois, demonstrée par la préface du Si-yu-ki, la traduction de cette préface par feu Stanislaus Julien défendue contre la nouvelle traduction du Père A. Gueluy*. Schlegel was dealing with the translation of Zhang Yue's preface, the Chinese text of which is in Xuan Zhuang, "Bian Ji," 13ff.

5. Schlegel first articulated this rule in his "Le stèle funéraire du Teghin Giogh et ses copistes et traducteurs chinois, russes et allemands," *Journal de la Société Finno-Ougrienne* 8 (1892):30; he refers to this in *La loi du parallélisme*, p. 1. The translation into English is mine.

6. For recent summaries of the scholarship, see Yin Gonghong, *Pianwen*, and Jiang Shuge, *Pianwen shi lun*.

7. Yin Gonghong, *Pianwen*, 57ff.

8. Jiang Shuge, *Pianwen shi lun*, 49ff. and 313ff.

9. Jingmen shi bowuguan, *Guodian Chu mu zhujian*. Peking 1998.

10. The sequence in *Laozi* A in the Guodian tomb is, in terms of the received text, 19, 66, 46, 30, 64 (in part), 37, 63, 2, 32, 25, 5 (part), 16, 64 (part), 56, 57, 55, 44, 40; in *Laozi* B the sequence is 9, 59, 48, 20, 13, 41, 52, 45, 54; and in *Laozi* C it is 17, 18, 35, 31, 64 (part).

11. Mawangdui Hanmu boshu zhengli xiaozu, *Mawangdui Hanmu boshu*; an edition with the transcribed texts only is Mawangdui Hanmu boshu zhengli xiaozu, *Mawangdui Hanmu boshu Laozi*.

12. MWD/A has the *zhang* sequence 38, 39, 41, 40, 42, 43, 44, 45–66, 80, 81, 67–79, 1–21, 24, 22, 23, 25–37, MWD/B 2 the sequence 38, 39, 41, 40, 42 etc. like MWD/A. Zhuang [Yan] Zun 莊 (嚴) 遵 is credited with having done a slightly different arrangement of the *zhang*. This, however, did not consist in breaking them apart but in linking a few of them to arrive at a lower number that could be interpreted in terms of the Yin/Yang doctrine. Cf. pp. 36–37.

13. D. C. Lau, *Tao Te Ching*, xiv, writes: "In my view not only is the Lao-tzu an anthology but even individual chapters are made up of shorter passages whose connection with one another is at best tenuous." On p. xv he writes: "Since we cannot expect a high degree of cohesion in the thought, the most sensible way of giving an account of it (i.e., the Lao-tzu) is to deal with the various key concepts, and to relate them wherever possible,

but also to point out inconsistencies when they are obstinately irreconcilable." L. Hurvitz, "A Recent Japanese Study of Lao-tzu: Kimura Eiichi's 木村英一 *Rōshi no shinkenkyū* 老子の新研究," *Monumenta Serica* 20 (1961):311–67, gives on p. 327ff. a translation of Kimura Eiichi's reading. See also Kimura Eiichi, "A New Study of Lao-tzu," *Philosophical Studies of Japan*, 1:93f.

14. Cf. D. C. Lau, trans., *Tao Te Ching*; Robert G. Henricks, *Lao-tzu Te-Tao Ching*.

15. D. C. Lau, *Tao Te Ching*, 14.

16. D. C. Lau, *Tao Te Ching*, 51.

17. A. Waley, *The Way and Its Power*, 129.

18. Cf. pp. 156ff.

19. Robert G. Henricks, "Examining the Chapter Divisions in the *Lao-tzu*," *Bulletin of the School of Oriental and African Studies* 45.3 (1982):501–524.

20. All references are to my critical edition and translation of Wang Bi's *Laozi* and his commentary to this text. Detailed philological documentation and discussion will be found there. *Wang Bi's Commentary on the Laozi: Critical Text, Philological Commentary, Extrapolative Translation* (in press).

21. In MWD A alone such inversions against the Fu Yi "old text" text occur no less than 9 times (*Laozi* 56.3–6, 61.3, 66 (處之上 ... and 處之前 ...), 80.4, 81.2f., 14.4, 15.3, 28.2–4, 31 (非君子之器/不祥之器); that is, they may be considered a frequent occurrence.

22. D. C. Lau, *Tao Te Ching*, 101.

23. D. C. Lau uses a different text from Wang Bi's, in which phrase 1, 古之, does not appear.

24. A. Waley, *The Way and Its Power*, 227.

25. L. Hurvitz, "A New Study," 359f. Cf. Kimura Eiichi, *Rōshi no shin kenkyū,* 489f.

26. A. Waley, *The Way and Its Power*, 197.

27. D. C. Lau, Chan Wing-tsit, and Kimura Eiichi do not differentiate between phrase 1 and 2 on the one hand and phrase 3 on the other. D. C. Lau, *Tao Te Ching*, 105; Chan, *A Sourcebook in Chinese Philosophy*, 161; Kimura Eiichi in the translation by L. Hurvitz, "A New Study," 348.

28. The other translators such as D. C. Lau, *Tao Te Ching*, 105; Chan, *A Sourcebook*, 161; Kimura Eiichi in L. Hurvitz, "A New Study," 348, do the same, writing "therefore."

29. In *Laozi* 15.4, Wang Bi comments justly that the *shu* 孰 in the twofold *shu neng* 孰能 "who is able to . . ." there "points at the difficulty to do this" 言其難; this means that it should be translated "who possibly could . . ." with the expected answer "no one" or "hardly anyone." In *Laozi* 23.2, the question is asked *shu wei ci zhe* 孰為此者? This refers to storm and heavy rains. The answer is naturally Heaven and Earth, and in this case it is actually appended. The question should be translated "Well, who is effecting them? Heaven and Earth naturally." In *Laozi* 58.3, the question is asked *shu zhi qi ji* 孰知其極? Wang Bi comments correctly in my opinion that this refers to the impossibility of recognizing this "utmost" as it is impossible to grasp it in terms of forms or names. The translation must run: "Who after all recognizes its ultimate?" (Answer: no one). In *Laozi* 73.4, Wang Bi reads the question *shu zhi qi gu* 孰知其故 as implying the answer "Only the Sage." This question is in fact followed, as in the case of *Laozi* 44, by a "therefore" 是以. This "therefore" would be nonsense if the answer would not have been actually implied by the text in the manner suggested by Wang Bi. The *shu gan* "who would dare 孰敢" in *Laozi* 74.1 obviously implies the answer "no one." In 77.2, the question "who after all is capable of having something in excess to offer to All Under Heaven 孰能損有餘以奉不足於天下者?" is followed by the evident answer: "Only he who has the Way, naturally," 其惟道者乎. These are all the instances where *shu* appears in the *Laozi*.

30. Fan Yingyuan, *Laozi Daode jing guben jizhu*, 2:16a (p. 46a).

31. Cf. *Zhanguo ce zhuzi suoyin*, 461.227.8: 明主愛其國忠臣愛其名 "the enlightened ruler will love his state, the loyal minister will love his name;" *Han shi waizhuan zhuzi suoyin*, 1.13.3.19 為能勝理而無愛名, which Hightower, *Han shih wai chuan: Han Ying's Illustrations of the Didactic Application of the Classic of Songs*, 23, translates "only by being able to rise above desire will one not have a love for fame." Cf. also *Sanguo zhi*, 1412 存身愛名.

32. Cf. "Wang Bi's Ontology," in my *Language, Ontology, and Political Philosophy: Wang Bi's Scholarly Exploration of the Dark (Xuanxue)*.

33. L. Hurvitz, "A New Study," 330.

34. Cf. Wang Bi's *Laozi weizhi lüeli*, in Lou Yulie, *Wang Bi ji jiaoshi*, 196f. See my translation in "The Structure of the *Laozi*'s Subtle Pointers" in the volume *Wang Bi's Commentary on the Laozi: Critical Text, Extrapolative Translation, Philological Commentary*, (in press).

35. *Laozi* 2, 28, 41 and other *zhang* contain rhymed parts. Cf. B. Karlgren, *The Poetical Parts in Lao-tsi.*

36. Cf. the chapter "Wang Bi's Ontology" in my *Language, Ontology, and Political Philosophy: Wang Bi's Scholarly Exploration of the Dark (Xuanxue).*

37. *Guanzi*, Nei ye, 270.

38. For another English translation, see Rickett, *Kuan-tzu*, 161.

39. Cf. S. Couvreur, *Mémoires sur les bienséances et les cérémonies* (Leiden: Brill, 1930), vol. II, 1:55.

40. Ibid., II, 2:428f.

41. Ibid., II, 2:518f.

42. Ibid., I, 2:514.

43. Sun Xidan. *Li ji jijie*, 605.

44. Chen Qiyou (ed.), *Hanfeizi jishi*, 1:1.

45. Ibid., 1:111.

46. *Mozi yinde*, 1, lines 1ff.

47. *Xiao jing*, 2:2560a.

48. *Zhouyi yinde*, 繫辭上 1.

49. See also my already published translation of this text, "Wang Bi: 'The Structure of the *Laozi*'s Pointers' (*Laozi weizhi lilüe*)," *T'oung Pao* 72 (1986):92–129.

50. *Wang Bi, Laozi weizhi lüeli*, in Lou Yulie, *Wang Bi ji jiaoshi*, 195.

51. For Shi Daoan, see his preface to the *Ren ben yu sheng jing* 55:45a f., which is entirely written in IPS. A passage from this is is translated in R. Wagner, "Die Fragen Hui-yuan's an Kumarajiva," Ph.D. dissertation, Munich 1969, p. 196; for Shi Huiyuan see his *Shamen bujingwangzhe lun*, II.86, line 12. The passage is translated in Wagner, "Die Fragen Hui-yuan's an Kumarajiva," p. 187.

52. Cf. Wang Bi, *Laozi weizhi lüeli*, 197, where Wang Bi sets off the *ming* 名 against the *cheng* 稱 in parallel statements. They are not really parallel, however, and he continues by subdividing the *cheng* into a subpair. See Wagner, "Wang Bi: The Structure of the *Laozi*'s Pointers," p. 119ff.

4. Deconstructing and Constructing Meaning

1. Liu Xie, *Wenxin diaolong yizheng*, 2:669.

2. The *Xici* is read here through Wang Bi's perspective; in this view, the *Xici* are an integral part of the text.

3. *Zhouyi* 7.10a.

4. *LZWZLL*, 3.1ff.

5. Cao Pi, *Dianlun lunwen*, 178.

6. Cf. Tang Yongtong, "Wei Jin xuanxue he wenxue lilun," *Zhongguo zhexueshi yanjiu*, 1(1980):37–45; Wang Baoxuan, *Zhengxhi xuanxue*, 350–56.

7. Zhou Jizhi, "Wei Jin wenlun de xingqi yu xuanxue zhong 'tian ren xin yi' de xingcheng," *Zhexue yanjiu* 5(1984):47f.

8. Liu Shao, *Renwu zhi*, 1, in W. Bauer (Bao Wugang), ed., *Renwu zhi yinde* 人物志引得.

9. Kong Fan, *Wei Jin xuanxue he wenxue*, 7. Oddly, in the plethora of recent studies about the relationship of Xuanxue with literature and literary theory, Wang Bi's discovery of the literary structure of the *Laozi* as a form of its philosophizing about the unspeakable has not been mentioned. Wang Bi's analysis of the *Laozi* and the *Zhouyi*, both of which clearly rank as *wen* 文 in the Chinese sense, is in fact far more elaborate and philosophically sophisticated than the other sources from the third century. Cf. Tang Yongtong, "Wei Jin xuanxue he wenxue lilun," *Zhongguo zhexueshi yanjiu* 1(1980):37–45; Zhou Jizhi, "Wei Jin wenlun de xingqi," *Zhexue yanjiu* 5(1984):45–53.

10. Cf. my "The Language of the *Laozi* and *Lunyu*" in my *Language, Ontology, and Political Philosophy: Wang Bi's Scholarly Exploration of the Dark* (in press).

11. *LZWZLL*, 3.1.

12. *LZWZLL*, 6.1.

13. See the studies by Hu Shi 胡適, Liang Qichao 梁啟超, Zhang Xu 張煦, Tang Lan 唐蘭, Gao Heng 高亨, Qian Mu 錢穆, Luo Genze 羅根澤, Feng Youlan 馮友蘭, Gu Jiegang 顧頡剛, Ma Xulun 馬敘倫, Tan Jiefu 譚戒甫, and others in the *Gushi bian*, vols. 3, 4, and 6. Homer Dubs joined in this debate with his "The date and circumstances of the philosopher Lao-Dz," *JAOS* 61(1941):215ff. and "The Identification of the Lao-Dz," *JAOS* 62(1942):300ff.

14. M. Soymié, "L'entrevue de Confucius et de Hiang T'o," *Journal Asiatique* 242(1954):311–92.

15. Sun Cizhou, "Ba *Gushi bian* disi ce bing lun *Laozi* zhi youwu," repr. in Luo Genze, ed., *Gushi bian*, 6:86ff.

16. *Zhuangzi yinde* 14.5.48. Cf. Sun Cizhou, "Ba *Gushi bian*," p. 84.

17. *Kongzi jiayu*, 3:11, cf. R. Wilhelm, *Kungfutse, Schulgespräche*, 60f.

18. *Liji zhengyi*, 19:1400 c; cf. S. Couvreur, Mémoires sur les bienséances et les cérémonies, I.2:434 and 463.

19. Guo Moruo, "Lao Dan, Guan Yin, Huan Yuan," *Gushi bian*, 6:631ff., has assembled many of the relevant passages that show that these texts "accepted" the *Laozi* as the teacher of Confucius, ibid. p. 637. Cf. A. Seidel, *La divinisation du Lao Tseu dans le taoisme des Han*, 12.

20. For the pictorial evidence for this motif, see Kaete Finsterbusch, *Verzeichnis und Motivindex der Han-Darstellungen*, 221f. Liu Peigui, "Han huaxiangshi zhong de Kongzi jian Laozi," pp. 35ff. has found that nearly all of these reliefs come from southern Shandong and northern Jiangsu, that is from an area in which the Gaoping Wangs had their seat.

21. Cf. Chen Dezhao, *Laozi sixiang dui Han chu zhengzhi zhi yingxiang*.

22. Sima Tan's 司馬談 comments "on the essential purport of the Six Schools" 六家之要指 are quoted by Sima Qian in his autobiography; cf. *Shiji*, Takigawa Kametaro, ed., *Shiki kaichu kosho*, 130:7ff. Sima Qian, *Shiji*, 130:3288–92.

23. B. Wallacker, "Han Confucianism and Confucius in Han," in D. Roy, Tsuen-hsuin Tsien, eds., *Ancient China: Studies in Early Civilization*, 222f.

24. Yang Xiong (Han Jing 韓敬 comm.), *Fayan zhu* 4.6 (p. 76f.).

25. Ban Gu, *Han shu*, 20:861ff. For an analysis of the *Gujin renbiao*, see my "Ban Gu and the End of History," unpublished paper, 1995.

26. Wang Baoxuan, *Zhengshi xuanxue*, 55.

27. *Lunyu* 6.21; Ban Gu, *Han shu*, 861.

28. *Lunyu* 17.2.

29. *Lunyu* 16.9.

30. *Laozi ming*, cf. A. Seidel, *La divinisation du Lao Tseu*, 128. In the same manner, the earliest commentator on Ban Gu's *Han shu*, Zhang Yan (third century CE), is quoted by Yan Shigu as also disputing the *Laozi*'s assessment by Ban Gu (*Han shu*, 862, note 13). The Tang ruling house of

Li 李, which claimed descent from Laozi actually proceeded to rewrite the *Han shu*. The Tang copies of the *Han shu* have transferred Laozi to the *shangshang* 上上 position of the sage according to an order given in 742. Cf. Liang Yusheng (Qing), *Renbiao kao* 人表考, in *Ershiwu shi bubian*, 1:285.b f. This arrangement can still be seen in the reprint of the 1739 edition of the *Han shu* in *Ershiwu shi* 1:457a. The classical formula of the Daoist tradition is in the Tang author Lu Xisheng's (fl. 888–903) preface to his *Daode zhen jing zhuan*, 2a f., where Lu claims that Laozi is a match for the sages Fu Xi, King Wen, and Confucius together and thus superior to each one of them; cf. Wang Baoxuan, *Zhengshi xuanxue*, 8. Li Yue (Tang) transfers in the preface to his *Daode zhenjing xinzhu*, Zhengtong Daozang, HY 692, Schipper, 692, p. 1b f., the statement to the texts ascribed to these persons by saying that "the Six Classics are only the branches and leaves of Huang/Lao." This assessment was not restricted to Daoists such as Lu Xisheng. The Tang ruling family, which claimed descent from Laozi, gave the honorific "emperor," *di* 帝, to him, while ranking Confucius only as a "king," *wang* 王. Wang Baoxuan, *Zhengshi xuanxue*, 9, has assembled this evidence.

31. Cf. Jao Tsung-i, *Laozi Xiang Er zhu jiaozheng*, 27. Cf. S. Bokenkamp, *Early Daoist Scriptures*, 113. Our translations agree.

32. Wang Baoxuan, *Zhengshi xuanxue*, 39f. Sun Chu 孫楚 (fourth century?) stated that Ban Gu established the nine ranks "to record the ranking order in the register of the spirits [of the dead]" and that "Chen Qun based himself on this in order to grade the living." Cf. *Taiping yulan*, 265; Wang Baoxuan, *Zhengshi xuanxue*, p. 55.

33. Quoted in Kong Yingda's subcommentary to Zheng Xuan's *Commentary to the Shijing*, in Ruan Yuan, *Shisan jing zhushu*, 586a end; cf. Wang Baoxuan, *Zhengshi xuanxue*, p. 10. From the argument and terminology, this piece looks authentic. We do not have to conclude that Wang Bi ever wrote a complete commentary to the *Xici*, which is highly unlikely. However, he wrote an essay to one section of it and used it as his basis for the *Zhouyi* interpretation. The quotation must have been taken from one of these texts.

34. Wang Bi, *Lunyu shiyi*, on *Lunyu* 7.1 in Lou Yulie, ed., *Wang Bi ji jiaoshi*, 623f.

35. *Shiji*, 63.2139. The pronounciations for Lai and Hu are taken from Sima Zhen's commentary. Wang Bi deviates from the *Shiji* biography in giving the family name of Lao 老 to Laozi instead of the Li 李 common in all other sources. Cf. Gao Heng, "Shiji Laozi zhuan jianzheng," *Gushi bian* 6(1938):444ff. This implies a rejection of the claim of the Li family to be descended from Laozi, a claim used by many rebels since the Eastern Han

to justify their ambitions for the throne; cf. A. Seidel, "The Image of the Perfect Ruler in Early Taoist Messianism: Lao Tzu and Li Hung," *History of Religions* 9.2–3(1969/1970):216ff. The assumption that Laozi's family name was Li eventually led to the establishment of Laozi as the ancestor of the Tang ruling family. The claim of the Lis to descend from Laozi was current in Wang Bi's time. Kong Rong 孔融, a descendant of Confucius, for example, managed to be received at the age of ten by the much senior Li Ying 李膺 by pointing at the longstanding friendly relationship between Li Ying's presumable ancestor Laozi and his own forefather; cf. *Shishuo xinyu*, 2.3, p. 56; R. Mather, *Shih-shuo Hsin-yü: A New Account of Tales of the World*, 26. The discussion about this passage of the *Lunyu*, however, was not over. A few decades after Wang Bi, Ge Hong 葛洪 (284–364) suggested that Lao Peng simply meant Laozi, *Baopuzi, neipian*, 10:43.

36. Jao Tsung-i, *Laozi Xiang Er zhu jiaozheng*, 12.

37. He Yan, *Lunyu jijie* 7.1. A Lao Peng is in fact mentioned in the Da Dai li, 大戴禮, 9:10b, and appears in Ban Gu's *Gujin ren biao, Han shu*, 20:884, where he belongs to the lowest grade of the highest category, *shang xia* 上下.

38. Quoted in Lu Deming, *Lunyu shiwen*, in Lu Deming, *Jingdian shiwen*, 3.1362; cf. Tan Jiefu, "Er Lao yanjiu," *Gushi bian* 6(1938):477.

39. An example is *Laozi* 67, where the "I" is not identified; in the commentary, however, Wang Bi explains phrase 4 of this *zhang* with phrases from other parts of the *Laozi* and from the *Xici*, both of which have the Sage as the subject; cf. my *Wang Bi's Commentary on the Laozi: critical Text, Extrapolative Translation, Philological Commentary* (in press). The attempt by Gu Jiegang in his "Cong Lüshi chunqiu tuice *Laozi* zhi chengshu niandai," *Gushi bian* 4(1933):485f., to present the quotations from the "Sage" in the *Laozi* as quotations from a different *Laozi* does not seem to be successful because these quotations are not all explicit and thus not unified so that it is difficult to assign them either way. Wang Bi himself, needless to say, relied on what he saw as the internal evidence in the *Laozi* and the *Lunyu*.

40. Cf. my *Wang Bi's Commentary on the Laozi: Critical Text, Extrapolative Translation, Philological Commentary* (in press).

41. *LZWZLL*, 198.

42. A. Waley. "Appendix I: Authorship in Early China," in *The Way and Its Power*, 101f.

43. Yang Xiong quotes the same *zhang* of the *Laozi* identifying the "I" with Laozi himself. In his rebuttal of charges of obscurantism, the *Jie nan*

解難 ("Explaining Difficulties"), he writes: "Lao Dan left a saying 'there are few who honor and understand me.'" Quoted in *Hanshu* 87b:3578.

44. Cf. Lu Xisheng's preface to his *Daode zhenjing zhuan*, 2a: "Ruan Ji called [Laozi] a superior worthy and second-degree Sage, agreeing [in this] with [Wang] Fusi [=Bi]." Cf. Wang Baoxuan, *Zhengshi xuanxue*, 8.

45. Wang Baoxuan, *Zhengshi xuanxue*, 16. Sun Sheng (302–73), *Lao Dan fei da xian lun*, 119–20.

46. *Laozi* 20.6.

47. *Laozi* 20.9.

48. *Laozi* 20.10.

49. *Laozi* 20.3.

50. *Laozi* 20.13.

51. *Laozi* 64.8.

52. *Laozi* 42.2. There, the "men of the crowd" are not explicitly mentioned, but I assume the text refers to them.

53. *Laozi* 8.1.

54. *Laozi* 20.9.

55. *Laozi* 8.1.

56. *Laozi* 20.15.

57. He Shao, *Wang Bi bie zhuan*, quoted in Pei Songzhi's commentary to the *Sanguo zhi*, 795.

58. Liu Yiqing, *Shishuo xinyu*, 4.8, p. 199. The standard translation of the core phrases by Richard Mather in his otherwise admirable work runs: "The Sages embodied the Non-actual. Furthermore, since the Non-actual may not be the subject of instruction, the Sages of necessity dealt with the actual (*yu*). Lao-tzu and Chuang-tzu, not yet free of the actual, were constantly giving instruction about that in which they felt a deficiency." Cf. R. Mather, *A New Account of Tales of the World*, 96. The term *shengren*, the Sage, routinely refers to Confucius in third- and fourth-century materials. The translation of 故言必及有 as "the Sages of necessity dealt with the actual" directly contradicts Pei Hui's statement that "the Sage was absolutely unwilling to discourse about it [about negativity]." The translation of *wei* 未 as "not yet" (not yet free of the actual) blurs the fundamental difference between Lao/Zhuang and the Sage. *Wei* 未 is frequently used in the *Shishuo xinyu* as a blank negation. The most important

point, however, is the last sentence, where Prof. Mather follows the reading implied in the punctuation of the phrase by most Japanese and Chinese scholars who give 恆訓其所不足, instead of 恆訓, 其所不足. W. Liebenthal translated the passage in his rendering of an article by Tang Yongtong in an even stranger manner: "When Pei Hui saw him [Wang Bi], he felt he was not like others. He asked: 'If No-Thing were really at the bottom of things, the Sage would have said so. But he did not. And Lao-tzu incessantly talked about it. Why?' Wang answered:'Though the Sage well conceived No-thingness 有 [sic], he did not broach this subject because it leaves no room for comment. Lao-tzu truly acknowledged Thingness, but he always said that it is insufficient (to represent the absolute).'" W. Liebenthal, trsl. T'ang Yung-t'ung, "Wang Bi's New Interpretation of the I-Ching and the Lun-yue," *Harvard Journal of Asiatic Studies* HJAS 10(1947):152. Most Chinese scholars also missed the structure and the content of the last phrase and thus the point of the entire story; cf. Liu Dajie 劉大杰, *Wei Jin sixiang lun*, 21; He Changqun, *Wei Jin qingtan sixiang chulun*, 64; Feng Youlan, *Zhongguo zhexue shi*, II.603; Tang Yongtong, Ren Jiyu, *Wei Jin xuanxue zhong de shehui zhengzhi sixiang lüelun*, 22; Hou Wailu et al., *Zhongguo sixiang tongshi*, III:97; Tang Changru, *Wei Jin nanbei chao shi luncong*, 326; Lou Yulie ed., *Wang Bi ji jiaoshi*, 639 and 645; Luo Minsheng, "Shi lun Wang Bi xuanxue dui mingjiao de pipan," *Zhongguo zhexueshi yanjiu*, 1:75 (1987). He Qimin, *Wei Jin sixiang yu tanfeng*, 94, misquotes the relevant portion from He Shao and inserts the *Shishuo xinyu* version here. Qian Mu's "*Ji Wei Jin xuanxue sanzong*," originally published in 1945, in id., *Zhuang Lao tongbian*, 346, seems to have been the first to set off the last three characters of the He Shao version with a comma, writing 故恆言無，所不足, which changes the entire text in the sense in which I have translated it. His example, however, has not been followed.

59. The capping ceremony normally takes place during the twentieth year of a young man's life. As Wang Bi was born in 226, this gives us a *datum ante quem* of 245. I believe, the Chinese editors have mispunctuated this passage, writing 弼父業為尚書郎時裴徽為吏部郎弼未弱冠往造焉 in the form of 弼父業為尚書郎. 時裴徽為吏部郎，弼未弱冠往造焉; this would prompt a translation "Bi's father Ye was a *shangshulang*. At the time Pei Hui . . ." In this reading, the first phrase about Wang Bi's father is perfectly unconnected information. I believe the punctuation has to run 弼父業為尚書郎時，裴徽為吏部郎；弼未弱冠往造焉, "When Bi's father Ye was a *shangshulang*, Pei Hui was a *libulang*," meaning that, as Wang's father and Pei Hui had both been lower-level officials at the same time, Wang Bi felt able to visit Pei, although he himself was still uncapped and Pei was by the time a famous intellectual and high-ranking official. Liu Rulin's calculation in his *Han Jin xueshu biannian*, II:161, is quite reliable proving that, by 244, Pei Hui had become Regional Inspector in Jizhou, but Liu had no source other than the misread-

ing of the present passage to argue that, at the time of his meeting with Wang Bi, Pei Hui was a *libulang* 吏部郎, an entrance job for youths from high families; there was nothing daring in Wang Bi's visit had Pei been just a *libulang*. Liu, ibid., 159, assumes that Wang Bi's *Commentary* must have been written before this encounter, namely in 243. There is little evidence to support this; obviously Wang Bi was known as a connoisseur of the *Laozi* long before he published his *Commentary*.

60. For the sources, see my "Wang Bi's Ontology."

61. *LZWZLL* , 195.

62. Cf. Jack Dull, "A Historical Introduction to the Apocryphal (Ch'an Wei) Texts of the Han Dynasty," 516ff.; Anna Seidel, *La divinisation du Lao Tseu*.

63. Some examples: Wang Bi, *ZYLL*, section *ming xiang* 明象 (Lou Yulie, ed., *Wang Bi ji jiaoshi*, 609), takes up the metaphor of the hare and fish traps from the *Zhuangzi* (*Zhuangzi yinde*, 75.26.48f.). Wang Bi, commenting on *Laozi* 38.2, quotes with 天地之心見 the *tuan* for *Zhouyi*, hexagram *fu* 復 (Lou Yulie, ed., *Wang Bi ji jiaoshi*, 336); Wang Bi on *Laozi* 17.1 quotes the *wenyan* to *Zhouyi* hexagram 1; Wang Bi's *LZWZLL*, 6.1 quotes Confucius from the *Lunyu* 2.2, and there are some quotations from the *Laozi* in Wang Bi's *Commentary on the Zhouyi*.

64. *Wenzhang xulu*, quoted in Liu Xiaobiao, *Shishuo xinyu zhu*, 4.10, 200. Some Chinese scholars have misread this passage as meaning that He Yan thought "[Laozi] was the same as a Sage," that is, ranked equally high with him. I believe this reading to be untenable in terms of grammar, content, and the evidence quoted above. Cf. Wang Baoxuan, *Zhengshi xuanxue*, 9f.

65. Cf. R. Wagner, "Die Unhandlichkeit des Konfuzius," in A. Assmann, ed., *Weisheit. Archäologie der literarischen Kommunikation III*, 455–64.

66. He Shao, *Xun Can biezhuan*, quoted in Pei Songzhi, *Sanguo zhi zhu*, 10.319f.

67. Cf. the chapter "The Language of the *Laozi* and the *Lunyu* and the Cognizability of That-by-Which the Ten Tounsand Entities Are," in my *Language, Ontology, and Political Philosophy: Wang Bi's Scholarly Exploration of the Dark (Xuanxue)*.

68. Lu Xisheng, *Daode jing zhuan xu*. The sources have been diligently assembled by Wang Baoxuan, *Zhengshi xuanxue*, 8.

69. Shi Daoan, *Er jiao lun*, 138; Zhou Yong, "Zhou chong da shu bing Zhou chong wen," 40b.

70. Wang Baoxuan, *Zhengshi xuanxue*, p. 11ff.

71. Ibid., 16.

72. Wang Baoxuan has assembled much evidence that the "famous intellectuals" of the Wei and Jin set themselves the goal of reaching reaching this second-highest level in the nine-tiered scale as a way of claiming for themselves the status of *yasheng*. Wang Baoxuan, *Zhengshi xuanxue*, 54ff.

73. See "The Structure of the *Laozi's* Pointers," in my *Wang Bi's Commentary on the Laozi: Critical text, Extrapolative Translation, Philological Commentary* (in press).

74. *Laozi weizhi lilüe.* Zhengtong daozang, Schipper 1255. Zhang Junfang. *Yunji qiqian.* Zhengtong Daozang, Schipper 1032, ch.1; this "comprehensive excyclopedia of Taoist learning" (Strickmann) was submitted to the throne in 1019.

75. Quotations from the *Xici* are in Wang Bi on *Laozi* 38.2, 47.1, 49.4, 64.1, 67.1, 70.4, 73.6 (2); from the *wenyan* in Wang Bi on *Laozi* 5.2 and 77.1, from the *tuan* and *xiang* to hexagram *fu* in Wang Bi on *Laozi* 38.2.

76. All *Laozi* quotations are read and translated here through Wang Bi's *Commentary.* For the details of text and translation, see my *Wang Bi: The Structure of the Laozi's Pointers and Commentary on the Laozi: Critical Edition of the Text, Translation and Commentary.*

77. Wang Bi on *Laozi* 38.2.

78. *Laozi* 80.4, cf. Wang Bi's commentary on *Laozi* 80.1.

79. Cf. "Political Philosophy" in my *Language, Ontology, and Political Philosophy: Wang Bi's Scholarly Exploration of the Dark (xuanxue)* (in press).

80. Cf. the translation of Wang Bi on *Laozi* 64.1 and note 1 in my *Wang Bi's Commentary on the Laozi.*

81. Cf. note 1 in the translation of *Laozi* 17.1 in ibid.

82. Cf. For Zhong Hui 鐘會 , see Pei Songzhi on *Sanguo zhi*, 786; for Xun Rong 荀融, see ibid., 316; for He Yan, see the excerpt from his biography quoted in *Taiping yulan*, 385.

83. Cf. my *Language, Ontology and Political Philosopy: Wang Bi's Scholarly Exploration of the Dark (Xuanxue)* (in press).

84. There are unmarked verbatim quotations in Wang Bi on 10.2 from *Laozi* 32.1, on 10.3 from *Laozi* 56.7, on 10.4 from *Laozi* 19.1, on 10.5 from *Laozi* 32.1, on 10.6 from *Laozi* 37.1–3.

85. For a list of all explicit references of this kind, see my "The Wang Bi Recension of the *Laozi*" in *Wang Bi's Commentary on the Laozi* (in press).

86. For He Yan being superior to his stepfather, Cao Cao, in reading military tracts, cf. the *Biography of He Yan* quoted in *Taiping yulan*, 385. For his precocious reading of the *Laozi*, cf. *Shishuo xinyu*, 12.2; for Wang Bi as in turn superior to He Yan, cf. p. 16f.; for Zhong Hui's reading, cf. the biography of his mother quoted in Pei Songzhi on *Sanguo zhi*, 785f. The entire chapter XII of the *Shishuo xinyu* is devoted to such examples of precocious intelligence.

87. For a translation of the *Shishuo xinyu* 4.10 reports about this encounter, cf. p. 15ff.

88. Cf. p. 275.

89. Zhong Hui's description of his education at the hands of his mother is quoted in Pei Songzhi's *Commentary to the Sanguo zhi*, 785f. Zhong Yu's writings are listed in Yao Zhenzong, *Sanguo yiwen zhi*; they are *Zhouyi xun* 周易訓 (3192 a–b), *Laozi xun* 老子訓 (3255a), and *Bishi lun* 筆勢論 (3273a).

90. Jao Tsung-i, "Wu jianheng er nian Su Dan xieben Daode jing canjuan kaozheng (jian lun Heshang gong ben yuan liu). The Su Tan Manuscript Fragment of the Tao-Te Ching (A.D.270)," *Journal of Oriental Studies* II.1:1–71 (1955).

91. Kong Yingda, subcommentary to Zheng Xuan's *Commentary to the Shijing*, 1.289a: "Those at the beginning of the Han who made 'traditions', *zhuan* 傳, and explanations, *xun* 訓, kept them separate from the classics; thus the texts of the three 'traditions' [to the *Chunqiu*] were not linked 連 [=intersected] with the classic. That is why the writing of the *Gongyang zhuan* in the classics on stone was throughout without the text of the classic [=*Chunqiu*]. The *Hanshu Yiwenzhi* has an entry '*Mao's Shijing* in 29 *juan*' 毛詩經二十九卷 and [separately from this another entry] '*Explanations and traditions to Mao's Shi in 30 juan* 毛詩故訓傳三十卷. Thus the Explanations 故訓 made by Mao were also separate from the classic [i.e., Mao's *Shijing*]. When it came to Ma Rong's writing his *Commentary on the Zhouli*, he said: '[I] want to save the scholars [the need] to read twice; that is why [text and commentary] together are carried in the present text.' Accordingly it began during the Later Han that the commentary [directly] followed the [individual passages of the classic]" 就經為注.

92. Tang Yongtong, "Wang Bi zhi *Zhouyi Lunyu* xinyi," 268.

93. Du Yu, *Chunqiu jingzhuan jijie*.

94. As we have seen "internal commentary" was already present in the *Guanzi* as well as in the Wuxing MS found in Mawangdui. The rearrangement of text and commentary coming at the end of the Eastern Han seems to differ in certain features of layout that makes the commentary into a distinct layer of text inserted into another and marked in some special way. The later technique of writing the commentary in smaller script so that two lines of it would fit a single line of the main text could hardly have been applied to bamboo strips as they are too narrow for two lines of text. By the end of the second century, however, paper was already much in use, and it might have been the availability of this medium that made this change in layout possible. The insertion of a character such as *zhu* 注 at the beginning of a comment was another option, but a weak one as it did not help to determine the end of the comment.

95. Yan Lingfeng, *Zhongwai Laozi zhushu mulu*, 4, assumes that the 安 and the 毋 are close in the old script and have therefore been mixed up. Wuqiu 毋求 is a well-recorded family name.

96. Fu Yi's report is quoted in Peng Si, *Daode zhenjing jizhu zashuo*, Zhengtong Daozang, Schipper 709, 2.13b. For a detailed analysis see my "The Wang Bi Recension of the Laozi" in my *Wang Bi's Commentary on the Laozi: Critical Text, Extrapolative translation, Philological Commentary.*

97. Rao Zongyi, "Laozi Xiang Er zhu xulun," 1155–71; Zheng Chenghai, *Laozi Heshang gong zhu jiaoli*; I. Robinet, *Les Commentaires du Tao Tö King jusqu'au VIIe siècle*; Ōfuchi Ninji, "Rōshi Sō Ji chū to Kajoko chū to no kankei ni tsuite," 103–8.

98. Ōfuchi Ninji, "Rōshi Sō Ji chū to Kajoko chū," 103–8.

99. "Dingzhou xi Han Zhongshan Huai wang mu zhujian *Wenzi* shiwen," *Wenwu* 12(1995):27–36. Li Dingsheng, "Wenzi lun dao" 文子論道, pt. 1, *Fudan xuebao (Shehui kexue ban)*, 3(1984):80–85; pt. 2:4:(1984):41–48. Li Dingsheng and Xu Huijun 徐慧君, eds., *Wenzi yaoquan* 文子要詮 (Shanghai: Fudan daxue Press, 1988).

100. Biography of Du Ji, *Sanguo zhi*, 502. Cf. Xu Kangsheng, "Lun Wei Jin shiqi de zhuzi baijia xue," *Zhongguo zhexue yanjiu* 3(1982):33; Tang Changru, "Wei Jin xuanxue zhi xingcheng ji qi fazhan," 313ff.

101. Cf. p. 159ff.

102. *Han shu, Yiwenzhi*, 10:1729.

103. Shima Kuniō, *Rōshi Kōsei*, 8.

104. *Daode zhen jing zhigui*, Zhengtong Daozang, HY 693, Schipper, 693; Meng Wentong, "Yan Junping Daode zhigui lun yiwen," *Tushu jikan* 6(1948):23–38.

105. Shima Kuniō, *Rōshi kōsei*, 8.

106. Cf. p. 45ff.

107. Chao Yuezhi, *Fuzhi ji*, in *Ji Tangzi Laozi Daode jing zhu*, 1.

108. Kusuyama Haruki, *Rōshi densetsu no kenkyū*, 168n32, and 19n6, identifies these even with An Qi Sheng Zhi 安期生之, who is mentioned in *Shiji*, 2436, as a student of Heshang changren.

109. Cf. his biography in the *Hou Han shu*, 1972.

110. Kusuyama Haruki, *Rōshi densetsu no kenkyū*, 199ff., has studied these fragments and the relationship of this commentary—which is sometimes ascribed in Tang dynasty sources (p. 205) to *Laozi* himself—with the Heshang Gong commentary.

111. Cf. Tang Yongtong, "Wang Bi zhi *Zhouyi Lunyu* xinyi," 266.

112. Ibid. Tang Yongtong believes that the Wei Feng rebellion in fact marked an opposition of the *qingtan* 清談 scholars to the Cao family's ascension to power.

113. Cf. Tang Yijie, *Wei Jin nanbei chao shiqi de daojiao*, 125ff.

114. Rao Zongyi, *Laozi Xiang Er zhu jiaozheng*, 3, based on statements in the *Zhuanshou jing jieyi zhujue* 傳授經戒儀注訣, Schipper 989, p. 3b.

115. Tang Xuanzong, *Daode zhenjing shu waizhuan*, Du Guangting, *Daode zhenjing guangshengyi*, both quoted in Rao Zongyi, *Laozi Xiang Er zhu jiaozheng*, 1.

116. Cf. Rao Zongyi, *Laozi Xiang Er zhu jiaozheng*, 3.

117. Published and edited by Rao Zongyi, *Laozi Xiang Er zhu jiaozheng*.

118. Yu Fan 虞翻, *Laozi zhu* 老子注 in 2 j., mentioned in his biography in the *Sanguo zhi*. *Wushu*, 1322. The *Sui shu* book catalog already lists it as lost.

119. Fan Wang 范望, *Laozi zhuxun* 老子注訓 in 2 j. is mentioned in the preface of Lu Deming's *Jingdian shiwen*, but not in the Sui and Tang book catalogues. Cf. Yao Zhenzong, *Sanguo yiwenzhi*, 26.

120. Sun Deng quotations will be found, for example, in Li Lin, *Daode zhen jing qushan ji*, 3.12b, 4.15b, 6.11b.

121. Zhong Yu 鍾繇, *Laozi xun* 老子訓, referred to in Liu Xiaobiao's *Commentary to the Shishuo xinyu* quoting a Weizhi 魏志. Zhong's commentary was lost before the *Sui shu* book catalog was compiled.

122. Referred to in the *Commentary to the Wenxuan*; cf. Shima Kuniō, *Rōshi kōsei*, 35. This commentary was lost early and is not registered in the *Sui shu* book catalog.

123. Zhong Hui 鍾會, *Laozi daode jing zhu* 老子道德經注 in two *juan*, mentioned among his sources in Lu Deming's *Jingdian shiwen*, 64, as well as in the book catalogs of the *Sui shu* and the two *Tang shi*. Fairly extensive quotations survive in Tang, Song, and Yuan collections of *Laozi* commentaries and the commentary is quoted, for example, in the *Commentary on the Wenxuan*. For a specimen of this work cf. pp. 241–49 further down in this chapter.

124. Xun Rong 荀融, *Laozi yi* 老子義, mentioned in the *Family Chronicle of the Xun clan*, *Xun shi jia zhuan* 荀氏家傳 as quoted in the commentary to the biography of Xun Rong's uncle Xun Shuang in the *Sanguo zhi, Wei*, 316. According to this Jin source, Xun Rong's commentary "circulated as widely in its time as the tracts by [Wang] Bi and Zhong [Hui] on the meaning of the *Lao[zi]* and *[Zhou]yi*."

125. For Zhong Hui and Wang Bi, cf. He Shao, *Wang Bi zhuan*, quoted in Pei Songzhi's commentary to Zhong Hui's biography in the *Sanguo zhi, Wei*, 795. For Xun Rong, cf. the *Xun shi jia zhuan* quoted in the previous note.

126. Dong Yu 董遇, *Laozi xun* 老子訓, mentioned in the *Wei lüe* 魏略 as quoted in Pei Songzhi's commentary to Wang Su's 王肅 biography in the *Sanguo zhi, Wei*, 420.

127. Meng Kang 孟康, *Laozi Mengzi zhu* 老子孟子注, mentioned in Lu Deming's *Jingdian shiwen*, preface, 64. The *Sui shu* mentions that a *Laozi Commentary* by a Mr. Meng 孟氏 was listed in the Liang catalog, but was lost. Zhang Junxiang's *Laozi jijie* 老子集解, which is wrongly entered into the Daozang as Gu Huan's *Daode jing zhushu* (Daozang, Schipper 404–6), quotes commentary sections from an "Older Meng" 大孟, and from a "Younger Meng" 小孟; the former is probably Meng Kang.

128. He Yan 何晏, *Laozi daode lun* 老子道德論, is mentioned in the *Commentary to the Shishuo xinyu* 4.6 and in Liu Xie's *Wenxin diaolong*. The Sui and Tang book catalogs list it as still extant. These essays seem to have contained those elements of He Yan's unpublished *Laozi* commentary that he felt were still worth publishing after he had heard Wang Bi give his interpretation of the *Laozi*. One surviving long fragment is studied in "Discerning the That-by-which: The Language of the *Laozi* and the *Lunyu*" in my *Language, Ontology, and Political Philosophy: Wang Bi's Scholarly Exploration of the Dark* (in press). According to the *Jin zhugong zan* 晉諸公贊, quoted in the *Commentary to the Shishuo xinyu* 4.12, both Ruan Ji and Xiahou Xuan 夏候玄 wrote a *Daode lun* 道德論; however, they are not

mentioned separately in the book catalogs of the Sui and Tang. Three fragments of Ruan Ji's text survive in *Taiping yulan* 1 and 77 and are quoted there as *Tong Lao lun* 通老論. Yao Zhenzong, *Sanguo yiwen zhi*, 3256, suggests that the two titles might refer to the same text. One fragment of Xiahou Xuan's text is studied in my "Discerning the That-by-which: The Language of the *Laozi* and the *Lunyu*," in *Language, Ontology, and Political Philosophy: Wang Bi's Scholarly Exploration of the Dark (Xuanxue)*, (in press).

129. Even then, however, some texts such as the Xiang Er commentary already assumed that the students were familiar with other commentators from the same environment, and took pains to refute them. Cf. the Xiang Er example given further down in this chapter on p. 225.

130. Cf. Ma Zonghuo, *Zhongguo jingxue shi*, 57f. Lu Shengjiang, "Han Wei xuefeng de yanbian yu xuanxue de chansheng," 92–96.

131. For a fine study of the set-up and teaching methods of such a private late Han school see Yoshikawa Tadao, "Sho Gen no gakujuku." Zheng Xuan had several thousand students, Ma Rong well over a thousand and of Cai Xuan 蔡玄 his biography in the *Hou Han shu* writes that "his students always counted in the thousands and there were over 16,000 people who copied his writings." Cf. Lu Shengjiang, "Han Wei xuefeng de yanbian," 93.

132. *Shishuo xinyu* 4.6 and 4.7.

133. Cf. the commentary to the biography of Zhong Hui in *Sanguo zhi, Wei*, 795.

134. Cf. p. 174.

135. Cf. the translation of this exchange on p. 129.

136. *LZWZLL*, 196.

137. Ibid.

138. Ibid.

139. I am grateful to Prof. Robin Yates to alert me to the strangeness of the rebuttal of an extinct school such as the Mohists.

140. Cf. *Han shu*, 3056. Note that the *Zhuangzi*'s name is also taboo, becoming Yan Zhou 嚴周 instead of 莊周 in this passage.

141. See my "Discerning the That-by-which: The Language of the *Laozi* and the *Lunyu*," in *Language, Ontology, and Political Philosophy: Wang Bi's Scholarly Exploration of the Dark*.

142. Wang Bi, *Zhouyi lüeli*, 609f.

143. The term used here for meaning is *yi* 義. In contexts like these it is used synonymously with *yi* 意. This phrase in fact seems to go back to the *Xici* A 12 statement, "The Sage established the *xiang* 象 in order to fully express the meaning *yi* 意"; Wang Bi, *Zhouyi zhu, 554*.

144. Wang Bi, *Zhouyi zhu*, 215f.

145. The complete translation of this passage is given further down in this chapter.

146. Cf. the documentation in the section dealing with this *zhang* in my *Wang Bi's Commentary on the Laozi: Critical Text, Extrapolative Translation, Philological Commentary*.

147. As Zhang Zhan's *Liezi* edition was very probably based on material from Wang Bi's library, Wang Bi might have known that this text assigns *Laozi* 6 to a *Huangdi shu* 黃帝書. Cf. Yang Bojun, *Liezi jishi, 3*.

148. For the different traditions of reading this phrase see S. Van Zoeren, *Poetry and Personality: Reading, Exegesis and Hermeneutics in Traditional China*, 37ff.

149. *LZWZLL*, 6.1.

150. *LZWZLL*, 6.1.

151. *LZWZLL*, 2.44.

152. Wang Bi, *Zhouyi zhu*, 215.

153. 212.

154. Ibid., 215.

155. Cf. my *Language, Ontology, Political Philosophy* (in press).

156. *Lunyu* 7.1; cf. Wang Bi, *Lunyu shiyi*, 623f.

157. Wang Bi, *Lunyu shiyi*, 626.

158. It should be pointed out that in the frequent Han-dynasty quotations of this passage, the phrase about the people's being unable to give a definition of Yao is regularly missing; cf. Ying Shao, *Fengsu tongyi* 1 : 1; *Han shu*, introduction to the *Rulin zhuan* 儒林傳, 3589. In both cases the emphasis is not on the ineffability of Yao's characteristics but on his leaving behind formalized social institutions, *wenzhang* 文章, in which his hidden agenda manifests 煥 itself, as most later commentators read this passage.

159. Shima Kuniō, *Rōshi Kōsei*, 65.

160. This more detailed argument about the punctuation was necessitated by the punctuation favored in the standard edition of Chen Qiyou, ed., *Hanfeizi jishi*, II:853. Against the *Hanfeizi* reading, he punctuates 太上，下智有之此言太上之下民無說（＝悅）也.

161. The *zhi* 智 of *Hanfeizi*'s *Laozi* text is to be read as a *zhi* 知. It is interpreted directly out of the phrase just preceding: "The people know 知 that punishment and rewards（賞 for 罰）both originate in their own [behavior]."

162. Chen Qiyou, ed., *Hanfeizi jishi*, II.852f.; cf. Liao, *The Complete Works of Han Fei Tzu*, II.179.

163. Li Dingsheng and Xu Huijun, *Wenzi yaoquan*, 1ff. The new finds are published and discussed in three papers by the Hebei sheng wenwu yanjiusuo Dingzhou Han jian zhengli xiaozu entitled "Dingzhou xi Han Zhongshan Huai wang mu zhujian *Wenzi* shiwen," "Dingzhou xi Han Zhongshan Huai wang mu zhujian *Wenzi* jiaokan ji," and "Dingzhou xi Han Zhongshan Huai wang mu zhujian *Wenzi* de zhengli he yiyi," all in *Wenwu* 12 (1995).

164. *Huainanzi zhuzi suoyin* 9.70.22ff.

165. Some texts erroneously write 民之 instead of 民知 here. I follow the Sibu congkan edition, which has also been followed in the text edited by D. C. Lau, *Wenzi zhuzi suoyin*, 42.8.16. The otherwise very fine edition by Li Dingsheng and Xu Huijun, eds., *Wenzi yaoquan*, 155, wrongly accepts the 之 reading.

166. *Wenzi zhuzi suoyin*, 42.8.7ff. Cf. Li Dingsheng, Xu Huijun, eds., *Wenzi yaoquan*, 154f. While D. C. Lau follows Yang Shuda, *(Zengbu) Laozi guyi*, 24, and leaves the phrase 故太上下知有之 without punctuation altogether, which creates a grammatical impossibility, Xu and Li punctuate 太上，下知而有之 with a reference to Wang Bi's *Commentary* in the notes, although this reading does not make much sense in the context.

167. Sadly, Rao Zongyi's edition of the text, most recently republished as *Laozi Xiang Er zhu jiaozheng*, does not seem convincing in many places both as far as critical textual handling and as far as punctuation are concerned. The Xiang Er commentary to *Laozi* 13.1 is a case in point. Rao Zongyi, 21, transcribes it 知道，上知也，知也。惡事，下知也。雖有上知，當具識惡事，改之不敢為也. The duplication of 上知也，知也 with a full stop after it seems meaningless and ends up generating another meaningless phrase, 惡事，下知也. The consequence of this construction is that the Xiang Er statement 雖有上知，當具識惡事 seems perfectly unfounded in the *Laozi* text. The text as given in the concordance of the *Xiang Er Commentary*

compiled by Mugitani Kuniō, *Rōshi Sō Ji chū sakuin*, 17, does not follow Rao Zongyi here. It uses full stops to separate textual units and writes 知道，上知也，知也惡事，下知也.

168. S. Bokenkamp, *Early Daoist Scriptures*, 103, did not spot this imperative in his translation. While there is much agreement between our translations of this *zhang*, the differences remain significant enough.

169. There is a small break in the parallelism between the two first sentences, where either 就 should be inserted before the 親, or 就 before 譽 should be deleted.

170. Rao Zongyi and the *Rōshi Sō Ji chū sakuin* both punctuate 見惡人，誠為説善, but, although I believe they would agree with my translation, I do not see how their punctuation would take care of the 為, which I read as meaning "to [that person]" in accordance with the next commentary by Xiang Er 為惡人説善, which both editions leave intact.

171. It is not clear to me why Rao Zongyi reads 悔 here against a MS that gives 侮. The *ren* 人 radical to the left is clearly separated in this MS against the heart radical; cf. MS p. 2 line 3 情性 for an example.

172. Rao Zongyi punctuates this phrase 百姓不學我，有貴信道言 . . . , although the subject in the previous commentary for the 但貴道言 clearly is the 得仙之士 who is identified in this commentary here as 我. The concordance edition, in my view, punctuates correctly.

173. This formula about the princes of oldest antiquity also occurs in the introduction to Ban Gu's "Tables of Personalities of Ancient and Recent Times," *Han shu*, 861.

174. This last passage is only in Qiang Siqi's *Daode zhenjing xuande zuanshu* of 964, from which Shima Kuniō, *Rōshi Kōsei*, incorporates it into his own edition, but it is not in the many other MSS and editions consulted by Zheng Chenghai, *Laozi Heshang gong zhu jiaoli*, 113. For the "Rules," cf. Zhang Shoujie, *Shiji zhengyi*, appended to *Shiji*, 18ff.

175. Shima Kuniō, *Rōshi Kōsei*, 87.

176. Eduard Erkes, *Ho-shang-kung's Commentary on the Lao-tse*, contains a translation of this commentary. Sadly, however, the translation is riddled with errors and thus of marginal use today.

177. Qiang Siqi quotes a much shorter text here, namely 説太上之君舉事猶貴重於言. This would rather call for a reading of the *you* 猶 as meaning "still": "This means that when the princes of high antiquity undertook something they were still paying great attention to their words." The duplication of 猶 in the text above which follows that suggested by Zheng

Chenghai eliminates this possibility, and forces a translation of 猶兮 as "planning" or "meticulously organizing."

178. Cf. Zheng Chenghai, *Laozi Heshang gong zhu jiaoli*, 113f.; Shima Kuniō, *Rōshi Kōsei*, 86f.

179. Yu Zhengxie 俞正燮 (1775–1840), *Guisi cungao* 癸巳存稿 (quoted in Yang Bojun ed., *Liezi jishi*, 4), cites passages from the *Bohu tong* 白虎通 as well as from Tang and Song texts that indicate that a *pin* 牝 is something like a hole (as in a tree). This reading, however, does not seem to have been an option present for Wang Bi or his contemporaries. From the symbolic interpretation of the the *pin* residing "in a lowly position," it is clear that Wang Bi thought of the female. This reading is reinforced by the *Zhouyi* reference to a *pin* given below.

180. *Zhouyi zhengyi*, 7.4a7f.

181. *Zhouyi zhengyi*, 9.2a10f.

182. Cf. "The Language of the *Laozi* and *Lunyu*" in my *Language, Ontology, and Political Philosophy: Wang Bi's Scholarly Exploration of the Dark* (in press) for a more detailed analysis.

183. *Zhouyi zhengyi*, 7.9b3ff.

184. Cf. Wang Bi on *Laozi* 1.5 and 52.3.

185. Shima Kuniō, *Rōshi Kōsei*, 85. The last two sentences take up a line in *Zhuangzi* 17.6.42. More closely, however, this argument is made in the *Liezi*; cf. Yang Bojun, *Liezi jishi*, 2. There it directly precedes a verbatim quotation of the *Laozi* 6 discussed here. The quotation is described there as coming from the *Huangdi shu* 黃帝書; ibid., 3.

186. Shima Kuniō, *Rōshi Kōsei*, 55, does not list this passage quoted in Qiang Siqi's 強思齊 *Daode zhen jing xuande zuanshu* 道德真經玄德纂疏 (*Zhengtong Daozang*, Schipper 711) and given in Meng Wentong, "Yan Junping *Daode zhigui* lun yiwen," *Tushu jikan 6(1948):26*. A further explanation of the four concepts of *daode, shenming, taihe*, and *tiandi* is in Zhuang Zun's notes to *Laozi* 44 in his *Daode zhen jing zhigui*, 8:9b: "That which entrusts my nature to become me is *daode*. That which grants to [my nature] to come alive, is the *shenming*. That which causes it to become completed is the *taihe*. And that which it relies on to take on shape is Heaven and Earth." The Great Harmony is here a force that leads to the full development of the particular nature of a person.

187. Shima Kuniō, *Rōshi Kōsei*, 65.

188. The same reading occurs in the Li Rong text in the Daozang, which belongs to the Xiang Er textual tradition. Cf. Shima Kuniō, *Rōshi Kōsei*, 64.

189. Shima Kuniō, *Rōshi Kōsei*, 65.

190. Li Dingsheng and Xu Huijun, eds., *Wenzi yaoquan*, 60. The *Liezi* contains a full quotation of *Laozi* 6 marked as coming from a *Book of Huangdi*; cf. Yang Bojun, *Liezi jishi*, 3. However, the interpretation is clearly marked by the philosophical shift coming with Xiang Xiu and Guo Xiang in the decades after Wang Bi's death. I therefore do not include this reading here.

191. Cf. N. Barnard, "The nature of the Ch'in 'Reform of the Script' as reflected in archaeological documents excavated under conditions of control," in David T. Roy, Tsuen-hsuin Tsien, eds., *Ancient China: Studies in Early Civilization*, 181ff.

192. S. Bokenkamp, Early Daoist Texts, 83, reads the term 擧 as meaning "rigid" and translates "therefore [their sexual organs] do not become rigid." The term only occurs once in the Xiang Er commentary. I think the context is provided by the calmness of the earth that the woman imitates and the warning that the male should not push ahead. But I am not familiar enough with early medical/sexual terminology to form a firm judgment.

193. Shima Kuniō, *Rōshi Kōsei*, p. 65.

194. This commentary repeats in part its predecessor.

195. The expression "administrator life and death," *sheng si zhi guan* 生死之官, which I think is identical with "administrator of death and life," occurs again in Xiang Er on *Laozi* 21.3, cf. infra.

196. This chatty last remark looks quite superfluous in the context. It might be a gloss added later on.

197. The plural here is deduced from Han dynasty thinking in texts such as the *Huangdi neijing* 黃帝內經, which commonly assumed that men would replenish their vital energies by having intercourse with many women.

198. *Liexian zhuan* quoted in *Hou Han shu*, 2741. Cf. R. van Gulik, *Erotic Color Prints of the Ming Period*, 3. Rao Zongyi, *Laozi Xiang Er zhu jiaozheng*, 68. The 其要 that I render "with the purpose" is translated by van Gulik as "the main point of his art." The "art" to which this might refer, is only mentioned two sentences later. Cf. Li Ling, *Zhongguo fangshu kao*, 357ff.

199. Rao Zongyi, *Laozi Xiang Er zhu jiaozheng*, 11.

200. Ibid., 28.
   a. Read 合精 for 結精.
   b. Read 令 for 名.

c. Read 合 for 結.

d. Read 無妻 for 妻.

e. Read 不可勤也 instead of 不可不勤也: Shima Kuniō, *Rōshi Kōsei*, p. 65.

201. S. Bokenkamp, *Early Daoist Texts*, 84, translates this quite differently, translating as "laboring [at intercourse]" what I read as "forcing oneself to it [a reduction of sexual intercourse]." As a consequence, his translation of the last phrase of the *Laozi* also is fundamentally different from mine.

202. Li Dingsheng and Xu Huijun, eds., *Wenzi yaoquan*, 124.

203. Ibid.

204. Chen Jingyuan, *Daode zhen jing zangshi zuanwei pian*, 2.10a ff. The text was compiled between 1068 and 1077. Strangely enough, neither Yan Lingfeng, *Ji Yan Zun Laozi zhu*, 10, nor Shima Kuniō have spotted this passage. The *Daode zhenjing zhushu*, 1.22b, preserves a statement on this phrase with the introduction "Yan [Zun], Gu [Huan] and others say." The different interpretations offered in the following statement are difficult to assign. The tenor of this commentary, however, fits neither the lines above nor those below.

205. Chen Jingyuan, *Daode zhen jing zangshi zuanwei pian*, 2.10a ff.

206. From the comments to the next *zhang*, it seems likely that Zhuang Zun read these two as one. Tradition ascribes to Zhuang Zun a *Laozi* text consisting not of 81 but of 72 *zhang*.

207. Zhuang Zun read *gu* 轂 as "cart" because he used the expression *tuigu* 推轂, "pushcart," to explain the term.

208. While, in the previous phrase, the vessels are indeed made of clay, the houses are not really made by cutting doors and windows. This remains awkward.

209. *Zhouyi, Xici* B2, *Zhouyi yinde* 45/繫下/2.

210. *Zhouli zhushu*, 39.269.

211. One example of the use of the term for a human being is *Lunyu* 2.12, "The gentleman does not function as a vessel."

212. Li Shan, *Wenxuan Li Shan zhu* 文選李善註, ed. Sibu beiyao, 11.3b7, 11.5a1, 53.4b3, 59.3b7, 59.12a1. Li Lin 李霖, *Daode zhen jing qushan ji* 道德真經取善集, ed. Zhengtong Daozang, HY 718, Schipper 718.

213. Zhong Hui, *Laozi zhu*, quoted in Li Lin, *Daode zhen jing qushan ji*, 2.20f.

214. In fact, Wang Bi also argues in the *LZWZLL*, 1.25ff. that the That-by-which can only "shine forth" because there are entities. On the other hand, Wang Bi never speaks of a "mutual dependency." The argument by Wang Xiaoyi, "Zhong Hui yu zaoqi xuanxue," *Zhongguo zhexueshi yanjiu* 2:31 (1987), who analyzes the same passage, that Zhong Hui's theory here is "the same" as that of Wang Bi is not convincing. True, both speak about a relationship between *you* and *wu*, but differ in the ontological status assigned to the two.

215. Tang Yongtong, "Guiwu zhi xue (xia)—Dao An he Zhang Zhan."

216. Kusuyama Haruki, *Rōshi densetsu no kenkyū*, p. 200f.

217. Gu Huan, *Dao de zhen jing zhushu*, 1.23bf.

218. See "Patronage and the Transmission of the Wang Bi Commentary," in my *Wang Bi's Commentary on the Laozi: Critical Text, Extrapolative Translation, Philological Commentary* (in press).

219. Cf. Gottlob Frege, *Funktion, Begriff, Bedeutung. 5 logische Studien.*

220. Rao Zongyi. *Laozi Xiang Er zhu jiaozheng*, 12.

5. The Craft of Wang Bi's Commentary

1. See the chapters "Ontology" and "Political Philosophy" in my *Language, Ontology, and Political Philosophy: Wang Bi's Scholarly Exploration of the Dark* (in press).

2. Verification will be found in the chapter "Patronage and the Transmission of the Wang Bi Commentary," in my *Wang Bi's Commentary on the Laozi* (in press).

3. Du Yu, *Chunqiu jingzhuan jijie.*

4. My reconstruction of the Wang Bi *Laozi* is largely based on these quotations. See "The Wang Bi Recension of the *Laozi*," in my *Wang Bi's Commentary on the Laozi* (in press).

5. Cf. note 1 in the translation of *Laozi* 5 in ibid. for a full translation of the relevant passages.

6. Cf. *Laozi* 11 and 28.

7. An example is the substitution of the "worthy," *xianren* 賢人 for the *qi* 其 in Xiang Er on *Laozi* 11.1 in 三十輻共一轂當其無有車之用 mentioned above.

8. Ruan Yuan, *Jingji zuangu.*

9. W. A. C. H Dobson, *Late Han Chinese*, uses this paraphrase or "translation" of the *Mengzi* into Late Han Chinese as the sample for describing this stage of the development of the Chinese written language.

10. See, for example, the 1850 *Shengyu guangxun* 聖諭廣訓, which is a reprint of a 1724 edition, *Shengyu xiangjie* 聖諭像解, distributed to the provinces for reprinting in 1903, or the *Shengyu guangxun zhijie* 聖諭廣訓直解 of 1876.

11. Wang Yi, *Chuci zhangju*; this commentary is contained in many editions of the *Chuci*. Mr. Schimmelpfennig, University of Heidelberg, is about to complete a Ph.D. dissertation on this commentary.

12. Such translations occur in Wang Bi on *Laozi* 10.1,2,3,5,6, 11.2, 16.1, 20.4, 21.8, 30,4,5, 32.2, 34.1, 53.1,2, 54.7, 58.3,5, 61.8, 62.4,6, 73.4, 78.1, 80.2.

13. Such paraphrases occur in Wang Bi on *Laozi* 1.8, 23.2, 6, 25.5, 10, 27.4, 28.5, 29.3, 30.3, 35.3, 55.3, 28.1, 69.2,3, 72.1, 75.1, 77.2.

14. Wang Yi on *Li Sao*, in *Chuci buzhu*, in Takeji Sadao, ed., *Soji sakuin*, 277.

15. Hermann-Josef Röllicke has offered a fine analysis of the origin and early development of the term *ziran* in his *Selbst-Erweisung. Der Ursprung des ziran Gedankens in der chinesischen Philosophie des 4. und 3. Jhs. v. Chr.* For *wu* 無, "negativity," Pang Pu has recently developed an early suggestion by Wen Yiduo 聞一多 that *Xuanxue* might have some forerunner in "some quite mysterious primordial religion, namely Shamanism" into a philological argument that *wu* 無 in fact has a family history in the terms 舞 and 巫. Cf. Pang Pu, "Shuo 'wu'," 63–74. The same case could of course be made for the One 一 with the Great One 太一 as a god mentioned already in the *Chuci*.

16. *Zhouyi zhengyi*, 8.8a3f.

17. See, for example, the social explanation of the term "The Highest Oneness 至一" in *Zhuangzi*, 41.16.6f.

18. There also is a link to *Laozi* 16.4: "Generally speaking, all of the entities, their diversity [notwithstanding], revert and return to their root" 根; this identifies the One with the "root," but there is no visible reference to this statement in the present commentary.

19. *Zhouyi yinde*, 39/繫上/I.

Bibliography

Ban Gu 班固. *Hanshu* 漢書. 12 vols. Beijing: Zhonghua Press, 1964.

Barnard, Noel. "The Nature of the Ch'in 'Reform of the Script' as Reflected in Archaeological Documents Excavated under Conditions of Control," in D. T. Roy and Tsuen-hsuin Tsien, eds. *Ancient China: Studies in Early Civilization*. Hong Kong: Chinese University Press, 1978, pp. 181–214.

Bauer, Wolfgang (Bao Wugang 鮑吾剛), ed. *Renwu zhi yinde* 人物志引得. San Francisco: Chinese Materials Center, 1974.

Bokenkamp, Stephen. *Early Daoist Scriptures*. Berkeley: University of California Press, 1997.

Cao Pi 曹丕. *Dianlun lunwen* 典論論文. In Zhang Pu, comp, *San Cao ji*, 177–79.

Chan, Alan K. L. *Two Visions of the Way: A Study of the Wang Pi and Ho-shang Kung Commentaries on the Lao-tzu*. Albany: State University of New York Press, 1991.

Chan, Wing-tsit. *The Way of Lao-tzu*. Indianapolis and New York: Bobbs-Merrill, 1963.

Chao Yuezhi 晁説之. *Fuzhi ji* 鄜畤記. In *Ji Tangzi Laozi Daode jing zhu* 集唐子老子道德經注, Guyi congshu. Repr. Yangzhou: Yangzhou guji Press, 1990.

———. *Songshan Jingyu sheng ji* 嵩山景迂生集. In Chao Yiduan 晁貽端, ed., *Chao shi congshu*. 晁氏叢書 Liuan: Daixuelou, 1826–32.

Ch'en Ch'i-yün. "A Confucian Magnate's Idea of Political Violence: Hsün Shuang's (128–190 A.D.) Interpretation of the Book of Changes." *T'oung Pao* 54 (1968):73–115.

Chen Dezhao 陳德昭. *Laozi sixiang dui Han chu zhengzhi zhi yingxiang* 老子思想對漢初政治之影響. Taipei: Daqian wenhua Press, 1981.

Chen Jingyuan 陳景元. *Daode zhen jing zangshi zuanwei pian* 道德真經藏室
纂微篇. Zhengtong Daozang, HY 714, Schipper 714.

Chen Qiyou 陳奇猷, ed., *Hanfeizi jishi* 韓非子集釋. 2 vols. Peking: Zhonghua
Press, 1962.

Chen Shou 陳壽. *Sanguo zhi* 三國志. 5 vols. Beijing: Zhonghua Press, 1973.

———. *Sanguo zhi* 三國志. Bonaben 百衲本 edition. Taipei: Shangwu Press,
1967.

———. *Sanguo zhi* 三國志 (Photomechanical reprint of the Wuyingdian
武英殿 edition of 1739). In *Ershiwu shi* 二十五史. Shanghai: Shanghai guji
Press, 1991.

Jingmen shi bowuguan 荊門市博物館. *Guodian Chu mu zhujian* 郭店楚墓
竹簡. Peking 1998.

Couvreur, Séraphin. *'Li Ki,' ou Mémoires sur les Bienséances et les
Cérémonies: Texte chinois avec une double traduction en français et en
latin.* 2 vols. Repr. Paris: Belles Lettres, 1950.

Da Dai Liji 大戴禮記. In Sibu congkan. Shanghai: Commercial Press, 1929–
34.

Daode zhenjing zhushu 道德真經註疏 [wrongly ascribed to Gu Huan 顧歡]. In
Zhengtong Daozang, HY 710, Schipper 710. Also in the Jiayetang
congshu 嘉業堂叢書 (1919) with a preface by Liu Zhenggan.

Demiéville, Paul M. "Philosophy and religion from Han to Sui." In D.
Twitchett and J. K. Fairbank, eds., *The Cambridge History of China,* vol.
1: *Ch'in and Han.* Cambridge: Cambridge University Press, l986.

"Dingzhou xi Han Zhongshan Huai wang mu zhujian *Wenzi* de zhengli he
yiyi." See Hebei sheng.

"Dingzhou xi Han Zhongshan Huai wang mu zhujian *Wenzi* shiwen," see
Hebei sheng.

Dobson, W. A. C. H. *Late Han Chinese: A Study of the Archaic-Han Shift.*
Toronto: University of Toronto Press, 1964.

Du Guangting 杜光庭. *Daode zhen jing guang shengyi* 道德真經廣聖義. In
Zhengtong Daozang, HY 725, Schipper 725.

Du Guoxiang 杜國庠. "Liang Han jing jingu wenxue zhi zhenglun" 兩漢經
今古文學之爭論." In *Du Guoxiang wen ji* 杜國庠文集. Beijing: Renmin
Press, 1977, pp. 299–318.

Du Yu 杜預. *Chunqiu jingzhuan jijie* 春秋經傳集解. 2 vols. Shanghai:
Shanghai guji Press, 1988.

Dull, Jack L. "A Historical Introduction to the Apocryphal (Ch'an
Wei) Texts of the Han Dynasty." Ph.D. dissertation, University of
Washington, 1966.

Dubs, Homer H. "The Date and Circumstances of the Philosopher Lao-Dz."
JAOS 61 (1941):215–21.

———. "The Identification of the Lao-Dz." *JAOS* 62 (1942):300–304.

Ebrey, Patricia. *The Aristocratic Families of Early Imperial China: A Case*

Study of the Po-ling Ts'ui Family. Cambridge: Cambridge University Press, 1978.

Erkes, Eduard, trans. *Ho-shang-kung's Commentary on the Lao-tse*. Ascona: Artibus Asiae, 1950.

Ershiwu shi kanxing weiyuanhui 二十屋史刊行委員會, ed. *Ershiwu shi bubian* 二十五史補編. 5 vols. Beijing: Zhonghua Press, 1956.

Fan Ye 范曄. *Hou Han shu* 後漢書. Peking: Zhonghua, 1965.

Fan Yingyuan 范應元. *Laozi Daode jing guben jizhu* 老子道德經古本集註. In Xu Guyi congshu 續古逸叢書. Yangzhou: Jiangsu Guangling guji Press, 1994.

Fang Xuanling 房玄齡. *Jinshu* 晉書. 10 vols. Beijing: Zhonghua Press, 1974.

Feng Youlan 馮友蘭. *Zhongguo zhexue shi* 中國哲學史. Shanghai: Shangwu Press, 1934.

Finsterbusch, Kaete. *Verzeichnis und Motivindex der Han-Darstellungen*. 2 vols. Wiesbaden: Harassowitz, 1966.

Fozu tongji 佛族統記 T.1035

Frege, Gottlob. *Funktion, Begriff, Bedeutung. 5 logische Studien*. Göttingen: Vandenhoek & Ruprecht, 1975.

Fu Juyou 傅舉有 and Chen Songchang 陳松長, eds. *Mawangdui Han mu wenwu* 馬王堆漢墓文物. Changsha: Hunan Press, 1992.

Gao Heng 高亨. "Shiji Laozi zhuan jianzheng" 史記老子傳箋證. In Luo Genze, ed., *Gushi bian*, vol. 6. Repr. Hong Kong: Taiping Press, 1962–, pp. 441–73.

Ge Hong 葛洪. *Baopuzi* 抱朴子. In Zhuzi jicheng 諸子集成. Shanghai: Shanghai shudian, 1990.

Gentz, Joachim. "Ritus und Praxis: Die *Chunqiu* Exegese des *Gongyang zhuan* von ihren Anfängen bis Dong Zhongshu." Ph.D. dissertation, University of Heidelberg, 1998.

Gu Jiegang 顧頡剛. "Cong Lüshi chunqiu tuice Laozi zhi chengshu niandai" 從呂氏春秋推測老子之成書年代. In Luo Genze, ed., *Gushi bian*, vol. 4. Repr. Hong Kong: Taiping Press, 1962, pp. 462–520.

———. *Handai xueshu shilüe* 漢代學術史略. Shanghai: Asia Books, 1936.

Gu Yanwu 顧炎武. *Rizhi lu* 日知錄. Huang Rucheng 黃汝成 comm. Shanghai: Shanghai guji 1985.

Guanzi jiaozheng 管子校正 (Dai Wang 戴望, ed.). In *Zhuzi jicheng*. Shanghai: Shanghai shudian, 1990.

Guo Moruo 郭沫若. "Lao Dan, Guan Yin, Huan Yuan" 老聃關尹環淵. In Luo Genze, ed., *Gushi bian*, vol. 6. Repr. Hong Kong: Taiping Press, 1962–, pp. 631–43.

Han shi waizhuan. See Han Ying.

Han shu. See Ban Gu.

Hanfeizi. See Chen Qiyou.

Han Ying 韓嬰. *Han shi waizhuan zhuzi suoyin* 韓詩外傳逐字索引. Liu

Dianjue 劉殿爵 and Chen Fangzheng 陳方正, eds. Hongkong: Commercial Press, 1992. See Hightower, *Han shih wai chuan.*

He Changqun 賀昌群. *Wei Jin qingtan sixiang chulun* 魏晉清談思想初論. Shanghai: Shangwu Press, 1946.

He Qimin 何啟民. *Wei Jin sixiang yu tanfeng* 魏晉思想與談風. Taipei, 1967. Repr. In *Zhongguo xueshu yanjin congshu* 中國學術研究叢書 12. Taipei: Taiwan xuesheng Press, 1984.

He Shao 何邵. *Wang Bi biezhuan* 王弼別傳. Quoted in Pei Songzhi, *Sanguo zhi zhu.*

He Yan 何晏 et al., eds. *Lunyu jijie* 論語集解. In Sibu beiyao. Shanghai: Zhonghua Press, 1930.

Hebei sheng wenwu yanjiusuo Dingzhou Han jian zhengli xiaozu 河北省文物研究所定州漢簡整理小組. "Dingzhou xi Han Zhongshan Huai wang mu zhujian *Wenzi* de zhengli he yiyi" 定州西漢中山懷王墓竹簡＜文子＞的整理和意義. *Wenwu* 12 (1995):38–40.

———. "Dingzhou Xi Han Zhongshan Huai wang mu zhujian *Wenzi* shiwen," 定州西漢中山懷王墓竹簡＜文子＞釋文. *Wenwu* 12 (1995):27–34.

———. "Dingzhou xi Han Zhongshan Huai wang mu zhujiuan *Wenzi* jiaokan ji" 定州西漢中山懷王墓竹簡＜文子＞校勘記. *Wenwu* 12 (1995):35–37, 40.

Henricks, Robert G., trans. and ed. *Te-Tao Ching. Lao-tzu. Translated from the Ma-wang-tui Texts, with an Introduction and Commentary.* New York: The Modern Library, 1993.

———. "Examining the Chapter Divisions in the Lao-tzu." *Bulletin of the School of Oriental and African Studies* 45.3 (1982):501–24.

Hightower, James, Robert. *Han shih wai chuan: Han Ying's Illustrations of the Didactic Applications of the Book of Songs.* Cambridge: Harvard University Press, 1952.

Holzman, Donald. *La vie et la pensée de Hi K'ang (223–62 Ap. J.-C.).* Leiden: E. J. Brill, 1957.

Hou Han shu. See Fan Ye.

Hou Wailu 候外盧 et al., *Zhongguo sixiang tongshi* 中國思想通史. 6 vols. Beijing: Renmin Press, 1957–.

Hou Han shu. See Fan Ye.

Hou Kang 候康. *Bu Hou Han shu yiwen zhi* 補後漢書藝文志. In *Ershiwu shi bubian,* 2:2105–30.

Huainanzi zhuzi suoyin 淮難子逐字索引 (A Concordance to the Huainanzi). Hongkong: Commercial Press, 1992.

Hurvitz, Leon. "A Recent Japanese Study of Lao-tzu: Kimura Eiichi's 木村英一 Rōshi no shin-kenkyū" 老子の新研究. *Monumenta Serica* 20 (1961):311–67.

HY= *Harvard-Yenching Institute Sinological Index Series Index No. 25: Combined Indexes to the Authors and Titles of Books in Two Collections of Taoist Literative,* repr. Taipei: Ch'eng-wen, 1966.

Ji Tangzi Laozi Daode jing zhu 集唐字老子道德經注. In Guyi congshu. Repr. Yangzhou: Yangzhou guji Press, 1990.

Ji Yun 紀昀 et al., eds. *Siku quanshu zongmu* 四庫全書總目. Taipei: Yiwen, 1961.

Jiang Shuge 姜書閣. *Pianwen shi lun* 駢文史論. Beijing: Renmin wenxue Press, 1986.

Jinshu 晉書. Cf. Fang Xuanling 房玄齡.

Johnson, David. *The Medieval Chinese Oligarchy*. Boulder, Colo.: Westview Press, 1977.

Kaga Eiji 加賀榮治. *Chugoku koten kaishaku shi. Gi Shin hen* 中國古典解釋史・魏晉篇. Tokyo: Keiso Press, 1964.

———. "Gi Shin ni ukeru koten kaishaku no katachi–To Yo no 'Shunju kyōden shukai' ni tsuite (1)–" 魏晉に於ける古典解釋のかたち--杜預の'春秋經傳集解'について (1)–. Part I: *Jimbun ronkyū* 13 (1955):15–34; part II: *Jimbun ronkyū* 14 (1955):24–74; part III: *Jimbun ronkyū* 15 (1955):32–58. (Parts II and III with subtitle "To Yo no 'Shunju kaishaku' ni tsuite" 杜預の'春秋解釋'について.)

Karlgren, Bernhard. *The Poetical Parts in Lao-tsi*. Göteborg, Sweden: Elanders boktryckeri, 1932.

Kimura Eiichi 木材英一. "A New Study on Lao-tzu." *Philosophical Studies of Japan* I (1959):85–104.

———, ed., Eon kenkyū 慧遠研究. 2vols. Kyōto: Sobunsha 1960, 1962.

———. *Rōshi no shin kenkyū* 老子の新研究. Tokyo: Sobunsha, 1959.

Kong Fan 孔繁. *Wei Jin xuanxue he wenxue* 魏晉玄學和文學. Beijing: Zhongguo shehuikexueyuan Press, 1987.

Kong Yingda 孔穎達, comm. *Zhouyi zhengyi*. In Ruan Yuan, ed., *Shisan jing zhushu*.

———. *Zhouyi zhengyi*. In Ruan Yuan, ed., *Shisan jing zhushu*.

Kongzi jiayu. See Wang Su.

Kusuyama Haruki 楠山春樹. *Rōshi densetsu no kenkyū* 老子傳説の研究. Tokyo: Sobunsha, 1979.

Kramers, Robert Paul. *K'ung Tzu Chia Yu: The School Sayings of Confucius*. Leiden: E. J. Brill, 1950.

Laozi weizhi lilüe 老子微旨例略. Zhengtong Daozang, Schipper 1255.

Lau, D. C. *Chinese Classics: Tao Te Ching*. Hongkong: Chinese University Press, 1982.

Li Dingsheng 李定生. "Wenzi lun dao" 文子論道. Pt 1: *Fudan xuebao (Shehui kexue ban)* 3 (1984):80–85; pt. 2: 4 (1984):41–48.

Li Dingsheng and Xu Huijun 徐慧君, eds. *Wenzi yaoquan* 文子要詮. Shanghai: Fudan daxue Press, 1988.

Li Lin 李霖. *Daode zhen jing qushan ji* 道德真經取善集. Zhengtong Daozang, HY 718, Schipper 718.

Li Ling 李零. *Zhongguo fangshu kao* 中國方術考. Beijing: Renmin zhongguo Press, 1993.

Li Shan 李善, comm. *Wenxuan Li Shan zhu* 文選李善註. 4 vols. Sibu beiyao. Shanghai: Zhonghua Press, 1930. Cf. also Liuchen zhu Wenxuan.

Li Yue 李約. *Daode zhenjing xinzhu* 道德真經新注. Zhengtong Daozang, HY 692, Schipper 692.

Liang Yusheng 梁玉繩. *Renbiao kao* 人表考. In *Ershiwu shi bubian*.

Liao, Wen-kuei. *The Complete Works of Han Fei Tzu: A Classic of Chinese Legalism*. London: Probsthain, 1939.

Liebenthal, Walter. "Wang Pi's New Interpretation of the I Ching and Lun-Yü." Harvard Journal of Asiatic Studies 10 (1947):124–61. Translation of Tang Yongtong. "Wang Bi zhi *Zhouyi Lunyu* xinyi."

Liji zhengyi 禮記正義. In Ruan Yuan 阮元, ed., *Shisan jing zhushu*.

Liu Dajie 劉大杰. *Wei Jin sixiang lun* 魏晉思想論. Kunming: Zhonghua Press, 1939.

Liu Peigui 劉培桂. "Han huaxiangshi zhong de Kongzi jian Laozi" 漢畫像石中的孔子見老子. Shandong Kongzi xuehui ed. *Lu wenhua yu Ruxue* 魯文化與儒學. Jinan: Shandong youyi Press, 1996, pp. 35–41.

Liu Rulin 劉汝霖. *Han Jin xueshu biannian* 漢晉學術編年. 3 vols. Beijing: Zhonghua Press, 1987.

Liu Shao 劉邵. *Renwu zhi* 人物志. Cf. W. Bauer (Bao Wugang 鮑吾剛), ed., *Renwu zhi yinde* 人物志引得.

Liu Xiaobiao 劉孝標. *Shishuo xinyu zhu* 世說新語注. See Liu Yiqing, *Shishuo xinyu*.

Liu Xie 劉勰. *Wenxin diaolong* 文心雕龍. In Sibu beiyao. Shanghai: Zhonghua Press, 1930.

———. *Wenxin diaolong yizheng* 文心雕龍義證, annotated by Zhan Ying 詹鍈, 3 vols. Shanghai: Shanghai guji Press, 1989.

Liu Yiqing 劉義慶. *Shishuo xinyu* 世說新語. Shanghai guji Press, 1982. Cf. also Yu Jiaxi, comm., *Shishuo xinyu jianshu*.

———. *Youming lu* 幽明錄. Linlang mishi congshu 琳琅秘室叢書.

Liuchen zhu Wenxuan 六臣註文選. 2 vols. Ed. Sibu congkan. Shanghai: Commercial Press, 1929–34.

Loewe, Michael A. N. "Manuscripts Found Recently in China: A Preliminary Survey." T'oung Pao 63.1–2 (1977):99–136.

Lou Yulie 樓宇烈, ed. *Wang Bi ji jiaoshi* 王弼集校釋. 2 vols. Beijing: Zhonghua Press, 1980.

Lu Deming 陸德明. *Jingdian shiwen* 經典釋文. 3 vols. Shanghai: Shanghai guji Press 1985.

———. *Lunyu shiwen* 論語釋文. In Lu Deming, *Jingdian shiwen* 經典釋文.

Lu Shengjiang 盧盛江. "Han Wei xuefeng de yanbian yu xuanxue de chansheng" 漢魏學風的演變與玄學的產生. Nankai daxue zhongwenxi-Nankai wenxue yanjiu–bianweihui 南開大學中文系·南開文學研究·編委會, ed., *Nankai wenxue yanjiu*, 1987 南開文學研究, 1987, pp. 92–127.

Lu Xisheng 陸希聲. *Daode zhen jing zhuan* 道德真經傳. Zhengtong Daozang, HY 685, Schipper 685.

Lunyu. See He Yan.

Lunyu yinde 論語引得. Harvard-Yenching Institute Sinological Index Series Suppl. 16. Repr. Taipei: Ch'eng-wen Publishing Company, 1966.

Luo Minsheng 羅民勝. "Shilun Wang Bi xuanxue dui mingjiao de pipan" 試論王弼玄學對名教的批判. *Zhongguo zhexueshi yanjiu* 1 (1987):73–75.

Ma Guohan 馬國翰, ed. *Yuhan shan fang ji yishu* 玉函山房輯佚書. N.p., 1884.

Ma Zonghuo 馬宗霍. *Zhongguo jingxue shi* 中國經學史. Shanghai: Shangwu Press, 1937.

Mather, Richard. *Shih-shuo Hsin-yü: A New Account of Tales of the World*. Minneapolis: University of Minnesota Press, 1976.

Mawangdui Hanmu boshu zhengli xiaozu 馬王堆漢墓帛書整理小組. *Mawangdui Han mu boshu Laozi* 馬王堆漢墓帛書老子. Beijing: Wenwu Press, 1976.

———. *Mawangdui Hanmu boshu* 馬王堆漢墓帛書. Vols. 1 and 2. Beijing: Wenwu Press, 1974.

Meng Wentong 蒙文通. "Yan Junping Daode zhigui lun yiwen" 嚴君平道德指歸論佚文. *Tushu jikan* 6 (1948):26–37.

Mengzi zhushu 孟子注疏. Sibu beiyao. Shanghai: Zhonghua Press 1930.

Miao, Ronald. *Early Medieval Chinese Poetry: The Life and Verse of Wang Ts'an (AD 177–217)*. Wiesbaden: Steiner, 1982.

Miyazaki Ichisada 科舉前史. *Kyūhin kanjinhō no kenkyū* 九品官人法の研究. Kyōto: Toyōshi kenkyūkai, 1956.

Morimitsu Kisaburō 森三樹三郎. "Gi Shin shidai ni ukeru ningen no hakken 魏晉時代における人間の發見." *Tōyō bunka no mondai* 東洋文化の問題 1 (1949):121–201.

Mozi yinde 墨子引得. Harvard-Yenching Institute Sinological Index Series. Suppl. No 21. Taipei: Ch'eng-wen Publishing Company, 1966.

Mugitani Kuniō 麥谷邦夫. *Rōshi Sō Ji chū sakuin* 老子想爾注索引. Kyōto: Hōyū Press, 1985.

Nakamura Keiji 中村圭爾. *Rikuchō kizokusei kenkyū* 六朝貴族制研究. Tōkyō: Kazama Shōbō, 1982.

Nan Qi shu 南齊書. See Xiao Zixian.

Nylan, Michael, trans. *The Canon of Supreme Mystery by Yang Hsiung*. Albany: State University of New York Press, 1993.

Ōfuchi Ninji 大淵忍爾. "Gotobeidō no kyōhō ni tsuite" 五斗米道の校法 について. *Tōyō Gakuhō* 49.3 (1966):40–68.

———. "Rōshi Sō Ji chū to Kajoko chū 老子想爾注と河上公注とのについて關係." In Yamazaki sensei taikan kinenkai, ed., *Yamazaki sensei taikan kinen*. *Tōyōshigaku ronshū*, 103–8.

Rao Zongyi 饒宗頤. *Laozi Xiang Er zhu jiaozheng* 老子想爾注校證. Shanghai: Shanghai guji Press, 1991.

———. "Laozi Xiang Er zhu xulun" 老子想爾注續論. In Fukui hakushi shōjū kinen rombunshū kankokai 福井博士頌壽記念論文集刊行會, ed., *Fukui Hakushi shōju kinen Tōyō bunka ronshū* 福井博士頌壽記念東洋文化論集, pp. 1155–71.

———. "Wu jianheng er nian Suo Dan xieben Daode jing canjuan kaozheng (jian lun Heshang gong ben yuan liu) 吳建衡二年索紞寫本道德經殘卷考證 (兼論河上公本源流): The Su Tan Manuscript Fragment of the Tao-Te Ching (A.D. 270)." *Journal of Oriental Studies* II. 1 (1955):1–71.

Pang Pu 龐朴. "Shuo 'Wu'" 說 "無". *Zhongguo wenhua yu Zhongguo zhexue*. Shenzhen: Dongfang Press, 1986, pp. 62–74.

Pei Songzhi 裴松之. comm. *Sanguo zhi zhu* 三國志注. See Chen Shou. *Sanguo zhi*.

Pelliot, Paul. "Les classiques gravés sur pierre sous les Wei en 240–248." *T'oung Pao* 23.1 (1924):1–4.

Pokora, Timoteus. *Hsin-lun (New Treatise) and Other Writings by Huan T'an (43 B.C.–28 A.D.)*. Michigan Papers in Chinese Studies No. 20. Ann Arbor: Center for Chinese Studies, The University of Michigan, 1975.

Qian Daxin 錢大昕. *Qianyantang ji* 潛研堂集 (Lue Youren, ed.). Shanghai: Shanghai guji Press, 1989.

Qian Mu 錢穆. "Ji Wei Jin xuanxue sanzong" 記魏晉玄學三宗. Orig. publ. 1945, repr. in Qian Mu, *Zhuang Lao tongbian*, pp. 345–65.

———. *Zhuang Lao tongbian* 莊老通辨. Taipei: Dongda tushu gongsi, 1991 (orig. publ. 1957).

Qiang Siqi 強思齊. *Daode zhen jing xuande zuanshu* 道德真經玄德纂疏. Zhengtong Daozang, HY 711, Schipper 711.

Queen, Sarah. *From Chronicle to Canon: The Hermeneutics of the* Spring and Autumn, *according to Tung Chung-shu*. New York: Cambridge University Press, 1996.

Ren Jiyu 任繼愈 (and Tang Yongtong 湯用彤?). *Wein Jin xuanxue zhong de shehui zhengzhi sixiang lüelun* 魏晉玄學中的社會政治思想略論. Shanghai: Shanghai Renmin Press, 1956.

Rickett, W. Allyn. *Kuan-tzu: A Repository of Early Chinese Thought*. Vol. 1. Hong Kong: Hong Kong University Press, 1965.

Robinet, Isabelle. *Les commentaires du Tao Tö King jusqu'au VIIe siècle*: Mémoires de l'Institut des Hautes Études Chinoises V. Paris: Collège de France, 1977.

Röllicke, Hermann-Josef. *"Selbst-Erweisung." Der Ursprung des ziran-Gedankens in der chinesischem Philosophie des 4. und 3. Jhs. v. Chr.* Frankfurt: Peter Lang, 1996.

———. "Hidden Commentary in Pre-canonical Chinese Literature." *Bochumer Jahrbuch zur Ostasienforschung* 19 (1995): 15–24.

Ruan Yuan 阮元, ed. *Shisan jing zhushu* 十三經注疏. 2 vols. Beijing: Zhonghua Press, 1987. *Sanguo zhi*. See Chen Shou.

Schipper, Kristofer M. *Concordance du Tao-tsang: Titres des ouvrages*.

Publications de l'École Française d'Extrême-Orient CII. Paris: École Française d'Extrême-Orient, 1975.

Schlegel, Gustave. *La loi du parallélisme en style chinois, demonstrée par la préface du Si-yu-ki, la traduction de cette préface par feu Stanislaus Julien défendue contre la nouvelle traduction du Père A. Gueluy.* Leiden: E. J. Brill, 1896.

————. "Le Stèle funéraire du Teghin Giogh et ses Copistes et traducteurs chinois, russes et allemands." *Journal de la Société Finno-Ougrienne* 8 (1892):30.

Seidel, Anna K. *La divinisation du Lao Tseu dans le Taoisme des Han.* Publications de l'École Française d'Extrême Orient LXXI. Paris: École Française d'Extrême-Orient, 1969.

————. "The Image of the Perfect Ruler in Early Taoist Messianism: Lao-Tzu and Li Hung." *History of Religions* 9.2–3 (1969/70):216–47.

Shengyu guangxun 聖諭廣訓. N.p., 1850.

Shengyu guangxun zhijie 聖諭廣訓直解. Anhui, 1876.

Shengyu xiangjie 聖諭像解. Lithograph print. Jiangsu, 1903.

Shi Daoan 釋道安. "Er jiao lun 二教論." In *Guang Hong ming ji*, ch. 8, T 2103:136b–43c.

————. Preface to the *Ren ben yu sheng jing* 人本欲生經. In *Chu sanzang jiji* 出三藏集記. T.55.45.a f.

Shi Huiyuan 釋慧遠. *Shamen bujing wangzhe lun* 沙門不敬王者論. In Kimura Eiichi, ed., *Eon Kenkyū*, 2:84–90. Also in Shi Sengyou, ed., *Hong ming ji.* T. 2102:29–32.

Shih, Vincent Y. C. *The Literary Mind and the Carving of Dragons.* New York: Columbia University Press, 1959.

Shima Kuniō 島邦男. *Rōshi Kōsei* 老子校正. Tōkyō: Kyūkoshōin, 1973.

Shishuo xinyu. See Liu Yiqing

Sima Guang 司馬光. *Zizhi tongjian* 資治通鑑. 20 vols. Shanghai: Zhonghua Press, 1976.

Sima Qian 司馬遷. *Shiji* 史記. 10 vols. Beijing: Zhonghua Press, 1973.

Soymié, Michel. "L'entrevue de Confucius et de Hiang T'o." *Journal Asiatique* 242.3–4 (1954):311–92.

Som, Tjan Tjoe 曾珠森. *Po Hu T'ung* 白虎通. *The Comprehensive Discussions in the White Tiger Hall: A Contribution to the History of Classical Studies in the Han Period.* 2 vols. Leiden: E. J. Brill, 1949–52.

Suiboku bijutsu taisei 水墨美術大系, Tôkyô: Kôdansha, 1975.

Suishu. See Wei Zheng.

Sun Cizhou 孫次舟. "Ba Gushi bian di si ce bing lun Laozi zhi youwu" 跋古史辨第四冊並論老子之有無. In Luo Genze, ed., *Gushi bian*, vol. 6. Repr. Hong Kong: Taiping Press, 1963, pp. 74–101.

Sun Sheng 孫盛. "Lao Dan fei da xian lun" 老聃非大賢論. In *Guang Hong ming ji* 廣弘明集 T.2103:119b–20a.

Sun Xidan 孫希旦. *Li ji jijie* 禮記集解. Taipei: Wenshizhe, 1990.

Suzuki Yoshijirō 鈴木田次郎. *Taigeneki no kenkyū* 太玄經の研究. Tōkyō: Meitoku Press, 1964.

Taiping yulan 太平御覽. 12 vols. Taipei: Xinxing Press, 1959.

Takeji Sadaō 竹治貞夫, ed. *Sōji sakuin* 楚辭索引 Kyōto: Chubun Press, 1979.

Takigawa Kametarō 雲瀧龜太郎. *Shiki kaichū kōshō* 史記會注考證. Repr. Taipei: Yinwen yinshuguan, n.y.

Tan Jiefu 譚戒甫, "Er Lao yanjiu 二老研究." *Gushi bian* 6 (1938):473–515.

Tang Changru 唐長孺. *Wei Jin nan bei chao shi luncong* 魏晉南北朝史論叢. Beijing: Sanlian Press, 1978.

———. "Wei Jin xuanxue zhi xingcheng ji qi fazhan" 魏晉玄學之興成及其發展. In Tang Changru, *Wei Jin nan bei chao shi luncong* 魏晉南北朝史論叢, pp. 311–50.

Tang Xuanzong 唐玄宗. "Daode zhen jing shu waizhuan" 道德真經疏外傳. In Tang Xuanzong, *Daode zhen jing shu*. Zhengtong Daozang, HY 679, Schipper 679.

Tang Yijie 湯一介. *Wei Jin nanbei chao shiqi de daojiao* 魏晉南北朝時期的道教. Xian: Shanxi shifandaxue Press, 1988.

Tang Yongtong 湯用彤. "Guiwu zhi xue (xia)–Daoan he Zhang Zhan" 貴無之學（下）－道安和張湛. *Zhexue yanjiu* 7 (1980):62–70 and 48. Repr. in Tang Yongtong, *Lixue. Foxue. Xuanxue* 理學，佛學，玄學, pp. 295–314.

———. *Tang Yongtong xueshu lunwen ji* 湯用彤學術論文集. Beijing: Zhonghua Press, 1983.

———. "Wang Bi zhi *Zhouyi Lunyu* xinyi" 王弼之周易論語新義. *Tushu jikan* 圖書季刊 NS 4.1 and 2 (1943). Repr. in *Tang Yongtong xueshu lunwen ji*, pp. 264–79. See Liebenthal, Walter for a translation.

———. "Wei Jin xuanxue he wenxue lilun" 魏晉玄學和文學理論. *Zhongguo zhexueshi yanjiu* 1 (1980):37–45.

(Tang Yongtong?), Ren Jiyu 任繼愈. *Wei Jin xuanxue zhong de shehui zhengzhi sixiang lüelun* 魏晉玄學中的社會政治思想略論. Shanghai: Shanghai renmin Press, 1956.

van Gulik, Robert H. *Erotic Color Prints of the Ming Period*. Tokyo: privately published, 1951.

Van Zoeren, Steven. *Poetry and Personality: Readings, Exegesis, and Hermeneutics*. Stanford: Stanford University Press, 1991.

Vervoorn, Aat. "Zhuang Zun: A Daoist Philosopher of the Late First Century B.C." *Monumenta Serica* 38 (1988–89):69–94.

Wagner, Rudolf. "Ban Gu and the End of History." unpubl. MS, 1995.

———. "Die Fragen Hui-yüan's an Kumarajiva." Ph.D. dissertation, University of Munich, 1969.

———. "Interlocking Parallel Style: Laozi and Wang Bi." *Études Asiatiques* 34.1 (1980):18–58.

———. *Language, Ontology, and Political Philosophy: Wang Bi's Scholarly Exploration of the Dark (Xuanxue)*. In press.

——. "Lebensstil und Drogen im chinesischen Mittelalter." *T'oung Pao* 59 (1973):79–178.

——. "Patronage and the Transmission of the Wang Bi Commentary." In *Wang Bi's Commentary on the Laozi: Critical Text, Extrapolative Translation, Philological Commentary*. In press.

——. Review of Alan K. L. Chan, *Two Visions of the Way: A Study of the Wang Po and Ho-shang Kung Commentaries on the Lao-tzu. T'oung Pao* 79 (1993):179–82.

——. "Twice Removed from the Truth: Fragment Collection in 18th and 19th Century China." In Glenn Most, ed., *Collecting Fragments: Fragmente Sammeln*. Aporemata 1. Goettingen: Vandenhoeck & Ruprecht, 1997, 34–52.

——. "Die Unhandlichkeit des Konfuzius." In A. Assmann, ed., *Weisheit. Archäologie der literarischen Kommunikation III*. Munich: Fink Verlag, 1991, pp. 455–64.

——. *Wang Bi's Commentary on the Laozi: Critical Text, Extrapolative translation, Philological Commentary*. In press.

——. "The Wang Bi Recension of the *Laozi*." In *Wang Bi's Commentary on the Laozi: Critical Text, Extrapolative Translation, Philological Commentary*. In press.

——. "Wang Bi: 'The Structure of the Laozi's Pointers' (Laozi weizhi lilüe)." *T'oung Pao* 72 (1986):92–129.

——. Wang Bi's Ontology." In *Language, Ontology, and Political Philosophy: Wang Bi's Scholarly Exploration of the Dark (Xuanxue)*. In press.

Waley, Arthur. *The Way and Its Power*. New York: Grove Press, 1958 (originally London: Allen and Unwin, 1934).

Wallacker, Benjamin E. "Han Confucianism and Confucius in Han." In D. Roy and Tsuen-hsuin Tsien, eds., *Ancient China: Studies in Early Civilization*, pp. 215–28.

——. "The Spring and Autumn Annals as a Source of Law in Han China." *Journal of Chinese Studies* 2.1 (1985):79–72.

Wang Baoxuan 王葆玹. *Zhengshi xuanxue* 正始玄學. Jinan: Qi Lu Press, 1987.

——. *Xuanxue tonglun* 玄學通論. Taipei: Wunan tushu Press, 1996.

Wang Bi 王弼. *Laozi weizhi lilüe* 老子微旨例略. In Lou Yulie, *Wang Bi ji jiaoshi*. See also the edition in Wagner, *Wang Bi's Commentary on the Laozi: Critical Text, Extrapolative Translation, Philological Commentary*.

——. *Laozi zhu* 老子注. In Lou Yulie, *Wang Bi ji jiaoshi*. Critical edition in Wagner, *Wang Bi's Commentary on the Laozi: Critical Text, Extrapolative Translation, Philological Commentary*.

——. *Lunyu* shiyi 論語釋疑. In Lou Yulie, ed., *Wang Bi ji jiaoshi*, 2:621–37.

———. *Zhouyi* lüeli 周易略例. In Lou Yulie, ed., *Wang Bi ji jiaoshi*, 2:591–620.

———. *Zhouyi* zhu 周易註. In Lou Yulie, ed., *Wang Bi ji jiaoshi*, 1:211–2:590.

Wang Can 王粲. *Jingzhou wenxue jiguan zhi* 荊州文學記官志. Fragments in Yan Kejun, *Quan shanggu sandai Qin Han sanguo liuchao wen. Quan Hou Han wen.*

Wang Chong 王充. *Lun Heng* 論衡. Beijing: Zhonghua Press, 1979.

Wang Deyou 王德有, ed. and annot. *Laozi zhigui* 老子指歸. Peking: Zhonghua, 1994. Cf. Zhuang Zun.

———. *Laozi zhigui quanyi* 老子指歸全譯. Chengdu: Bashu, 1992.

Wang Su 王肅. *Kongzi jiayu* 孔子家語. In Sibu beiyao. Shanghai: Zhonghua Press, 1930.

———. *Shengzheng lun* 聖證論. In Ma Guohan, *Yu han shan fang ji yishu*, vol. 2.

Wang Su 王素, ed., *Tang xieben Lunyu Zheng shi zhu jiqi yanjiu* 唐寫本論語鄭氏注及其研究. Beijing Wenwu Press, 1991.

Wang Xianqian 王先謙, ed., *Shiming suzheng bu* 釋名疏證補. Shanghai: Shanghai Guji Press, 1984.

Wang Xiaoyi 王曉毅. "Jingzhou guanxue yu sanguo sixiang wenhua" 荊州官學與三國思想文化, *Kongzi yanjiu* 孔子研究 1 (1994):44–49.

———. Wang Bi guli xintan "王弼故里新探 *Kong Meng xuebao.* 75 (1998): 169–85.

———. *Wang Bi pingzhuan* 王弼評傳. Nanjing: Nanjing daxue Press, 1996.

———. *Zhongguo wenhua de qingliu* 中國文化的清流. Beijing: Zhongguo Shehuikexueyuan Press, 1992.

———. "Zhong Hui yu zaoqi xuanxue" 鐘會與早期玄學. *Zhongguo zhexueshi yanjiu* 2 (1987):28–32.

Wang Yi 王逸. *Chuci zhangju* 楚辭章句. Ming print.

Wei Zheng 魏徵. *Sui shu* 隋書. 6 vols. Beijing: Zhonghua Press, 1973.

Wenzi zhuzi suoyin 文子逐字索引 (A Concordance to the *Wenzi*). Hong Kong: Commercial Press, 1992.

Wilhelm, Richard. *Kungfutse. Schulgespräche.* Düsseldorf: Diederichs 1961.

Xiao Zixian 蕭子顯. *Nan Qi shu* 南齊書. 3 vols. Beijing: Zhonghua Press, 1972.

Xiao jing zhushu 孝經注疏. In Ruan Yuan, *Shisan jing zhushu.*

Xu Gan 徐幹. *Zhonglun* 中論. In Zhongguo xueshu mingzhu. Taipei: Shijie dangju, 1956–61.

Xu Kangsheng 許抗生. "Lun Wei Jin shiqi de zhuzi baijia xue" 論魏晉時期的諸子百家學. *Zhongguo zhexueshi yanjiu* 3 (1982):31–42.

Xuan Zhuang 玄奘 and Bian Ji 辯機. *Da Tang xiyou ji jiaozhu* 大唐西遊記校注. (Ji Xianlin 季羨林, ed.) Beijing: Zhonghua Press, 1985.

Yamazaki sensei taikan kinenkai 山崎先生退官記念會, ed., *Yamazaki sensei taikan kinen. Tōyōshigaku ronshū* 山崎先生退官記念　東洋史學論集. Tōkyō: Yamazaki sensei taikan kinenkai, 1967.

Yan Kejun 嚴可均, ed. *Quan shanggu sandai Qin Han sanguo liuchao wen* 全上古三代秦漢六朝文. 4 vols. Beijing: Zhonghua Press, 1985.

Yan Lingfeng 嚴靈峰. ed., *Wuqiubeizhai Laozi jicheng* 無求備齋老子集成. Taipei: Yiwen Press, 1965.

————. *Zhongwai Laozi zhushu mulu* 中外老子著述目錄. Taipei: Zhonghua congshu weiyuanhui, 1957.

Yan Zun 嚴尊. See Zhuang (Yan) Zun.

Yang Bojun 楊伯峻, ed., *Liezi jishi* 列子集釋. Beijing: Zhonghua Press, 1985.

Yang Shuda 楊樹達. *(Zengbu) Laozi guyi* （增補）老子古義. Shanghai: Zhonghua Press, 1936.

Yang Xiong 揚雄 (Han Jing 韓敬, comm.). *Fayan zhu* 法言注. Beijing: Zhonghua Press, 1992.

————. *Taixuan jing* 太玄經. In Sibu beiyao. Shanghai: Zhonghua Press, 1930. Cf. P. Nylan, trans., *The Canon of Supreme Mystery by Yang Hsiung*.

Yao Zhenzong 姚振宗. *Sanguo yiwenzhi* 三國藝文志. In Ershiwu shi kanxing weiyuanhui, ed., *Ershiwu shi bubian*, 2:3189–3300.

Yates, Robin. *Five Lost Classics: Tao, Huanglao and Yinyang in Han China*. New York: Ballantine, 1997.

Yin Gonghong 尹恭弘. *Pianwen* 駢文. Beijing: Renmin wenxue Press, 1994.

Ying Shao 應劭. *Fengsu tongyi* 風俗通義. In Sibu congkan. Shanghai: Commercial Press, 1929–34.

Yoshikawa Tadaō 吉川忠夫. "Shō Gen no gakujuku" 鄭玄の學塾. In Kyōto daigaku Jimbun kagaku kenkyūjō, ed., *Chūgoku kizoku shakai sei no kenkyū*, pp. 321–59.

Yu Jiaxi 余嘉錫, comm. *Shishuo xinyu jianshu* 世説新語箋疏 (Zhou Zumo 周祖謨 and Yu Shiyi 余淑宜, eds.). Revised edition, Shanghai: Shanghai guji Press, 1993.

Yu Zhengxie 俞正燮. *Guisi cungao* 癸巳存稿. Congshu jicheng. Taipei: Yiwen, 1971.

Yu Yingshi 余英時. "Han Jin zhi jishi zhi xin zijue yu xin sichao" 漢晉之際時之新自覺與新思潮. *Xinya xuebao* 新亞學報 41 (1959):25–144.

Yunji qijian 雲笈七籤. See Zhang Junfang.

Zhan Ying 詹鍈, ed., *Wenxin diaolong yizheng* 文心雕龍義證. 3 vols. Shanghai: Shanghai guji Press, 1989.

Zhang Pu 張溥, comp. *San Cao ji* 三曹集. Changsha: Yuelu shushe, 1992.

Zhang Junfang 張君房, comp. *Yunji qijian* 雲笈七籤. Zhengtong Daozang, HY 1026, Schipper 1032.

Zhang Junxiang 張君相. *Laozi jijie* 老子集解. Wrongly entered into the Zhengtong Daozang, HY 710, Schipper 710, as Gu Huan 顧歡, *Daode zhen jing zhushu* 道德真經註疏.

Zhang Shoujie 張守節. "Shiji zhengyi" 史記正義. In Sima Qian, *Shiji*, vol. 10, appendix, pp. 11–33.

Zhang Zhan 張湛. *Liezi zhu* 列子注, Zhuzi jicheng 諸子集成. Shanghai: Shanghai shudian, 1990.

Zhanguo ce zhuzi suoyin 戰國策逐字索引. Hong Kong: The Commercial Press, 1992.

Zhao Qi 趙崎. "Tici jie 題辭解". *Mengzi zhushu*, 5.

———. *Mengzi zhangju* 孟子章句. In *Mengzi zhushu*.

Zheng Chenghai 鄭成海. *Laozi Heshang gong zhu jiaoli* 老子河上公注斠理. Taipei: Zhonghua Press, 1971.

Zheng Xuan 鄭玄. *Mao shi jian* 毛詩箋. In Ruan Yuan, ed., *Shisan jing zhushu*, 1:262–64.

———. "Shipu xu" 詩譜序. In Ruan Yuan, ed., *Shisan jing zhushu*, 1:262–64.

Zhengtong Daozang 正通道藏. Repr. Taipei 1962 of the edition Shanghai: Commercial Press, 1923–26.

Zhou Jizhi 周繼旨. "Wei Jin wenlun de xingqi yu xuanxue zhong 'tian ren xin yi' de xingcheng" 魏晉文倫的興起與玄學中"天人新義"的形成. *Zhexue yanjiu* 5 (1984):45–53.

Zhou Yong 周顒. "Zhou chong da shu bing Zhou chong wen" 周重答書并周重問. In *Hongming ji*, juan 6.

Zhouli 周禮. In Sibu beiyao. Shanghai: Zhonghua Press, 1930.

Zhouli zhushu 周禮注疏. See Ruan Yuan, *Shisan jing zhushu*.

Zhouyi yinde 周易引得. Harvard-Yenching Institute Sinological Index Series No. 10. Repr. Taipei: Ch'eng-wen Publishing Company, 1966.

Zhu Yizun 朱彝尊. "Wang Bi lun." *Pushuding ji* 曝書亭集. In Sibu congkan. Shanghai: Commercial Press, 1928.

Zhuang (Yan) Zun. *Daode zhen jing zhigui* 道德真經指歸. Zhengtong Daozang, HY 693, Schipper 693.

———. *Ji Yan Zun Laozi zhu* 輯嚴遵老子注. In Yan Lingfeng, ed., Wuqiubeizhai Laozi jicheng.

Zhuangzi yinde 莊子引得. *A Concordance to Chuang Tzu*. Harvard-Yenching Institute Sinological Index Series Suppl. No. 20. Cambridge, Mass.: Harvard University Press, 1956.

Zhuanshou jing jieyi zhujue 傅授經戒儀注訣. Zhengtong Daozang. Schipper 989.

Index

ambivalence: seeming in *Laozi*
due to misreading, 271–272;
translation as way to eliminate,
276–281
Anqiu Wangzhi: *Laozi*
commentator, 154
aristocracy: Wang Bi and, 11, 13
author: status of determining
reading strategy, 131–132
authority: bases of commentaries',
175

baby: metaphorical value of
different terms for in *Laozi*,
284–287
Ban Gu: and *zhangju*, 39; origin of
structure of *Gujin renbiao* by,
122; personality evaluations in
Gujin renbiao by, 119, 122–123
Bao Xian: on Confucius and Lao
Peng, 126
ben / mo (root/offspring): Wang Bi
insertion of concepts of into
Laozi analysis, 290–292
Bi Zhi: and *zhangju*, 40;
technique of reading *Zhouyi*,
35; Wang Bi and, 35, 175

Cai Rong: and commentary of
meaning, 43; as Pure One, 43;

Library of, 12; parallel style in,
56
Cao Pi: on *wenqi*, literary
endowment, 118–119
Cao Shuang: as regent, 14; and
Wang Bi, 17
chan wei texts: as classics, 40;
coding of and Yinyang wuxing,
34; as secret transmission of
Confucius, 32
Chao Yuezhi: on Wang Bi's
commenting, 37
Chen Qun: *Jiupin zhongzheng*
system by, 124
Cheng brothers: Indebtedness to
Wang Bi, 26
chizi (baby): See baby
Chunqiu: as lead classic in Han,
33; commentary techniques for,
33. See also *Gongyang zhuan*,
Zuozhuan
classics: eunuchs' refusal to
recognize authority of, 156;
hegemonic control over
meaning of, 157; source for
interpretation of, 46; unified
meaning of, Zheng Xuan on, 41;
Xun Can on as being dregs of
Sage, 145
cock: metaphorical value of, 268

and earth by, 182; status of in
Gujin renbiao, 123; Wang Bi on
difference between and worthy,
124–125
Schlegel, Gustave: on parallel
style, 55; insufficiency of rule
by, 56
schools, philosophical: faulty
methodology of in reading
Laozi, 163; Sima Tan on, 160–
161; Wang Bi sequence in
criticising, 167–168; Xuanxue
assessment of, 133
sequence: hierarchical meaning
of, 167
sexual practices in *Laozi*: of
Huangdi, Xuannü, Gongzi, and
Rong Cheng denounced by
Xiang Er, 225; Xiang Er on,
222–229
Shangshu: as part of implied
reader's education, 144
Sheng zheng lun, 47
shi (beginning): Wang Bi analysis
of *Laozi* term of, 288–289
Shi Daoan: on Wang's assessment
of Laozi and Confucius, 136;
use of Interlocking Parallel
Style by, 110
Shi Huiyuan: use of Interlocking
Parallel Style by, 110
shifa method of transmitting
teaching, 155
Shijing: *Mengzi* interpretation of,
33; interpretation technique
used for, 33
Shipu: quoted on unified meaning
of classics, 42
Shishuo xinyu: on Wang Bi and
Pei Hui discussing Confucius
and Laozi, quoted, 129–130
Sima Guang: on self-assessment
of He Yan, 17
Sima Shi: He Yan on qualification
of, 17; mourning Wang Bi, 18
Sima Tan: on status of Confucius
and Laozi, 121; Wang Bi
treatment of *Treatise on the Six*

Schools by, 160–181; Wang Bi
changing sequence of schools in
Treatise by, 167–168
Sima Yi: as regent, 14
Song Zhong, 46, 154
spirit: definitions of, 211
structural writing: explanation of,
66
Su Dan: *Laozi* manuscript by, 150
subject: list of *Laozi* passages
without, 270; Wang Bi'
technique of insertion of, 270–
275
subtle words: imitation of, 20–21
Sun Deng: *Laozi* commentary by,
155
Sun Sheng: assessment by of
Wang Bi's *Zhouyi* commentary,
27–28; criticism by of He Yang
and Wang Bi, 25; treatise
"Yixiang miaoyu jianxing lun,"
translated, 27–28
straw/dogs in *Laozi* 6: different
interpretations of symbolic
meaning of, 266
systematic argumentation: by
Wang Bi, 27
systematization of classics: Wang
Bi and, 30; in Han, 30–31

taiji (Great Ultimate): identified
with *men* (door) in *Laozi*, 6,
214
Taixuan fu: and *Laozi*, 38. See
also Yang Xiong
Taixuan jing: Role of in Jingzhou,
36, 46
teaching institutions, collapse of,
10, 156
terms, philosophical: merging of,
281–298
That-by-which: constituent
elements of, 212, 297–298
translation: as commentarial
strategy, 276–281
True Text on Causes and Effects:
reading of *Laozi*, 11, 235–236,
237–238

Printed in Great Britain
by Amazon